AGAINST INEQUALITY

Studies in Critical Social Sciences Book Series

Haymarket Books is proud to be working with Brill Academic Publishers (www.brill.nl) to republish the *Studies in Critical Social Sciences* book series in paperback editions. This peer-reviewed book series offers insights into our current reality by exploring the content and consequences of power relationships under capitalism, and by considering the spaces of opposition and resistance to these changes that have been defining our new age. Our full catalog of *SCSS* volumes can be viewed at https://www.haymarketbooks.org/series_collections/4-studies-in-critical-social-sciences.

Series Editor
David Fasenfest (York University, Canada)

Editorial Board
Eduardo Bonilla-Silva (Duke University)
Chris Chase-Dunn (University of California–Riverside)
William Carroll (University of Victoria)
Raewyn Connell (University of Sydney)
Kimberlé W. Crenshaw (University of California–LA and Columbia University)
Heidi Gottfried (Wayne State University)
Alfredo Saad-Filho (Queen's University, Belfast)
Chizuko Ueno (University of Tokyo)
Sylvia Walby (Lancaster University)
Raju Das (York University)

Against Inequality

Contributions to a Discourse
of Social Emancipation

Alejandro I. Canales
Dídimo Castillo Fernández

Translated by
David Stiles Sparks

Haymarket Books
Chicago, IL

First published in 2024 by Brill Academic Publishers, The Netherlands
© 2024 Koninklijke Brill NV, Leiden, The Netherlands

Published in paperback in 2025 by
Haymarket Books
P.O. Box 180165
Chicago, IL 60618
773-583-7884
www.haymarketbooks.org

ISBN: 979-8-88890-549-4

Distributed to the trade in the US through Consortium Book Sales and Distribution (www.cbsd.com) and internationally through Ingram Publisher Services International (www.ingramcontent.com).

This book was published with the generous support of Lannan Foundation, Wallace Action Fund, and the Marguerite Casey Foundation.

Special discounts are available for bulk purchases by organizations and institutions. Please call 773-583-7884 or email info@haymarketbooks.org for more information.

Cover design by Jamie Kerry and Ragina Johnson.

Printed in the United States.

Library of Congress Cataloging-in-Publication data is available.

Contents

Foreword VII
Preface XIII
List of Figures XXVII

Introduction 1

1 New Perspectives and Imperatives in the Face of Inequality 9
    1   Imperatives of an Emancipation Strategy in the Face of Global Inequality 18
        1.1   *An Ethical Imperative* 19
        1.2   *An Existential Imperative* 20
        1.3   *A Political Imperative* 22
    2   Preliminary Reflections 27

2 Underlying Metadiscourses within Scientific Discourses on Inequality 29
    1   A Critique of Methodological Nationalism 29
    2   Methodological Androcentrism and Its Feminist Critique 31
    3   Development and Progress as Metadiscourses of Modernity 34
    4   The Discourse against Inequality as a Critique of Progress and Development in the Social Sciences 40
    5   Summary 47

3 Social Inequality: a Totality Approach 50
    1   Social Inequality: a Total Social Fact 50
    2   Critique of Individualistic Approaches 53
    3   Multidimensional Perspectives of Inequality 65
    4   Inequality and Society: Analysis Model from Its Totality 71

4 Debates on Inequality throughout History 85
    1   Inequality in Ancient Greece 85
    2   Inequality in the Christian Era and Feudal Society 88
    3   The English Poor Laws and the Transition to Capitalism 94
    4   Political Economy's Critique of the Poor Laws and the Formation of the Capitalist Labor Market 97
    5   Social Inequality under Capitalism: Rousseau and Marx 103

5 The Debate on Social Inequality in the 20th Century   114
   1 Functionalist Sociology   115
   2 Neoclassical Economics   122
   3 Gunnar Myrdal and the Principle of Circular and Cumulative Causation   132

6 The Death of Class and the Historical Resilience of a Social Category   141
   1 The Death of Class   143
   2 Argument 1. From Class Structure to Social Stratification   144
   3 Argument 2. From the End of Class to the End of Marxism   146
   4 Argument 3. The Historical Obsolescence of Class   149
   5 Class Is Dead, Long Live Class!   154
   6 The Death of Class: Ideology or Theory?   157
   7 Critique of the Alleged Obsolescence of Class Analysis   162
   8 Against Determinism   166
   9 Class: Critical Function of a Concept   178

7 The Return of Class   182
   1 Giddens and Class Structuration in Contemporary Capitalism   183
   2 Erik Olin Wright: Marxism and Social Classes Revisited   196
      2.1 *Discussion Points on Erik Olin Wright's Approach*   202
   3 Charles Tilly and Categorical Inequality   207
   4 Reproduction and Social Inequality in the Thought of Pierre Bourdieu   216

8 Social Classes and Inequality in Global Capitalism   227
   1 On Globalization and Class Inequality   229
   2 Neoliberalism and Globalization: Ideological Foundations in the Reconstitution of the Ruling Classes   235
   3 The Reconstitution of the Ruling Classes in Global Capitalism   239
   4 The Constitution of the Working Class in Global Capitalism   246
   5 Class Structure and Social Antagonism in Global Capitalism   260

9 Final Reflections: for a Project of Social Emancipation   265

   References   275
   Index   287

Foreword

When the authors first honored me with the request to write the foreword to this book, I did not think I would find within its pages a seminal work. The text you have in your hands is the result of a profound reflection that goes beyond a scholastic enumeration of theories and interpretations of inequality. The authors have made an effort that is difficult to surpass. Writing with four hands represents a choice in which the authors must share principles, values, and show coherence. When this is achieved, the result is unbeatable. Alejandro Canales and Dídimo Castillo have united experience, academic history, and a theoretical praxis whose scope places them at the pinnacle of Latin American critical thought. Knowledgeable about the reality of Our America, they dissect the dynamics of inequality in all its forms. Their objective is to visualize the origin and causes of the phenomenon in order to act accordingly.

It is no easy task to delve into the study of inequality when it can be said, without fear of being mistaken, that it is one of the problems that has been most treated in the social sciences. This has led the authors to make an extra effort to avoid falling into clichés. With clear language and fluent writing, they make the text a reference work. It is not a mere descriptive study in which statistical methods and methodological options are listed and end up describing all types of inequalities, be they social, economic, gender, cultural, or ethnic.

What distinguishes their proposal is their theoretical conception that exposes the inequality trap. The authors resist a sweetened version that transforms inequality into an endemic problem. Their horizon seeks to broaden our view of the issue, and to achieve this, they confront the different schools of thought that have examined inequality, exposing the weaknesses they present, the contradictions in which they incur, and the limits of their arguments. From their broad research and analysis, Alejandro Canales and Dídimo Castillo open up a certainly novel perspective in studies on inequality. They warn us of the danger of limiting ourselves to take for granted analyses based on a sea of abstractions, the results of which at times does nothing more than perpetuate inequalities, as if they were an insurmountable reality. On the contrary, the authors propose a dialectical adventure, which makes it easier to understand, if I may paraphrase Marx, the fetishism of inequality.

The theoretical and political praxis that is presented in the pages by Canales and Castillo is truly at the service of the emancipatory causes of our day; it is knowledge linked to the struggles faced by Latin American critical thought. In this sense, the authors take sides, breaking the accommodating neutrality that describes and thinks of inequalities as a phenomenon whose consequences can only be mitigated. They exercise what Wright Mills identified as sociological imagination. They unite the action of the social scientist with political praxis as part of their civic responsibility in order to question power, governments, and those responsible for applying policies. In this way, Canales and Castillo evidently follow the mandate of academic and public intellectuals in the sense Mills (2000 [1959]: 185) intended with the idea of the sociological imagination:

> To those with power and with awareness of it, [they impute] varying measures of responsibility for such structural consequences as [they find] by [their] work to be decisively influenced by [the] decisions and [the] lack of decisions [by the powerful]. To those whose actions have such consequences, but who do not seem to be aware of them, [scholars direct] whatever [they have] found out about those consequences. [They attempt] to educate and then, again, [they impute] responsibility. To those who are regularly without such power and whose awareness is confined to their everyday milieux, [they reveal] by [their] work the meaning of structural trends and decisions for these milieux, the ways in which personal troubles are connected with public issues; in the course of these efforts, [they state] what [they have] found out concerning the actions of the more powerful.

They present their results, refute arguments, recover concepts, put them in to play, and give them prominence. Under this dimension, inequality is redefined as part of a social order—capitalism—and at that moment, the great forgotten—social class—emerges with force. They recover the analysis of class and Marxian thought to underline that the thesis on the end of classes and the obsolescence of "sinful" Marxism, in general, lies on the same weak double characteristic: its superficiality in the critique and the caricaturing of Marxism as a social theory. In defense of the explanatory capacity of the concept of social class and Marxism, Canales and Castillo deploy a theoretical arsenal of deep depth. Their arguments are difficult to refute. They go to the roots, which is why their proposal is radical and transforming. They break down and mark the contradictions of those previous scholars who have caricatured and abandoned class analysis in the study of inequality.

The authors question the classics and take their arguments to the limit. Under this perspective, inequality is redirected to incorporate it structurally to the evolution of capitalist development. Taking Marcel Mauss and his essay *The Gift* (2002) as a starting point, inequality is defined as a total social fact. Inequalities take root, become institutionalized, and configure a social relationship within the economic, political, religious, military and family orders. As a total social fact, it comes to life in education, technological transformations, symbols, and culture.

Implicitly, Alejandro Canales and Dídimo Castillo become co-participants of the analysis present in Pablo González Casanova's *The Sociology of Exploitation* (2006). In it, González Casanova points out that:

> the measurement of inequality is not a purely scientific phenomenon and far from any value; sometimes it takes on obviously ideological forms that appear in the Pareto coefficient and in different types of graphic analysis; but even when formulas are used that more faithfully express inequality, such as the Gini index or the Schutz coefficient, at the base of their application lies the central dogma of a new type of political and social order to which Tocqueville referred, speaking of the capitalist society of his time. Irrationalism, fascism and racial or colonial discrimination will not be able to do away with it, as a value, nor with the empiricist analysis of inequalities.

This work by Canales and Castillo shows how keenly aware they are of the forms that inequalities take in the contemporary world within global capitalism. Their conclusion, because of its rotundity, leaves no room for doubt: It shocks the conscience. Inequality, they say, kills. For the authors, we are experiencing a crisis of inequality as a pattern of development of capitalism, to which we must incorporate the transition from analog capitalism to digital capitalism. In their characterization, however, Canales and Castillo sustain in this monumental work that this is:

> not only another industrial revolution but also a radical and structural transformation in the social and political, sexual and cultural, ecological and spiritual, demographic and human spheres, among many others that make up contemporary social life. The digital age and microelectronics redefine and restructure all social forms, including class structure and social inequality.

Once again, their proposals are in line with one of the most influential economists in Latin America, González Casanova, who in the late 1980s highlighted in his essay "Poverty and Inequality in Latin America" (González Casanova, 2015) the consequences of a style of capitalist development in which:

neoliberal conceptions came to legitimize the accentuation of inequality as the price of growth. Modernization and external openness. The hierarchization of exports as the main source of dynamism, the growth of imported supplies, the provisions of all kinds in favor of capital, the contraction of public employment and the internationalization of ways of life and consumption, were all factors that strengthened historical relations that lead to the constant reproduction of inequality.

Alejandro Canales and Dídimo Castillo practice the noble art of thinking. They link social knowledge and intellectual processes to a solid proposal. Therein lies the greatness aspect of the work, while giving meaning and amply justifying the subtitle: contributions for a discourse of social emancipation. Their text is an open plea against inequality, both politically and epistemologically.

In their debates with modernity, the reader finds the guide to follow Canales' and Castillo's reasoning. From its pages emerge ideas, concepts, and categories on which the discourse of inequality is built. It is not by chance that they begin their journey by quoting J.J. Rousseau. How could they not? His work marks a before and after in studies on inequality. Therefore, recovering one of the most outstanding theorists of the 18th century, whose work inspired the French Revolution and the Latin American emancipation process, is a wise move. The authors quote Rousseau to remind us of the difference and distance between natural and social inequalities, reinforcing the idea that social inequalities arise from the "forms and conventions established by human beings in their social coexistence. It would correspond to the different privileges and benefits enjoyed by some individuals to the detriment of others, such as wealth, power, status and authority." Thus, there is little to add.

It is difficult to find those who, since Marx, rescue Rousseau. In this sense, the courage of the authors is palpable through their theoretical rigor, which will act as a referential part of Latin American critical thought. They do not engage in theoretical syncretism; instead, they express the need to incorporate within their analysis emancipatory and revolutionary thought. Canales and Castillo reject reductionist visions and place the struggle against inequality as part of humanist thought. Only in this way can we understand the relationship they establish between Rousseau and the denunciation of inequalities.

I take the liberty of quoting Rousseau to support Canales and Castillo in their recovery of the Genevan. In his *Discourse on the Origin and Foundations of Inequality among Men* (1761) [1755], he stresses:

> If we follow the progress of inequality through the different revolutions, we shall find that the establishment of the Law and the Right of property

was its first term, the institution of the Magistracy the second; that the third and last was the change of legitimate power into arbitrary power; so that the condition of rich and poor was authorized by the first epoch, that of the powerful and the weak by the second, and, by the third, that of Master and Slave, which is the last degree of inequality and the goal to which all others finally lead, until new revolutions ... bring the government back to being a legitimate institution.

Alejandro Canales and Dídimo Castillo have achieved an orderly reflection. A filigree work, the two authors have successfully unraveled the asymmetries of social relations founded on the contradiction of capital and labor and on the social relations of exploitation. If the statement 'inequality kills' serves as an initial alert to the direction the authors will explore, it primarily grounds us in the tangible reality, from which they subsequently embark on a journey to challenge conventional perspectives through their work. Above all else, they highlight that the alternative is not to live in inequalities, to make them endemic, to make them bearable. The goal, rather, is to put an end to them. Canales and Castillo understand inequality in the same way that Zygmunt Bauman understood the Holocaust. Inequality and the Nazi Holocaust are linked by their meaning. They are proposals of death incorporated into the rationality of the West. They are modernity. They are not extramural: they are constituted in its womb and history.

In short, I believe that the work that you, the reader, have in your hands is destined to become a classic in the fight against inequality. And that makes its reading obligatory—I would even say, essential—for those who from the academy and political praxis seek to break the siege of socially conformist thinking, of empty answers. Alejandro Canales and Dídimo Castillo encourage social scientists of today to think in radical ways in order to win and draw a rupturist alternative to capitalism. Thus, they distance themselves and warn against falling prey to descriptive studies that are incorporated into the logic of capitalism with a human face: "they are not public policies, no matter how progressive they were, the strategy to overcome inequality, but rather strategies of social emancipation." The authors question the idea of progress that legitimizes capitalism on which the world of inequality is built. Inequality is not "a pending issue of modernity, it is one of its contradictions." It is a question, they will say, of capitalist modernity.

Their knowledge is placed at the service of emancipatory causes, drawing on the accumulated body of knowledge of great Latin American intellectuals. In its pages, we will recognize those who have forged the critical thought of Our America. But we also find the main representatives of the different traditions that give life to the cultural reason of the West. The authors take a look at these texts from the global south, joining those who have not hesitated to question power, uncover the inconsistencies, make explicit the limits of capitalism, and propose an alternative to overcome the exploitation of human beings by human beings.

To conclude, it is possible to affirm that the authors bring inequalities to the ground. We can feel inequality in an era where it expresses a lacerating reality. We walk through cities in which, as soon as we focus our gaze, we are assaulted by inequalities. Children at traffic lights selling Kleenex, swallowing fire, dressed as clowns, or begging for alms. Helpless elderly people lying on the sidewalks, the poverty of those who are marginalized, excluded and persecuted. Young people sniffing cans of glue. Women with their babies begging for sympathy and a few coins. Jobless workers, with disjointed gestures. They are the forms of inequality that oppresses and destroys the human condition and, in its worse cases, kills; they are explicit ways of denying human dignity.

The authors raise their voices in denouncement. In other words, they show how people live, get sick, and die as a consequence of the social class structure in contemporary capitalism. Only in this way can harsh realities truly be understood, like the fact that members of the ruling classes have a life expectancy that in some cases exceeds that of members of the working classes by 15 years. Social inequalities are class inequalities.

Alejandro Canales and Dídimo Castillo are aware of this reality. For this reason, their text, *Against Inequality: Contributions to a Discourse of Social Emancipation*, is not just another work. It is an option for social change and for struggles for human dignity, as well as a profound analysis of capitalist modernity. Now, the reader has the floor. Think to win and act accordingly.

Marcos Roitman Rosenmann

Preface

> The entire strength of the modern labor movement rests on theoretic knowledge.
> ROSA LUXEMBURG

Globalization, postmodernity, the information age, digital capitalism, labor flexibility, *precariousness*: All terms that point to the transformations of capitalism in the current era but which, in their uses and meanings, fall prey to the theoretical-ideological dominance of contemporary conservatism. In the face of this, leftist thought is unable to emerge from the political defeat it has suffered in recent decades. But it is not only a defeat in class struggle, it is something deeper. Its theoretical-political foundations have been questioned—in a certain way, displaced—by the expansion and consolidation of a new mode of capitalism, with new political and ideological underpinnings and foundations, and in the face of which, as leftists, we are still trying to take our first critical steps.

Both revolutionary socialist and reformist social democratic thought, which dominated the debate and the political programs of the left in the twentieth century, have become, supposedly, "outdated," obsolete in the face of the new ways of constituting social conflict and class struggle. The now urgent need for a political and theoretical re-foundation of the left is evident. It is not only the case that many of its leaders, parties, unions, movements, are today explicitly or implicitly embracing neoliberal postulates. Faced with the almost absolute power of a singular ideology (conservative, neoliberal), it would seem that there is no other option but to adapt to it, even from positions that could open some space for a social progressivism, but which, nevertheless, does not question either the social and political bases or the ideological and comprehensive bases of the neoliberal doctrine.

Confronted with this political defeat of critical thinking, the left has tended to take refuge in its ideological discourses, trying to reinvent itself from the humanist principles of its philosophy. This serves as a foundation from which it gives meaning to its political praxis, at whatever level it may occur. The left and critical thinking, thus, find solace in their always valid and legitimate ethical principles and moral values concerning the human being, society, and the proper way to act in it. However, they are still ethical principles, not political ones.

If a young elementary school child, embodying the innocence that defines them, were to ask a leftist militant, be it a grassroots member or, more significantly, one of its leaders, the simplest question of all: "*What for do you do politics?*", the answer from that militant or leftist leader would, in most instances, be remarkably similar. It would be centered around guiding their actions based on principles and humanist values. To caricature that response, the militant or leftist leader might aptly express: "*To make the world a better place to live in.*"

This is, undoubtedly, a totally unquestionable argument from an ethical and moral point of view. But it is also an argument not far from the one that any Miss Universe contestant would answer when faced with a similar question.[1] The truth is that, beyond the corny and emptiness of this answer, it must be acknowledged that politicians, both on the left and the right, in the present political landscape, wouldn't offer more profound answers if confronted with the same question. They would say that it is for the social good, to advance social justice, and so on, a long peroration of good intentions. In the end, and in the best of cases, it is a set of humanist ideals. Of *dreams and utopias*—valid, legitimate, necessary and unquestionable—yet undoubtedly insufficient in today's context, as they remain just that: *mere dreams and utopias*.

Faced with this situation of the left, the basic question seems to be the same as the one faced in the mid-nineteenth century: What is the strategic sense—that is, the horizons of reason that give transcendence to a political program of the left[2]—that give sustenance to the praxis of its militants and leaders and allow them to go beyond themselves? What are those theoretical-political premises (and not only philosophical ones) from which all of us—militants, leaders, and social classes themselves—can presently utilize to construct a sense of transcendence extending beyond the ethical principles and moral values of humanism? In our view, this would mandate establishing comprehensive frameworks about social and historical reality (its theoretical and political principles), from which the left and social classes can formulate a political strategy for transformation and social emancipation.

Obviously, we are not addressing the academic theories of contemporary society per se, but rather their potential application as comprehension categories for supporting transformative practices within that reality. Faced with

---

1 And with this, we neither want to denigrate nor disrespect this contestant or the Miss Universe competition; however, we wish to illustrate, by taking the matter to an extreme situation and comparison, the theoretical-political weakness of critical thinking in the contemporary left, both in its reformist wing as well as in its revolutionary wing.

2 In this sense, we are referring to political programs, distinct from government programs. These are ideas forces that surpass immediate circumstances, aiming to transform society rather than merely govern it.

these academic theories, we must adopt a twofold critical approach: (1) a critical theoretical use that unveils the extent and limitations of this knowledge, revealing the philosophical and political agendas they uphold. And (2) a critique political that unveils the rational horizons that can be derived from such theoretical critique. The latter necessitates that political critique is both sustained and constructed from a class position within the social and political topography of this society, encompassing not only an understanding of social reality but also a commitment to its transformation through a project of social emancipation.

To do this, we believe that it is necessary to reframe that child's initial question. The question isn't so much about *what for* an individual, identifying as a leftist, holds a particular office and political commitment today. Rather, it involves turning the question around and asking *why* that militant or leftist leader believes that, from the field of politics, they can make progress toward realizing the answer they initially provide: *making a positive difference in our current social realities.* In essence, *why* does this militant or political leader of the left believe it is *possible* to attain such ideals and humanist utopias?

At this point, the response takes us beyond the realm of ideals and abstract idealism, steering us toward the domain of materialist thought and philosophy. It is about supporting the "why" in a Theory of History that refers to historical processes and social subjects that make this utopia of humanist ideals possible. Consequently, the *historical possibility* of the socialist project would no longer be based only on its ideals, but would have theoretical and political foundations. These foundations not only provide *why it is possible* but also *why it is necessary* a socialist project of transformation and social emancipation.

On the one hand, it would be based on a theoretical argument, rooted in a political philosophy of the subject matter. Consequently, it embodies a material and historical perspective for comprehending and interpreting the world and its everyday nature. And, on the other hand, it would allow the identification of social subjects, equally historical and mundane, *capacity* of materially constructing that utopia, from their historical and circumstantial conditions.

Another clarification is in order here: The fact that we can distinguish and identify subjects with the material *capacity* to execute such a political program does not necessarily imply that they possess the *power* to enact it. This differentiation between the *capacity* to perform an action and the actual *power* to do so is neither trivial nor superficial. The former pertains to the subject's inherent material conditions and *capacities*, while the latter is contingent upon the historical conditions in which the subject operates. This, in turn, involves the capacities and *powers* of other subjects with whom they interact in an ongoing struggle to safeguard their respective material and worldly interests. *Capacity* is intrinsic to the subject themselves, while *power* is contingent on their position in relation vis-à-vis other subjects.

Paraphrasing Silvio Rodríguez, the Cuban singer songwriter, we can assert that *History is made by hand and without permission*. And that is the point. Firstly, History (the dream) is made by historical actors. And, on the other hand, these dreams and utopias are built from historical contexts, full of conflicts, struggles, interests and materialities, risks, uncertainties and with and against (without the permission) of other equally historical and material subjects.

Due to this *historical materiality* of the social world, the socialist project, whether revolutionary or reformist, requires being supported by a theory of History that explains its possibilities of construction and transformation. Ultimately, it involves the *making* of History, extending beyond its historicities. Idealisms (dreams and utopias) do not materialize based on their goodness, desirability, or universal acceptance. Instead, their realization depends on material and historical conditions that either possible or impossible them. It is never a matter of *capacity* to bring them to fruition but always a matter of *power* to do them.

It is paradoxical, moreover, that it is precisely the fact that these interests become possible (a question of *power*), that is, materialize as concrete facts, which ends up, in many cases, making them equally acceptable, although not necessarily desirable. The historical materialization of these principles and values, their materialization in the social structure, as vectors of the foundational matrix of society, is what ends up making them acceptable. There is, at the end of the day, a form of pedagogy, of education of society and its populations in those principles and values, which makes them act according to those material interests. They are not accepted because they are desirable purely and simply, but because that acceptability is achieved, has been made possible by and from their very *imposition* as social praxis, and therefore, that it has been done from positions of power, from concrete and specific material interests, particular, not global, proper to certain sectors, classes, genders, races within society, positioned in positions and *locus* of power within the political, social and economic structure of society.

Neoliberalism, for example, is currently accepted (and, in some cases, even projected as desirable) not because of the goodness of its proposals but because it was *imposed* and materialized as a project, because it was built from a social practice, from which its acceptance and its current potency as a desirable project was founded. But this construction was made from positions of power. It was imposed from the outcome in its favor of a particular class struggle, where the defeated included not only specific subjects (such as workers, industrial capitalists, middle classes, small and medium traders, state officials, etc.) but also long-standing historical projects (like industrial capitalism, the social-democratic and socialist left, the liberal right, etc.). This defeat marked not just the loss of concrete social subjects but also a historical mode of constitution and social formation that had reached its phase of exhaustion. This mode was the basis for sustaining forms of power, particularly the political power to organize society, the State, the Nation, the economy, and politics around its interests and principles.

At the end of the day, it is not about ideals but about interests, concrete projects, and material conditions—specifically, structural and historical conditions. These conditions make the aforementioned possible and form the bedrock that creates and sustains the *historical and material possibility* of a project.

However, the concept of *possibility* carries a philosophical significance of no lesser importance. It signifies that no project is given or preordained; instead, every project is actively constructed by concrete subjects. This construction does not occur in a social or ahistorical vacuum but, rather, within the context of an ongoing struggle with other subjects, who pursue alternative "ideals," aiming for the materialization of equally material and worldly interests. In essence, *praxis* becomes the arena of politics, construction, transformation, and, consequently, *theorization.*

Returning to our initial reflection, the question, then, centers on the theoretical-political (or philosophical) frameworks from which a leftist politician today derives the historical feasibility of their project. In essence, why does a leftist politician believe that their socialist (or social-democratic, as the case may be, considering them equivalent for our purposes) project is *historically and materially possible*? The response, in this instance, cannot and should not be confined to the field of principles and ideals alone. It necessitates grounding on the level of theories and philosophies of history. It is within this realm that the left finds itself grappling with a substantial void, entangled in a defeat from which it has yet to emerge.[3]

It Is not the *desirability* of a project (its humanist philosophy) that gives it political meaning; rather, it is the material foundations of the *historical necessity* of that project that gives it political meaning. Thus, socialism and social

---

[3] The answers that Marxism elaborated in the past are insufficient today. This does not stem from the shortcomings of Marxism as a theoretical body in itself or as a philosophy of history, but because society, the social reality to which those Marxist theories alluded at the time of their writing, was transformed due to the influence of conservative and right-wing projects that shaped alternative modes of capitalism, consequently altering the constitution and formation of classes and class conflict within capitalism.

democracy are posed as *necessary* because they would make it possible to overcome the structural contradictions that capitalism generates and is unable to resolve. The recurrent crises of accumulation, labour exploitation, oppression and injustice, and social inequality, to name just a few, are all material conditions in the face of which the *historical need* for a radical transformation of capitalism is posed. The critique and reflection on these structural contradictions (material conditions) leads us to the formulation of theories of history and capitalism that explain the *reason* for the need to transform society.

However, no theory of history resolves the question of *how* these transformations can be made possible. Following Luxemburg, this necessity can materialize if the subjects (classes) are constituted not only with the *capacity* to do so but, above all, are constituted as subjects with the *power* to make it possible. If the *capacity* of a certain class rests on the objective contradictions of capitalism, the *power* to actualize this capacity involves its formation as a class with consciousness in itself and for itself. And it is in this process, which entails constructing the social and political consciousness of class, where the paramount significance of the theoretical dimension becomes apparent.

On this point, Marxism, or more specifically, Marx himself, provided us with an answer. However, today, that theory is being scrutinized and questioned, not due to potential fallacies, but because it experienced a political defeat. Hence, the initial step is to reclaim that political stance from which it was displaced. It is a moment to reignite with politics, to recommence a struggle for transformation. Yet, to undertake this, we require theoretical underpinnings that not only provide a sense of transcendence but also offer a perspective of historical possibility.

In response to the child's initial question, we would say: *we do politics because we firmly believe that another world is not only desirable but also possible*. This prompts the need to delineate the distinction between the *possible* and the *desirable*.

If we assert that *another world is possible*, it is because we are based on a theory that identifies material forces, not just individual *wills*, that can drive it. Specifically, we recognize a material realm of struggle from which the construction of this alternative world is *possible*. It is not merely a matter of *voluntarism*, but always involves material and historical *possibilities*, which are built and rebuilt trough social praxis.

In articulating this stance, we deliberately distance ourselves from the conservatism of the possible. Unlike the conservative view that regards politics as *the art of the possible*, that is, the possible as *limitations* to politics, we advocate for a perspective where politics is viewed as the art of *making it possible*, that is, the possible as praxis political. The former takes a conservative, conformist stance, while the latter represents an active commitment to transformation, grounded in knowledge and a theory explaining why this transformation is possible. From this standpoint, the socialist (and even social-democratic) project is not only desirable but *is possible*. And it is possible because there are material and historical forces that *can make it possible*, more precisely, because there is the possibility of unleashing the material forces that *make it* possible.

In this line of reflection, we must unravel what the *possible* means for us and what is a *possibility* in the realm of history. Socialism is not the fruit of a historical determination but is a *possibility* of History. The material processes—the material structures that construct History—do not determine it but arise as possibilities. And it is precisely because there is the possibility of socialism in History that we do politics—that is, we develop a political praxis that makes it possible. If socialism were already determined by material structures, then politics, the art of making it possible, would be meaningless; there would be no *point in* doing politics, nothing more to do than to sit and wait for the evolution of history, which will inevitably lead us to socialism. In the best of cases, the meaning of politics would be to facilitate that historical determination, not to actively construct it.

The crucial point is that History doesn't progress in a predetermined manner but unfolds through struggles whose outcome remains undecided, wrought within the very course of the struggle itself. History is the product of the class struggle, yet it is a struggle whose conclusion remains open-ended. This is precisely why we do politics—to render that outcome possible and no other. However, for this very reason, we require a theory, and a philosophy of history that elucidates why socialism is necessary and fundamentally possible.

This inevitably leads us to rethink Marx and undertake a re-foundation of Marxism rooted in Marx and previous iterations of Marxist thought. It is not a question of post, neo, trans Marxist proposals but rather to re-found Marxism from its own roots, essentially making Marxism by returning to Marx. In this context, the pivotal concept is not merely Marxism itself but the active process of *making* Marxism.

For this, it is necessary to return to the elemental idea-force of Marxism: the founding thesis of the revolutionary character of Marx's thought. And it is revolutionary not because it is radically situated against capital, but because it is situated from a political philosophy, a theory of praxis, where the very meaning of theory, philosophy, politics, and history is reconfigured. It is the return to the theses on Feuerbach, in which the importance for Marx of the Theory-Praxis link is synthesized.

On the one hand, the validity of a theory is not merely an academic issue but fundamentally a political one. Its sense of truth is not demonstrated through "empirical researches", but from social praxis. Its measure of *truth* lies in its capacity to become social practice, and in our case, praxis of social transformation.

On the other hand, the conditions in which this praxis unfolds and which the theory seeks to theorize are not pre-existing but, instead, are in a constant state of construction and transformation. This dynamic evolution is a direct consequence of the specific trajectory of social praxis during each historical moment. Within this praxis, individuals possess the possibility (both the capacity and power) to make and transform such historical circumstances.

Lastly, we must revisit Marx's most renowned and frequently cited thesis: that theory serves not only as a means of comprehending history but also as a tool for its transformation. In other words, it enables intervention in history.

Within these three arguments resides the integral connection between Theory and Praxis, embodying a revolutionary essence. From our viewpoint, this conception of history embraces possible horizons, framing the future as a realm of historical possibility (in the words of Zemelman).

What is paradoxical is that this dual principle of theories, serving as a framework for understanding and as a model for praxis and transformation, is also at play in the realm of right-wing theories and philosophies, such as liberalism, among others. All liberal theories have consistently been employed for both comprehending and actively influencing society, guiding its trajectory. These theoretical frameworks propose ways of organizing society, whether from an economic, political, or cultural standpoint. A couple of examples can be found in the field of economic, such as in popular theories of economic development that have not merely functioned to comprehend capital accumulation in advanced economies but have also operated as theoretical frameworks to impose their perspectives on the structuring of the economy, labor, politics, and populations within Third World societies.

Likewise, in recent decades, the neoliberal economic doctrine not only constitutes a framework for comprehending production and distribution processes; more significantly, it functions as a program of intervention, particularly in the construction of a new political economy. Neoliberalism serves as the theoretical foundation for the conservative political agenda that has set the groundwork for the process of global capital accumulation.

What is relevant, in any case, is that all liberal theories have always had a political sense, as orienting a political and social praxis that contributed to consolidate a mode of domination and exploitation. In the face of this, we understand that critical theories must go beyond understanding and unraveling these modes of construction and use of theories for the purpose of preserving the *status quo* and, instead, advance in ways of understanding the material bases that make their social transformation possible.

It is in this context that this book is inserted. It is a political-intellectual effort that seeks to contribute to the formulation of a political theory on the need for social change, one that hopes to lead to a program of social transformation in the present times. We seek to contribute to the foundation of the historical need for socialism, not from the level of its ethical principles and moral values, neither from its humanist philosophy or the desirable that it may present, but from a political perspective that allows us to unveil the material bases and structural foundations of the possibility of this political program of social transformation. We want to move from the foundation of the *need* for socialism in its *desirability* to a foundation in its *historical possibility* as a political program.

In our understanding, the challenge is to theoretically sustain a policy of socialist transformation that articulates the humanist perspective of the project of social emancipation, while maintaining a materialist philosophy of history. It is, in short, a theoretical contribution that points to how to make the *desirable possible*, how to make *historical necessity* a *historical possibility*.

This happens, in the first place, by understanding that the possible is constructed—that is, it is not given but *becomes possible* from its own historical conditions, not as determinations but as the foundation of that possibility. In this sense, if class struggle is the space from where History moves and is structured, then it is in that same space from where we must base the *historical possibility* of the socialist program, as a necessary and desirable program.

Luxemburg grounds the historical inevitability of socialism in the Marxist thesis on the anarchy of capital and capitalism, manifested in their propensities towards recurrent crises and the consolidation of economic and political power. We position the issue of inequality as an integral domain of this tumultuous nature and a factor contributing to the cyclical crises of capital accumulation. Hence, we suggest concentrating on the analysis and comprehension of *social inequality* as one of the factors that could propel us forward in the aforementioned theoretical-political project.

In fact, inequality serves as a gateway to transcending capitalism, given its role as a social realm and a mode of organizing society that has been a constant throughout the formation of all human civilizations to date. Specifically, each society has been upheld by a distinctive combination and arrangement of what we term the fundamental forms of social inequality, namely, *class*, *gender*, and *race* inequality. Why do we assert that the class-gender-race triad constitutes these elemental forms?

1. Class is significant because, in each social structure, classes constitute the framework through which the labor process is organized, thereby shaping the conditions for the material reproduction of the population.
2. Gender plays a crucial role as the means by which the issues of social and biological reproduction of the species are organized within each society.
3. Race is pivotal as the manner through which, in every social formation, the question of the struggle between ethnicities, groups, and cultures (and consequently, the social and political construction of the "other") is addressed. These aspects have consistently played a role in the organization of material production and social reproduction.

Capitalism corresponds to a historical form of organization of the economy, politics, culture, and populations that, when intricately combined in a particular way, constitute the elementary forms of social inequality. This makes them, at the same time, the elementary forms of constituting and making individuals as social subjects, embodying social categories of class, gender, and race.

This underscores the necessity for a social theory of inequality—a comprehensive framework exploring its origins and the historical methods through which its fundamental forms are constituted. In this context, Luxemburg's thesis on the historical inevitability of socialism demands progress on two distinct yet entirely complementary (mutually imbricated) planes.

1. At the theoretical level: Involves a theoretical critique of capitalism and its foundational principles. This entails theorizing about the elementary forms of social inequality as structuring elements of the foundational relationship of capitalism—the capital-labor relation—and, consequently, the inherent social conflict, the class struggle.
2. At the political level: Entails contributing to a program of political and social emancipation—a path towards human liberation from these fundamental forms of social inequality.

At the theoretical level, the focus here is on the necessity for a comprehensive framework or theory that elucidates social inequality as an inherent structuring process within society. In this regard, the book serves as a contribution to a theory of social inequality, rooted in a philosophical and political perspective of the world and society. It fundamentally aligns with Marx and Luxemburg's understanding of theoretical contributions as tools for praxis—aiming to enhance comprehension for practical application and advance the formation of class as a historical subject for social change.

From this standpoint, this book contributes to unraveling the historical foundations of inequality, conceptualized not solely as social differentiation but also as processes and dynamics of *social oppression*. These processes shape classes, genders, and races, rendering them socially and politically unequal and distinct—positioned in various and conflicting roles within the social structure. These positions, in turn, arise from the interconnections and relationships established among them. They manifest as social relations characterized by *domination, exploitation*, and social *exclusion*, playing a pivotal role in the constitution of subjects as unequal subjects. These relations give rise to social conflict and the ongoing struggle between these categories in terms of their conflicting interests and the rights structured by these relations.

Our perspective on inequality suggests that the social subject (class, gender, race) is formed through two interrelated processes or dimensions. Firstly, it is shaped by the convergence and interweaving (the conjunction-imbrication) of various processes and social relations that structure social inequality, encompassing *domination, exploitation*, and *exclusion*. These elements are present in each dimension of inequality and serve as the *foundational relationships and processes underlying every form of social inequality*. Secondly, it is influenced by the combination and interweaving (the conjunction-imbrication) of various domains of social inequality, namely *class, gender*, and *race*. These constitute *the fundamental fields and forms of inequality*.

Within each field of inequality (race, class, gender), there is a reproduction of relations characterized by domination, exploitation, and social exclusion. Each of these social relations is shaped by the interplay and overlap of each social field: race, class, and gender.

The conjunction-imbrication of these two moments of inequality—the elementals forms of inequality, and the processes and relations that structure them—gives shape to the modes of *social oppression*. These modes, in turn, constitute the fundamental subjects that struggle among themselves; some strive to reproduce this structure of inequality and oppression, while others attempt to dismantle or destructure them. From our perspective and political positioning, it constitutes the basis for the struggles for social emancipation, in each and every one of these fields of constitution of the elementary forms of social inequality.

Thus, our theoretical-political perspective on inequality is grounded in the notion that social struggle (the struggle between classes, genders, races) is not merely a confrontation against the other, but rather against the material structures that shape us as unequal subjects—some in positions of oppression and others in positions of being oppressed. For instance, the feminist struggle would be misguided if it were solely framed as a battle against men for mere gender equity, without progressing towards a broader struggle against patriarchy as a societal and historical structure of gender oppression.

When contemplating slavery, we can ask ourselves if it is conceivable a master-slave system that isn't rooted in the oppression of the former over the latter? Clearly not, as both social categories, the master and the slave, are products of a slave system. Similarly, why should we think that it is possible to establish a social construct of gender (marked by gender equity and equality) without contemplating the liberation (emancipation) of individuals from the shackles of gender oppression, namely, patriarchy?

Just as master-slave inequality as a system of oppression can only be eliminated with the abolition of slavery, gender inequality can only be overcome on the basis of the destructuring (abolition) of the patriarchal system that gives rise to gender inequality. It is not by making the master good and empowering the slave, neither is it by constructing modes of equity in the master-slave relationship, that the problem of the subjugation of the slave by the master is solved. It is not a matter of there being good masters, who know how to behave towards their slaves. The issue is structural and is based on the social forms, relations, and structures from which the master-slave relationship is founded and, therefore, the constitution of some as masters and others as slaves. And it is this structure and structural relations that must be destructured and abolished at their very root.

The inequality between men and women represents a manifestation of this oppressive and subjugating structure. These structures constitute power dynamics, relations of dominance, exploitation, and oppression that give rise to concrete subjects: men and women positioned as unequal entities across various dimensions, including power and the economy. It is ineffective to solely address the patriarchal values and machismo ingrained in men without transforming the structures and systems of relations that construct these patriarchal forms of both men and women. Feminism must remain cognizant that its objective is not only the pursuit of equality but, more fundamentally, a struggle for emancipation and liberation.

Here lies the radical nature of our proposition: because we understand the issues of inequality and oppression as comprehensive and total realities, then, the struggle for emancipation is an all-encompassing struggle. Consequently, the battle against inequality is inherently a pursuit of *liberation*, extending beyond mere equalization. This perspective arises from recognizing that the foundational point of inequality lies in structures that bind subjects to relationships, anchoring them in positions of oppression. The primary inequality manifests in the disparate forms of freedom that characterize each societal category and subject, with some existing as liberated beings exercising control over the social forms of freedom for others.

The struggle for equality transforms into a struggle for liberation from the shackles of oppression, from those chains that tether subjects to structural positions, molding them into oppressed and subjugated entities. Inequality has deprived us of our freedom because it thrives on a foundational, inherent inequality: we face uneven circumstances in terms of freedom. The lack of equal freedom is the root cause of inequalities in other societal realms. However, this original inequality in freedom is not a natural state; it has been historically constructed. *Some* individuals have deprived *others* of their freedom. Hence, the fight against inequality is synonymous with a struggle for emancipation and liberation.

Inequality unfolds as a historical process that constitutes both oppressors and the oppressed (classes, genders, nationalities, races), delineating the foundations of their conflict. This perpetual dynamic gives rise to the *historical possibility* of a project of emancipation from those chains and social relations that fix them in such positions of inequality—some as oppressors and others as oppressed. Consequently, the struggle for emancipation doesn't revolve around the subject itself but rather targets the structures of social relations rooted in exploitation, domination, and exclusion, upon which the oppressive system is built. It is a confrontational struggle between historical subjects—classes, genders, races, nationalities—in determined historical and structural circumstances.

The political role of theory is to reveal both the structural and historical conditions, along with the modes of political formation of the subjects involved in class struggle. These dual functions of theory can only be cultivated through active engagement in the struggle itself, rather than from the confines of an academic setting or the offices of public institutions, including those affiliated with leftist parties. Struggle and knowledge (theory) emerge from the perspective and circumstances of the oppressed, the exploited, the dominated, the subjugated—those from below.

That is the purpose of the book. We neither claim to possess the answers to these questions nor do we pretend to. Our satisfaction in our work, however, lies in two aspects: firstly, raising questions that we deem relevant and essential for advance on such path; and secondly, offering analytical frameworks, fields, and categories of analysis, modes of thought that aid in developing those answers. We acknowledge that these answers will always be constructed within and emerge from the ongoing class struggle. But we recognize too, that this theoretical and, if you will, philosophical reflection, is a crucial and indispensable element within the broader context of the class struggle.

Figures

1. Progress as a metadiscourse in the social thought of Modernity   43
2. Fields of constitution of social inequality   72
3. Erik O. Wright's typology of class definitions   199
4. Graphic difference between equality, equity and emancipation   271

Introduction

> For as long as there is inequality, as long as some work so that others may consume, as long as the words "bourgeoisie" and "plebs" exist, there will be no peace.[1]
>
> RICARDO FLORES MAGÓN, Mexican anarchist and social reform activist, 1912

∴

Inequality as a phenomenon has been observed in practically all social-historic formations, in all cultures and civilizations. If anything seems to characterize class societies, it is that all of them are constituted on the basis of various forms of inequality among the subjects that compose them. Currently, the gap between rich and poor in the world is not only economic and in terms of resources but also in terms of life options and horizons. The arrogance and indolence of some—of the richest 1%—in the face of poverty and inequality configure a social scenario without precedent in history.

As Therborn (2013: 1) notes, inequality is unacceptable in our societies because it constitutes "a violation of human dignity; it is a denial of the possibility for everybody's human capabilities to develop." Inequality is, thus, not only a question of wealth and poorly distributed resources: It constitutes a whole social, political, and cultural order that limits and restricts the possibilities of human fulfillment. Inequality takes many forms and affects us in different ways: premature death, ill health, humiliation and submission, exploitation, powerlessness, repression, rape and aggression, discrimination and segregation, loss of dignity and self-pride, as well as calling into question our own identities and limiting our actions and performance in society.[2]

---

1 Original quote in Spanish: "*Porque mientras haya desigualdad; mientras que unos trabajan para que otros consuman; mientras existan las palabras 'burguesía' y 'plebe', no habrá paz*".
2 Even in the face of the effects of climate change, which would highlight Condorcet's prophetic phrase, it should be pointed out that it is not the planet that limits our perfectibility, but the capitalist mode of exploitation of labor and nature that dominates us, which, in its desire for limitless accumulation, is destroying the two main sources of its wealth: labor and nature. As Marx himself anticipated, "[c]apitalist production, therefore, only develops the techniques and the degree of combination of the social process of production by simultaneously undermining the original sources of all wealth—*the soil and the workers*" (Marx, 1996: 507–08, our emphasis).

In the eighteenth century, the discourse of Modernity conquered the world with its proposal of the inevitable progress of the human spirit, under the utopia and promise of full and limitless self-realization. For Condorcet (1795: 11), for example, "the perfectibility of man is absolutely indefinite; that the progress of this perfectibility, henceforth above the control of every power that would impede it, has no other limit than the duration of the globe upon which nature has placed us". However, today in the 21st century, we can affirm that the limits to this improvement do not come only from nature or from external structures but from the very way in which we as a collective or as individuals have organized our life in society.

Inequality is not only appalling in its sheer magnitude. It is that and more. Following the reasoning of critical thinkers of Modernity such as Rousseau, Condorcet, Godwin, and others, there is no doubt that the structures of social inequality, which have been strengthened in capitalism, directly attack the human spirit and reason, since they constitute structures that limit and attack the development of the human being. If this is so, the question is why inequality has never been attributed the weight and importance it deserves in social analysis. Except in the case of its most radical critics—Marx and Engels—inequality used to be assumed as a mere phenomenon; although not desired, it was thought as inevitable and intrinsic to any class society, even considered by some as a natural determinant of justice and equity, as Clark (1908) argued at the end of the nineteenth century. Likewise, *inequality* as a category of analysis was always subsumed in one of its most evident representations: poverty, marginality, or social exclusion. However, although these social and political phenomena are linked to inequality, they are not necessarily faithful and logical correlates of it. What we can affirm is that inequality as a social issue, although perhaps not conceived as such in previous scholarship, was always mediated by other categories and social processes (Therborn 2013).

Inequality is not only a matter of numbers and statistics—it is a phenomenon that directly affects the living conditions, health, and death of populations. As early as the beginning of the 1980s in Latin America, conversations about social inequality in the face of death were underway, with the role of social class as a factor of discrimination with respect to the health-illness-death process already being discussed (Bronfman and Tuirán 1984). Social classes and the social inequality, thus, act in a dual role. On one hand, it shows that social inequality in the face of death is itself a class inequality. On the other, it makes the class structure and the concept of class an essential theoretical basis for constructing frameworks for understanding and explaining social inequality in health, illness, and death. It is not only a matter of individual situations that differentiate people but a question of entire social structures from which the inequality that divides society and its population into social classes is constituted.

More recently, Therborn (2013: 7) has been emphatic in literally pointing out that "inequality kills." And it is not only about inequality in major regions of the world—even within the United States as well as in Europe, social inequality is expressed as a factor of death and an attack on people's health. In the case of the United States, for example, Therborn points out that inequalities of race and educational level together generated a gap of more than 12 years in life expectancy, which is practically equal to the difference in national averages between the United States and Bolivia (7). In this sense, the Black population and, in general, the less educated population of the United States would have a standard of living similar to that of the population of Bolivia, the least developed country in South America. Likewise, in the case of Europe, while life expectancy among the poorest and least educated strata tends to stagnate or grow very slowly, in the more privileged and better educated social strata it shows sustained growth, thus widening the gap between the life horizons of the poorest and most privileged populations. Even in very 'egalitarian' countries and societies with a strong welfare state, such as Finland, the gap in life expectancy between the richest quintile and the poorest increased between 1988 and 2007 (10).

In the face of this and other evidence, we can only agree with these authors and affirm that social inequality not only stunts the ability of individuals to develop fully, but also constitutes a major cause of death, and in the last decade, inequality as a force has killed more people than wars and terrorism. We contend that inequality is not some conjunctural situation typical of the many crises, distortions, and readjustments of the economy in recent decades, but it is a structural and intrinsic component of the dynamics of development and the capitalist way of life.

Likewise, although emphasis is commonly placed on the inequality of economic classes, it should be noted that it is not the only one that generates this type of deadly consequences. We tend to overlook other modes and structures of inequality that are also differentiating in terms of the mortality of individuals. It is becoming increasingly evident to us that gender inequality—that is, machismo, patriarchy, as well as homophobia—also kills; that ethnic-racial inequality—that is, discrimination and racism—also kills; that inequality based on migratory status and national origin—that is, xenophobia—also kills; that geographical and territorial inequality—that is, segregation or residential and spatial marginalization—also kills; and we could go on and on, pointing out other forms of inequality in the face of death in our current times.

Faced with this situation, in various international forums, academic, and political circles, as well as in civil society, critical voices have arisen that question the indolent tolerance that has been maintained for decades and centuries in the face of inequality. Thus, for example, there has been insistent talk of considering equality as a good of humanity. This is intended to elevate the principle and value of equality to the rank of a universal human value and/or right. While appreciating the scope that this formulation represents, it should be noted, however, that this proposal still needs to be complemented with its logical and natural corollary. If equality is a universal human value, it must, then, be understood that any form of inequality is, in the same sense, an attack on humanity itself, and, therefore, could very well be classified as *a crime against humanity*.

However, so far no one has stood up to affirm anything of the sort. On the contrary, in important centers of power and decision-making, not only does an indolent tolerance of inequality still prevail that would outrage anyone, but, in addition, voices are even raised to justify and defend inequality as a process that originates in the *natural* and intrinsic difference between human beings, thus ignoring the role of social and historical factors in the determination and genesis of the different forms and structures of social inequality.

Critical approaches, however, question these visions, pointing out that inequality merely reflects the inequitable and unjust nature of our societies, as it evidences the various contradictions and dilemmas that expose indolence in the face of exclusion and the pain of others (Stiglitz 2015; Sen 2009). In the United States, for example, contemporary inequality highlights the myth of a middle-class society in continuous advancement and progress, according to which each generation enjoyed better living conditions and welfare than the previous ones. A rich country, but full of poor people; a land of opportunities where a child's future depends more on his or her parents' income and education than on his or her own abilities and talents. A country where the richest are taxed less than the poorest in relation to their relative incomes; where justice is a function of the level of people's ability to pay. Based on this evidence, Stiglitz (2015: 86) concludes that "[t]hese are the contradictions that the United States is gradually and painfully struggling to come to terms with as it begins to comprehend the enormity of the inequalities that mark its society—inequities that are greater than in any other advanced country."

Contemporary societies have entered globalization bearing the burden of crushing social inequality. Contrary to apologetic discourse, globalization has only exacerbated the very structures of capitalism. Political institutions, social structures, ways of life, work, and reproduction—in short, the most basic structures of contemporary societies—function as ways of reproducing the privileges of some while at the same time excluding the majorities from those same privileges (Callinicos, 2003).

In the face of this reality, various discourses emerge. Terms and concepts such as *equity, equal opportunities, egalitarianism*, among others, are used indiscriminately to construct political and social positions and proposals against inequality and its manifestations. The debate on inequality, thus, crosses the academic frontiers and is placed, with full rights, in the social and political debate. In view of this, our interest with this book is to contribute to this debate from a critical and radical perspective,[3] which is nonetheless essentially conceptual and academic. On this occasion, we are not interested in the political debate itself but rather in providing arguments and theoretical and methodological reflections to support a radical critique. We are interested in providing a *theory of inequality* that allows an understanding and comprehension of its genesis and not only of its manifestations or consequences.

In the face of inequality, it is necessary and urgent to develop theoretical and methodological frameworks that, in addition to contributing to its understanding, make it possible to explain the forms and dimensions it assumes in contemporary society, as well as the ways to reduce and eventually abolish it.

We do not understand inequality as a form of differentiation pure and simple—that is, as a result of unjust distribution processes related to economics, income, power, capital, etc.—but as a founding structure of society. We do

---

3 By the use of the adjective *critical*, we understand a way of thinking and analysis that seeks to have a discernment with respect to the facts it analyzes, in such a way that it is possible to separate, judge, and distinguish, the different components of a social fact. It is not by chance that *critical* has the same root as *criterion* and *crisis*, since both terms help us to explain the meaning of what we understand by a critical perspective; on the one hand, the *criterion* and the *criterious* as a way or norm to know the truth of the facts. On the other hand, *crisis* as a category that allows us to identify and distinguish in each phenomenon its *critical* points—that is, inflection points—that account for eventual moments of rupture and transformation. Thus, a critical perspective is one that seeks the critical points and moments that give rise to possible processes of crisis as options for change and transformation and that, therefore, define the border points—that is, the limits and edges of each concept and social category and analysis—from which we can apprehend and think about the possibilities of transformation, change, and evolution of the facts and social structures to which these categories, theories, and concepts refer. With this we can construct a form of understanding of the social that is not only restricted to explaining the facts, but also to establishing horizons of reason—in other words, frontiers (critical and inflection points)—from which future options (transformation and change) can be thought of. And it is *radical* because our critique points to the root of the phenomena—to their very genesis—from which emerge both the forces that drive and consolidate it at one moment, as well as those that allow its evolution and transformation at other moments and that, together, determine the dynamics and movement of society, its evolution, and its history.

not analyze or use inequality on a more/less plane but on a structural plane, i.e., of structuring factors and processes. Based on Giddens, we see inequality as a matrix of society's constitution.

It is not that we consider irrelevant the analysis of social inequality as a result of distributive forms but that we place ourselves in another plane of analysis of this same situation of distributive inequality, electing not to describe or explain inequality in its determinants but rather to understand it as a way of constituting society.

Synthesizing these ideas, we can point out that in the face of inequality two main theses emerge:

a) Either inequality is understood as a consequence, a structure and process determined by the forms of Modernity, or
b) Inequality is seen as a process, a 'structuring structure' of Modernity itself.

This is not merely an academic distinction but one with profound political and ideological implications.

In the first case, from Modernity itself, it is possible to establish strategies and ways of confronting inequality that can lead to situations and processes for overcoming it. These are strategies of equality, equity, egalitarianism, and a focus on rights, in the most progressive cases.

In the second case, where we are situated, we analyze the way in which societies have been historically structured or constituted, based on structures of inequality and processes of inequality. It is, as we said—and taking up Giddens again—the perspective of inequality as a component in the constitution of society itself.

In this sense, we understand our critique of inequality—our discourse *against inequality*—as a critique of Western Modernity and, therefore, of the vary constitution of our societies as capitalistic societies—centered on capital and its accumulation as its founding social relation—and with it, of inequality as a foundational process and relation within capitalist society.

Our position not only seeks to understand inequality but to do so through a process of epistemological critique on a double plane. On the one hand, *criticism of the theories*, in the perspective proposed by Zemelman (1987)—that is, of critical reflection on the concepts, categories, indicators, and frameworks for understanding inequality. On the other hand, that of social criticism confronting inequality as a social phenomenon and, therefore, historically situated and structured.

It is an epistemological critique that not only questions and reconstructs the concepts and categories of analysis of inequality, but also one that fundamentally confronts inequality as a social fact in itself and, therefore, contributes to a strategy to overcome it.

It is an epistemological critique, since, if we consider inequality as a social fact, and, therefore, as historically situated, the analysis and critique of this social fact is also a process of social and historically situated reflection. Returning to Santos (2016), we look at inequality from an *Epistemology of the South*, that is, from a position of social critique insofar as we seek its critical points, its moments of inflection and possible ruptures from which we can think about the horizons of social and political transformation of inequality as a social fact. Thus, our critique of inequality is also a critique of capitalist Modernity. This is not only because we consider inequality as a pending issue of the progress and development promised by the modernist and capitalist narrative, but also, fundamentally, because we see inequality as one of the founding social matrices of this capitalist form of modernization and progress.

If inequality is not a remnant of traditional or pre-modern socio-historical structures, but, rather, constitutes a vector of the foundational matrix of Modernity, then overcoming inequality can only be achieved on the basis of a strategy of overcoming Modernity itself, or at least this capitalist form of Modernity we intimately know today. For the same reason, this radical restructuring is a strategy of social emancipation, which allows us to restructure the foundations of the constitution of this Modernity and with it, to restructure the foundations of society and its future history.

In synthesis, if we position ourselves epistemically within a discourse against inequality, it is because, from there, we want to further argue for a strategy of emancipation and liberation in the face of all forms of inequality. Therefore, it is not only a matter of reducing the extreme forms of inequality, or its contemporary manifestations and consequences. Nor is it a matter of governance or 'equalization' policies—equity, egalitarianism, or similar. We hope to frame all articulations of inequality in a larger proposal for social emancipation, fighting against all forms of inequality.

Discourses and proposals that purport equality—whether as equity or egalitarianism—adequately confront and face the manifestations and consequences of inequality, especially when framed within a rights-based approach. However, they do not necessarily address the fact that all societies have been constituted on the basis of structures of inequality and that, therefore, inequality is a constituent factor, a structuring structure of all social forms. For the same reason, equity, egalitarianism and other similar approaches do not resolve the fundamental fact that inequality refers to the way in which social subjects are constituted, not only to the way in which something is distributed among them.

The unequal distribution of wealth, power, privilege, and status has undoubtedly reached outrageous and indecent levels as of recent times. However, equalization as a method to diminish inequality only points to the most direct and immediate manifestation and consequence of inequality, but it does not point to the articulation of unequal subjects. What is required in this understanding is the *abolition* of these modes of constituting such subjects as unequal and, therefore, their *emancipation* from the structures (processes and relations) that constitute them as unequal.

These are the theses that we want to develop and argue in this book. It is not so much a study of inequality in itself but, rather, a critical reflection on the ways in which inequality has been thought of conceptually and politically at different moments in history, with special reference to the way in which inequality has been thought of and understood in modern and capitalist society. The sense of this reflection is none other than a theoretical and political demand *against inequality*—which is understood here as a mode of submission and social subjugation—and one that is in favor of an equally theoretical and political proposal for social emancipation against all forms of human inequality.

Marx pointed to the class struggle as the motor of history. He pointed this out in a correct, though partial, sense: It is not only the inequality and antagonism of classes that move history, but all forms of inequality that, in the processes of their construction, oppose and confront human beings by establishing modes of oppression of some over others, of discrimination of some with respect to others, and of exploitation of some by others. It is not only the social class struggle that moves history, but it is also the violence of patriarchy and the various struggles for gender, racism and ethnic-racial confrontation, geopolitical and territorial inequalities, intergenerational confrontations, among so many other ways of constituting inequality in our contemporary societies.

CHAPTER 1

New Perspectives and Imperatives in the Face of Inequality

> For a society where we are socially equal, humanly different, and totally free.
> ROSA LUXEMBURG

∴

In an early work on social inequality, the political philosopher Rousseau (1761) points out two kinds of general inequality in the human species:

1. A form that he calls 'natural' or 'physical', which refers to the intrinsic differences between individuals of the human species. This would include factors of the human body itself, such as age, health, bodily strength, to which he adds the qualities of the spirit or soul.
2. A social form that he calls 'moral' or 'political', which arises from the forms and conventions established by human beings in their social coexistence. This would correspond to the different privileges and benefits enjoyed by some individuals to the detriment of others, such as wealth, power, status, and authority.

The first form of inequality corresponds to the forms of differentiation inherent to individuals of any species, including human beings. As individuals, we are not physically equal or identical to one another—that is an irrefutable truism. Natural differences between individuals are even a fundamental factor for reproduction itself as a species. However, an important point to note is that not every difference leads to inequality—or, more precisely, that the genuine natural difference between human beings is not a reason for any form of social inequality. The fact that human beings are not *naturally equal* to one another is no reason for us to be *socially unequal* with respect to one another.

Thus, for example, men and women are not equal or undifferentiated individuals—that is obvious. Our bodies, our reproductive apparatus, our physiognomy and physiology are different and establish a natural and necessary distinction for the reproduction of the species. However, the fact that men and women are not naturally equal is no reason to build some form of social inequality on that natural difference. The differences in our natures define just that, natural differences, but not necessarily social differences. For a natural difference to become social inequality, it requires the mediation of social-historic processes from which such natural difference is reconstructed and redefined. In this process of mediation—where the natural ceases to be natural and becomes social—it is not nature that creates inequality but those social processes that act as mediators between nature and society. In the case of the difference between men and women, for example, it corresponds to patriarchy and the forms of sexual division of labor and power, from which relationships of exploitation and domination of men over women and discrimination of women against men are built. Therefore, the construction of difference and inequality implicate political, economic, cultural, and demographic processes, all of which are essentially social and historical and constitute the basis on which all forms of social inequality are built. The socially transformed differences of nature only refer to their immediate, directly observable forms, never arriving to the genesis of such forms of inequality or their complex articulations.

In this line of thought, Rousseau points out that social inequality constitutes a historical phenomenon that arises with the creation of private property, which he exemplifies by referring to inequality as that difference in the possession or appropriation of resources, privileges, and benefits among individuals. In this case, inequality does not stem from the differences between the forms of individuals, their characteristics, or profiles but, rather, from the material resources they may possess or appropriate. Inequality, therefore, does not refer to an intrinsic—natural—difference between individuals but to their position in a social structure that implies a differentiation in terms of the resources and privileges they possess—something that is, in its essence, the result of certain underlying social relations.[1]

From this perspective, which emphasizes the social-historical character of inequality, there has always been a debate about its causes and origins, as

---

1   Social inequality between men and women, for example, does not arise from the differentiated form of their bodies, structures, minds, etc., but is the product of a social process: the sexual division of labor or, in other words, the different form of appropriation and enjoyment of the labor of others and, therefore, a relationship of exploitation and domination of some (men) over others (women). The same can be said with respect to other ways of dividing social relations, such as class, ethnic-racial, nationality, intergenerational (age), geographic and territorial inequality, among many others.

well as about what to do about it. Lenski (1984) points out that, from antiquity to the present day, two major positions have dominated human thinking on inequality: This is the eternal debate between conservatives, on the one hand, and critics or radicals, on the other. The former "is essentially supportive of the status quo, viewing the existing distribution of rewards as just, equitable, and frequently also inevitable. The other is highly critical, denouncing the distributive system as basically unjust and unnecessary" (p. 5). For centuries, these two views and positions on inequality have been debated over and over again by scholars, laymen, political leaders, and officials at all levels. According to Lenski, the form of the debate changes, of course, but the arguments underlying both perspectives are the same at their nucleus. For some it is fair, equitable, and even essentially necessary and functional, while for others, it is unjust, unacceptable, and harmful. What is relevant, in any case, is that, faced with the issue of inequality, these different positions have been maintained with few variations throughout the history of civilizations, especially in the West (Harman, 2008).

From our perspective, however, we do not see the issue as something so simple. The differences in perspectives on inequality are not only in terms of moral and political principles vis-à-vis its consequences and manifestations but also refer us to the confrontation between two major modes of understanding the social and the ways of constituting societies. We refer to what Tilly (1999) points out as two major ontological and epistemic perspectives, namely:

1. On the one hand, we identify an individualistic approach, centered on having, which defines inequality as a *function of distribution* among individuals. In this approach, inequality is understood as an uneven distribution of attributes, resources, privileges, rights, or other elements among a set of individuals. *Having, distribution* and *individuals* would be the fundamental categories of analysis on which the discourse on inequality is built.

2. On the other hand, we identify a structuralist and relational approach, according to which inequality would correspond to structures of differentiation between social subjects, which are constituted as such on the basis of a system of relationships that link them to each other. *Being, relations*, and *social subjects* would be the fundamental concepts that underlie the discourse on inequality. Unlike the previous one, this perspective considers that inequality expresses a social division between social categories called classes, genders, races, nationalities, or others, which are constituted on the basis of relations of domination, exploitation, and discrimination that give rise to this social division, and from which forms

and modes of identity and belonging to these social categories are constructed. Inequality is, thus, always a categorical inequality.

In the first case, from individualistic and distributive ontologies, inequality is understood as an essentially inevitable phenomenon, although it is governable and manageable in terms of its forms, dimensions, and magnitudes that it can reach. The inevitability arises from the irrefutable fact that human beings are inherently different individuals among us, both in terms of the talents and capabilities we possess and the needs we demand (Sen, 2009). Thus, there will always be forces driving an unequal distribution of payoffs (whether in resources, prestige, privilege, welfare, status, etc.), as all payoffs are always a function of the merit/need duality, and around which differentiation and inequality among human beings is built.

This perspective of the supposed governable nature of social inequality exists because it is a perspective that focuses on the field of *having*, rather than on the sphere of *being*. If inequality refers to what people have with respect to a "something" (Sen, 1992)—be it income, privileges, status among others, etc.—then it will always be possible to establish public policies and programs that can *re-distribute* those "somethings"—that original phenomenon that created unequal individuals—in order to correct the excesses in the original distribution function of those "somethings". That is, it will always be possible to reduce, to certain socially and politically tolerable parameters, the range of differentiation in the original distribution of each "something" that originates the inequality between individuals in a population.

The key question in this rhetoric, then, centers on determining the socially acceptable limits of inequality, which defines the general framework for State action and public policies (social policy, economic policy, among others). The action of the State (and the political negotiations between the different social actors involved) corresponds, then, to a mode of governance and management of the forms, manifestations, and magnitudes of inequality. This on two levels. On the one hand, it is effectively aimed at reducing inequality to politically tolerable and socially acceptable levels, for which redistributive strategies of various kinds are established. On the other hand, it aims to create conditions of equality and equity among individuals, so that it is only the natural difference in merit and capabilities, as well as needs, that determines the forms and magnitudes of social inequality. The aim, then, of policies forged in this rhetoric is to control the effects that social and cultural structures generate as 'supposed' distortions in the natural differentiation between individuals and, therefore, to reduce their impact in determining social inequality.

In the second case, however, the issue is seen from a totally different perspective. Inequality does not refer to *having* but to *being*. What constitutes inequality is not the difference in what each *has* in relation to the other, but, rather, what each *is* in relation to the other. This turns the traditional relationship of inequality upside down. We are not unequal because we have different possessions (income, resources, talents, opportunities, privileges, status, etc.), but we have different possessions because we are unequal. It is not the distribution function and its possible modes of redistribution that defines the structure of social inequality, but, rather, it is categorical inequality that determines the shape of the distribution function of possessions among individuals according to their constitution and membership in a given social category.

Thus, in this perspective, class inequality does not mean that workers are workers because they have less income than professionals, and, in the same line of thought, that professionals have less income than capitalist entrepreneurs, but more than general employees or office workers. That is to say, an individual is not a worker because they have this or that level of income, resides in this or that neighborhood, has this or that access to education and health, among other fields of distinction related to social inequality. Rather, it is the other way around: an individual, because they are a worker, has such socioeconomic living conditions (health, education, housing, work, income, etc.). While the concept of generalized socioeconomic inequality may be complex, it is undeniably evident in the context of gender or ethnic-racial disparities. In these cases, one's gender plays a significant role in determining access to various social realms, influencing standards of living, income, employment, and more. Similarly, ethnic-racial inequality operates on a similar principle. It is not an individual's possessions that define their ethnic-racial status, but rather the mandated condition that, to a certain extent, dictates the goods, resources, and various forms of capital that each person can acquire.

This example allows us to illustrate this distinction between a perspective of inequality centered on *being* vs. one centered on *having*. The former, unlike the latter, establishes that inequality is constructed on the basis of processes and relations between subjects and social categories. Thus, inequality in terms of having something is, in reality, determined by this unequal constitution of subjects and social categories. Therefore, the basis of inequality is not in what one *has* but in what one *is*. Thus, the genesis of inequality will not be found within the function of material distribution—that is, the way in which individuals are distributed according to the volume of their possessions and holdings—nor the way in which such possessions and holdings are distributed among individuals. Rather, the genesis of inequality lies in those social processes on which such social subjects and categories are constituted as socially unequal—processes that, as we shall see in the following chapters, refer to relations and structures of social *domination*, *exploitation*, and *discrimination*.

It is also relevant to point out that these relational processes and structures refer to ways of constituting society itself. This is why we say that categorical inequality, thus understood, is a foundational process of society itself.

Thus, if inequality is the product of a system of categorical relations—that is, between classes, races, genders, nationalities—and not a function of the distribution of something among individuals, then it is not the differences in talents and capacities among human beings that determine the forms and structuring of social inequality. It is not that the presence of differentiated talents and capacities is denied, only that their explanatory and inequality-determining potential is restricted and limited. For one thing, any physical differentiation between individuals, at most, allows us to explain the inequality between these different individuals, but it never allows us to explain the social reproduction of this form of inequality, nor how it is transferred and inherited to the following generations. In other words, these individualistic ontologies of inequality fail to explain how individual inequality becomes a social structure between subjects and individuals that is transferred from one generation to another and, then, passed on from one epoch to the next.

Likewise, if it is assumed that the origin of inequality is the natural difference between individuals, this perspective does not explain how and why inequality is systematically presented as modes of differentiation between the same categories of subjects—that is, why one category, women for example, is systematically placed in inferior and subordinate positions with respect to another, men in this case. When the differences between categories of individuals refer more to the character of such categorization of distinction and less to the individual character of such distinction—that is, to the individuality of individuals—then, it is evident that inequality is not between individuals but between social categories and, therefore, that inequality is not due to a supposed individual differentiation but, rather, to a social construction of categorial differentiation—that is, to the social and historical structuring of social categories of differentiation and inequality.

Again, inequality between categories—gender, ethnic-racial, class, among others—does not refer only to attributes of such subjects but to a grandiose social structure that is constituted from the relationship that gives rise to such social categories—that is, to a social and historical structuring of inequality between such categories of social subjects. Thus, categorical inequality refers not only to *categories of analysis* but to inequality between social subjects. Each category of inequality is itself a *social category*, a concrete social subject, a historically and socially situated collective, and, therefore, inequality itself is also a historical and socially situated process, not a result of the naturally given attributes and differences in the individual profiles of human beings.

The difference between individuals is real and undeniable, we want to clarify. But this does not imply that this difference alone is the origin of social inequality between individuals. Individual differences can never explain the persistence of social inequality, as Tilly (1999) reminds us. And even less can individual differences explain the persistence of concrete and recurrent modes of social inequality, such as gender inequality, class inequality, ethnic-racial inequality, among many other modes of social inequality.

Faced with this stark contrast between individualist and structuralist paradigms, a third perspective is often put forward by theorists, which corresponds to the idea of *social stratification*. In this vision, society would not be divided into classes but, rather, into social strata, a more flexible category of analysis. Although this perspective represents aspects of the social structure, the understanding of its configuration at each moment is also intrinsically linked to the characteristics and attributes of individuals. Structural-functionalism is inscribed in this line, although sociology with Weberian roots is also often included.[2]

However, from our perspective, any theory of inequality based on the social stratification approach must solve the following dilemmas in order to pose its particular approach to the origin of the inequality that stratification wants to represent:[3]

1. Whether the social strata themselves are constructed on the basis of individual difference from the form that the distribution function between individuals assumes at each moment and in each place;
2. or if, to the contrary, the distribution function is the result of the historical form of the structuring (constitution) of these social strata.

The first case is usually the most common, where the use of 'strata' refers to categories established by the researcher, the politician, or the social analyst, with respect to the form assumed by the distribution function that renders individuals unequal. That is, a categorization based on the way in which something—power, resources, income, privileges, social status, etc.—is distributed among individuals. Categories of analysis, in this case, are constructed on the basis of this unequal distribution that refer to specific strata within that form of the distribution function. Or, more simply put, researchers construct these analytical categories based on perceived, visible inequity in the social realms they

---

[2] In both cases, we discuss this approach to stratification in more detail in subsequent chapters, especially the functionalist theories of Parsons and Davis.
[3] What is relevant is that any solution to this dilemma necessarily leads to adopting one of the two major ontological perspectives already outlined. In the first case, it leads to an individualistic ontology, while in the second, it leads to a structuralist one.

consider. In this perspective, strata would be aggregates of individuals, differentiated on the basis of a categorization that reflects the relative position of each individual in the distribution function.

The extreme cases—and, therefore, the ones that best reflect this situation—refer to the strata constructed based on statistical procedures, such as quintiles, deciles, or percentiles. Or inequality measured on the basis of other quantitative indicators, such as the Gini index, inter-quartile interval, or any other model that estimates the distance between different strata within the distribution function in our social worlds. In all these cases, it is evident that, despite the construction of an idea of inequality related to social stratification, the individualistic paradigm predominates contemporary discourses and debates of inequality, where inequality is the result of the banal and even natural form taken by the distance of individuals with respect to their access to a given thing—income, privileges, status, etc. But in fact, social stratification itself is constructed on the basis of that same distribution function of that 'something' among the individuals that make up any given society.[4]

Therefore, it is easy to understand that under this mode of stratification the premise of the individualistic paradigm of social mobility is maintained as a matter of the characteristics, talents, merits, and capacities of individuals, not so much of structural factors. Mobility, indeed, is the transit of an individual from one stratum to another, which is achieved according to their capacity to access a greater volume of resources, income, privileges, or whatever is shaping the particular distribution function. This common, even popular, model of mobility is possible because the current understanding of the social stratification of individuals is dominated by the individualist paradigm in terms of the origin of social inequality.

In the second way of considering social stratification, the structuralist paradigm predominates. In this model, the distribution function is the result of a particular historical form of social structuring of inequality and, therefore, reflects a structure of inequality among social subjects: classes, ethnicities, races, genders, nationalities, among many others. Therefore, in this model, the social constitution of the subjects and categories of inequality is prior to and at a higher level of analysis than the distribution function. In fact, every

---

4 Whether considering the question from data of income strata, for example, which are constructed on the basis of statistical methods (percentiles), or on the basis of ad hoc categories or ways of representing social classes (upper, middle and lower class), the method of analysis does not alter the central argument, since in both cases the resulting stratification is constructed on the basis of the income distribution function among individuals in a population and not fundamental rights based on constructions of power.

distribution function (of income, privileges, status, etc.) derives from this historical form of constitution of the social categories of inequality and, therefore, from the structure of social relations and processes that at each historical moment constitute the social structure of inequality between classes, genders, races, nationalities, or others.

From this perspective, if there is any sense or utility in using a social stratification perspective constructed on the basis of the distribution function in research considering inequality, it is to have an empirical approximation to the social structures of categorical inequality between subjects, classes, races, ethnicities, genders, and others—but in no case does such a perspective constitute a method or theory that allows the substitution of structural, sociohistoric particularity. Even when it is not made explicit, in this model, social inequality is, again, essentially a structural issue, constituted on the basis of processes of categorical inequality, in Tilly's terms.

As we can see from this discussion, the social stratification approach does not constitute a unique paradigm or model, *per se,* and, therefore, cannot be considered as an alternative to the individualist and structuralist approaches; rather, any stratification model is necessarily inscribed in one or the other paradigms of inequality, without offering a true alternative to them in terms of the way of understanding the origin and constitution of social inequality. However, as an approach, it does have a certain heuristic and methodological value, since it contributes to the design of methodologies, indicators, and modes of empirical reconstruction of social inequality, regardless of the theoretical and ontological paradigm assumed.

If inequality refers not to the possessions that one or the other has but to the social constitution of one or other as unequal beings within hierarchical social categories, then the analysis of the genesis and modes of social structuring of inequality does not refer to particular modes of distribution of those possessions—those "somethings" to which Sen alludes—but, rather, to the very modes of constitution of such social categories—that is, of the social-historical structuring of classes, genders, ethnicities, races, nationalities, generations, and geographies. In this perspective, the analysis of the distributive functions of supposed "somethings" only makes sense as a mediation for the analysis of the essences of inequality (Tilly), that is, it demonstrates the links and structures of the larger social processes that configure subjects as unequal, which is manifested in the distributive inequality of these "somethings".

1   Imperatives of an Emancipation Strategy in the Face of Global Inequality

If our understandings of inequality refer to structures of differentiated constitution of individuals as unequal social subjects, and not so much to a matter of distinction between individuals, purely and simply, then there are no measures of equity and egalitarianism that would ever allow us to break these structures that generate categorical inequalities. From this perspective of understanding inequality as categorical structures, the only exit strategy must be one that confronts these structures directly, dismantling them and reconstituting new social forms on the basis of principles of equality and equity. Therefore, they are not public policies, no matter how progressive they were, the strategy to overcome inequality, but rather strategies of social emancipation.[5]

Let's put it simply with a very illustrative example: Currently, the promotion of gender equity policies, parity forms of power distribution, among many others, has become very popular. However, these are strategies that are more concerned with the form of the distribution function and less with its genesis. How far away in time are we from those early, radical discourses of feminism that advocated not for gender equity in our current capitalistic world but simply for the liberation and emancipation of women.

Surely, what is being proposed today in the 21st century in the face of patriarchy and its global forms, i.e., strategies of equity, no one would have dared to propose such an idea in the face of slavery in the 19th century, when slave forms of social inequality still prevailed. From whatever perspective, it is undoubtedly unwise and unreasonable to propose to an enslaved individual that the best strategy to confront their current condition of oppression, subjugation, and discrimination is that of mere master-slave equalization, as part of a larger strategy of equity within the system of slavery itself. On the contrary, the only sensible and realistic approach to any situation of marked inequality such as this is to propose what was actually implemented in those years: a strategy of *emancipation* from their condition as slaves based on the abolition of all forms of slavery—that is, the dissolution of the social structures and relations that gave rise not only to the condition of masters and slaves but of the very slavery that constituted some as masters and others as slaves. While in the case of slavery, a emancipatory strategy seems to be clear common sense, but when it comes other issues of drastic inequality, such as gender inequality,

---

5   It is not from above—from the State with their equity policies and programs—where we will see legitimate fights for and strategies of overcoming inequality but from below—from and with the social subjects as protagonists of social emancipation processes.

class inequality, ethnic-migratory inequality, and so many other contemporary forms of social inequality, an emancipatory strategy is distorted and covered up with a thousand political rhetoric.

This is why, from our critical perspective that explicitly argues against all forms of inequality, the only strategy that makes sense and has historical transcendence is that of social emancipation. This strategy implies, however, confronting various imperatives, of which three seem to us to be the most relevant for our discussion: (1) an ethical imperative, (2) an existential imperative, and (3) a political imperative.

1.1   An Ethical Imperative

Because any form of inequality is a form of social exclusion that always results in the social construction of limitations on people's lives, it implies an ethical imperative. As Therborn (2013: 21) points out, inequality, "when it doesn't literally kill people, … it stunts people's lives." It is, in any case, a situation that entails a deep social division, where some can access a full development of their capacities and potentialities as human beings, while others see their options to fully participate in social and political life as limited. By limiting people's options for development and life fulfillment, inequality not only implies shortages, injustices, or inequities but, above all, a denial of the ethical principles and values on which the condition of every human being is based.

Those who are in a position of inequality are not only exposed to risks and vulnerabilities of all kinds, but are also, first and foremost, prevented from achieving their full realization as human beings. All forms of inequality, along with social exclusion and discrimination, also subordinate and subjugate, preventing the realization of people as free and sovereign beings. They are forms and social ties that constitute modes of dependence of some on others and modes of imposing the condition of some by denying that of others. Inequality does not only refer to having fewer resources than others but also involves essentially denying, even partially, the human condition of some for the full development of others. As Therborn (2013: 1) points out, "inequality, then, is not just about the size of wallets. It is a sociocultural order, which (for most of us) reduces our capabilities to function as human beings, our health, our self-respect, our sense of self, as well as our resources to act and participate in this world."

Therefore, any discourse against inequality entails an ethical imperative, which makes it necessary to confront all forms of exclusion as a way of restoring people's *dignity*, that is, of restoring their condition as human beings, which is violated on a daily basis by exclusion and inequality. Any debate on inequality must necessarily cover this ethical and moral imperative. It is in our opinion that any rigorous debate on inequality must, first, be undertaken from an essentially humanistic perspective to adequately debate its forms, causes, consequences, policies, and strategies. The first thing that should be in question is not the "something" that makes us unequal, not the degree or level of inequality with respect to a "something", but the fact that all inequality is an attack on human dignity, insofar as it prevents and limits the full realization of the basic and primary condition of every human being: the realization of their humanity.

In traditional, pre-modern societies, inequality did not pose an ethical dilemma, since the issue was resolved on the basis of an ideological matrix according to which individuals are neither equal nor alike. Inequality was, thus, due either to natural factors or to divine causes. We were unequal because of our unequal human nature or because some god wanted it that way; in no case did it imply a moral dilemma. In modern society, which is based on the principle of equality of all human beings, regardless of their social, ethnic, gender, nationality, or any other category of social distinction, any form of inequality is, by the same token, an attack on that principle of universal value on which Modernity itself is founded. In other words, any form of inequality is not only a way of restricting the lives of the people who suffer it but is also, in essence, an attack on humanity itself.

1.2 *An Existential Imperative*

If inequality refers not so much to the sphere of *having* as it does to the sphere of *being*, then all inequality necessarily refers to people's forms of existence. Every form of inequality (of class, gender, race, geography or any other) is based on a form of social division of people, which refers not to what each individual possesses or has the option of accessing, but fundamentally to his or her way of *being* and *existing* in this world. Social division does not only refer to forms of distance between some individuals and others (for the same reason, it does not refer to the degree or size of that distance), but it refers to a division between social categories, that is, between subjects socially and historically constituted on the basis of social relations and structures. In this sense, we can affirm that all forms of inequality not only divide individuals but also separate and regroup them insofar as they constitute strata, classes, different and unequal social categories in terms of their options and conditions of *existence* as social subjects, not only as individuals (Tilly, 1999).

Inequality not only implies the division between social categories but also the shaping of socially differentiated identities, belongings, and forms of existence. Thus, all social inequality refers to a division between differentiated forms of human beings, establishing a distinction in terms of the forms of social existence of these social categories. For the same reason, all inequality, while being based on a profound social division into classes, genders, races, etc., is also based on diverse modes of existence of these classes, genders, and races. It is on this level that we refer to inequality as an *existential* phenomenon, since it refers to modes of social construction of the very existence of people insofar as they are constituted as social subjects and not as mere individuals.

The corollary of this ontological perspective is simple and radical: If inequality is not a matter of distribution of something between individuals but is always referred to as a categorical inequality, then a redistributive solution, that is, one that focuses on the search for and construction of conditions of distributive equity, pure and simple, is neither enough nor sufficient in any case.

Any redistributive strategy aims at creating conditions of equity in terms of *having*, but it never attempts to solve the problem itself in terms of the unequal forms of *being* of subjects—of their unequal forms of identity, belonging, and existence. Faced with this insufficiency of such redistributive proposals, what is required is a *strategy of social liberation* and *emancipation* that implies the *abolition* of the structures of social inequality, that is, of the links and relationships on which the categories of social inequality themselves are constituted.

In the case of gender inequality, for example, the proposal of *gender equity* is not enough, however progressive and liberal such a strategy may seem.[6] What is required is a return to the original proposal of feminism that proclaimed *women's liberation* as a process of social emancipation that would abolish the structures of patriarchy. For one thing, it is not only equity or equality of access to different spheres: power, resources, privileges, etc., since it is not only a struggle for the emancipation of women but of society as a whole. It is not about the equalization of women with men, but about the abolition of the social division between men and women and, therefore, the abolition of the categories of man and woman, masculine and feminine as categories of social, political, economic, family, cultural, demographic and other distinctions used to inscribe inequality.

The greater struggle against racism and slavery referred to the abolition of slavery as a process from which the master-slave relationship was constituted and, with it, its corresponding social categories; just as in the nineteenth century, today, the struggle against gender inequality (and any other mode of social inequality) must also refer to the abolition of patriarchy as a social process from which the male/female, masculine/feminine relationship is constituted,

---

6 In this regard, a clarification is in order to avoid misunderstandings: We mean here that equity-focused strategies are *not sufficient* in larger fights for structural inequality, although they are *undoubtedly necessary* and, therefore, welcome. We only wish to warn of their structural limitation as a strategy *against* inequality.

and, thus, the corresponding gender categories that divide and render the population and society inequal.

The structures of inequality are much deeper than their immediate forms that are reflected as distribution functions. That is why the strategies of equity and equalization of forces between social subjects are just that, a change in the correlation of forces between such subjects, never a social and historical overcoming of the conditions and structures that gave rise to their constitution as socially unequal subjects.

1.3 A Political Imperative

All inequality implies a form of social division itself that is sustained by patterns of social exclusion. The political question arises when we ask ourselves: How it is possible to maintain forms of social cohesion and integration in a community divided by the exclusion of some in favor of others? How is it possible to maintain and reproduce forms of life in common among subjects socially divided and traversed by dynamics of social exclusion? How is it possible that those who are unequal in material and status do not rise up at every moment against these social structures that subject and subordinate them to positions of inequality? This contradiction is resolved at the political level, that is, through the exercise of power, particularly in two distinct ways. On the one hand, it is resolved through forms of domination and oppression of some over others and, on the other, through forms of legitimization, both of inequality and social division as practices and of the forms of domination themselves.

Inequality does not refer to any simple division between one and others in the distribution of wealth. It is neither the envy of the poor for the luxuries of the rich that arouses anger, resentment, dissatisfaction and frustrations. In fact, the wealth and luxuries of football and entertainment celebrities, for example, arouse not only morbidity, but also generate a certain admiration among 'common' people. While, on the other hand, in the case of other rich people, things are totally different, because we know that they, "the captains of finance and the rest of the economy, are not entertaining us. *They are ruling us*" (Therborn, 2013: 21; emphasis ours). That is why their wealth arouses neither morbidity nor admiration in the masses but, rather, a type of rage and frustration for the sheer fact of knowing that the rich are not only rich but also incredibly powerful and that, deep down, their wealth and luxuries are sustained by the very power of domination and subjugation of us, the others, the poor and unequal.

Inequality implies not only a social division between the rich and poor, but it also suggests a large gap in the distribution of power between the powerful rich and the powerless poor, between the dominant and the dominated.

This division between the included and the excluded cannot be sustained by itself but only on the basis of these other forms of social division of power and domination over society and its forms of inequality. In other words, the social division between classes, genders, races, nationalities, and other forms is always and at all times resolved from relationships of power, establishing hegemonic forms of domination in each of the planes in which social inequality is manifested and constituted: domination of classes, domination of gender, domination of races, domination of nationalities, etc. What is relevant in this discussion is that, in all these cases, domination is not necessarily and at all times exercised in authoritarian ways and with the use of brute force, but it is also fundamentally structured on the basis of cultural hegemonies that legitimize the various forms of inequality and social exclusion, as well as the use of force and oppression to maintain and reproduce them over time. For this reason, these hegemonic separations are modalities that contribute to the perpetuation and reproduction in time and history of these forms of inequality, exclusion, and social division.[7]

One way of exemplifying this situation of domination and hegemony is based on the unequal social valuation of some subjects (classes, genders, races, nationalities, etc.) with respect to others, that is, the unequal legitimacy attributed to each social category in each mode of inequality. Bauman (2011), with his usual acuity, exemplifies this when he analyzes the issue of inequality and exclusion from the perspective of the so-called "collateral damage" of global and postmodern society.

It is generally accepted that inequality places the most unequal in conditions of greater vulnerability to natural and social catastrophes. The question is why and how they accept this greater propensity to be part of the collateral damage of capitalism. This could be explained, in part, by the fact that the poor

---

[7] Gender inequality exemplifies this. Male dominance over women has been with us since the beginning of our history as humanity, to such an extent that there is no lack of males who believe that their power is a condition of human nature. Likewise, male power is sustained both by forms of daily violence against women and by a narrative that legitimizes this daily violence and the supposed supremacy of men over women. Male domination, like other modes of domination, is, thus, exercised both from the field of force and from violent and stark imposition, as well as from the field of ideology and consciousness, creating cultural, political, and ideological hegemonies that seek to legitimize this masculine violence and larger systems of gender inequality (Bourdieu, 2000). The clearest example, in this sense, is when women who are victims of rape, harassment, or other type of patriarchal violence are held responsible for that same violence suffered by them, with discourses such as: it was her fault because of where she walked, how she dressed, because woman are the provocateurs, among other discursive forms, which seeks to delegitimize the position of women even when it comes to their defense against the violence of male domination (Segato, 2016).

and the unequal, natural candidates for collateral damage of any human or natural endeavor, are "branded permanently, as they tend to be, with the double stigma of non-importance and unworthiness" (Bauman, 2011: 8). In other words, while for the rich and the 'equal' every harm against them is considered an attack on society itself, when it comes to the poor and unequal, these same harms are understood as collateral effects and consequences, situations that are totally acceptable and tolerable for the sake of achieving a greater end that benefits society as a whole. They become mere "collateral damage," thus demonstrating that these are situations and consequences that, although dramatic, are irrelevant and unimportant to such an extent that they do not reach the minimum status to be considered in any assessment of risks and vulnerabilities for society and, therefore, do not reach the minimum value necessary to be incorporated as a relevant factor, or at least to be considered, in the decision-making process regarding any human undertaking, be it in economics, politics, or war. The unequal is thus, in a historic trend of violently placed hierarchies, socially categorized and signified as "the rejects of order and the refuse of modernization ... victims of order maintenance and economic progress" (Bauman, 2011: 7).

The fact that a person in unequal conditions loses their house as a result of a real estate crisis is irrelevant, a mere collateral damage compared to the social and economic damage that would result if that situation were to affect a bank manager or one of the financial brokers who contributed with their speculation strategy to that same real estate crisis. The damages and negative effects of any social and human undertaking are not only unequally distributed, but above all, they are unequally legitimized and valued by society. It is this inequality in the legitimacy of the condition of being and existing of each social category, of each class, gender, race, etc., that allows sustaining and giving legitimacy to the same social inequality, to the same inequality in the self-perception and public recognition of the value and social and cultural meaning of each social category, again of each class, race, gender, or nationality.

This inequality in the social recognition of each subject and their unequally valued position is reflected in the tendency, which is already a constant, that every time there is an economic or financial crisis, rescue policies tend to prioritize big businessmen, managers, and CEOs, who are also usually those who bear the main brunt of the responsible for these crises, substantially postponing and restricting aid to those most in need (Stiglitz, 2012).

Although the damage may be the same (and even tends to be relatively more serious when it affects the most unequal), the social valuation of the damage is not because it is constructed from conditions of social and cultural hegemony, that is, from positions of power and ideological dominance that configure an unequal valuation and relevance of some subjects with respect to others. Although in the liberal discourse of our Western democracies all individuals are equal before the law, we are, in fact, not equal before the State, the market, or social institutions, nor are we equal within the categorizations of class, gender, race, and/or nationality.[8]

One of the glaring instances of unequal valuation, and consequently, the social and public significance or 'importance,' in the realm of contemporary social violence is observed in discussions surrounding acts such as aggressions, rapes, murders, and other crimes. Distinct treatment is accorded to victims based on their gender identity and expression. For instance, violence, particularly against women, inherently categorized as gender-based violence, is so prevalent that public discourse often tends to attribute responsibility to the victim or, at the very least, highlights perceived recklessness in her behavior as a supposed precursor to such acts of aggression (Segato, 2016).

Another example that shows the ways in which these situations of privileged valuations are manifested through unequal strategies of resource allocation, can be found in the provisions of technological surveillance devices and staffing for public protection and security in the more affluent neighborhoods compared to the poorest and most economically impoverished neighborhoods. Both cases above quickly illustrate the unequal social valuation of the damages and consequences of any economic and social policy, not to mention the unequally distributed effects of natural disasters and other social ills such as violence.

Inequality, thus, reflects one of the weakest and most contradictory aspects of Western democracies and, therefore, at the same time, puts the concept of democracy itself into constant questioning and political tension. As Bauman (2011: 13) points out, in our brand new and dominant Western democracies, social inequality poses an irresolvable "contradiction between the formal universality of democratic rights (accorded to all citizens equally) and the less than universal ability of their holders to exercise such rights effectively; in other words, the gap separating the legal condition of a 'citizen de jure' from the practical capacity of a citizen de facto."

The corollary is simple and clear: social inequality does not allow ordinary citizens to fully exercise their political rights, thereby limiting the conditions for the full exercise of their political freedom. This reflection by Bauman leads us to return to the old discussion on the supposed—and, in our opinion,

---

8   Thus, for example, within the same family context, the wife losing her job does not have the same impact and meaning as when it is the husband who loses it, even if it is the case that the wife is the main breadwinner in the family.

false—dilemma between freedom and equality. Following Bauman's reasoning, we can then affirm that without a full and equitable exercise of social rights (equality) of all and for all, political rights (freedom) become meaningless and useless for most individuals. In other words, just as equality is a necessary and indispensable condition for establishing the full enjoyment of freedom, conversely the condition of freedom is also a necessary and indispensable condition for establishing social structures and relations among equals. Freedom and equality are mutually imbricated phenomena, embedded in each other. Without the condition of one, the other becomes fictitious, that is, a social fiction that only contributes to maintaining situations of domination and power of some over others.

This is where Rosa Luxemburg's widely quoted phrase with which we began this chapter takes on its full meaning: A person is not totally free if that freedom implies some form of inequality with respect to others. Conversely, social inequality can only be abolished when the total freedom of subjects is restored on all planes.[9] This is necessarily so because equality and freedom refer ontologically to the sphere of existence of subjects, that is, to their modes of being, socially speaking. As discussed above, it does not refer to the various modes of distributing goods or to the sheer possession of some type of resources, privileges, and/or other economic, social, and cultural devices themselves. Rather, freedom can only be constituted between socially equal subjects and individuals, and, conversely, equality can only be constituted between totally free subjects and individuals.

In this sense, we understand that any discourse against inequality, further, necessarily entails a political imperative, since any form of inequality is in itself a way of preventing and limiting the full exercise of the political and citizens' rights of individuals and social subjects. For the same reason, and from this political imperative, a critique of inequality cannot be resolved purely and simply on the basis of strategies of equity and redistribution of rights, resources, or privileges. A radical critique of inequality is essentially political, and subversive, because it is based on a project of emancipation and social and political liberation, where the term *liberation* refers not only to the abolition of

---

9   Thus, for example, the abolition of slavery in the 19th century was undoubtedly an important step, but it did not restore either equality or full freedom of the former slaves, since such abolition was only formal and limited to the legal, maintaining racism as a dominant and hegemonic mode in the idiosyncratic construction of many nations and peoples of the Western world, a situation that prevails to this day, as exemplified by Barack Obama, when in his farewell speech he explicitly stated that "race remains a potent and often divisive force in our society" (*The New York Times*, 2017, January 10).

the chains of inequality but also, and through this same process, to the restitution of the conditions of freedom of individuals.

This proposal leads us to a profound critique of the way in which equality and freedom are treated in Western societies. In this regard, and returning to the critical writing of Amartya Sen, we can ask ourselves why in Western democracies "any violation of liberty, significant as it is, [is] invariably ... judged to more crucial ... than suffering from intense hunger, starvation, epidemics, and other calamities ... treating the slightest gain of liberty—no matter how small—as enough reason to make huge sacrifices in other amenities of a good life" (Sen, 2009: 300).

Nothing better exemplifies this unequal valuation given to equality and freedom, than the fact that while freedom is safeguarded by and from the State, equality is left to the free will of the markets and the economy. In other words, while freedom is elevated to the rank of supreme value and universally validity, which requires the State and the authorities to set up various institutions and mechanisms to guarantee and safeguard it, equality, on the other hand, is relegated to a private matter to be resolved on the basis of the resources, capital, and strategies that people can deploy in their economic relations with other actors and agents.

In other words, while the risks of freedom are resolved by the State, the systemic risks and contradictions inherent to the economy and markets, such as inequality, are relegated to biographical and individual solutions (Beck, 1998). While freedom is a matter of public interest and, therefore, a matter of the State, equality is a matter of private interest and between private individuals, a matter of allocation of scarce resources that is resolved through the action of markets. While freedom is essentially a question of politics and power, equality is a matter of economics and distribution. If there is any sense in state action on equality, it is restricted to reducing excesses in distributive inequality, never to confronting inequality as a political and state matter.

2   Preliminary Reflections

Modernity was presented to us as a hope for progress, sustained by human reason as its main historical engine. In its beginnings, philosophers such as Condorcet, Godwin, and others went so far as to affirm that there would be no possible obstacle that could limit the power of human reason and that progress itself could not finally resolve. However, already in the second half of the 19th century, and more appropriately throughout the twentieth century, Modernity has been presented to us as an incomplete project (Habermas, 2014).

From our perspective, this unfinished character of Modernity lies in one of the vectors that make up its own foundational matrix: persistent social inequality, which not only has not been abated by progress and human reason as promised but, rather, constitutes one of the pillars of Modernity itself. The founding matrix of modern society includes and reproduces different forms of inequality that are structured on the basis of relations of exploitation, domination, and discrimination that sustain capitalist progress. Inequality is not a pending issue of Modernity; on the contrary, it is one of its underlying contradictions, which cannot be resolved unless a radical questioning of capitalist Modernity itself is established.

In this sense, it is the ethical, existential, and political consequences of all forms of inequality that persist in Modernity, which configure it as an unfinished project with a great pending issue that is none other than that of *social emancipation* with respect to all forms of inequality among individuals. It is this historical debt of Modernity that forms the basis of a new political and social project in this era of reflexive and global modernity. Our project and discourse *against inequality*, thus, constitutes a theoretical, epistemic, and ideological matrix from which to project the new "great transformation", in Polanyi's terms, that will support a project of *emancipation and social liberation*.

CHAPTER 2

Underlying Metadiscourses within Scientific Discourses on Inequality

Modern social sciences are heirs of the geopolitics of the world-system (Wallerstein, 1999). The metadiscourses that underlie the narratives of social science reflect this. The metadiscourses that underlie the narratives of social science reflect this. The discourse of modern social science is sustained by various metadiscourses, that is, underlying categories that give meaning to science itself. In this following chapter, we will analyze and refer to only three of them: methodological nationalism, androcentrism, and developmentalism.

1   A Critique of Methodological Nationalism

The first of these meta-discourses is methodological nationalism, initially criticized by Ulrich Beck (2000b) in his study on globalization. According to this author, in modern society, social thought and theory were built on the principle of correspondence between State, Nation, and Territory. This metatheoretical perspective permeated the social sciences, particularly in approaches to scientific observation, as well as in the construction of the object of study by many social scientists. Sociology, thus, became the science of modern society. This historical moment in which sociology and, in general, modern social thought arose coincided directly with the advent of Modernity; thus, as a modern social science, its intellectual development was directly influenced by the social, historic, economic and political contexts that allowed national societies to be theoretically constituted as objects of study and studied as independent units (Goic, 2007).

In line with the Modernity thought, the spatial dimension of social phenomena was circumscribed to the territorial limits of the Nation-State. It is not that a world geography could not be thought of—evidently there was a clear concern and priority for world geopolitics—only that this concept was conceived as a process of articulation of national geographies and, therefore, on the basis of national territorialities. In other words, in this perspective, all social processes are theoretically and analytically constructed on the basis of this principle of methodological nationalism. What happened at the world level corresponded, then, to *inter*national processes and relations, that is, relationships between (*inter*) nations. Such a logic would never be able to arrive at a supranational category that, while itself encompassing the nation-states as important actors, would account for their dynamics, characteristics, patterns, and territorial structures at a more abstract and global level (Canales, 2002). It is not only that there was no global space as such, but above all, there was no way of thinking about society in terms of global spaces, since the categories and concepts used were soaked in that methodological nationalism, which hindered a vision and conception of social and economic processes based on spatialities other than those of the Nation-State.[1]

With the advent of global and postmodern society, these approaches are outdated. They fail to grasp the global forms of social processes. In view of this, the larger social sciences are now faced with the challenge of seeking new approaches, concepts, and categories that allow us to think of the world as a global society and, more precisely, in terms of globalized societies. This not only implicates a change in the territorial scale of analysis, that is, it is not a question of moving from a national to a global scale purely and simply, since it is not a problem of levels of aggregation or abstraction of the analysis but, rater, something more complex and profound.

The critique of *methodological nationalism* is a questioning that refers to a theoretical and an epistemological rupture: What is needed in the social sciences are new views and perspectives from which to observe and study contemporary societies, new approaches that transcend the epistemological limits of methodological nationalism and allow the construction of a new "narrative that accounts for the global from globality itself, that breaks with the predominant historicist conception and, finally, that eventually includes within its same narrative the totality of regions where these dynamics come to life and are expressed" (Fazio, 2011: 92, our translation).

In this regard, Ianni (1996) puts forward an interesting thesis. Just as the classic paradigms of political life within Modernity (left and right) were based on a certain conception of national society,[2] the emerging paradigm or paradigms must develop and mature on the basis of a renewed conception of global

---

1 The Nation-State is one of the institutions of modernity that is increasingly being questioned (Ohmae, 1995). Thus, for example, unlike the liberal ideologies of the nineteenth century that promoted the concept and practice of national sovereignty, our contemporary orthodox neoliberalism, on the other hand, seeks to dismantle it at the state and national level, shifting allegiance to corporations and organizations at the global level.
2 Whether from the perspective of its conservation (right) or its transformation (left)—or from the infinite number of intermediate positions—the various paradigms of Modernity shared the same substratum: national society, its development, and modernization. (On this point, see Wallerstein 1995).

society. For one thing, "society" in this case must allude to a multitude of "societies." The use of prodigal categories or traditional paradigms (of Modernity and national society, for example) must be used as a basis for our theorization but with an epistemological twist that allows for their conventional space-time connotations to be annulled or dislocated.[3]

In a world where societies are globalizing, where social, economic, cultural, and all kinds of processes cross and dissolve national borders on a daily basis, it is anachronistic to continue to assume that the nation-state is the natural social form of the contemporary world (Wimmer and Glick Shiller; 2002). In this context, we argue that, just as in the past the scientific discourse of Modernity resulted in a social science that circumscribed its object of study to the social and territorial limits of the nation-state, today the delimitation of the field of social science research and the problematization of its objects of study must overcome and go beyond the contours of the nation-state and begin to think of problems in terms of its globalization.

In this framework, it makes sense to ask how to analyze processes that only have meaning in a global sense with categories constructed for national levels. Or, in other words, how to analyze processes in which national categories are not sufficient to grasp them because such processes are simply not contained in the national level but have surpassed and fragmented that level of analysis. Such seems to be the challenge in the case of inequality and its links with development processes. In a globalized world, that is based on global economic models and patterns of accumulation, there is no doubt that inequality, as well as society itself, must also be thought of and analyzed in global terms.

2   Methodological Androcentrism and Its Feminist Critique

A second underlying assumption in scientific discourse is what we call here *methodological androcentrism*, which has been widely criticized and combated by feminist theorists and scholars (Butler, 1999). It is not only that science has

---

[3] As Ianni points out, "reflection on global society reopens fundamental epistemological questions: space and time, synchrony and diachrony, micro and macro, singular and universal, individualism and holism, small story and big story. These are questions that are approached on the basis of the recognition of global society as a complex and problematic totality, articulated and fragmented, integrated and contradictory. … They are forces that feed integrating and fragmentary tendencies and ascribe nation and nationality, group and social classes, provincialism and regionalism, localism and cosmopolitanism, capitalism and socialism" (Ianni, 1996: 168, our translation).

been essentially built by men and the presence of women has been minor. Undoubtedly, this is present and has had a fundamental influence on the way in which science has developed and on the reproduction of patriarchal modes in its conformation. However, from our perspective and from the approach we wish to discuss at this time, this is not the determining factor. Our approach points to the fact that this lower female presence is a consequence of a structural situation of male dominance in practically all areas and spheres of society, which is also manifested in the scientific field.

The essential point here is threefold: First, the delimitation of research problems, as well as scientific agendas and programs, are constructed from and for a logic of male domination. At the same time that they deal with and concern themselves with masculine problems, science itself is oriented to reinforce this masculine dominance. Secondly, the methodological frameworks for analyzing these problems—as well as the conceptual and theoretical frameworks for understanding and comprehending them—are defined from a condition of hegemony of the masculine over the feminine, thus reflecting male dominance in the construction of knowledge and science. And, thirdly, this way of constructing science is also a way of reproducing patriarchy as a dominant mode of social organization. Both the frameworks of social understanding, that arise from this androcentric model, and the modes of social intervention, that derive from them, represent modes of reproducing gender inequality.

The clearest example is in the area of sexual and reproductive health. In the second half of the 20th century, two pills revolutionized the sexual and reproductive behavior of populations: contraceptive pills and Viagra. Both arise from research and scientific agendas that reflect the androcentric nature of the development of medical science and health. The issue of sexual and reproductive health is undoubtedly a relevant topic of major social, political, and demographic importance. However, these two pills reflect the character of research in this regard. The scientific research agenda on reproductive behavior is constructed from the position of men and for the benefit of male interests. These are two distinct ways of patriarchal problem solving related to the reproductive behavior of men and women.

On the one hand, pregnancy and fertility are resolved by controlling the reproductive capacity of women and, therefore, once again establishing the female body as the field of domination of a patriarchal society. It is not the reproductive capacity of men that is in question and exposed to social and political control but that of women, thus reproducing the position of female subordination vis-à-vis society and the State, that is, vis-à-vis other social subjects: men and the dominant classes.

On the other hand, sexuality problems are also treated from a position of male dominance. What matters is impotence and erectile dysfunction in men, not the conditions that affect women and their sexuality. What medical science must solve is how to maintain favorable conditions for male sexual pleasure, relegating to the background the problems that women's sexual health and well-being may present in this regard.[4] Once again, the female body is seen and conceptualized as an instrument at the service of male pleasure, and women are not seen as subjects with rights and needs, with problems of their own and equally relevant as those of the male body.

These two examples taken from medical science with clear repercussions in society show us how the sciences and their research agendas are constructed from the perspective of the masculine, thus reproducing patriarchal forms of domination. Likewise, these examples also show us that science and its discourses are part of the reproduction of forms of male domination and the subordination and submission of women, at least in a double sense. On the one hand, as we have already mentioned, it is accomplished by prioritizing male topics in the research and theorizing agenda, relegating female topics and approaches to the background. On the other hand, and from a deeper vision, we see that the very frameworks of meaning—the conceptual and methodological approaches to knowledge, the research paradigms, and even the very social facts to be observed—are constructed on the basis of male narratives, that is, meta-discourses based on patriarchal positions that reproduce the vision and paradigm of male domination.

Such a perspective implicates approaches that are concerned not only with the fact studied (sexuality) but above all the construction of the fact as a social problem (male sexuality as a priority over female sexuality), as well as its social and symbolic representation, its analytical understanding, and methodological apprehension, which all fall within this field of male domination of the larger discourse and work of science. And this is true regardless of whether or not the scientist in question is a man or a woman themselves. Undoubtedly, the female presence in the world of science contributes to unveil

---

[4] Thus, for example, vaginal atrophy, now called genitourinary syndrome of menopause (gmms), has never received the attention and importance that has been given to erectile dysfunction in men, even though both diseases usually occur at the same stages of a person's life course and, in both cases, directly affect the individual's sexuality. The different treatment of one problem and the other reflects the male predominance in determining research agendas in this area, thus reproducing forms of male domination over women. Medical knowledge is neither neutral nor objective, but ultimately obeys a mode of male domination that fixes and conditions its development.

and criticize this situation, but this is not enough, since it is not a matter of *presences* but of *essences*. The issue lies in the gender coordinates, in this case, from which the meanings and senses of scientific research are constructed. From the delimitation of the problems and fields of observation to the theoretical and methodological frameworks of analysis, everything is crossed by these underlying masculine narratives, and this is so because in science—as in every field of society—exactly the same thing happens: the dominance of the masculine as the underlying narrative that constructs the meaning of social fields (Butler, 2001).

As Mires (1996: 17, our translation) rightly points out, "a science created by men, in times when patriarchal rules predominated, can hardly have a neutral or objective character." In this context, a feminist criticism of science refers not only to the theoretical and methodological aspects of the construction of science and its discourses. It is neither merely a matter of critique of the androcentrism underlying the discourses of science, but, rather, one that purports the need to construct new narratives and discourses that aim at social emancipation, the radical transformation of these structures of power and male and patriarchal domination. As Butler (2001: 1) points out, "feminism is about the social transformation of gender relations"; therefore, a feminist critique of scientific discourses and, in particular, of the androcentrism underlying them is fundamental, not only to unveil the forms of male domination but also (and mainly) to oppose them with the construction of alternative political and scientific discourses that point to processes of emancipation of women and of society as a whole.

3   Development and Progress as Metadiscourses of Modernity

Tocqueville (2010 [1835]) affirmed that no society can prosper or exist without dogmas that constitute it.[5] And in modern-western society, there is no greater

---

5 For Tocqueville, however, dogmas are not necessarily a burden of past visions. They can also form supporting statements of the new, of the positive; therefore, they are dogmas in affirmation. Among these, he pointed out the importance of the "dogma of the sovereignty of the people" and how it "became the law among laws," the founding narrative of the nascent American nation (Tocqueville, 2010 [1835]). It is not our interest to question the scope of this dogma; rather, we are only interested in highlighting its value as a founding narrative of contemporary (modern) society and to illustrate through this example the value and function of dogmas as constitutive narratives of societies in each historical era. The value of dogma is not what it says but rather what convinces; its value lies in its role as structuring collective imaginaries, and they are dogmas precisely because they are assumed without question.

dogma than the idea of *progress*, that is, that humanity advances inexorably towards higher stages of knowledge, culture, and moral perfection. Along the same lines, Nisbet (1980) points out that, in its more than three thousand years, there has been no more important and transcendental idea in the West than that of progress. This idea has come to be "more than something cherished or to be cherished; that is an essential element of historical movement, from the past through present to future. Such a value can then be transposed from the merely desirable to the historically necessary" (Nisbet, 1980: 4).

Throughout history, *progress*, as the advancement, improvement, and perfection of society and humanity, has been understood primarily from two different and sometimes antagonistic perspectives:

1. On the one hand, in a spiritual way, that is, of progress of the human spirit towards a higher and superior stage of existence and human happiness.
2. On the other hand, in a secular form, that is, of the progress of human reason, expressed in the knowledge and progress in scientific and technical knowledge that allow man to create unlimited resources to face the various problems, risks, and contingencies posed by both nature and society.

The Westernized and modern way of understanding progress, especially from the eighteenth century onwards, is the attainment here on earth of moral or spiritual virtues, with the ultimate goal of the ever-increasing perfection of human nature, for which the essential thing is the systematic advancement in the second plane of the idea of progress—that is, the advance and perfection of human reason as the driving force of our history. Condorcet (1795: 11) is perhaps the one who best expresses this idea, when he points out:

> [N]o bounds have been fixed to the improvement of the human faculties; that the perfectibility of man is absolutely indefinite, that the progress of this perfectibility, henceforth above the control of every power that would impede it, has no other limit than the duration of the globe upon which nature has placed us.[6]

They do not admit criticism, since this would unveil them for what they are, losing their founding (convincing) power in the symbolic constitution of concrete and historically situated societies.

6 Condorcet was aware of the obstacles and challenges facing Western society in advancing along the path of perfectibility of the human spirit. In this sense, and considering our discussion on inequality and progress, it is relevant that this author considered, precisely, inequality as the greatest of these obstacles. In this regard, he points out: "Our hopes, as to the future condition of the human species, may be reduced to three points: the destruction of inequality between different nations; the progress of equality in one and the fame nation; and lastly, the real improvement of man" (Condorcet, 1795: 251). In other words, for Condorcet, progress

In this sense, the idea of progress as we understand it today reached its peak between the eighteenth and twentieth centuries, when the secularization of the term was consolidated. It is thanks to this idea of progress that other founding ideas of modernity such as freedom, equality, and popular sovereignty, ceased to be mere desires and wishes and became objectives, concrete goals to be achieved in this earthly and secular world. The idea of progress led these other related concepts to end up becoming objectives "not merely desirable but historically necessary" (Nisbet, 1980: 171).

The project of Modernity supports a process of differentiation and delimitation from the past through which modern society has to be founded on itself, as opposed to traditional societies (Beriain, 1996).[7] In order to achieve this social reflexivity, Modernity had to be capable of disarticulating not only the social and material structures of traditional society but also of deactivating the potential of the conceptual and epistemic system on which its worldview was built and which supported a way of thinking and acting. In this process, Modernity had to be capable of replacing the ways of thinking and acting predominant in traditional societies with modern forms of action and thought. In short, it was a matter of imposing a modern vision of the world whose superiority would be sustained by the potential of reason and science.

This movement of Modernization manifested itself as the secularization of thought and worldview. It was the transfer of the concept of transcendence from the field of religion to that of history, politics, and science (Mires, 1996). Modernity, thus, proposed a project of transcendence that was not religious but secular, based on human reason and, in particular, on the free development of science. In this way, modern thought sought and continues to seek to establish a worldview based on a rational and scientific perspective, thus expressing the modernist thesis of the predominance of reason over other forms of understanding the social and natural world.

Based on the project of Modernity, the West was assumed as the embodiment of a civilizing process that would lead to a continuous progress of the social and human condition (Wallerstein, 1999b). Although it constitutes in essence as a moral ideal, this civilizing and modernizing project is based on the intellectual triumph of rational and experimental science over pre-modern or traditional worldviews, based on cognitive structures and understanding

---

(perfectibility of man) could not be understood without solving the problem of social inequalities.

7 Beriain (1996) points out various concepts that illustrate the reflexive character of modern society, such as self-valorization (Marx), self-production (Touraine), self-confrontation (Beck) and self-reference (Luhmann), to which we can add that of self-organization (Maturana).

of a religious, magical, and/or "irrational" nature. Reason, thus, becomes the main weapon of Modernity against the forces of obscurantism and conservatism, represented by and in the traditions and other social institutions of premodern societies.

According to the project of Modernity, the modern subject sees themself at the center of a process of natural and social evolution in which progress becomes its concrete manifestation and reason and science, its main driving forces. In this way, Modernity expresses a meta-narrative in which the idea of progress is glorified in terms of a "conviction that the history of man marches in a determined directionality in which the future is, by definition, the surpassing of the present" (Hopenhayn, 1988: 61, our translation). In a sense, the idea of progress constitutes at its very base the central inspiration of the whole philosophy of modern thought.

Likewise, the predominance of reason is not gratuitous. Scientific thought and the development of technology, the material underpinnings of modernization, are, of course, based on reason. The modernist thesis is that traditional institutions hindered the development of reason and science, as well as its manifestation in technological development, thus limiting the possibilities of social and material progress of societies. In this way, and by virtue of elevating progress to the status of Modern Reason, it was necessary to sustain a project of secularization of society, especially in the field of scientific and technological production. According to Habermas (1985: 9), "the project of Modernity ... intended to release cognitive potentials ... [so] to utilize this accumulation of specialized culture for the enrichment of everyday life – that is to say, for the rational organization of everyday social life".

In Enlightenment thought, progress is seen as not only an inevitable process but also as the embodiment of a teleological vision of human history. Western civilization becomes an ideological construction according to which its omnipresence was both inevitable and necessary and desirable, where the capitalist economy represented the essence of progress because it was in essence a civilizing process (Wallerstein, 1999b; Blaut, 1993). In this sense, the secularization of scientific and technological reason would allow the liberation of the forces of social and material progress, thus opening a path of modernization to progressive and uninterrupted economic development.

Modernization corresponds precisely to this process of social evolution from traditional societies to modern societies, where the notion of progress configures the teleological framework that gives meaning to the modernization of society. Underlying this worldview is the notion that modernization, as a strategy for the future, defines a path of evolution and progress that is assumed to be continuous, permanent, and infinite. In fact, modernization implies the overcoming of traditional forms and their replacement by modern forms, within a framework of growing rationalization of social life, of its institutions, and even of the very "traditions" that modernity generates.

The Social Sciences, along with studying the social problems of their time, do so from the paradigms of the historical epoch that constitutes them. Undoubtedly, the social worlds we study exists independently of those who observe them. However, whoever observes it can only do so through the vision they have of society, a perspective that is based both on the observer's position in the society they observe and, on the narratives, and metadiscourses that give meaning to their systems of observation. Without these narratives, without these organizing myths, we can affirm absolutely nothing. There are no universal concepts; they are all plural and partial and historically situated (Wallerstein, 1999).

In this sense, the Social Sciences have been sciences of Modernity and, therefore, imbued and constructed from the paradigm of social progress and the limitless expansion of knowledge and human reason. Progress as a metadiscourse of Modernity is the matrix that founds and gives foundation to the science of society. From this underlying discourse, objects of scientific observation are constructed, which become the disciplinary fields of the Social Sciences.

In this regard, we can point out two ways in which the notion of development and progress underlies the construction of the Social Sciences:

1. On the one hand, as an object of study: Here the criticism is that, as an object, it does not refer to development itself but to the modern-western form of development and its social structures, which operate as devices for the construction of meaning in social research. On this plane operates the dominant logic of comparing contemporary society with past ones in a format of modern society versus traditional society, where the modern is the European form, which invisibilizes other modernities, while the traditional is an abstraction that invisibilizes the different societies prior to the modern era (Dussel, 2017). It is development understood as modernization, a transition from the traditional (without distinguishing its origin, structures, and social and historical forms but only as an abstract category) to the modern, understood in its European-Western form, making abstraction of other possible forms of modernity.
2. On the other hand, as a worldview and metadiscourse: It is not development itself as a social process but as a system of values, prejudices, and worldviews of the social world in all its spheres and levels: production, culture, politics, population, history, etc. Here, development operates not as a heuristic category, but as an ideological-cultural category: development

as a necessary and desirable state to be achieved and not as a historical and possible process. This is when Western forms become social dogmas, assuming the founding and constituent function that Tocqueville attributes to dogmas. The critique is that these are dogmas with a specific historical and social origin, whose function is both to found and distinguish one's own society (Europe, North, Center, Metropolis) and to constitute the modernization project to be imposed on the other societies under the domination of Western power (Third World, South, Periphery, Colonies) (Blaut, 1993).

In both cases, the progress-development duo is present in the construction of the field of each discipline of the Social Sciences, since it is part of the perspective from which the representations of the objects (societies) observed are constructed. However, progress, whether as a dogma of Modernity or as a meta-discourse of it, is imbued with a European-Western rationality and opens another flank of criticism: It went from being an idea of self-reference and self-identification to a discourse of domination and expansion of a social and cultural form (Quijano, 2014).

A good starting point for the critique of development and progress as narratives of Modernity is from an analysis of the very situation of those who have not yet developed, that is, the countries of the Third World. Initially, they were called "backward"; then, they were called "underdeveloped"; later, they were politely called "less developed"; and, more, recently they were called "developing countries." Regardless of the title or descriptor, the point is that all of these denominations are only euphemisms that fail to refer to the true essence of the situation of these "Third World" countries. They seek to denominate a situation from the perspective of the North (of the developed countries) without understanding the circumstances of these other dispossessed regions of the world, which, being a central part of the development of the central countries, are not developed like them. As Castoriadis (1979: 189) pointed out, from the perspective of the West "other countries or societies were considered to be naturally less mature or less developed, and their main problem was defined as the existence of 'obstacles to development'."

The scientist, the politician, and even the citizen of the global North, seeks in the Third World the same manifestations that development has had in their societies, without stopping to question the meaning that their own development and modernization once had. But this same frustration is suffered by the scientist, the politician, and the citizen of the Third World. This is because both first and third worldists, are not aware that "the paradigm of 'rationality' with which the whole world lives today, which also dominates the discussions on 'development', is nothing more than a particular, arbitrary, contingent historical creation" (Castoriadis, 1979: 214). They are, therefore, neither aware of the fact that in order to position oneself against this paradigm of rationality and progress, it demands an epistemological criticism of the discourse and narratives of progress that opens the way to further critical thinking and to the construction of other horizons of reason and rationality different from those of progress and development. This crisis of development does not arise because it does not generate the transformations it promises, the progress and maturity it promotes, but because it stems from the questioning of its ontological and epistemological bases themselves.

In this sense, and contrary to Castoriadis (1979), it is not the *crisis* of development that leads to the questioning of its postulates but, rather, the *critique* of development and progress as narratives of Modernity that can lead to a proposal to overcome its imaginary meanings. This critique is what drives us in this text.

Criticism as an act of social self-reflexivity (analysis, judgment) contributes to becoming aware of the realities of the social and of our position in our social worlds; thus, it can be the basis for a discourse and a praxis of emancipation. In this sense, and taking up the thesis of Horkheimer (2002), for whom a social theory is critical to the extent that "its goal is man's emancipation from slavery" (246), that is, to emancipate human beings from situations that enslave them, our interest in a discourse against inequality is in its use as a critical theory of hegemonic discourses and, with it, a contribution to a social theory for a praxis of liberation and social emancipation.

4   The Discourse against Inequality as a Critique of Progress and Development in the Social Sciences

The discourse against inequality is a critique of the narrative of Modernity, insofar as it constitutes the basis of both the system of discourses of science about society and of the discourses of legitimization of the representations and projects of society in its various fields: economic, social, demographic, political, cultural.

Modern reason, exemplified in the notion of progress, is not only a category of self-understanding but also configures a historical project and, as such, is also a colonizing project of other modes of understanding, of other epistemological constructions of the world and society. The discourse of progress and Modernity, constructed from the West (Europe, in particular), is a project with universalist pretensions; however, it does not cease to be a locally situated enterprise. As a project, it not only aims to coax other ways of life and understanding in its image, but it is also a way of imposing itself on them through violence. As a historical project, modern Western reason becomes a project of domination, exclusion, and colonization of other worlds (Bautista, 2014).

Modernity imposed both a way of seeing the world from the reason of progress and from the reason of patriarchy, from the reason of the national and the nation-state, from the reason of the white-European race, among other ways, and in all of them as a reason of affirmation of the dominant and negation of the dominated; reason of the center-developed, denying and annulling the reason of the peripheries and the undeveloped world; reason of the man and the masculine, annulling and invisibilizing the reason of the woman and the feminine; reason of the nation, denying the reasons of the people, ethnic groups, and communities; reason of the white, denying and dominating the reasons of other ethnic groups and races. Likewise, it is a way of constituting societies from those same metadiscourses, transforming via domination, colonization, and subjugation of other types of social discourses, of the other modes of self-understanding as societies and, therefore, of self-conformation as societies, peoples, and communities.

The social construction of gender, family, work, State, economy, population, religion, race, class, among so many other categories and social processes, are constructed from the dominant reason, in this case the reason of progress and Modernity. From there they are imposed on other worlds as part of the process of colonization and political and cultural domination. In this sense, the discourse against inequality as a critique of progress and modern reason is not only from a perspective of critical theory, from a critical epistemology, but also and fundamentally as a political epistemology.

Our interest is not only to unravel the original myths and dogmas on which the discourse of Modernity and progress is built, but to do so from a political sense, that is, from a political critique, since we see in them both a mode of self-understanding and modes of domination and exclusion, that is, a colonizing project in every sense of the word. In this respect, we use inequality as a category on which we can base our epistemological critique, as well as construct a political theory of social emancipation.

We see inequality neither as a remnant of pre-modern times nor as a pending agenda of Modernity and progress. On the contrary, inequality is a founding component of Modernity, a pillar on which progress rests. Modernity as a colonizing project is also based on inequality between the colonizing world and the colonized world, between classes, races, genders, all dominant and dominated. In the same way that progress in its economic mode is sustained in relations of unequal development, progress is also sustained in social and material relations of class, gender, race, ethnicity, geography, and territory that are equally unequal. It is in this sense that we claim that the discourse against inequality is the starting point of our epistemological and political critique of Modernity and progress.

In the case of progress, for example, it is a meta-narrative that is at the basis of practically all scientific and disciplinary discourses in the social sciences, to such an extent that, until now, it has become an underlying category that gives meaning and reason to the scientific discourse on societies. Thus, for example, modern Economics is constructed on the basis of discourses on productive development; Sociology, on the basis of the discourse of social modernization. Similarly, in Demography, the dominant discourse has been that of population growth and demographic transitions. In these three cases—Economics, Sociology and Demography—we use different terms for the same meaning. The theoretical ideas of development, modernization, and growth-transition conform disciplinary formats for the same social narrative: progress as a meta-discourse of Modernity that gives meaning to the sciences of society (see Figure 1).

In addition to writing against this prevalent discourse of progress, we, further, oppose this discourse in the same way we theorize against inequality, on the same two levels on which Modernity constitutes progress as a social and historical narrative:

1. If progress was presented as a necessary, desirable, and even inevitable historical project, our critique points to the fact that it was neither necessary, nor desirable, and even totally avoidable. The discourse against inequality presented here points, precisely, to those situations, contexts, and histories where progress is not desirable and, therefore, is unnecessary.
2. If progress as a project was affirmed in the imposition and consolidation of social, economic, and political structures, the critique of this historical project from a discourse against inequality becomes a device of and for social *emancipation*, that is, of liberation from the structures of domination, exploitation, and discrimination on which the project of progress of Modernity is based. On this plane, we see critique and feminist theory as a path to follow in terms of elevating the critique of inequality, that is, the discourse against inequality as a way of taking this logic of critique/emancipation to all spheres of society.

The method to achieve this goal is through the critique of modern reason itself, that is, a critique of progress, considering inequality, understood as those very structures hidden and concealed in the discourse of Modernity, as part of larger social structures that are made invisible and silenced, obscuring their true obscene and indecent character. If inequality as the founding matrix of

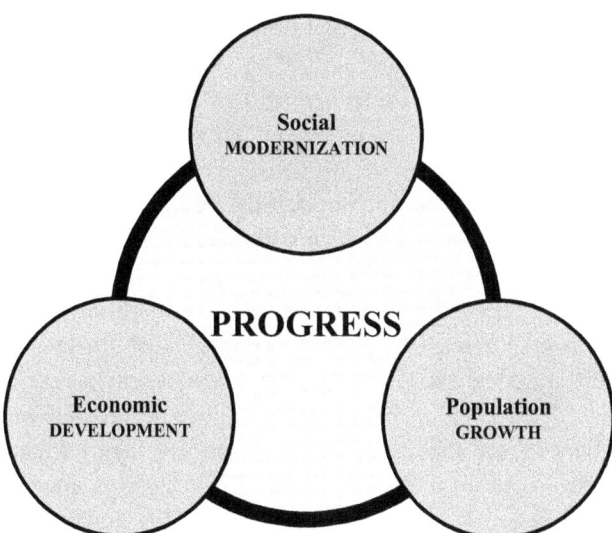

FIGURE 1 Progress as a metadiscourse in the social thought of Modernity

society is the hidden face of progress, then the critique of this discourse begins with placing inequality as a constitutive process of our social realities, which allows us to build our critique of progress as the reason for Modernity.

In this same process, the critique of Modernity becomes a first act of social emancipation, to the extent that it derives from and gives way to a process of self-awareness of the limits of the discourse of reason and progress. It is not an anti-modern discourse but one based on the *critical use* of Modernity as a social narrative, taking it to its limits, to its edges, to its frontiers, in order to free itself from the cognitive and epistemological chains that sustain its modernizing project.[8] And one of these frontiers of the discourse of progress is precisely what it silences: inequality as the founding structure of Modernity. Therefore, just as the theories of development and modernization were once discourses *For Progress* and Modernity, today we propose that a critical theory of modernity and progress is essentially a discourse *against inequality*, that is, against these forms of modernity and progress historically constituted on the

---

8 For this reason, a critique of Modernity is not a postmodern project or one that adds to the postmodern narratives but, rather, a *transmodern* project, as Dussel (2013) puts it. It is not only to situate itself *after* modernity, nor is it an anti-modern project, but, rather, a critique of Modernity implicates a project that *transits* from Modernity in order to situate itself *beyond it*.

basis of structures of social inequality, whether it be of class, gender, race, ethnicity, age, geography, among many others.[9]

Having said this, it is worth asking the following: in what sense does our critique of progress become a discourse of emancipation and not merely a postmodern and conservative discourse? We consider that in at least two senses our critique distances itself from and opposes the postmodern critique, so much in vogue a few decades ago and which still permeates many social, political and, scientific discourses:

1. On the one hand, because our discourse is a bet on a *possible* future based on a *horizon of reason* (Zemelman, 1992) that seeks to transform and not to restore. It is not a discourse against progress purely and simply but one against inequality. Therefore, it is not anti-modern or anti-progress but a position that tries to take the discourses of progress to their ultimate consequences, that is, the total liberation from all chains of inequality, from all forms of exploitation, from all forms of domination, and from all forms of discrimination.
2. On the other hand, because it is a discourse that is based on a critical view from the South of the world, theorization from the South of Modernity. Let us look at this second aspect in more detail.

We understand that an epistemology of the South (Santos, 2016) alludes to a way of considering society that makes explicit and aware the particular sociotopographical positionality of researches that, to an extent, determines our certain perspectives of analysis and understanding and, therefore, of social praxis in general. It is not a perspective of analysis looking at the South of society or looking at the society of the South, but, rather, it is a position looking at society positioned from the South, from perspectives and considerations of the South, without losing sight of the fact that this perspective as well is a totalizing view of society. However, what makes the critical difference is the perspective (the zeta axis, in Zemelman terms) from which we as investigators place ourselves to look at and examine society, from the South itself. And to do so from the South is to establish a radical first point of distance and critique with respect to other dominant views from the North of society that also have their

---

9 Here, we follow the tradition of critical thinking in pursuit of liberation projects, initiated by Marx with his critique of political economy, continued by the development of Critical Theory by the Frankfurt School, as well as with important contributions from Feminist thought and theory and its critique of patriarchal society. In all of these cases, critique is used as a mediation for the construction of discourses, consciousness, and praxis in the name of social emancipation.

own totalizing theories within Western research that seek their ways of understanding and action on this same society that concerns us all, including us.

An epistemology of the South is, above all else, an epistemology of resistance, that is, an epistemology of opposition to the Northern perspectives underlying hegemonic narratives and discourses on contemporary society (Santos, 2006). If every dominant narrative is nothing but the narrative of the dominant classes (Wallerstein, 1999b), then every contested and radical narrative is critical of that official narrative and, therefore, critical of the very condition of domination of the dominant classes.

The debate regarding Progress as a constitutive metadiscourse within the large narrative of Modernity is illustrative of the character of the critique we point out: The discourse against inequality is our way of confronting the narratives of progress, hegemonic visions of domination with their greatest phantom: inequality. By confronting the civilizing project of Modernity with its founding structures of inequality, we are confronting it with the uncivilized, which is intrinsic to that same Western civilizing project.

The discourse against inequality turns the civilizing progress of the capitalist world-economy upside down, laying bare the structures of inequality, domination, and exploitation on which it is based. It is also a discourse of contestation and emancipation. Although the civilizing project of the West (capitalism and its modern world-system) was ultimately inevitable, this does not mean that we should accept it as necessary and, even less, as desirable. In this sense, the critique of progress and its narratives constructed from the hegemonies of the North is, also, a bet for other possible projects, for other civilizing narratives based on social matrixes against all forms of inequality.

Undoubtedly, we are not the first to situate inequality as the starting point for a critique of contemporary society. There have always been voices of protest against the domination and hegemony of some over others and of critique of social forms based on structures of social inequality. In the case of capitalist society, Rousseau and Marx were perhaps the first to raise a critique of capitalism based on inequality. In both cases, it is a discourse against conservative thought, which, from Aristotle to the present day, seeks either to naturalize or to divinize the structures of inequality. On the contrary, Rousseau and Marx were the first to propose the historicity of the structures of inequality, as well as their founding and structuring character of the very society of which they are a part. For both authors, societies are intrinsically unequal, insofar as every society is founded on structures of property, that is, of private appropriation of goods and the product of labor.

Now, if more than two centuries ago, authors of such high level of transcendence, such as Rousseau and Marx, raised the issue of inequality as a central axis of contemporary societies, it is worth asking why this has not become a scientific research program since then. In this regard, we understand that this undervaluation of inequality as the axis articulating scientific work is not so much a characteristic of science itself as it is a manifestation of the hegemonic values in society within scientific endeavors.

For capitalist society, the soundness of the economy and the well-being of the population refer more to its potential for growth, development, and progress than to the conditions of inequity, inequality, and social injustice that it creates and reproduces. For this reason, the fundamental measure of a society's soundness is its average and growth indices: per capita income, production and productivity level, etc. Measures and indicators of injustice, inequality, and inequity have always remained in the background. As Bauman (2011) points out, it is no coincidence that societies are measured and compared with each other more often by the value of their GDP per capita than by the Gini Index or some other measure of social inequality. This reflects the dominant priorities and values of contemporary Western culture. The central interest on an economic growth and development was because these particular issues, and not inequality, were and are the main concerns of the West with respect to the economy and production relations. The point is that this hegemonic position has been systematically transferred to the Social Sciences, especially in the way of defining its research, modes and methods of analysis, and the theorization of problems. In this larger hegemonic discourse, it is not that inequality is not relevant but that it is constituted as a component of secondary value, related to and dependent on the predominant values of growth and development.

It is no coincidence that both from developed countries and from the various international and multilateral institutions—the World Bank, the IMF, the United Nations, the ILO, among others—inequality has always been conceptualized as a consequence of non-development, a perversion of the prevailing modes of development in the Third World, and never as a constituent process of economies and societies, especially as a constituent of asymmetrical power relations. For the same reason, the structures of inequality as the result of modes of underdevelopment are perceived and conceptualized as reversible structures within the same society, without the need to achieve a radical transformation of the same.

On the contrary, from alternative perspectives, that is, from the position of those of us who are in a situation of inequality, whether it be social, geographic, political, gender, ethnic, or racial, the issue of looks very different. From this side of growth and development, the situation of inequality is not a secondary issue, even less so when it constitutes one of the vectors that make up our social and historical matrix. That is why, in a consideration from the South, from below, from the periphery, from the underdeveloped, or whatever you want to call it, inequality constitutes one of the central axes in the construction of the meaning and transcendence of Social Science, that is, a fundamental and founding factor of a scientific undertaking that seeks to understand and comprehend the situation of our social realities as a whole and lay the foundations for its emancipatory transformation. It is not a matter of studying inequality purely and simply: its origins, causes, consequences, and manifestations. Rather, it is about making inequality the point from which to look at society and, from there, to build a scientific knowledge of it. If we speak of looking at the world from the South, it is because it is a matter of looking at society from what constitutes us within it: the structures of inequality.

Just as within contemporary feminist theory the question is not only the construction of frameworks of understanding of the social situation of women, but what is relevant and emancipating in these discourses is the construction of frameworks of understanding of the relation of domination of men over women, in our case, it is a question of constructing a framework of understanding of inequality that allows us to understand how society is constituted based on relations of exploitation, domination, and exclusion, in order to construct projects of social emancipation against these structures of social inequality.

5 Summary

Much of the theorization and problematization of the dynamics of inequalities in our peripheral societies has been constructed from the perspective of the central countries and, in particular, from the perspective of the dominant interests and hegemonic classes in those societies. Returning to Santos (2016), we can say that the discourse on inequality has been constructed from an Epistemology of the North, where the knowledge and criteria of validity and legitimacy of the proposals and analytical and categorical frameworks have been established on the basis of the cognitive practices and underlying interests of the classes and social groups that have historically been hegemonic and dominant in modern societies, thus reproducing and renewing various forms of colonialism both in the gestation of scientific knowledge and in the social and political connotation assigned to social processes and to the subjects and classes involved.

Our proposal is to contribute to the critique of this traditional discourse found within the Social Sciences. In order to sustain this critique and make it transcend the field of contingent politics and also appropriate the fields of science and knowledge production, we need to simultaneously develop two cognitive processes, namely:

1. To position ourselves epistemically from the perspective of the social groups and classes that have been systematically subordinated and dominated in this form of global capitalism (Dussel, 2017; Quijano, 2014). This is why we emphasize that our discourse against inequality is for a proposal of social emancipation from and for Latin America. The point here does not refer so much to the fields of validity of observation as to the geo-social and topographic position from which we observe inequalities.
2. To reinvent the categories and methodologies of analysis based on cognitive practices and alternative criteria of validity, based on new horizons of reason (Zemelman, 1992) that, together with giving understanding to the analyzed phenomena, configure new paths to processes of social emancipation through the transformation of our societies.

In this sense, if we are interested in the analysis and study of inequality, it is because we see in it an epistemological, theoretical, and political potential unparalleled in current times. Critical reflection on the debate on inequality leads us to rethink its terms and scope. In particular, to redefine the categories of understanding and methodologies of analysis that we use to understand it and to propose the need for a critical use of these categories, concepts, and theories. This epistemological critique of theory allows us to unveil the authoritarian and imposing character of, for example, the set of policies and programs that are constructed and designed from the North as forms of management and governance of inequalities in our societies and that are expressed in the various forums and world conferences on the subject.

This same epistemological critique allows us to see how the terms inequality, exclusion, equity, among others, have ceased to be categories of analysis that refer to social processes and have become categories that denote and connote a social problem—a "social issue"—whose scope and meanings are constructed from dominant and hegemonic positions in advanced societies.

Likewise, this *critical use of theory* (Zemelman, 1987) should lead us to the formulation of new theoretical frameworks, that is, new fields of meaning of these categories as new forms of understanding and comprehension of social phenomena, in this case, of inequalities and social exclusions. What we seek in this critique is precisely new theoretical frameworks for understanding inequalities in contemporary society, constructed from and for the South, that is, from and for the subjects who are usually subordinated and dominated by the political and cognitive practices of the dominant groups of the social and political North.

It is a double process of reflection: on the one hand, reflection as critique of the other and of their cognitive practices; on the other, reflection as self-knowledge, self-identification, and revaluation of our own social, political, and cognitive practices. All this is with the goal to reflect, and reflect us, into the contradictions of contemporary society, to identify the points of confrontation and of social and political debate, and to strengthen of critical positions from the formulation and consolidation of theories and methodologies that give them support.

In short, it is a matter of assuming as a founding epistemological premise the fact that on this side of inequality there are not only populations, poverty, and underdevelopment, but, above all, there are one and multiple societies, one and many Histories, one and thousands of Communities and Cultures, one and many political and cognitive practices, and all of them are reproduced in each population and in each society. It is a question, then, of constructing horizons of reason and understanding from this side of social processes, from this side of domination and exclusion, from this side of globalization and postmodernity.

CHAPTER 3

Social Inequality: a Totality Approach

1 Social Inequality: a Total Social Fact

Inequality is commonly referred to as an essentially economic phenomenon, referring to the concentration of resources, income, privileges, status, and capital in certain social groups. Inequality in this perspective becomes more a category of analysis of a distribution function, rather than a social process constituted by social, cultural, political, demographic, and economic practices. This way of understanding and analyzing inequality entails a methodological bias that is not minor. It implies a virtual dissociation of the phenomenon itself—inequality vis-à-vis a "something", as Sen (1992) calls it—from the social practices that constitute it, which are developed in the various fields of society.

Our theoretical and political proposal is based on a different epistemological principle. We understand all social practice as a *total social fact* in the sense that Mauss (2002) and Bourdieu (2005) give to this concept.

In his studies on the function of the gift in traditional societies, Mauss (2002: 6–7) pointed out that in the social game of exchange of presents, services, and gifts in reality what is exchanged is not "is not solely property and wealth, movable and immovable goods, and things economically useful. In particular, such exchanges are acts of politeness: banquets, rituals, military services, women, children, dances, festivals, and fairs, in which economic transaction is only one element, and in which the passing on of wealth is only one feature of a much more general and enduring contract." Mauss calls this whole complex process, which involves different levels and planes of social reality, a *total system of giving*, that is, a set of total social phenomena in which "all kinds of institutions are given expression at one and the same time – religious, juridical and moral, which relate to both politics and the family; likewise economic ones, which suppose special forms of production and consumption, or rather, of performing total services and of distribution. This is not to take into account the aesthetic phenomena to which these facts lead, and the contours of the phenomena that these institutions manifest " (Mauss, 2002: 3–4).

Bourdieu, in various writings, recovers Mauss' concept of exchange as a *total social fact* and extends its use to all social practice, beyond just economic relations. As he points out, sociology in its most complete and general definition refers to the set of practices involved in production and reproduction, not only economic but also social and cultural reproduction (Bourdieu, 2011).

Even contemporary neoliberal economics, with its enormous power to dictate political norms at a global level and to present itself as universally valid, owes its fundamental characteristics "to the fact that it is immersed or *embedded* in a particular society, that is to say, rooted in a system of beliefs and values, an *ethos* and a moral view of the world, in short, an *economic common sense*, linked, as such, to the social and cognitive structures of a particular social order" (Bourdieu, 2005: 10. Our emphasis).

In fact, economics, as we usually understand, it is actually constituted from a process of abstraction that dissociates "economic" practices from the social order of which they are a part, like all human practices. The exigency of the analysis is, then, to recover this totality of dimensions of the social that are immersed in all social practices, including economic ones. It is to take up Polanyi's concept of *embeddedness*, according to which the economy refers not only to economic relations, but, rather, to a process that is embedded in social, political, cultural, and economic relations, and vice versa.

In this sense, following Mauss and Bourdieu, we can point out that every economic act is in fact a *total social fact*, that is, although in the analysis of any economic phenomenon we can make abstraction of diverse non-economic conditions and contexts (culture, politics, society, demography, territories, etc.), this does not mean that these conditions are not present—embedded—in the very constitution of the analyzed economic act.

The fact that we can analytically abstract these conditions of the phenomenon under study, does not imply that the phenomenon is circumscribed only to those conditions explicitly included in the analysis. Rather, it is a process of thought that requires these moments of abstraction in order to construct models of understanding our social realities. Given our inability to apprehend these social realities in all of its totality directly, we use these mediations in our analysis that are based on, at times limiting, processes of abstraction. For the same reason, every model is only an abstraction of the real. Any process of understanding the real must, therefore, go beyond the current models that we have designed to apprehend it, integrating those other dimensions and levels of analysis that have been abstracted in the theoretical and methodological models we have constructed.

This process starts from the premise that we cannot understand reality directly but that we do so from processes of abstraction, which are represented in the categories and concepts that we use as theoretical and methodological devices for apprehending reality. For the same reason, every concept, every model is always partial and incomplete, which, however, does not invalidate them in themselves but poses a demand for continuous reflection and epistemological critique so as to use these concepts according to their own limitations and partialities, placing ourselves in their border points, that is, those regions of the concept in which we can appreciate what has been included and what has been abstracted. This is what makes up the critical use of theory, as Zemelman (1989) calls it, which demands, by the same token, a reconstruction articulated from a vision of totalities.

The case of inequality is illustrative of the above. It is common for its analysis to refer preferentially to the economic dimensions of inequality (inequality of income, resources, capital, consumption, among many others). In our case, on the other hand, we understand inequality as a total social fact, that is, it does not refer to the sheer forms of distribution of the different "somethings" (privileges, income, capital, etc.) in our economic relationships, but, rather, to a complex social process that, as such, is constituted by a set of social practices that subjects develop in various fields of society.

It is, then, a matter of thinking about inequality as a totality in itself. As a total social fact, inequality is not only economic or only about differences related to class, gender, ethnic-racial, age, geographic, or other various dimensions that may be added to the list. It is all of them at once and none of them in particular. As a total social fact, inequality is the articulation of all its dimensions, each one *embedded* in the others at the same instance. The categories of analysis that we usually use (economic capital, social capital, classes, gender, ethnicity, citizenship, among so many others) are only partial and restricted modes of reconstruction of the social fact itself, inequality. While these perspectives and categories are at times useful and can contribute meaningfully to our understanding of inequality, they can never achieve its total apprehension, only offering us analysis in a partial and disjointed way.

The exigency before us, then, is to initiate from these partial categories a process of critique and reflection that takes us beyond them, to discover in that same process the diverse aspects of the totality embedded in inequality as a social fact. It is a demand of thought, that is, to critically think of concepts and theories as categories of mediation between the concept itself and the social fact to which it refers, questioning the concept and the theory for what they do not make explicit in their understanding of the social fact but which, in a certain way, have included it as an abstraction. It is an exigency to theoretically reconstruct the social fact as an articulated totality (*thought totality*), in the understanding that we will never be able to recover the social fact as a real totality (*experienced totality*) (Zemelman, 1987).

In synthesis, and taking up Bourdieu (2005: 3) when he points out that "the social world is present in its entirety in every 'economic' action," we can equally affirm that the social world is in its *totality* in every form and in every practice of social inequality, whether we refer to class inequality, gender inequality, ethnic-racial inequality, or geographical and territorial inequality. At this level, the methodological and theoretical requirement now is how we equip ourselves with instruments of knowledge (categories and concepts, methods of analysis, mediations) that allow us to recover the multidimensionality and multifunctionality of social practices that we can reproduce in historical models.[1]

2   Critique of Individualistic Approaches

According to Tilly (1999), the debate on inequality can be synthesized in the confrontation between two major modes of understanding. On the one hand, we find an individualistic approach, which understands inequality as an uneven distribution of attributes, resources, privileges, rights, or other elements among a set of individuals. On the other hand, we find a structuralist approach, from which inequality is understood as structures of differentiation between social subjects, which are configured on the basis of relations of exploitation, domination, and social discrimination between classes, genders, ethnicities, races, ages and geographies. In our case, we subscribe to the second approach, which we will develop in this chapter.

If inequality is consequence of a system of categorical relations—that is, between classes, races, genders, nationalities, etc., and not of the distribution of something among individuals—then it is not the differences in talents and capacities among human beings that determine the forms and structures of social inequality. It is not meaning the presence of differentiated talents and capacities is denied, only that their explanatory and inequality-determining potential is restricted and limited. Let us take a closer look at this critique of the talents/capabilities/needs approach.[2]

Amartya Sen (1992) raises an interesting dilemma regarding equality and inequality. The issue according to this author is that whenever there is talk against inequality and in favor of equality, the central question is with respect to what field or sphere such equality refers to. For Sen, any strategy of equality always refers to a "something" that, therefore, necessarily implies inequality

---

1   What lies behind this limitation in our way of understanding social reality is the fact that although we can assume it as a directly *experienced totality*, we cannot, therefore, register it as a directly *thought totality*; we must, rather, do so through theoretical, methodological, and epistemological mediations.
2   The term *capabilities*, in this case, is used in its generic meaning, not necessarily referring to the concept used by Amartya Sen. On this point, see Excursus 1 in this chapter.

with respect to other "somethings." The debate around inequality no longer refers to it in itself but is "the central social exercise in which equality is to be demanded" (Sen, 1992: IX), that is, to what would be the social field that is established as the foundation of inequality. Therefore, the debate around inequality is no longer about inequality itself but, rather, about the political and ideological principles on which the vision of society is built in each particular case.

The point is that this dilemma is in practice irresolvable. According to Sen, the issue of inequality and of any egalitarian proposal is that it faces two basic conditions of differentiation: on the one hand, the heterogeneity of human beings and, on the other, the multiplicity and diversity of variables from which inequality can be constructed. In our case, we wish to focus on the first of these two conditions regarding inequality, with the understanding that if our critique of the heterogenous consideration is valid and sustained, then it is irrelevant to discuss and question the second.

Sen (1992) basically points out two arguments and definitions that should be taken up in this regard. On the one hand, he indicates that

> [E]quality is judged by comparing some particular aspect of a person (such as income, or wealth, or happiness, or liberty, or opportunities, or rights, or need-fulfilments) with the same aspect of another person.
> SEN, 1992: 2

On the other, Sen states that

> [H]uman beings are thoroughly diverse. We differ from each not only in external characteristics (e.g., in inherited fortunes, in the natural and social environment in which we live), but also in our personal characteristics (e.g., age, sex, proneness to illness, physical and mental abilities). The assessment of the claims of equality has to come to terms with the existence of pervasive human diversity. (1)

These arguments summarize what we pointed out with respect to individualistic ontologies. According to the first argument, Sen is explicit in considering inequality as a matter between individuals (human beings in abstract, not social categories in concrete and historical sense) with respect to the distribution of "specific conditions"—resources, etc.—, and arises from the comparison with respect to what one has in terms of these resources, opportunities, needs, etc. The underlying question remains how the distribution of those "specific conditions of individuals" is determined and, based on that, how to determine whether the inequality resulting from that distribution is unjust or not (Sen, 2009).

Curiously, in the second argument, he does not consider the fact that both the external characteristics and the intrinsic attributes of individuals that he points out, are, in fact, social and historical constructs and express a situation of structural inequality that transcends them. In both cases, the structuring conditions of inequality are abstracted in these individualistic and distributivist ontologies that attribute to properties and attributes of individuals (whether external conditions or personal characteristics) what in reality is a social and historical construction. It is evident that inherited patrimony, social environment, sex, age, and other personal attributes are not individual conditions but social processes from which structures of inequality are constructed. Thus, for example, what differentiates a man from a woman is not his or her sexual condition but a socially constructed condition based on that sexual difference that gives rise to a social system of gender differentiation and inequality, which transcends the male/female dichotomy. In other words, the social and historical conditions that give rise to gender inequality, as well as to patrimonial inequality and inheritance, inequality in health and illness and death—among other aspects cited by Sen—were simply abstracted from his analysis, annulled as such, remaining only as differences intrinsic to individuals.

And from this perspective of inequality, understood as the distribution of these "specific conditions" among individuals, it could not be otherwise. For example, if instead of considering sex as an intrinsic attribute of the person and it is analyzed as a social construct, it is no longer possible to refer to inequality as a process of differentiation between individuals but must necessarily be made as a categorical comparison between genders—i.e., a comparison of social categories that refer to collectives, not to individuals. Likewise, the founding relationship of inequality would no longer be a function of distribution between these abstract individuals but a structure of social relations of exploitation, domination, and discrimination between such categories of analysis, i.e., between genders. In other words, the definition of inequality indicated in the first argument cannot but be based on the second, which only abstracts the social and historical aspects of inequality, considering it as an abstract entity that relates equally abstract individuals, never social and historical subjects.

The methodological error of the premise that human beings are heterogeneous, different, and diverse, is that it places the difference in the individuality of the person and not in their social form as a historical subject. The question is not so much with respect to *what* we are unequal in, as Sen (1992) puts it, but *who* are those that are placed in one category or the other in regards to inequality.

EXCURSUS 1   Amartya Sen's Capabilities Approach

Amartya Sen's thought is more a reflection on equality than a discourse against inequality, although evidently important lessons and references for the latter can be drawn from the former. Likewise, we can affirm that Sen's approach is more normative in nature with respect to equality than being comprehensive or achieving an understanding of inequality as a social phenomenon. For him, the debate on equality and inequality is part of a broader reflection on the idea of Justice (Sen, 2009).

For Sen, the issue of equality refers to "a person's capability to achieve functionings the he or she has reason to value" (Sen, 1992:4, 5). With this, it is evident to question the social, individual, family, and historical conditions that contribute to such achievement, that is, to question what would be the social conditions, structures, and situations that limit and hinder the attainment of such an achievement or social norm of equality of capabilities. From this perspective, and in contrast to the individualist and distributivist ontological models, Amartya Sen's proposal is undoubtedly much more complex and profound, both in analytical-comprehensive and normative and political terms. His approach focused on the capabilities of each human being to function fully as such implies in a certain way that inequalities would be a form of human rights violations, since they would prevent the human development of thousands of people relegated to various modes of exclusion and social inequality that constrain their own freedom as human beings (Therborn, 2013).

Thus, the question of capabilities refers not only to what one has but, also and fundamentally, to the freedom to fulfill oneself and become, that is, to achieve those functions that have value for each person. In this analysis and assessment of what is just and ethical in terms of inequality based on capabilities, "individual claims are not to be assessed in terms of the resources or primary goods the persons respectively hold, but by the freedoms they actually enjoy to choose the lives that they have reason to value. It is this actual freedom that is represented by the person's 'capability' to achieve various alternative combinations of functionings" (Sen, 1992: 81).

Capacity, thus, refers to the freedom to choose between alternative lives, between combinations of differentiated valued functionings. Primary goods or resources do not represent the capabilities of a person, but they do represent conditions for the realization and for the exercise and enjoyment of freedom, of personal fulfillment. As Sen points out, "primary goods are, thus, general purpose means or resources useful for the pursuit of different ideas of the good that the individuals may have" (Sen, 1992: 81).

With this approach, Sen moves the inequality debate from the field of economics and resource distribution, purely and simply, to the field of politics and ethics, in terms of how social inequality constrains people's capabilities to achieve their fulfillment and, in particular, limits the "overall freedom a person enjoys to pursue her well-being" (Sen, 1992: 150). The unequal would be, then, people with insufficient basic capabilities.

In our opinion, this proposal has the great merit of politicizing the debate on inequality, broadening its problematization beyond sheer economic considerations, including other spheres equally relevant and fundamental to our understandings of inequality.

The question of *what* we are unequal in is based on an abstract and unified concept of the individual. It considers all human beings as equally individual—innately and inherently similar to each other—and this is only possible through the abstraction of our social and historical forms. In this perspective, we are all *one* and undifferentiated from the *others*: we are all individuals similar between *us*, but none of us is an *other* from which we can build our own identity (Canales, 2003). We are all the same: individuals. We differentiate ourselves not by what we are—identities, memberships, or social belongings—but by some possession that places us further above or further below in a function of distribution. Our position as individuals is easily interchangeable, and we can move from there to here and vice versa; it is a type of mobility that does not alter our condition as individuals nor our identity or sense of belonging, since these have been abstracted.

The constitution of all of us as individuals is constructed from this abstraction, which necessitates the annulment of our social forms and, therefore, of the social and historical differences that constitute us as social subjects, that is, as categories of social differentiation and inequality: class, race, gender, nationality, among many others. All these categories are abstracted in their essence and remain only as mere personal attributes. Not only is the social category abstracted, but also the social relations from which these categories are constructed as modes of social distinction and division are abstracted. With this, categorical inequality is annulled as such and remains as mere individual difference. The social and historical root and foundation of categorical inequality are, likewise, annulled and abstracted, remaining as what it is not: a mere difference between individuals.

A political corollary of this perspective of analysis is that a black man can occupy the position of a white man and vice versa, just as a woman can occupy the position of a man and vice versa. To accomplish this goal of equality, it is only necessary to modify the distribution of that "something" that distances them, black and white or man and woman; therefore, it is not necessary to abolish either racism or patriarchy, on which racial or gender inequality is based. This political strategy against inequality becomes a matter of equity and redistributive justice, not a matter of social emancipation. Thus, male-female inequality is reduced to a mere matter of distributive inequity and not to a matter of social construction of gender differences; social inequality only refers to the distribution of these "somethings" and not to the social and historical constitution of the possessors/owners of these "somethings".

However, people are not individuals undifferentiated from one another, distanced only by our possessions or positions in a distribution function. Our differences are not individual, nor can they be individualized, but will always be referred to structures and collectives, insofar as we constitute ourselves as social subjects and, therefore, socially constructed categories. As Aristotle said, the human being is in essence a *zoon politikón*, a social, civic animal. Therefore, what constitutes us at our nucleus are social, i.e., political and historical relations and conditions. Paradoxically, even when we see and conceptualize inequality as a function of distribution between individuals with respect to a *what*, the idea is in itself a social and historical construction. Inequality is not something given, something already structured, but a process in the making that is structuring itself.

Differences according to sex (gender), age, race, class, nationality, etc., are not between individuals; therefore, they are not individualizable differences and inequalities in their origin and constitution. Gender, race, class, etc., are social constructs that overdetermine the individual conditions of people, such as sex, age, etc. Individual differences with respect to "something" are nothing more than a way of personalizing a categorical inequality, which is annulled by these individualistic ontologies. The paradox of it all is that from these perspectives we speak of social inequality, but by abstracting from the social character of all inequality.

This way of individualizing the social is nothing more than one of the many *Robinsonades* that Marx accused of neoclassical economics. Ontologically in every society every individual is a social construct. Individuality as a condition of existence of persons is overdetermined by a higher plane of existence: their condition of being a *zoon politikón*, a social and civic being. In this sense, our individual forms of existence—that is, as individuals—are reconstructed and re-signified from the social plane, that is, from the social structures that condition us as social beings, as socially and historically constituted individuals. It is not that these individual differences (our individualities) disappear, but rather that their sense, function, meaning, structuring, etc., are reconfigured and reconstituted from the social as a higher plane of our existence. Thus, in any society, the differences between men and women do not disappear, but are re-signified from the social plane and, in this case, from patriarchy as a structuring social structure of gender relations and, therefore, of inequality between men and women. The same can be said with respect to differences of class, race, nationality, and a long etcetera.

Based on this ontological critique of the discourses that individualize inequality, we can now move on to the critique that sustains inequality in differences with respect to talents, capabilities, and other forms of individual distinctions. As Sen (1992) rightly says, human beings are profoundly heterogeneous; however, we add, this does not imply that this heterogeneity is the basis of the social inequality that separates and divides us as subjects, classes, genders, or races.

The social conformation of a person (in this case, as an individual) is from their constitution as a social subject and not from their individuality as a person. At the moment in which an individual-man established a relationship with an individual-woman that implied some form of social division, in that moment, one and the other ceased to be individuals to become social subjects linked to each other by relations of social inequality, relations on which the social division between individual-men and individual-women is built. Thus, it is not the difference between a given individual-man and a given individual-woman that is the basis of inequality between men and women but the way in which they socially relate to one another that produces the division of some as men and others as women.

The difference between individuals *becomes* inequality but not by itself: Rather, it is produced and constructed as inequality on the basis of social processes that relate and constitute individuals as social subjects. Individual differences do not cause inequality. What causes inequality is the way in which individuals relate to each other. Not every form of difference between individuals becomes a form of social inequality. However, every form of inequality entails a resignification of some form of differentiation between individuals. It is the latter that usually leads to confusion, as it is often misunderstood by equating difference with inequality (Therborn, 2013). Difference (individual) and inequality (social) correspond to two ontologically different planes of social reality, that is, their core perspectives on the constitution of the human being as a social being, where the latter, individualistic perspective tends to overdetermine the former. But, to reiterate, every form of individual difference is socially reconstructed as a social form of distinction, which, in many cases, entails forms of social inequality. In our social realities, there are no individual beings as such but social beings. In any society, every individual is, above all else, a social being, not an individual. If it were truly otherwise, it would cease to be a society in categorical and analytical terms.

We can only theorize and refer to individuals in terms of their individuality, isolated and separated from the rest of society, that is, in the form of a Robinson Crusoe novel, with an individual and socially isolated existence. But, what a paradox! In this context, it is impossible to speak of difference or inequality in the first place because to do so it is necessary to compare the individuality of one person with that of another who is equally isolated and individual, that is, another who is equally abstracted from the social reality that constitutes them as supposed individuals. This is to say that even to speak of individual differences it is necessary to speak in a more complex register than that of individuality and to refer, therefore, to some social form of existence in relation to other individuals. But this implies, then, to stop speaking and referring to individual-individuals but to social-individuals, where if in the first case (the Robinson Crusoe type) the accent is placed on the individual character of the individual, while in the second it is necessarily placed on the social character of that individual. So, we are back to the same thing: It is not individual differences that cause inequalities but the social forms of these individual differences (emphasizing *social forms*).

A good way to exemplify this ontological contradiction in the individualist and distributivist approaches to inequality is to analyze the thesis that the basis of social inequality is the intrinsic difference of human beings and, therefore, the unequal retribution of income, rights, privileges, among others is a product of the differences in the talents, capacities, and potentialities that characterize human beings and their difference.

In his reflection on equality, Sen (1992: 3) is reiterative in pointing out as a substrate of inequality the "basic heterogeneity of humans." In this regard, he is explicit when he points out that "the pervasive diversity of human beings intensifies the need to address this diversity of focus in the assessment of equality", or when he states that "the assessment of the claims of equality has to come to terms with the existence of pervasive human diversity" (1, 3).[3]

Liberal thought also argues that inequality is a totally valid and legitimate situation, since it corresponds to the unequal distribution of talents and merits among people. According to the principle of meritocracy, if we are not all equally talented and meritorious, then it is totally fair and the basis of a relationship of equity that we obtain differentiated retributions according to the abilities and merits of each person.[4] In this framework, it is even a sign of justice and equity that the most deserving receive more.

The problem with this approach is that it considers talents as well as merits, capacities, or potentialities as an attribute of distinct persons, as a part of their rugged individuality, when, in fact, every talent is a social construction and as such reflects a social condition of the individual that differentiates and renders them unequal from other individuals in some respect, whether that be class affiliation, gender, ethnic-racial origin, nationality, geographic origin, among many other ways of configuring categorical inequalities.

There is no doubt that human beings are intrinsically diverse and heterogeneous. As in other species of the animal kingdom, diversity among humans, including their genetic diversity, is a necessary condition for our evolution and reproduction as a species. But there is nothing to indicate that this intrinsic diversity must necessarily be constituted as social inequality. It is true that among animals' genetic diversity and diversity of "talents" (capacities and strengths) is the basis of a division among them in terms of their position, roles, capacities, and needs. In every herd there is always a leader, and males and females fulfill differentiated roles. However, the key difference lies in the fact that not even the most evolved animal species, apart from our own, can be considered as constituting a social form of life. Only human beings construct their lives on the basis of the social. For one thing, there is no history in the division of roles and functions in any animal species, i.e., there is no form of reproduction that allows transferring the position of an individual animal to

---

3 Sen (1992) further qualifies these assertions when he puts forward his thesis on human capabilities, which leads to understanding inequalities as veiled forms of human rights violations, inasmuch as they constitute social conditioning that limits the freedom and capacity of one to develop fully as a human being.

4 At the end of the nineteenth century, Clark (1908 [1899]) also established the principles of neoclassical economic theory, which would explain why income and remuneration should be differentiated according to the productivity levels of workers—i.e., according to their different abilities and talents.

the next generation. On the contrary, within each new generation, we find the division of individuals according to their talents, strengths, and capabilities, where order is re-established and re-constructed.

Only the human species exists as a society and community, where the historic differentiation of roles and functions is constituted as social inequality in such a way that positions are no longer assigned on the basis of individual conditions but of their social form, that is, of the social condition of each individual, of each person. Among human beings, thinking of them as social beings, inequality is not constructed on the basis of the individual talents or merits of each one with respect to those of others but, rather, on the basis of social and historical relations that denote forms of power, domination, exploitation, and discrimination among individuals. More specifically, discrimination and distinctions between individuals according to their talents is in reality a fallacy—a fetish—insofar as it assigns social and historical functions to individual and personal attributes. Every talent, every merit, and every ability is, in itself, a social and historical fact and is distributed according to social and historical forms and rules derived from social structures of inequality, in particular from power relations that divide individuals into different and unequal social subjects.

If talents, merits, etc. were indeed an individual attribute—part of the conformation of each person's innate individuality—then it is worth asking why they are not randomly distributed among the population but, rather, tend to be concentrated in a certain type or profile of individuals. For example, why do women tend to be systematically "less talented" than men in sports, such as soccer or others? Why does "entrepreneurial talent" tend to be concentrated in male, white, and affluent individuals and not in women, Indigenous people, and migrants? Why do men from low-income and popular sectors prevail in national soccer teams, while, on the contrary, white men from First World countries prevail in company boards of directors? Why is the proportion of workers' sons who ascend and become company directors or managers as low and insignificant as the proportion of businessmen's sons who become salaried workers?

These questions refer us in turn to another equally radical questioning. In the end, we are all talented for something, with our own distinct abilities and merits. The point is that we are not all equally talented, nor do we all have the same capacities in the same fields. But, again, we all have some talent or special capacity for something, that is for certain. The critical point to consider here is that those "somethings" are not the same, and are not equally valued socially. For the same reason, inequality does not lie in the different endowment of talents and capacities—in the individual merits of each person—but in the social construction that lies behind the unequal valuation and social significance of different talents, that is, in the social construction of merits, capacities, and talents. The underlying issue is not that inequality arises from the greater talent or merit of one person with respect to another, but from the fact that the talent, capacity, or merit of one person has more social value than that of another person. And this difference is not constructed on the basis of the talents themselves, nor on the basis of the individuals who have such talents or merits, but on the basis of the social structures from which such social inequality of talents and merits is configured. In this way, the social ideas of merit, capacity, and talent are nothing but mediations, ways of transferring to individuals a condition of social inequality constructed and determined in other social spaces and fields.

Social inequality is not a matter of talent or merit purely and simply, even in its consideration in the abstract, but, rather, of socially constructed and meaningful talents and merits, where their unequal valuation is also a social and historical construction. Thus, for example, the renowned soccer player Leo Messi is undoubtedly an individual with great talent for the game, which has allowed him to become a successful person, both socially, economically, and financially. However, Messi himself, with the same talent and innate ability for soccer, 100 years ago would have been just another son of an Italian immigrant in Argentina. It is not talent purely and simply what gives Messi his status of success and fame, but the social value that contemporary society assigns to that talent. For the same reason, what is at the basis of inequality (of Messi's wealth, in this case) is not talent in itself, but the historical structures from which that talent becomes a social condition of inequality.

Let us look at another example that contrasts with Leo Messi. The case of Professor Jaime Escalante and his achievements in training and teaching mathematics and calculus to low-income students, mostly Latinos, in a public school in East Los Angeles is widely known. However, despite being one of the most talented teachers in the United States, he did not achieve the fame, wealth, or worldwide recognition of a high-performance athlete. So, why is it that a talented, highly trained and capable teacher, with graduate training and studies, nevertheless fails to achieve the levels of success, fame, and wealth of a soccer player like Leo Messi or a basketball player like Michael Jordan, when in their respective fields they are undoubtedly the most talented?

Evidently, it is not the talent that distances them, but the field or scope of that talent.[5] For this particular society, sports seem to have a social function

---

5 This is without considering the weight of contextual factors: Jaime Escalante was of Bolivian origin and taught Latino students in a low-income, Mexican neighborhood. In other words,

of greater value, prestige, and fame than teaching. For the same reason, it is not the degree of talent, ability, and genius that may characterize an individual that contributes to eventual success, fame, and wealth but the social and historical context that determines the social value of talents and, therefore, the forms of inequality between the different social fields in which these talents may stand out. In any case, it is illustrative that this distance is not only between the great talents of one social field and another but also, in general, between the income, resources, wealth, prestige, and other material and symbolic goods perceived and achieved by athletes, regardless of their personal talent, which are usually higher than those of any teacher or professor, regardless of their individual talents. Undoubtedly, a more "talented" teacher achieves a better social position than a less "talented" one, but, even so, any teacher is still below the socioeconomic position achieved by any professional athlete. This example teaches us that social inequality is not the result of the differentiation of talents purely and simply, but of an underlying social structure that establishes a social inequality in relation to particular talents, granting a social function of higher rank, value and, prestige to some talents over others, regardless of the individualities and personal talents in each case.

Similarly, a meritocratic society is also a fallacy, a way of fetishizing social inequality, attributing the social ordering of our worlds as natural results of the individual properties of citizens. But it is not the differentiated merits between individuals that give rise to social inequality between them, but rather the reverse: it is the social inequality of merits that gives rise to the distinction of individuals, that is, it is the inequality in the construction of the valuation and social meaning of merits that explains the social inequality between individuals.

It is curious but totally illustrative that the fields where people's talents and merits are usually more highly valued imply a selectivity among individuals not because of their individualities but because of social and categorical selectivity. The unequal valuation and significance of merits, and, therefore, the social structure that arises from a meritocratic society, leads to a selection of people of a certain social profile that, curiously enough, is directly associated with certain structures of categorical differentiation, such as race, gender, class, nationality, among others.

---

surrounding Escalante was a series of structural conditioning factors and circumstances that were combined to construct various modes of categorical inequality, which, undoubtedly, also had an impact on this particular social construction of social inequality of the personal talents and abilities of Escalante himself as a social actor.

The issue of selectivity is not only that the rich have access to better education and professional training—and thus access to positions of social, economic, and political leadership in society—but the fact that education is one of the few fields that society establishes for access to these positions of leadership and social dominance. In other historical contexts, formal education has not been the mediation established for access to power, but other social devices such as religion (the priesthood), the militia, or marriage arrangements have. In other words, these fields of construction of social differentiation and inequality—education, the priesthood, the militia, depending on the historical context—are in themselves socially constructed, obey social forms of reproduction of power relations, and in no case correspond to fields of free and natural exercise of differences in terms of merits and capacities of each individual.

The corollary is both obvious and eloquent. In any society, even the most meritocratic, it is not individual differences (talents, merits, abilities) that form the basis of social inequalities—i.e., what divides people into unequal social categories—but the other way around: it is categorical inequality that usually manifests itself as inequality between individuals. Therefore, what we have to analyze as social scientists are the structures from which such categorical inequalities are constructed and reproduced, i.e., those social structures and processes that configure forms of inequality of classes, genders, races, ages, nationalities, among others.

3 Multidimensional Perspectives of Inequality

When Amartya Sen (1992: 12) asks the question "equality of what?" he opens the debate to the multiple spaces and variables from which equality and inequality can be judged and analyzed. He also attributes this wide multiplicity of spaces to the profound diversity that characterizes human beings.[6] Although he does not explicitly state it, this multiplicity of fields of inequality opens up the possibility of a multidimensional approach, that is, to think of the articulation of

---

6 Sen is equally aware that it is not only about interpersonal inequalities, but also about spaces of inter-group relationship and inequality, that is, such as classes, genders, races, or other forms of social grouping (Sen, 1992). However, his analysis of inequality between groups is much more limited and restricted in his theoretical proposal on capabilities than the analysis he makes regarding interpersonal inequality. Even when he recognizes its relevance, he does not analyze or delve into the origin of the making of these social groups, nor their connection with the spaces of inequality that emanate from them.

two or more of these spaces of constitution of inequalities. This is, in a way, the proposal made by the Economic Commission for Latin America and the Caribbean (ECLAC) in relation to what it calls the social inequality matrix (ECLAC, 2016).

According to ECLAC, social inequality is a multidimensional problem, whose original matrix recognizes several structural roots. The first and most basic axis of inequality is economic or class inequality, which is determined by the economic-productive matrix, as well as by the structure and forms of ownership and distribution of economic power among social strata and classes. Its most evident manifestation is the unequal distribution of income and rents, and it has secondary (yet vital) effects in other areas such as education, health, and the labor market.

Along with this class inequality, other forms of inequality are manifested in various spheres of social development such as gender relations, ethnic-racial status, life cycle, and life trajectories, as well as territorial and regional heterogeneities which include the rural-urban distinction. Thus, social inequality has at its origin a multiplicity of structuring axes that starting from the class structure include various fields of social life. For ECLAC, what defines this structuring character of inequality with respect to each of these axes "is their constitutive and determining weight in the process of producing and reproducing social relations and people's experiences; or, in other words, their impact on the depth of inequalities and their reproduction in different areas of development and the exercise of rights" (ECLAC, 2016: 16).

Although the social inequality matrix is not an approach that seeks to analyze and understand the origin and genesis of social inequality *per se*, and neither is it a perspective that considers inequality in the different axes that make up the larger inequality matrix, its contribution is nonetheless relevant in that it proposes a model of analysis that, on the one hand, is based on a multidimensional approach to inequality and, on the other, considers inequality in terms of distinction and social division between social subjects, whether it be classes, genders, races, or generations, and not only as interpersonal differences.

In this multidimensional model, the term *matrix* is rather metaphorical and alludes more to an approach that focuses on the interactions and intersections of these different fields or social axes in the configuration of social inequality and not so much on the genesis or origin of social inequality itself. The term matrix is used more to refer to a space of interaction and conjunction of different dimensions of inequality and not so much as a space where social inequality is created and produced. Therefore, it does not focus so much on the processes and relationships from which inequalities are created and constructed as it does on the spaces and dimensions where these inequalities are manifested. However, its relevance, as we said, is its overall vision, which allows for an articulated reconstruction of social inequality that goes beyond the classic view of it as a mode of distribution of 'something', whether it be resources, powers, rights, privileges, among others.

However, this model proposed by ECLAC does not depart from a normative perspective regarding inequality and equality. In other complementary texts, the organization does advance on the imperatives of equality, but while rescuing the centrality of more orthodox thinking concerning equality that has been seen in ECLAC thinking since its founding more than 70 years ago (Bárcena and Prado, 2016; Bielschowsky and Torres, 2018). In fact, this social inequality matrix model, which emphasizes the intersections of the various forms of inequality, is much more oriented to designing strategic indicators as well as guidelines for public policies in Latin America and the Caribbean, than to designing methods and categories of analysis for the understanding and comprehension of the processes and social relations that generate inequality, as well as the different fields (*vectors*) from which it is constituted.

Therborn (2013), for his part, also questions inequalities beyond the economic sphere—i.e., of income and wealth. For this author, the concern about inequality is still a matter of normative positions regarding lifestyles and the state of well-being of populations, where the principle of equality acquires a supreme value, sometimes unquestionable. However, Therborn's perspective recognizes that a comprehensive and analytical vision of inequality is also necessary to contribute to the understanding of the basic mechanisms and processes that generate inequality and equality. Based on this, he proposes a more complex analysis model.

Therborn starts by recognizing the multidimensional nature of inequality and, therefore, the methodological and theoretical mandates of thinking about it from categories of analysis and modes of thought open to the necessary and multiple articulation of levels, processes, and dimensions in which inequality is manifested and produced. In this regard, he considers three types of inequality, each of which would be sustained in some basic dimension of human life:

1. Firstly, *vital inequality*, which refers to socially constructed differences in terms of life options and survival opportunities. This idea of inequality stems from the fact that humans, as living beings, are susceptible to pain, suffering, and death on unequal terms.
2. Secondly, *existential inequality*, which refers to the socially constructed difference with respect to the attributes and conditions that constitute each person. In this field, we find the operation of the dimensions of family, gender, and race, as well as different modes and operations of social

status. This type of inequality derives from the fact that human beings are people who live our lives in social contexts that, along with determining these systems of distinction, are also the basis for the construction of our sense of identity and belonging, as well as for the development of emotional bonds between us.
3. Finally, the *material* or *resources inequality* to which we have access, which may limit or enhance as the case may be our condition as social actors with the capacity to act in pursuit of objectives and goals, whether material, emotional, or symbolic. The basis of this form of inequality are the economic, political, and cognitive systems (education, knowledge, etc.) from which we humans are constituted as actors in a structural context.

Vital inequality is perhaps the clearest and most evident form, around which there is no moral, ethical, or political principle that can justify it. Existential inequality, on the other hand, is a term and approach that has not yet achieved consensus among social scientists. Nevertheless, several of the manifestations of this type of inequality are already part of the theoretical and methodological heritage of the greater social sciences. This is the case for studies of gender inequality, ethnic-racial inequality, as well as national inequalities.

Inequality of resources, on the other hand, is undoubtedly the concern that has concentrated the greatest interest both in the field of the social sciences and in the political institutions and organizations of the State and civil society itself. The most conventional studies concentrate on inequality of income and wealth, but they do not stop there. For example, Bourdieu's studies on education and cultural capital or on distinction and taste show other areas in which inequality of resources is manifested, which go beyond sheer monetary income and material wealth.

Along with this classification of various types of inequality, Therborn advances in the analysis of the mechanisms that themselves generate and produce these forms of inequality. Considering that inequalities are produced and sustained socially as a result of both systemic processes and individual and collective distributive action, he points out four mechanisms that help us understand the social processes from which diverse modes of inequality are produced and maintained:

1. *Distantiation*: This mechanism refers to the result of continuous competition among individuals for access to resources, power, prestige, among other aspects. From liberal thought, this process of generating inequality is conceptualized as social achievement and is not seen as a mode of inequality but as a legitimate allocation of rewards. For Therborn, on the other hand, although achievement is an aspect to be considered, this

mechanism refers to a more complex situation, which is not reduced to the strictly individual sphere. In this regard, he points out "it is important to emphasize the systemic context of distantiation, as opposed to all individualist ideology, that success is the singular achievement of the successful individual" (Therborn, 2013: 56). It is necessary to go beyond the ideological connotations in the notion of achievement of the liberal perspective and consider it as part of a larger social libretto, with considerations of interdependencies and relationships that go beyond individual relationships. It is not that personal attributes and individualities do not contribute to the distancing between people but that this process is more of a result of systemic contexts that cannot be abstracted in analyses based on the individual level in order to fully understand this mechanism of inequality.

2. *Exclusion*: This arises from the social division between those who belong to a category and those who do not belong to it and results from conditions that allow the advancement of some and impede the advancement of others. It refers to discrimination and segregation of various kinds or to social and economic forms such as monopoly, that limit the access to and enjoyment of the right to something, restricting it to certain groups in society. Exclusion is the basic form of inequality, insofar as it creates a social division between people, which takes the form of classes, genders, races, or other social categories. As a social fact, exclusion institutionalizes the idea that not everyone can be like everyone else but that there is a social division that implies the inclusion of some in the higher strata and the exclusion of the rest of those social strata.

3. *Hierarchy*: This refers to "some institutionalized ranking of social actors, some high, others low, from super and sub-ordination" (Therborn, 2013: 59). All hierarchy is supported by a formal organization. In extreme cases, it takes the form of estates, castes, or other modes of division of society that not only establish a hierarchical order but also limit and constrain the possible mobility between its different hierarchical orders.

4. *Exploitation*: This refers asymmetrical relations between social classes and estates, where "freedom and property versus unfreedom and propertylessness has been the classical categorical divide underlying economic exploitation" (Therborn, 2013: 57). Every form of exploitation is sustained by a condition of freedom of some with respect to others, as well as the ownership of some and the absence of ownership of others. In the case of slave and servile labor, this seems obvious. But it is also true in the case of wage labor. Not only is the wage laborer not the owner of the means of production, but this very situation does not allow them to

enjoy the freedom that the capitalist enjoys, forcing the worker to depend directly on the sale of their labor power. The lack of resources and the lack of access to property are limitations to their freedom as an economic subject and, therefore, as a social and political actor, that is, as a social class.

Based on these four mechanisms, the dynamics of inequality and the processes that generate it can be analyzed and evaluated. It also makes it possible to consider alternative ways of overcoming or at least reducing inequality. This model analysis of inequality not only contributes to its comprehension and understanding but also, and in a certain normative way, to establishing principles for overcoming it. For one thing, each mechanism of inequality would be matched by an opposite one, aimed at generating situations of social equality.

In our case, we take up part of Therborn's approach, but we reformulate it based on a different theoretical and epistemological perspective. Our underlying assumption is that inequality and, therefore, the processes that constitute it, are not only a manifestation of society but, at the same time, a structuring process of society itself. According to our approach, the question of interest does not only concern the fact that in societies there are structures, situations, and contexts of inequality, of whatever type, but rather that societies themselves are unequal and are structured and constituted as such. In this sense, our interest in the study and analysis of inequality is because it is through inequality that we wish to study and analyze our societies. As the structuring axis of society, inequality also becomes a form of mediation in its analysis. We analyze inequality not as a category in itself but, as a historical form of society. Inequality, thus, alludes to a founding dimension of the social, of society itself. To analyze the processes, fields, relations, and structures that generate inequality is to analyze the processes, fields, and relations that are the foundations of society itself. It is a question, therefore, not only of constituent processes of inequalities but, and through this, of constituent processes of society.

The corollary of this approach is radical in terms of its critique of inequality. *A discourse against inequality is, therefore, a discourse against the historical social formation of our societies.* In other words, there is no possibility of a critique of inequality if it is not at the same time a critique of society. Likewise, every strategy of exit and overcoming inequality is, at the same time, a strategy of exit and overcoming this form of constitution of society. This perspective is not always present in the discourse of Therborn and other authors, nor in that of ECLAC, however progressive and advanced they may be in terms of analysis and understanding of inequality. However, this does not mean that these discourses and authors are wrong in their approaches—we hope to propose nothing of the sort. Rather, it is a matter of adequately situating the position of each one in terms of larger social debates, which always implies and refers to an essentially political debate. Therefore, on this plane, there are no right and wrong positions but, rather, political and social positions in legitimate confrontation.

4 Inequality and Society: Analysis Model from Its Totality

We understand social inequality as a complete social totality. As such, we can analyze it on the basis of three fields that compose and structure it. In each field, in turn, we identify a system of relations on which that field is constituted and from which is the genesis of all forms of inequality. Acting all together, these fields compose the matrix of all forms of social inequality. In this context, we use the term matrix to refer to the set of vectors—processes and social fields—that generate and found inequality, which, in turn, constitute fields and processes that construct society.

Every society is constituted on at least three fields of social relations:[7]
1. Economic (*oikos*), which refers to material reproduction;
2. Social and political (*polis*), which refers to the reproduction of power and its forms;
3. Population (*demos*), which refers to the demographic reproduction of the population that constitutes every society.

All forms of social inequality (of gender, class, ethnicity, nationality, among others) are also constituted on the basis of the articulation and interdependence, embeddedness, of these same three social fields. Likewise, each of these fields is constituted as such on the basis of a system of relations and processes that characterize it, while at the same time giving rise to social forms of inequality. In the case of the economy, the founding process is the relation of *exploitation* and is reflected in class relations. In the case of politics, the founding relationship is that of *domination* and is reflected in relations of power and hegemony, of domination and subjugation, oppression, which divide the different social groups. Finally, in the case of population, the fundamental relationship that interests us here is that of *discrimination* and *exclusion* between individuals

---

[7] Each of these fields, in turn, has given rise to the conformation of disciplinary fields of the Social Sciences: Economics, Sociology, and Demography, respectively. In this sense, from the perspective of totalities, the challenge that faces us as social scientists is to reconstruct the interrelationships between these disciplines, as well as the way in which each is reproduced and reconstituted in the others.

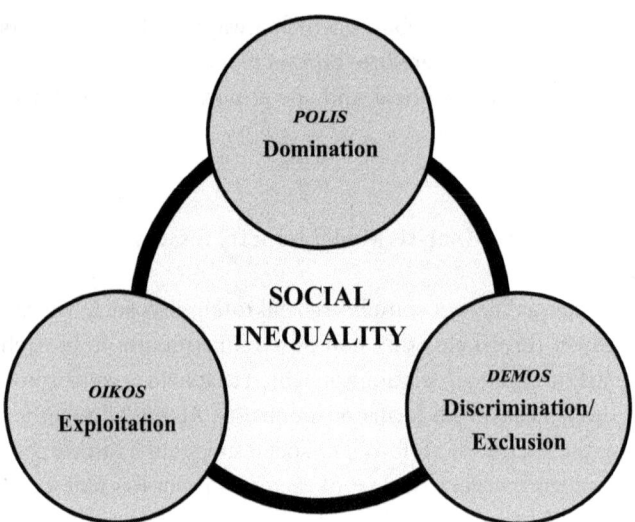

FIGURE 2   Fields of constitution of social inequality

on the basis of social and demographic categories. Figure 2 illustrates this perspective of understanding inequality.

With respect to the first field, *oikos,* we can affirm that all forms of social inequality have an economic basis and a substratum in the social relations of production, and this is true for inequalities based on class relations, gender, race, nationality, among others. Thus, the distribution of resources, wealth, income, which is usually analyzed as the basic form of all inequality, has its origin in these social relations of production that are constituted in the labor process and define the character of each society and each economic-social formation. This inequality is usually approached from the distribution function; thus, we speak of inequality of income, property, material conditions of life, etc., or other categories that acquire distributive forms. Although, in reality, all these distributive forms have a material substratum referring to the social form of production and the historical mode in which the labor process is constituted based on the forms assumed by the ownership of the means of production, as well as the two main means of generating wealth: nature (land and natural resources) and labor.

The division into social classes that arises from a particular mode of production—that is, from the social relations of production—is constituted on the basis of the relations of exploitation of labor, which, although they vary in each social-historic formation, always refers to the same type of class opposition: those who live from the fruit of their own labor against those who live from the fruit of the labor of others.[8] Precisely, the appropriation of this surplus labor of others is based on a relationship of exploitation and is what gives rise to all forms of division of society into social classes and, by this means, to the constitution of society on the basis of *class inequality*.[9]

The same can be said with respect to inequality in the field of the *POLIS*, that is, the forms of power and politics that constitute each society and that materialize as modes of *domination*. All forms of social inequality are based on an unequal distribution and exercise of power, that is, of forces and hegemonies that result in the division of society into classes, genders, races, nationalities, and, in general, all forms of differentiated strata. This inequality is based on a relationship of *domination* of some over others, which arises from the ability to subjugate and subordinate, oppress and rule, from some social subjects over other. Often this power arises from the control of some founding vector of the social formation, such as the ownership of the means of production, access to and control of military force, or the control and access to other modes of construction of social and cultural hegemonies.

---

8 This distinction, which is usually assumed to have Marxist roots, was in fact already pointed out by Aristotle in ancient Greece and, later, by Rousseau in the eighteenth century to refer to the origins of social inequality. For more details, see the following chapters of this book.

9 Although the term exploitation usually has a negative connotation in terms of the rejection it generates because it is supposed to be an unjust and inequitable relationship, in reality, it is the result of an ideologized reading of Marxist texts, which does not take into account that it is a category of analysis that refers to what it directly indicates: the extraction of value and wealth. Thus, for example, it is used to speak of the exploitation of a mine, agricultural exploitation, and exploitation of labor. In all three of these cases, the term refers to the extraction of value or wealth: from the mine, from the land, or from the labor, as the case may be. Likewise, in the particular case of labor exploitation, the same is true whether it refers to exploitation based on class relations (social division of labor), based on gender relations (sexual division of labor), or based on ethno-racial relations (ethno-racial division of labor). In this sense, if any critique should be made of the Marxist use of this category, it is its reductionism to understand it only for the analysis of class exploitation, without considering its heuristic and theoretical potential to account for other modes of exploitation and extraction of labour value. Such a shift would allow us to, therefore, analyze and consider the constitution of forms of social inequality equally structural and structuring of capitalist society, such as gender inequality or ethnic-racial inequality, among others, which account for the genesis of patriarchy, racism, and xenophobia. Finally, it should be noted that the use we make of the category of exploitation does not indicate anything about the fairness or unfairness of the form that this relationship takes, nor whether it is an equitable exchange or not. What is relevant, in any case, is the social form that the relation of exploitation assumes in each historical epoch and the fields from which it is constituted as such.

In this respect, Miliband (1987: 329) points out that in any class society, the ruling class is constituted not only by virtue of its capacity to control the means of production but, also, and fundamentally, "by virtue of its effective control over ... the means of state administration and coercion, and the main means of communication and consent." That is, domination is constituted from an adequate combination of control and exercise of the means of force and consensus, of repression and persuasion, of authority and hegemony. Thus, for example, in feudal societies power was constituted around access to and control of faith and religion, while in capitalism it is constituted around control of the means of production and the State.

In the third field of our model—the *DEMOS*—the relationship on which inequality is based is social *discrimination* and *exclusion*, on the basis of which forms of division and classification of the population into differentiated social groups are constructed. All type of segmentation of the population into social strata is based not only on strictly economic or political factors but also on "extra-economic" processes of social distinction and distancing, especially related to factors of cultural, ethnic, gender, or demographic differentiation, in general (Canales, 2003).

On the social differentiation into classes already referred to in this discussion—*OIKOS*/exploitation and *POLIS*/domination—a structure of inequality is reconstructed based on demographic factors of social differentiation. In this way, the classic categories of demographic differentiation (male-female, migratory status, ethnic origin, among others) become categories of social inequality. Likewise, these categories of demographic differentiation are used to construct social identities that reinforce this demographic structuring of social inequality, utilizing symbolic, political, and cultural dimensions. It is the configuration of social and cultural minorities (women, elder, migrants, ethnic groups, among others), whose condition as social minorities is constructed on the basis of modes of social exclusion and discrimination that imply a devaluation of their living and reproductive conditions. What is relevant for our reflection is the role that the categories of demographic differentiation assume as a representation of these conditions of social fragmentation of populations.

In other texts, we have referred to this phenomenon as a *demography of inequality* (Canales, 2003 and 2021b), a way of focusing attention on how the structures of demographic differentiation become structures of social inequality. We understand that it is not the characteristics of the subjects that generate discrimination or exclusion but, rather, the concrete social and economic structures from which social inequality is constructed as a form of differentiation between demographic groups. Many of the categories of decomposition/

disaggregation of populations usually used in demography are, in fact, categories of persistent inequality, in the sense that Tilly (1999) gives to this term. Sex, ethnicity or race, age and generation, rural-urban origin, citizenship/foreign status, occupation, income stratum and poverty status, among many others, are forms of sociodemographic distinction that are based on many other social relations of persistent inequality. These categories do not refer solely and exclusively to individual attributes but are the result of social and historical constructions, on the basis of which not only forms of categorical distinction between individuals are established but also forms of social inequality between demographic categories. Categorical distinction, which in demography takes the form of distance between one individual and another, is actually based on a relationship of social inequality. In short, sex, age, national origin, among many others, correspond to "categories of demographic differentiation, which are socially reconstructed and redefined in terms of the configuration of *demographic subjects* that are differentiated and exposed to unequal conditions of vulnerability, exclusion, and social discrimination" (Canales, 2003: 71, our translation).

Normally, within classical Marxist approaches, the emphasis is placed on the modes of production and exploitation, in the *OIKOS* as the founding social field of class inequality and, therefore, of the constitution of the class struggle. The relation of exploitation, thus, acquires a central place in the explanation of the origin of classes and in the constitution of society in social classes. It is not a question of denying the importance of the economic-productive field (*OIKOS*) nor of the relations of exploitation as motors of development and progress in capitalist societies. Rather, we are interested in discussing the notion—in our opinion, a mistaken one—that the relations of exploitation are circumscribed only to the sphere of the social division of labor into social classes and—the equally mistaken notion—that in the field of economy and production only the relation of exploitation is relevant for the constitution of class inequality, discarding the explanatory power and understanding that other fields and processes of generation of social inequalities, such as domination and discrimination, that is the *POLIS* and *DEMOS*.

On the contrary, the central thesis we wish to illustrate in this work is that, if we think of inequality as a social totality, then we assume that each of these fields—*OIKOS, POLIS,* and *DEMOS*—does not have an autonomous and independent existence from the other two. On the contrary, this division into three fields is only analytical and abstract in the understanding that in each of them the founding processes and relations are explained only in relation to the founding and constituent processes of the other two analytical fields. Thus, for example, it is unthinkable to consider the process of exploitation without mediating in it the relations of political domination that sustain the conformation of classes and modes of property; as well it is equally unthinkable to consider exploitation without considering the relations of discrimination and social division of populations that structure it in unequal and differentiated social categories, inserted in different positions of power and domination and at the same time exposed to different modes of exploitation and/or appropriation of the labor of others. Let us see this in relation to class inequality and the division of society into classes, commonly referred to as the mode of production.

It is now commonplace to say that all societies are based on various forms of exploitation of labor, insofar as all social formations are based on the social division between those who live from the fruits of their labor and those who live from the product of the labor of others. The same was true in ancient Greece as documented by Aristotle, as well as in the Roman Empire, the fiefdoms of the Middle Ages, or modern capitalism, both in its industrial and post-industrial forms. As Marx (1973 [1857]: 344–345) points out:

> Capital has not invented surplus-labor. Wherever a part of society possesses the monopoly of the means of production, the laborer, free or not free, must add to the working-time necessary for his own maintenance an extra working-time in order to produce the means of subsistence for the owners of the means of production, whether this proprietor be the Athenian χαλος γαχαθος [well-to-do man], Etruscan theocrat, *civis Romanus* [Roman citizen], Norman baron, American slave-owner, Wallachian Boyard, modern landlord or capitalist.

What distinguishes one society from another is not the presence or absence of relations of exploitation, but the form in which this relation of exploitation is making, and, therefore, the form in which social groups are constituted around the process of work and exploitation of labor power. Here, more relevant than the forms of property are the forms that the labor power adopts in relation to the various forms of property. Slave forms are not the same as forms of servitude or wage forms of labor power. Each of them poses a particular historical formation, where the concrete form of labor is the counter-side of the forms of ownership of the means of production, both formed and assumed by the process of the exploitation of labor. Thus, it is the relations of exploitation (extraction and appropriation of value and surplus value) that sustain and give rise to social classes, not the mere ownership of the means of production.[10]

---

10   This distinction is particularly relevant in view of the new forms of constitution of the ruling classes in global, post-modern, and post-industrial society, where ownership of the means of production is replaced as a central factor by the domination and control of

It is not the ownership of the means of production, purely and simply, that constitutes the genesis of social classes, but it is, rather, the forms of exploitation that manifest themselves in every society as social relations of production. The labor process as an abstraction always exists; the extraction of surplus value, on the other hand, does not. The relation of exploitation can only exist when the development of the productive forces has permitted the generation of a surplus of the fruit of labor that can be appropriated by some sector of society. But this is not enough in itself. It is necessary, in addition, that a division of society be constituted, in which some can be constituted as owners of the means of production and others as non-owners. But this social division does not arise directly from economic-productive relations but from power relations, that is, from the domination of some over others. It is from a structure of domination of some over others that subjects with different power over property are constituted, which makes it possible for this inequality of power and domination over others to be transferred to the economic-productive field in the form of a relation of exploitation of labor, that is, extraction of surplus. Thus, inequality in the field of power—*POLIS*—is reproduced in the field of production—*OIKOS*—as class inequality. What in one field is constituted on the basis of modes of domination in the other is constituted as modes of exploitation. What is relevant, in any case, is that neither one nor the other relation of inequality—domination and exploitation—can be understood and manifested without the concurrence of the other.

Such is the case, for example, of slave relations. Slaves do not exist in themselves, but are socially and politically produced from the domination by force of some over others—they are actively enslaved. The same is true of servile labor, and although it may be hard to believe, it is also what happened with wage labor. As both Polanyi (2001 [1944]) and Marx (1973 [1857]) point out, the construction of the working class—that is, of the wage form of labor and workers and, therefore, of the labor market—was a historical process that arose from the confrontation between social forces with different degrees of power and domination of some over others. Until the end of the eighteenth century,

---

the labor process by other actors. Managers, CEOs, and other high-level business officials make up the elites of large corporations, but they are not necessarily their owners, only their administrators. Curiously, the supposed critique of the class approach based on this relative loss of explanatory power of the concept of private property in recent times, overlooks the key fact that owners have always exercised their power through such figures. Such is the case of the overseers in the haciendas and fiefdoms, as well as of the military and their generals in the case of the slave systems of antiquity. In the following chapters, we will go deeper into this analysis.

wage labor existed only as a marginal and circumstantial form. As a dominant mode, it was produced by a "someone"—a social class, the capitalist—with sufficient power to do so. It was not made at any particular moment, but on the basis of certain historical and social conditions: when the industrial bourgeoisie achieves sufficient power to do so and faces the need to advance in the accumulation of capital, that is, when the bourgeoise manages to constitute itself as a dominant and powerful class (see *Excursus* 2). It is interesting to note that the primary and original power of the capitalist bourgeoisie did not arise from the relation of exploitation, purely and simply, but from its capacity (power) to constitute and generate a specific form of relations of exploitation and, in particular, to convert the worker into a subject susceptible of being exploited under the form that most suited the new dominant class, that of the wage laborer. And this power does not come solely and exclusively from the position of the bourgeoisie in the labor process but from the conjunction of their mode of political, economic, and social constitution.

Indeed, we know that in any social formation what gives rise to the class structure and the division of society into classes is not the relation to the means of production (property), purely and simply, but the relation of exploitation that opposes owners and workers, that is, those who live off the labor of others and those who live off the fruit of their own labor. However, this relation of exploitation does not occur in a vacuum, in the abstraction of the processes of production and extraction of surplus value, but is mediated and conditioned by social relations of domination and power, which make some constitute themselves as owners and others as non-owners and workers. The concrete forms of labor and property in each society do not arise by themselves but as modes of domination and power of some over others that characterize each society. And there is no greater power of domination than the capacity to socially and historically construct the social subject that is the object of exploitation and domination. Such is the case of slave labor in slavery, of servile labor in serfdom, and of wage labor in capitalism.

In this way, we see that every relation of exploitation is sustained by forms of domination. And *vice versa*, every relation of domination is sustained by forms of exploitation. Or put another way, political power is sustained by economic power, although not in a direct and deterministic way, but in an interdependent way. And by this we are not referring to the fact, very common nowadays, that the businessman corrupts the politician. Rather, we are referring to the fact that every mode of exploitation can only exist on the basis of its articulation with a mode of domination. It is not so much a question of relations between concrete actors acting at specific junctures, but of the founding of constitutive structures of society. They are not the actors as persons and individuals but as classes and subjects, as collective and historical actors.

Every form of exploitation is based on the social and historical construction of subjects that participate in this relationship with asymmetrical power: some as owners and others as workers. Labor as a category of exploitation has always exists, but this is nothing more than a truism, insofar as it is nothing more than a mere abstraction. What exists, in reality, are historical forms of labor and labor power, that is, historical forms of the labor process. These historical forms are what determine and are expressed in the forms of social inequality and the class structure of each society. The concrete (historical) form assumed by labor and labor power and its counterparts—the means of production and their ownership—is what characterizes and defines each social-historical formation. The concrete form of existence of labor—as slave, serf, or wage-earner—is constructed from fields of social and political domination. The same can be said with the forms of property. As fiefdoms, oligarchy, or bourgeois forms (capital), they do not exist in and of themselves but are historical products, arising from the forms of domination of some over others.

Thus, the *OIKOS* cannot be understood without the *POLIS*, and exploitation cannot be understood without domination. It is the *embeddedness* of both fields, of both processes, of both relations, that gives rise to the division of society into social classes. Likewise, this model of understanding becomes even more complex if we incorporate the third field indicated in the model, the *DEMOS*, and the relations of discrimination and social exclusion.

What is worth remembering here is that, when we speak of workers, in reality this is also an abstraction, which hides and makes invisible the demographic and social subjects that make up both the working class and the capitalist class. Workers, and capitalists, don't exist in abstract, but as *demographic subjects*, differentiated according to social categories and social processes of distinction, established on the basis of modes of social exclusion and discrimination. They are not only workers, or capitalists, purely and simply, but also women, indigenous people, migrants, older adults, rural people, people with little formal education, people from the Third World, and so on. They are workers exposed to various modes of social differentiation and exclusion, which entail various modes of social and demographic vulnerability. What is relevant is that these sociodemographic categories refer to various modes of domination and exploitation to which these demographic subjects are exposed.

In this regard, an example will help us to understand this complex situation. In her book *Mujer, inmigrante y trabajadora: la triple discriminación* [*Woman, immigrant, and worker: Triple discrimination*], Sonia Parella (2003) analyzes the situation of migrant women in Spain at the beginning of the 21st century and draws a very interesting conclusion. She points out that working women of migrant origin face a triple process of discrimination: as women (gender discrimination), as migrants (discrimination based on national origin), and as workers (discrimination based on class). Thus, the situation of this particular labor subject is determined by the concrete way in which the axes of the matrix of social inequality are articulated in a given geographical space. This triple discrimination, as Parella calls it, reflects the three fields that we have pointed out as the basis of the constitution as unequal subjects in a general sense: (1) in terms of economics, as exploited workers; (2) in terms of demographics, as women facing discrimination because of their gender and migratory condition; and (3), finally, in terms of the underlying relations of domination, which include modes of male domination, modes of ethnic-national domination, and modes of class domination. This situation of triple discrimination described by Parella is but a way of bearing witness to the larger, triple mode of constitution of social subjects; it is, therefore, a way to see the particular ways that these three fields that constitute inequality—*OIKOS, POLIS* and *DEMOS*—operate, as well as a way to note their role in the articulation of the three processes that generate social inequality: exploitation, domination, and discrimination.

What this model allows us to observe is that every relation of exploitation is not only constituted on the basis of owners of means of production with respect to workers and non-owners of such means of production, which in capitalism would be the relation between capital and labor or between capitalists and workers. Along with this, every form of exploitation is also a form of domination and is manifested in that it is a relationship between a dominant class (entrepreneurs, etc.) and classes dominated and subjected to relations of subordination and power of others. Likewise, it is not only relations of domination and subjugation, but also of discrimination and exclusion. Not only do capitalists dominate workers, but, curiously, it is generally white, urban, male capitalists from central countries who dominate and exploit women, indigenous, migrant, rural, and Third World workers (or other combinations of forms of social exclusion and discrimination). In other words, every form of exploitation is also a form of domination, as well as a form of social exclusion and discrimination, and vice versa. Every form of exploitation is, in fact, experienced as a form of social domination and discrimination, while every form of discrimination is also experienced as a form of exploitation and domination.

Thus, class inequality is itself a combination of these three fields that represent the social constitution of inequality. It is, first, a relation of exploitation. But it is also a relation of domination, in the sense that this exploitation does not occur in a vacuum but from a specific (social and historical) context of

EXCURSUS 2   Polanyi and the Formation of the Labor Market

Contrary to what is commonly thought in present times, the wage form of labor power has not existed forever but was created and socially constructed by capitalism. Likewise, it was not a simple and peaceful constitution, but involved a double struggle of capital. On the one hand, a struggle and antagonism against the power of the European aristocracy and seigniory that still maintained important forms of domination until the end of the eighteenth and beginning of the nineteenth centuries. On the other, a struggle put up by the workers themselves, who always resisted being transformed into wage labor.

In this regard, Polanyi (2001 [1944]) relates precisely the various vicissitudes of capital and capitalists in shaping the labor market. First, he discusses the conformation of labor as a commodity, despite the fact that not only had it never been one, and the fact that it does not behave or structure itself like other commodities, especially with regard to the meaning of its price: the wage. For one thing, labor is "no other than the human beings themselves of which every society consists" (75). Against this, Polanyi calls labor a fictitious commodity, the same as he does with respect to land and money. As Polanyi (2001 [1944]: 75–76) points out:

> labor, land, and money are obviously not commodities ... Labor is only another name for a human activity which goes with life itself, which in its turn is not produced for sale but for entirely different reasons, nor can that activity be detached from the rest of life, be stored or mobilized ... The commodity description of labor, land, and money is entirely fictitious.

However, in all three cases, and especially in the case of labor and money, these are fundamental commodities for the constitution of capitalism as a social mode of production and exploitation of labor power, whose organization through specific markets is totally arbitrary and fictitious.

This process, which Polanyi associates with the making of the labor market, takes place in a historical context, which we can even date between the end of the seventeenth century and the first half of the nineteenth century. This involved a great struggle of industrialists and capitalists against the English Poor Laws, which maintained various forms of protection for the worker but did not allow them to free themselves from their social and economic ties; in particular, we see various forms of subsidies or other forms of semi-servile work, which prevented their salaryzation.

Marx puts forward a similar thesis in relation to the historical formation of wage labor and links it to the process of the original accumulation of capital (Marx, 1982, Chapter XXIV). It is not only a question of the formation of workers and the labor market, in Polanyi's terms, but also of the formation in the same process of capital and its necessary accumulation to exercise predominance as a mode of production, that is, as a mode of exploitation of labor power.

What is relevant in any case is that both, Marx and Polanyi, put forward the thesis of the historical formation of both wage labor and capital and, therefore, of the capitalist relation as a mode of exploitation.

domination of some classes over others. This is reflected in property relations. Property is not something natural or that arose spontaneously, but is the result of modes of domination and subjugation, where limiting property ownership and making it private is used to restrict and limit the freedom of the classes in terms that establish systems and relations of dependence between them, a type of dependence that is determined on the basis of relations of power of some classes over others, which make possible the subjugation of some with respect to others. Finally, both exploitation and domination, manifest themselves as a social division of the population, which takes the form of various categories of socio-demographic distinction. These categories not only divide individuals and classify them into different groups, but, in turn, they form the basis of modes of social, political, and economic discrimination between these groups. This categorization of others is, thus, the basis of the processes of social inclusion/exclusion in such a way that, based on these categories of sociodemographic differentiation, modes of inclusion of some and exclusion of others are constituted, making forms of social division of the population.

What has been said so far with respect to class inequality can be said in the same way with respect to gender inequality, or ethnic-racial inequality, or any other mode of categorical distinction. In the case of gender, for example, social inequality refers both to a form of exploitation (sexual division of labor and exploitation of women's labor by men) and to a form of male domination and various modes of social discrimination and exclusion to which women are exposed. All this results in the constitution of society on the basis of a profound division between men and women, which is, therefore, irreducible if it is not considered and based on a radical critique of patriarchy, as a historical process that gives rise to all forms of gender inequality. What is relevant, in any case, is that gender inequality cannot be reduced to mere discrimination against women because of their condition as women, nor to a form of male domination, nor to a mode of exploitation and sexual division of labor. It is the structuring of all of them simultaneously in ways that are reciprocally imbued, *embedded* in its constitution and social structuring.

In keeping with this reflexive character of our way of understanding inequality, we can give an additional twist to this mode of analysis and understanding: As a totality, this model also implies thinking not only of inequality as an articulation of its fields of constitution, but also thinking of each field in itself as an articulation of modes and forms of social inequalities and, therefore, of the constitution of subjects and categories of social differentiation. In each field, modes of social division are constituted, which are translated into various forms of categorical inequality. Thus, in the relations of exploitation, not only social classes are related and constituted, but also genders, races, nationalities, etc. In this social field of the *oikos*, the relations and processes of exploitation manifest themselves as class division, sexual division, and/or racial division of society, as well as other modes of social construction of categories of inequality. In other words, exploitation as a social process of production, is the material substratum of the division of society into different forms of categories of social inequality. Just as from a perspective of class relations, we understand social inequality as the social division of labor; from a perspective of gender relations, we can understand and analyze it as the sexual division of labor; and from a perspective of ethnic-racial relations, as the racial division of labor (racialization), and so on. In other words, and considering only these three axes, class-race-gender, we see that each of them and all three together make up what we can call the mode of exploitation that characterizes and accounts for the character of inequality in each society. Exploitation as a process and social relation is not only economic (class based) but it is also sexual (gender based) and ethnic-racial (racially based), among other forms.

The above is based on our notion that every process of exploitation is in itself a totality—a total social fact—which is constituted on the basis of the articulation, *embeddedness* of different fields, modes, and social dimensions and, therefore, admits an analytical reading and reconstruction from each of these fields, modes, or dimensions. Each of these possible readings, although valid and legitimate in itself, is equally partial and limited theoretically and methodologically. Only the articulated reconstruction of the whole allows access to it as a *concrete totality* (Zemelman, 1987) as a *total social fact* (Bourdieu, 2005).

The same can be said of the processes of domination in the field of the POLIS and those of discrimination-exclusion in the field of the DEMOS. In both cases, the underlying idea is that we are dealing with social processes that refer to totalities—to total social facts—which involve more than one mode or dimension in their constitution as such. The possible emphasis on some particular axis—class, race, or gender—is undoubtedly valid and legitimate, but this does not derive from some analytical-comprehensive criterion, but from political and action-oriented criteria, i.e., social intervention and transformation. The point is that these two levels of analysis are often confused, that is, between which are the fundamental axes for understanding and explaining social inequality and which are the fundamental axes for designing a strategy for social transformation. Undoubtedly, the latter will always be mediated both by the interests and ideological perspectives of social actors and their reading of the particular historical scenario in which they act.

CHAPTER 4

Debates on Inequality throughout History

1 Inequality in Ancient Greece

In ancient Greece, Aristotle was the main defender of the forms of inequality prevailing at the time, supporting not only private property as a social institution but, also, slavery and other forms of social exclusion of foreigners, women, and children. In this regard, he argued that inequality did not refer to social facts as such but to forms inherent to human nature, thus attributing the social form of inequality to a natural form. If some have more resources than others, it is because it is something natural, derived from the natural differences between one and the other, not because of some social or political factor that causes some to be free and others slaves. Inequality is not human made but a result of human nature, which establishes differences between individuals from birth.

Thus, for example, regarding inequality among men, he affirmed that it derived from a natural form of division of labor and power, which was not only necessary but also just and convenient for all parties. In this regard, in *Politics* (2012: 37, 41, 42) Aristotle stated:

> For that which has the power to foresee by thinking is *naturally* ruling and *naturally* mastering, but what has the power to carry out those things with the body is ruled and is *naturally* slavish; hence the same thing is advantageous to a master and to a slave ... For ruling and being ruled are not only among the necessities but also among things that are advantageous, and some things diverge right from the moment of birth either toward being ruled or toward ruling ... It is clear, then, that some people are free and others slaves *by nature*, and that of the latter it is both advantageous and *just* for them to be enslaved. (our emphasis)

For Aristotle, this same principle of differentiation between free men and slaves also serves to differentiate the social position and power between men and women. In this regard, he textually points out that "the relation of male to female is by nature that of superior and inferior, and ruler and ruled" (Aristotle, 2012: 42).

Aristotle made a clear distinction between the affairs of the *OIKOS* (economy, household finances) and those of the *POLIS* (public affairs of the city, politics). In the former, class relations and divisions concerned reproduction, both familial and generational as well as material reproduction—i.e., food, protection, and the like. The affairs of the *OIKOS* were, thus, organized on the basis of relations of domination derived from the ownership of means of production, instruments, and slaves. The *OIKOS* referred, then, to the administration and government practiced based on relations of domination exercised by the father and the master over women, children, workers, slaves, and animals (Campillo, 2012). In this sense, the social (class) division of labor was evident and, moreover, naturalized as such, while juxtaposed with forms of sexual (male-female), family (father-children), and ethnic-racial division of labor (master-slaves).

As for the affairs of the *POLIS*, for Aristotle it was no discovery that the city should be divided into classes with different roles, functions, profiles, attributions, and positions. Thus, for example, in "Chapter IV" of "Book Four" of the *Politics* (Aristotle, 2012, 120–124), along with describing the two main classes that make up the city (rich and poor, principal and people), he describes within each of them various categories of internal differentiation. In the case of the people (workers, peasants, merchants, etc.), the distinction is established according to the type of activity they perform, while in the case of the rich or principal classes, the distinction would be according to the type of attribute or property they possess (wealth, nobility, merit, education, etc.).

Likewise, the social division into classes refers not only to the distinction between citizens (free men) and non-citizens but also in reference to property and wealth. Thus, for example, he justified that property should be vested in the citizens, since they should have the necessary economic freedom to devote themselves to the virtues demanded by the government of the *POLIS*. Likewise, he considered that those who live from the fruits of their own labor (non-proprietors), even if they could attain the status of free men, would not have the time and dedication necessary to devote themselves to the task of administering the common good. As he puts it textually, "citizens need to live a life that is devoted neither to the mechanical trades nor to the trade of the marketplace. For a life of that sort is ill-bred and not conducive to virtue. Indeed, those who are going to be citizens ought not to be farmers either, since they need leisure both for the formation of virtue and political activities" (Aristotle, 2012: 205). With this, Aristotle linked economic inequality (property) with political inequality (access to magistracies and public offices).

In contrast to these approaches, that tend to naturalize inequality among men, is often pointed out the writings of Plato, who is credited with having defended the communist thesis of "the communal ownership of all forms of property, and the establishment of a ruling class which would have even wives and children in common" (Lenski, 1984:6). Based on this reading and interpretation of some sections of *The Republic* (Plato, 1992), an attempt has been made to compare this philosopher and his theories with the proposals of both primitive communism and contemporary communism and socialism, believing that in Plato's political ideology everything was common and shared by all.

However, the truth is that Plato proposed something very distant from a communist and egalitarian *POLIS* (Fernández-Galiano, 1988). In this respect, at least three arguments can be made:

1. Plato's proposal would correspond rather to what we could call *class communism*, insofar as it refers to forms of communion and social equality that were restricted only to the dominant classes, never to the whole of society, which maintains and reproduces a structure of class inequality.

2. Plato does not oppose either private property or the shaping of society on the basis of highly differentiated class structures. In this respect, referring to the fable of the metals, he sustains the natural and necessary character of the division of society into social classes.[1] Furthermore, if this were not enough, it should be noted that he uses this fable only to refer to the division of classes among free men. On the contrary, for him, slaves, *metecos* (foreigners), and women were still totally subordinate classes without any right to property or citizenship; as such, it was not necessary to elaborate any story to legitimize and justify their unequal and subordinate origin.

3. Plato's proposal of the community of family and property is by its essence and form something that cannot even remotely be confused with and is in stark opposition to modern communism and socialism, both in terms of the persistence of a class structure and in terms of the subordinate role of women as mere objects of reproduction and, moreover, property of a class of men.

In opposition to Plato and Aristotle, Phaleas of Chalcedon is usually pointed out as an outlier of the time who would have proposed a radical critique of the forms of inequality prevailing in the Greek polis. This philosopher allegedly

---

[1] The myth of the metals refers to a fable that Plato relates and with which he seeks to convince the citizens of the different origins of each social class. He begins: "Citizens we shall say to them in our tale, you are brothers, yet God has framed you differently. Some of you have the power of command, and in the composition of these he has mingled gold, wherefore also they have the greatest honor; others he has made of silver, to be auxiliaries; others again who have to be husbandmen and craftsmen he has composed of brass iron; and the species will generally be preserved in the children" (Plato, 1992:125). This fable reinforces our idea that Plato was at no time promulgating a form of communism or egalitarian society.

advocated for a social system based on equality in the distribution of property and wealth among all citizens, thus confronting the very basis of all class structures and social inequality (Mossé, 1984). To this end, he did not propose forms of expropriation but rather mechanisms of redistribution of possessions, as well as placing limits on the wealth and possessions of citizens.

However, very little is known about him, as the main references we have in the historic record come basically from the texts of Aristotle, who makes some reflections and approaches on Phaleas' thought and philosophy. In any case, what is certain is that Phaleas' proposal, much like Plato's and Aristotle's, referred only to the classes of freemen, that is, only to citizens of the Polis and not to all the people who inhabited Greece. Once again, slaves, *metecos,* and women were left out of the social structure and, in the particular case of slaves, were rather part of the structure of possessions to be distributed among the freemen.

In reality, Greek thought faced great difficulty in referring to population as a whole. Not only did it not have a category of analysis or a concept that would allow such a reference (the concept of population as an aggregate of undifferentiated individuals is much later), but also, its very conception and philosophy of society were based on what they directly perceived and experienced: a society of classes, castes, and strata clearly differentiated by conditions and property relations on the basis of gender, race, age, and geographic and national origin. Thus, the distinction between rich-poor, city-village, men-women, citizens-*metecos,* adults-children, among others, constituted the horizon of reason from which the very constitution of the *POLIS,* the *OIKOS,* and the *DEMOS* was thought. The distinction between classes, genders, and origins was not only a categorical representation of people, but a systematic form of historical and cultural constitution, there being until then no possibility of reaching a higher degree of abstraction that would allow the naming or creation of a category of analysis that would encompass them all equally. Inequality between one and the other was as much a form of social constitution as of its conceptual representation. In this context, the naturalization of social inequality and the division of society into classes, castes, genders and origins were but a logical and obvious corollary that reflects the meta-narratives from which the thought and philosophy of the time were constituted.

2 Inequality in the Christian Era and Feudal Society

In the Christian Era, the debate takes a turn in terms of the philosophical matrix from which the forms of social inequality of the time are sought to be legitimized and founded. It is no longer a matter of a larger processes inherent to human nature that establish a division of men into distinct social classes, but, rather, social inequality acquires the value and representation of a divine matter, an order established by decision and arbitration of the gods. The predominance of religion and the consolidation of Christianity and its institutionalization in the Catholic Church of Rome give a twist to the debate on social inequality and class differentiation, attributing its origin to religious forms of legitimization of differences and inequalities. Inequality and the differentiation of society into social classes was no longer the product of economic, demographic, or political processes—all of them, always, of earthly and historical origin—nor was it attributed to any difference in the nature of each individual but was a divine mandate, and in the face of which, only submission was possible at the risk of falling into sin and heresy. As Rousseau (1761: 10) states,"[r]eligion commands us to believe, that Men, having been drawn by God himself out of a state of Nature, are unequal, because it is his pleasure they should be so."[2]

However, despite this religious and theological vision, the issue of social inequality—and especially the debate on wealth and poverty—continued to develop. In the case of the Catholic Church, in particular, one manifestation of inequality focused on the basis of the wealth of the Church as an institution and hierarchy, as opposed to the origins and poverty of Christ and his life witness and vocation in the face of power and wealth.

From its beginnings, the question of class inequality as we understand it today was present as a field of alternative visions within the doctrine of the Catholic faith. It did not necessarily translate into a debate about the origins, causes, and consequences of inequality but rather about what to do about it. In this regard, Lenski (1984) points to St. James (Santiago) as more inclined to accept the communitarian forms in the distribution of goods of the early Christians, as opposed to St. Paul and St. Peter, who would focus more on the

---

[2] It is illustrative of this divinization of social inequality that even in the 21st century in the midst of the advances in secularization and individualization of social life religious institutions—such as the Catholic Church, Evangelical churches, as well as those of the Muslim world—prevail and maintain these quasi-divine principles in the social distinction between men and women, systematically denying the most basic rights of women to control their bodies, their sexuality, as well as access to instances of power and decision-making in these religious institutions and in public life in general. Again, this is done through mediations of claiming not only earthly and social issues as bases of inequality but even divine and sacred origins of such inequality. It would seem that in these respects (and in others) these religious institutions remain anchored in the philosophies and ways of thinking about social inequality of more than two thousand years ago.

consecration of the divine and natural origins of the division of society into social classes.

The issue appears more complex and less clear regarding these initial assumptions. On the one hand, St. James focused more on a questioning of the so-called *sin of partiality*, questioning the favoritism that is normally expressed towards the rich against the poor and giving rise to forms of discrimination and exclusion against the latter.[3] In other words, St. James does not question inequality in itself, that is, he does not question the existence of rich and poor, but argues for an attitude of non-favoritism that a good Christian should have towards one or the other.

In the case of St. Paul, on the other hand, he argues in favor of social and class inequality. In particular, he calls for *contentment*, that is, to be content with the situation of inequality, because in the end all forms of inequality would be a natural fact sanctioned by God. Specifically, in his epistles he calls on slaves to maintain obedience and submission to their masters, since slavery itself would be a legitimate right of the latter, which comes from some divine mandate.[4]

With the consolidation of the Catholic Church and its economic and political power, the debate on inequality and poverty took other directions and arguments. Regardless of the validity of one position or another, what is certain is that the debate transcended the strictly theological and philosophical and had as its background the economic power and political role of the Church in this earthly world and in medieval society. What was being debated then (and to current days) is not inequality and poverty in themselves, their origins, and the attitudes of a good Christian towards them, but the role of the Church vis-à-vis political and economic power and its incidence and action as a political and economic power in society.

It is not by chance, then, that from the Catholic Church itself emerged approaches that based on various theological and religious arguments sought to justify and legitimize the forms of social inequality and the stratification of society into differentiated and unequal classes. One of the main exponents of

---

[3] "My brothers and sisters, believers in our glorious Lord Jesus Christ must not show favoritism. Suppose a man comes into your meeting wearing gold ring and fine clothes, and a poor man in filthy old clothes also comes in. If you show special attention to the man wearing fine clothes and say, 'Here's a good seat for you,' but say to the poor man, 'You stand there' or 'Sit on the floor by my feet'" (James 2, 1–3).

[4] "All who are under the yoke of slavery should consider their masters worthy of full respect, so that God's name and our teaching may not be slandered" (Timothy, 6, 1).

"Slaves, obey your earthly masters with respect and fear, and with sincerity of heart, just as you would obey Christ" (Ephesians 6, 5).

this conservative vision was John of Salisbury. This thinker of the twelfth century takes up the organicist visions as metaphors to understand the order and functioning of the social body (Jakubecki, 2013). In "Book V" of the *Policraticus*, he exposes a reformulated vision of the metaphor of the human body as a social analogy.

The organicist approach proposes that society functions and is organized like the human body, where each part not only performs a specific and differentiated function, but also establishes a hierarchical order among them, giving rise to a form of organization. Taking this view, Salisbury points out that society is organized like the human body, where the prince would be the head; judges and governors would be the eyes, ears and tongue; the senate, the heart; and those surrounding the prince would be the sides of the body. In this metaphor, the hands would represent soldiers and various officials, while the common people would be the feet. The clergy and the Church would be the soul of the human body (Lenski, 1984).

This Salisburyian vision breaks in a certain way with the traditional organicist visions in that Christ is no longer the head of the body but the prince, while the Church represents the soul. However, what is relevant for our discussion is that this ordering maintains the hierarchical structure of the Augustinian, organicist scheme of this same metaphor (Faci Lacasta, 1984). Likewise, Salisbury's vision incorporates elements proper to society and its social and economic forms, which makes it more correctly an analogy of the way in which society is organized, not so much of the divine order of the world and life as is the case in the Augustinian vision.

In this sense, it is evident that the description of social inequality as the result of a social structure that divides the population into social classes established this particular organicist vision. On the one hand, at the top is the prince, whose power comes directly from God; at the bottom, the workers of various orders (artisans, peasants, serfs, slaves, etc.); in the middle, and in an equally hierarchical manner, the various strata of administration and social control (officials, politicians, army). Likewise, while the prince owes obedience and submission only to God and his representatives on Earth (clergy and Church), all the other estates owe obedience and submission to the prince, since their power and status come directly from a divine mandate. Social inequality and the stratification of society into social classes, thus, constituted a necessary condition, the origin of which could not be questioned at the risk of falling into heretical positions.

In the face of this growing conservatism—which has predominated in the Catholic hierarchy ever since—dissident voices of different types, strengths, and radicalism have arisen. In the twelfth century, various social and religious movements appeared and consolidated, which, based on criticism of the concentration of wealth, promoted various forms of asceticism and community life. Among the former, the Franciscans stood out as the main Catholic mendicant order and in the second case the Cathars, as a social movement that promulgated communitarian forms of social life. The historical destiny of one and the other, however, was very different and reflects to a certain extent that the underlying theme within these religious orders is always political and refers to the unequal distribution of power between social classes.

This debate of inequality arises in a historical context: progressive impoverishment of the people and enrichment and concentration of power in the hands of the ecclesiastical hierarchy, a process resulting from the consolidation of Christianity as the official and dominant religion, first of the Empire and then of the various Germanic and European monarchies. This is when the Catholic Church ceased to be a Church of the people to become the Church of the powerful, making Catholicism a religion of Power, that is, becoming an instrument of ideological and theological support of kings and emperors. This led it to become an institution of Power itself with economic and political influences, ceasing to be only an institution of faith.

In this historical framework and in the face of the growing political power and economic wealth of the Church, Francis of Assisi emerged in the debate to call for a life of poverty as a way of reproducing the testimony of Christ and bringing it to the popular classes of the time. His act of stripping himself of all material possessions—including his clothes—and assuming a life of poverty dedicated to love of thy neighbor is widely known. His testimony led to the establishment of the Franciscan order, which consolidated begging as a Christian act of renunciation of material goods and luxuries. Beyond its theological and philosophical bases, what is certain is that the mere testimony and action of Francis of Assisi and, later, the Franciscan order, constituted a form of social criticism of the opulence and economic power acquired by the Catholic Church. Without departing from the key teachings and tenants of the Church, the Franciscans constituted a critical vision of their contemporary religious authorities, although they did not necessarily conform a position of radical confrontation with its hierarchy and, rather, ended up tolerating these deviations as part of the diversity necessary to maintain the unity of the people around the Church (Pulido, 2007).

The Cathars, on the other hand, did represent a radical critique, although in a different sense from both the Franciscans and modern Liberation Theology. They promoted community life through the sharing of goods, resources, and wealth. The theological basis was a radical dualism, according to which the universe would be made up of two worlds in continuous and absolute conflict.

On the one hand, the spiritual world created by God and, on the other, the material world created by Satan or the Devil. Faced with this duality, life's main challenge was to confront the temptations and forms created by the Devil, which is why wealth, luxury, property, and, in general, all forms of power were seen as a manifestation of sin and evil. In the face of this, there was only room for community life. If they attacked the Church, it was because they considered it to be an instrument of corruption, which distanced them from the faith and acting as a Christian witness (sharing faith in a public manner). And, of course, seeing the ways of life and the luxuries and riches of the Church, it was not difficult to sustain their criticism of the clergy, who had entered into a process of corruption by associating itself with the political power of kings, princes, and monarchs.

In this framework, the dispute both within the Church and in medieval society took the form of a debate about the poverty of Christ as opposed to the wealth of the Church. In this regard, the Italian medievalist and cultural critic Umberto Eco gives a detailed and entertaining account of this discussion in his historical murder mystery *The Name of the Rose* (1986), where in the form of a police thriller and mystery he places the central character, William of Baskerville, in a dual role: On the one hand, as a modern detective he follows the clues of a series of crimes and murders, which leads him to unravel dark and hidden mysteries that enclose the prestigious library of the Benedictine abbey where the events take place. On the other hand, he presents himself as one of the main spokesmen of the Franciscan order in the debate on the poverty of Christ and the wealth of the Church.[5] Beyond reproducing a debate that at this point in history may prove fruitless, it is worth focusing on the conclusions reached by Eco (1986: 204), which he presents in the voice of the central character of his novel:

> My good Adso, ... the question is not whether Christ was poor: it is whether the Church must be poor. And 'poor' does not so much mean owning a palace or not; it means, rather, keeping or renouncing the right to legislate on earthly matters.

Following Eco, we can affirm that, as in many other issues, the debate was not only restricted to the question of wealth/poverty, but had as its background

---

5 It is interesting the way in which Eco reproduces this power struggle within the Catholic hierarchy and transfers it to the same detective investigation, generating a confrontation between characters at different levels of the story but at the same time reflecting in each one of them the different positions in the larger struggle.

differences between groups and social classes in a long dispute over the very power of the Church here on Earth. In any case, it is equally relevant that both Franciscans and Cathars, as well as the Church itself and its hierarchy, did not question the origin of inequality, but, rather, the dispute revolved around what Christians, the Church, and the population in general, should do in the face of forms of inequality, which were assumed to be the result of either natural forms or divine mandates. At bottom, the question was always eminently political—referred to the affairs of the *POLIS*—and Eco summarizes it in the right of the Church to legislate and act on earthly things, that is, a contingent and political right related to questions of management and government and, therefore, of political power in the face of modes of social, economic, and cultural domination.

In this regard, it could be thought that the Franciscans and their testimony of poverty would have represented a radical strategy against inequality. In reality, it is rather an individual option, not a collective one, which, moreover, was not based on a critique of class structures nor on a strategy to overcome them, but only referred to a testimonial option in the face of a social situation. In this sense, it is worth noting the profound differences between the doctrine of the Franciscans and other similar Christian doctrines of the 20th century, such as Liberation Theology, which like them base their theological proposals on a radical critique of the forms of wealth and inequality prevailing in society and in the Catholic Church. However, they are essentially different doctrines. While that of Francis of Assisi sustains a preferential option for poverty, Liberation Theology sustains a preferential option for the poor. The distinction is not a minor one. While the former promotes a testimonial option of life in poverty, it does not question or propose a change in the social and religious structures that sustain this social inequality. Liberation Theology, on the other hand, proposes precisely an option for a particular social subject, the poor, in pursuit of a strategy and project of liberation from these structures of domination and exploitation that keep them in both material and spiritual poverty (Dussel, 1995). Thus, while the Franciscans have always been a critical order—but tolerable and assimilable by the ecclesial hierarchy—Liberation Theology, on the other hand, has been questioned and directly combated by this same Catholic hierarchy.

3 The English Poor Laws and the Transition to Capitalism

The debate on poverty and inequality in medieval Europe took a major turn in the 16th century, especially in England where the transition from feudalism to capitalism began. The question no longer focused on the origin of inequality—divine or natural—but on what to do about the growing number of people living in poverty and begging in the English cities of the time. In this context, various regulations were formed to provide aid to the poor, establishing the mechanisms for this aid and assistance, as well as defining the groups to which said aid and assistance should be directed. These regulations were aimed at reducing vagrancy and begging, so characteristic of England in the first half of the sixteenth century. This system of aid, with important transformations throughout the following centuries, took shape under the name of the *Poor Laws*, which would last until the middle of the 20th century when they were replaced by the emergence of a welfare state through which modern mechanisms for the social protection of the population were established (Villarespe, 2002).

The first Poor Law is a compilation of these initial regulations, which took shape as a legal decree in 1601 under the reign of Isabel I. This law is also known as the *Old Poor Laws*, since it was the basis for the implementation of other ordinances in the same sense; it regulated assistance and aid to the poor until the end of the eighteenth century, when the debate on this issue took another course and was framed in the consolidation of industrial capitalism, as well as in the rise and consolidation of political economy as a nascent science of this historical process (Himmelfarb, 1984).

According to Rodríguez Caballero (2003: 120, our translation), the Old Poor Laws were characterized by the following elements:

> (a) the parish was the basic unit of application; (b) aid was financed primarily through local property taxes; (c) management was carried out by officials appointed by local judges; and (d) aid varied depending on the type of poor: alms and asylums for the incapacitated poor (elderly and sick), apprenticeships for children, work for the able-bodied poor, and punishment or imprisonment for those who were able and unwilling to work.

In other words, this first Poor Laws establish three aspects to be considered, which will be debated in later centuries: (1) it defines the subjects susceptible to benefit from aid, differentiating the type of aid in each case; (2) it establishes the rule that the poor in order to receive aid had to remain in a parish, through which the aid system was channeled; and (3) it defines the legitimate mechanisms for exercising aid, which was derived directly from taxes levied on the parishes where the poor resided (Santolaria Sierra, 2003).

In 1662, this first Poor Law was supplemented by the Poor Relief Act 1662, also known as the *Settlement Law*, which along with reinforcing the principle of channeling aid through the parishes, strengthened the requirements for the settlement of individuals in each parish and, most importantly, the restrictions on the mobility of the poor outside their parish of residence. This principle will later be harshly criticized by the forerunners of Political Economy, who advocated free mobility of workers.

In 1782, a new modification was made under the name Relief of the Poor Act 1782, which would also be of great importance for the subsequent debate. Also known as *Gilbert's Act*, this law introduces the principle of foreign aid, that is, aid to a new subject not contemplated in the first Poor Laws. Under the term of aid to the able-bodied poor, this system was based on a form of subsidies to unemployed workers who up to that time were outside the aid system, corresponding only to support for residence in asylums.

In the last decade of the eighteenth century, the *Speenhamland Agreements* were added to these changes, through which special subsidies were instituted for those workers who as a result of the crises of the time and the hardships derived from the Napoleonic wars did not have sufficient income to support themselves and their families. This institutionalized a new subject of the poor: the *impoverished worker*, those who although employed received very low incomes and remunerations.

The consolidation of capitalism in the second half of the eighteenth century—as a result of the nascent Industrial Revolution, together with demographic growth and recurrent economic crises—generated various pressures that led to the reformulation of the Poor Laws. Begging and the volume of poor to be served increased, which represented an excessive burden at various times. On the other hand, the demands for urban and industrial labor were transformed and industrial activity expanded, requiring other arrangements in terms of population and labor dynamics.

All this led to the need to modify the Poor Laws. Based on the *Poor Law Report of 1834*—prepared by a parliamentary commission that included the participation of renowned economists such as Nassau William Senior—the *Poor Law Amendment Act*, better known as the *New Poor Law*, was passed that same year. Essentially, this new system was based on two measures: (1) the suspension of foreign aid and its replacement by a system of workhouses, where aid was offered in exchange for work done by the poor in highly precarious and exploitative conditions; and (2) the aid system would no longer be operated at the local level but by a centralized body of national scope created for this purpose (Rodríguez Caballero, 2003).

The consequences of these new Poor Laws were the consolidation of forms of forced labor, which, however, would be harshly criticized by classical economists, as they substantially restricted the mobility and availability of labor for the nascent Industrial Revolution. It is in this context that the discussion among classical economists on the Poor Laws and the formation of a working class took shape in the debate on the political economy of the time. It is a debate that involved people like Adam Smith, Malthus, and Ricardo, as well as Marx and Engels, and it is one that would be taken up by the neoclassical economists in the second half of the nineteenth century.

4 Political Economy's Critique of the Poor Laws and the Formation of the Capitalist Labor Market

For the nascent discipline of political economy—a science that sought to account for the transformation of English and European society in the eighteenth century—both the theoretical and political principles, as well as the measures implemented through the Poor Laws in all their forms, constituted serious obstacles to the development and consolidation of capitalism, particularly for the formation and constitution of a self-regulated labor market that would function as a mechanism for the allocation of labor power among different economic and productive activities.

Industrial activity had reached such a level that, in order to maintain its dynamic of growth and consolidation, it had to have a free and unlimited supply of labor, which at the time was bound and restricted by the effect of the ordinances arising from the Poor Laws. In this sense, Adam Smith, Malthus, and Ricardo all questioned these laws, focusing their argumentation on three main axes, namely:

1. The Law of Settlement, together with the channeling of aid to the poor through parishes and rural districts, only contributed to fix the labor force, preventing its mobility and free availability for industrial capital.
2. Subsidies, and especially the Speenhamland Act, were counterproductive in that they did not allow wages and labor to be freely regulated by a labor market.
3. The financing of these subsidies through taxes for aid had a negative impact on the possibilities of expansion of industrial capitalism, by reallocating funds and surpluses to the reproduction of the non-working population and not to productive investment and consolidation of industrial activity.

As we can see, the arguments of that time are not very different from those currently used by neoliberalism against income distribution and poverty reduction policies. Both in those years and today, the central argument is that any redistributive policy undermines the functioning of the market, generating major distortions in the allocation of economic resources and jeopardizing the options for economic growth and capital accumulation.[6]

In order to fully consider the scope of the ideological and political substratum of these criticisms, it is necessary to understand the historical moment in which they arise. It is in the moment of the consolidation of capitalism as an economic-social formation, sustained in the productive sphere by the industrial revolution and in the economic sphere by its social organization through the functioning of markets as mechanisms for the allocation of resources. In this historical context, the interest of political economy of the time was not concerned with understanding and explaining the origin of poverty and inequality but rather with how the persistence of certain social and political structures hindered the development of the productive forces of capitalism. For the classical economists, the problem was not poverty per se, but the Poor Laws as mechanisms that hindered its necessary transformation into free labor power, that is, into a working class freely available to capital.

Until the end of the eighteenth century and in spite of all the progress made in the capitalist organization of the economy and society, a proper labor market had not yet been created. Various paternalistic forms of protection of labor and workers still persisted, preventing their transformation into wage labor and, thus, hindering the ability of capital to generate economic surplus and capital accumulation. For the classical economists, the problem of inequality did not focus on the class structures that gave rise to that inequality, but their interest was centered on the consolidation of that class structure characteristic of capitalism for which the formation of a class of free workers was necessary in at least four senses:

1. Free of the means of production that tied them to a pre-capitalist economic-social form (servility, guilds, etc.).

---

6 In this point, Malthus (1966: 86) points out that contrary to common sense, "the parish laws of England … have therefore contributed to impoverish that class of people whose only possession is their labour." To this end, throughout chapter 5 of his First Essay on Population, he gives a series of arguments, all related to the distortions that these subsidies generate in the functioning of markets and the behavior of economic agents, advancing more than two centuries the same arguments currently offered by neoliberal economists in the face of similar policies against poverty and inequality.

2. Free of other ties such as those established by the Poor Laws, which allowed the social and material reproduction of the population without the need to sell their labor force as a fundamental means of livelihood.
3. Free to move to the different places of employment located in the various localities and regions of England, where the capitalist mode of production was installed and consolidated in industry, agriculture, and commerce.
4. Free to decide to sell their labor power for a wage and not be subsumed in relations of subjugation and extra-economic domination that would restrict their free discernment.

In the face of this, the ordinances arising from the Poor Laws constituted anything but an advance in the formation of a working class understood in the aforementioned format. In Marxist terms, we can point out that the Poor Laws did not allow the consolidation of the social relations of production proper to capitalism, which gave rise to a social division of labor between owners of the means of production and workers dispossessed of those means who only possessed their labor power as the only resource for their material sustenance. In this context, it was necessary *to free* the worker from all ties, so that they could *freely* transform their labor power into a commodity that could be traded in the market, becoming in this process a wage earner, that is, dependent on a salary for reproduction and, therefore, on the continuous and permanent sale of the only good or property in their possession: labor power. As long as this perfect condition did not exist, capitalism would face obstacles to the development of its productive forces and, therefore, to the capacity to exploit labor—extraction of surplus value—and its accumulation in the form of capital. In the face of this, one understands, then, the true nature of the discourses of classical economics against the Poor Laws and other similar ordinances and institutions. It is not a discourse in favor of free labor—although it may take that discursive form—but it is a discourse in favor of capitalism as a model of production and as the institutionalization of the social division of labor, a discourse in favor of the liberation of the social and productive forces of capital for its unlimited accumulation.

In the same logic but from a different perspective, Karl Polanyi understands the criticism of classical economists against the Poor Laws as a discourse in favor of the formation of a labor market, a necessary institution for the consolidation of the great social and economic transformation of the time, that is, the transition to a market society. According to Polanyi (2001), the consolidation of capitalism confronted in the eighteenth-century various institutions of the *Ancient Régime* that hindered the transformation of society into a market economy. Until before capitalism, markets constituted nothing more than accessories to economic life. As a rule, the economic system was subsumed in the social system, such that the economic order was only a function of the social order, not its constituent matrix as it begins to be in capitalism as a mode of production and distribution.

If "a market economy can function only in a market society," then to achieve this transformation requires the institutional separation of society into an economic and a political sphere (Polanyi, 2001: 60). For this, capitalism requires that all social and economic life be regulated by the action of markets, including labor, land, and money, which were institutions that until the end of the eighteenth century remained regulated and ordered based on non-market criteria and institutions, external to the free functioning of the market.[7] This is the moment when, for the defenders and promoters of the market economy (classical economics, in particular), it becomes evident that it is no longer possible to advance in the consolidation of the market society without the conformation of the labor market, as well as the land and money market. In all three cases, however, it required "nothing less than the total destruction of the traditional social fabric" (81). This implied, in the case of labor, going against the Poor Laws, the Settlement Act and the Speenhamland Act, as all of them only reinforced pre-capitalist and non-market forms of labor organization.

In the case of the conformation of the labor and land market, the formation of a working class was required, while restricting the power of landowners, *hacienda* owners, and feudal lords to control labor and land, freeing both resources from the social institutions that impeded their transaction in the market. But to free these commodities to market forces, it was simultaneously necessary to constitute those markets where they could be traded freely and self-regulated. In this context, Polanyi speaks of a process of *disembeddedness* of these commodities from their respective social and political orders in pre-capitalist societies and their economic liberation through their commodification.

---

7   For us, inhabitants of the 21st century, it may seem somewhat strange that the market (or markets) is not a constituent factor of society, especially when we were born and raised in a market society. But this was not always the case. What appears to us as something natural, in reality, had its historical origin in the eighteenth century, when the transition from feudalism to capitalism was consolidated and the Ancient Regime began its retreat in the face of the social and economic force represented by the capitalist mode of production. Until before those years, society and the economy were organized on the basis of other principles and institutions, where the market was only an accessory—one more device of the economic order—and where the economy was only one more institution within the social order. Hence, Polanyi defined all this as *The Great Transformation*, referring to this historical process of the constitution of market society and the capitalist economy.

These three categories—Land, Labor, and Money—face, in addition, the challenge that they do not constitute commodities as such, at least not like any other product of labor, but are what Polanyi calls *fictitious commodities*. A commodity is an object (or service) produced for sale and transaction in the market. Land, Labor and Money, on the other hand, although essential for the development of the market economy, are not commodities, since they do not fulfill one of the fundamental conditions of all commodities: none of them has been produced and even less with a mercantile sense, that is, a saleable item or good. Labor is, in reality, the name we give to one of various human activities, which, in itself, has no mode of existence but as a moment of the very existence of the worker as a person and is not separable from it. Likewise, the Land is but the name of nature. Although it generates wealth, it itself is not the result of the action of labor. Although it is through labor that wealth is extracted from land and nature, neither is the product of human labor. Finally, money is only a form of symbolizing purchasing power. While its possession undoubtedly confers great power, it does not in itself generate that power or the wealth it claims to represent. To transform labor, land, and money into commodities, then, requires a *fictional* process that gives them a property they do not have, functioning for the sustenance and development of the market economy as a whole.

Of these three fictitious commodities, he highlights the case of Labor. As Polanyi (2001: 79; emphasis ours) points out:

> [L]abor is the technical term used for human beings, insofar as they are not employers but employed; it follows that henceforth the organization of labor would change concurrently with the organization of the market system. But as the organization of labor is only another word for the forms of life of the common people, this means that the development of the market system would be accompanied by a change in the organization of society itself. All along the line, *human society had become an accessory of the economic system.*

The problem with this artificial (or fictitious) construction of labor as a commodity, is that since labor power is constituted as such it is exposed to be traded in the market and, therefore, susceptible to manipulation and indiscriminate use only determined by the laws of supply and demand, like any other commodity. However, labor is not just any commodity: Any manipulation and use of labor power has direct repercussions on the human being, who is the bearer and material support of the commodity labor power. In other words, it is impossible to make the labor power commodity independent of its human support: the person, the worker. Whatever happens to the labor force has direct repercussions on the person, and vice versa; the separation of the person beyond the labor market has direct repercussions on the labor force as a commodity. Thus, Polanyi points out that this separation—*disembedded*—is an act of fiction, an abstraction that is imposed on us as a form of "the real" but which fails to construct it as such. Work remains a human activity, impossible to de-scale itself from its human substrate.[8]

Thus, for example, if the price of potatoes is reduced, its only impacts are a reduction in potato production. However, if wages are reduced, there is a direct impact on the living conditions of the worker and their family. Thus, in capitalism the commodification of labor leads to the dehumanization of labor itself and, therefore, of the person who is its human support. In this sense, human society becomes a mere accessory of the economic system, thus inverting the relationship that characterized pre-capitalist societies.

Polanyi's thesis on *disembedding* and the transformation of labor power as a commodity allows us to broaden our reflections on social inequality. According to Polanyi, the *disembedding* of the market economy would be nothing other than its autonomization with respect to the other orders of the POLIS (social, cultural, political, demographic, among others), establishing the dominance of the market (economy, OIKOS) over the organization of society (POLIS).

However, it is worth asking whether this disembedding is really taking place as an autonomous form of the economic with respect to the social, or whether it is rather a matter of making the market a preferential field for resolving the question of power and class inequality inherent to all human society up to now. In this sense, we can put forward our thesis of understanding the market as a field of mediation in the relationship between POLIS, OIKOS, and DEMOS (politics-economy-population). Let us look at this in more detail.

The structure of classes and inequality does not arise from the economy or the market itself; rather, it is through the economy (the market) that the forms of social domination of some over others and, therefore, class inequality (in its broad sense, beyond the productive) are constituted. Through the market, a class of owners—of means of production, power, status, etc.—exercises its domination and hegemony over other social classes. The class structure, that is, the social division into social classes, is not only economic-productive but

---

8 The consequences of this thesis are many, and they allude to the processes of alienation which indicate that the conditions of work have direct repercussions on the conditions and forms of existence of workers as human beings, on their very humanity and, by that means, on their forms of self-consciousness, as workers and as human beings. We will return to this thesis when we discuss the *precariousness* of contemporary labor in global capitalism.

social and political, demographic and cultural. Property is not restricted to means of production but also to social status, forms of power, and, in general, to the wide variety of capitals pointed out by Bourdieu.

In this scheme, then, social inequality is institutionalized as such through the market, and as a class structure, it is presented as the dominant form in the organization of society, hiding and making invisible its social and political origin beyond the economy and the market. It is through the market that class inequality and the form of social division into social classes is exercised and reproduced. If before in pre-capitalist societies the reproduction of inequalities and class structures occurred through social institutions as diverse as the customary right to land and property, guild forms of work and production, slave or servile forms of labor, military and political power, religious forms, among many others, in capitalist society, on the other hand, it is through its economic form and its institution par excellence, the market.

The basic question remains pending: what is the origin of social inequality? As we have seen in this discussion, attributing it to the market or to the mode of production does not solve the problem: It only points to the social field from where the class structure reproduces social inequality, the field of power of that social division of classes, but not of the ultimate constitution of that division or class structure. Ultimately, class inequality is a political issue that implies differentiation in terms of the power held of some over others, which allows the imposition of some over others. This imposition, hegemony, or domination—whatever you want to label it—is what is transferred to the market, to religion, to the military, to the State, or to other fields or any combination of them, which is where it exercises its dominion over society as a whole. But, in any of these cases, it remains a political issue, one of confrontation and opposition between subjects and social classes.

5   Social Inequality under Capitalism: Rousseau and Marx

In his *Discourse on the Origin and Basis of Inequality Among Men* of 1755, Rousseau is perhaps the first to give an answer to the question of the origin of inequality. Until then, the debate concerned the ways in which inequality manifests itself, its consequences, and even its legitimacy and morality. But except for those who pointed to its divine origin, in general, there was no social and historical basis for its origins and evolution. Rousseau focuses the origin of inequality on the private ownership of things, a phenomenon that, contrary to what might be thought, is not a natural act of the human species but arises from certain social and historical conditions, which Rousseau analyzes and supports in the aforementioned text.

Rousseau differentiated between two forms of inequality: (1) what he calls natural or physical inequality, whose origin and cause is evident and is in the name itself; and (2) social inequality, which he calls moral or political inequality. The latter is the one we are concerned with here and refers to the forms and social patterns of distribution of the surplus of human labor. Rousseau's thesis is that there is nothing in the nature of the human being that gives rise to this form of inequality, which is always the result of social and historical processes.

In the first part of his text, Rousseau devotes himself to demonstrating this thesis, arguing from various angles how human beings in their natural state never generated processes or forms of inequality that went beyond the natural differences between individuals, which referred to each individual separately and did not generate differences that transcended them in time and were, rather, passed on to the following generations. In any case, all forms of inequality that prevailed naturally languished when compared to the forms of social inequality prevailing even in the most egalitarian societies.

It is often said that the stronger oppress and dominate the weaker, that the more astute take advantage of those less privileged with reason, that the more skillful impose themselves over the less skilled, and so forth and so on, we could go on pointing out various ways in which natural differences between humans could give rise to social differences between them. Faced with this question, Rousseau (1761: 90, 91) wonders how it was possible that these natural differences could become social inequalities, that is, forms of servility and domination among 'savage' men in their natural state, considering the fact that these same men "into whose heads it would be a hard matter to drive even the meaning of the words domination and servitude. ... [W]hat chains of dependence can there be among men who possess nothing?"

The truth is that social inequality was practically non-existent in the state of nature. In contrast to this idea of an eventual natural inequality, Rousseau (92) affirms that:

> [T]he bonds of servitude are formed merely by the mutual dependence of men one upon another and the reciprocal necessities which unite them. It is impossible for one man to enslave another, without having first reduced him to a condition in which he cannot live without the enslaver's assistance; a condition which, as it does not exist in a state of nature, must leave every man his own master, and render the law of the strongest altogether vain and useless.

In this context, it is worth asking whether it is really possible then to attribute the origin of inequality to factors of human nature, to sheer physical and natural differences between individuals.[9] In this respect, Rousseau points out that there is no plausible link between natural differences and social inequalities among human beings. However, we are confronted daily with arguments, theories, approaches, and policies that often point to the contrary, arguing the supposed natural origin of inequalities among humans. The issue in these cases is that all this argumentation is based on a process of transference by means of which ideas, attitudes, prejudices, theories, visions, and policies are taken from society and from the particular position of each subject within the social structure and are usually projected onto the state of nature (the natural difference between humans). In this process, properties, effects, powers, and other attributes that only exist in their social form are attributed and transferred to the natural form of the human being; in this way, processes that are essentially social and historical are *naturalized*.

Having said this, it is worth asking what would be the trigger that drives the process of inequality among humans and what would be the historical conditions for it to occur. In this regard, Rousseau (97) answers that it was none other than private property:

> The first man, who, after enclosing a piece of ground, took it into his head to fay "This is mine," and found people simple enough to believe it, was the true founder of civil society. How many crimes, how many wars, how many murders, how many misfortunes and horrors, would that man have saved the Human Species, who pulling up the Stakes or filling up the Ditches should have cried to his fellows: Be sure not to listen to this Impostor; you are lost if you forget that these fruits of the Earth belong equally to us all, and the Earth itself to nobody!

But the right of ownership over something does not arise out of nothing. The private (privative-prohibitive) appropriation of means of production, of utensils and other devices, requires, of course, the prior existence and production of those means of production, utensils and other devices. For this, natural man had to transit from his savage state to a social state, a state of communal life.

---

9 This is not an idle question. As we shall see below, neoclassical economic approaches and functionalist sociological theories have put forward precisely this thesis on the origin of social inequality. These approaches tend to highlight the natural conditions of differentiation among human beings as the main factor triggering social inequalities among them. They correspond to what Tilly (1999) calls individualistic ontologies of inequality.

First the family was the basic community nucleus, then the union of families, the community, tribe or clan, which allowed them to face the task of survival with greater efficiency and efficacy, and so we continue until the formation of social life.

In this process, what today we would call division of labor arises: first in its domestic form, as a sexual division of labor, some (women) in charge of work inside the home (reproductive), others (men) of activities outside the home (productive); then, in social form, where some are in charge of one type of activities (crops) and others of others (instruments, etc.). In both cases, the division of labor gives rise to another social phenomenon: the distribution of the product of labor and its surplus. As long as men were engaged in activities, tasks and works that did not require the assistance of several other humans, they were able to maintain their independence, freedom and equality. This situation is broken with the very development and progress that community life provided. As Rousseau (119) points out:

> As long as [individuals] ... undertook such works only as single person could finish and stuck to such arts as did not require the joint endeavors of several hands, they lived free, healthy, honest and happy, as much as their nature would admit, and continued to enjoy with each other all the pleasures of an independent intercourse ... [B]ut from the moment one man began to stand in need of another's assistance; from the moment it appeared an advantage for one men to possess the quantity of provisions requisite for two, *all equality vanished* ... [P]roperty started up; labor became necessary, and boundless forests became smiling fields, which it was found necessary to water with human sweat, and in which slavery and misery were soon seen to sprout out and grow with the fruits of the earth.

In other words, when the subsistence of the species required the labor of others, establishing a form of division of labor between one and the other, the social basis that gave rise to inequality among humans arose. But this is a contradictory process. Social life and the division of labor allow for greater efficiency in the reproduction and survival of the human species but also condemns it to a life of misery marked by the inequality that this same efficiency of labor entails. Life in collective, social life, allowed the development of the productive forces of labor, the control of agriculture, metallurgy, the generation of means for production that facilitated it and made it more efficient. It is a process that derived, in addition, in the development of the arts and science and conscience in a greater development of the spirit and human reason. But, in that same process, those developments that "civilized man ... ruined mankind" (120).

The development of the social division of labor not only allows for greater surpluses that facilitate and improve the survival of the species but is also the basis for the emergence of private property and inequality. This gives rise to competition and rivalry among human beings, expressed in the formation of groups and classes in opposition interests. The expansion of private ownership of the means of production was transferred to the equally private appropriation of the products of labor and, thus, gives rise to various forms of domination, including serfdom and forced labor (slavery). In doing so, Rousseau demonstrates that the spirit of society and the inequality it engenders alter and pervert the natural forms of existence of the human species. For him, the natural state of man in no case gives rise to the forms of social inequality that characterize contemporary societies. In this regard, he points out that "whatever definition is given to it ..., it is evidently against the law of nature that infancy should command old age, folly conduct wisdom, and a handful of men should be ready to choak with the superfluities, while the famished multitude want the commonest necessaries of life" (182, 183).

In this sense, for Rousseau, private property and the right that it generates and institutionalizes in society would constitute a kind of original sin that breaks the natural equality of the human species. Private ownership of means, resources, and the product of labor ultimately leads to a corruption of the human spirit, perverting its nature and enshrining social inequality and consolidating various modes of domination and exploitation of some over others. Based on this argumentation, Rousseau explains and substantiates the origin of social inequality and does so by considering its origin as a social and historical form, disassociating it from the natural forms of differentiation among human beings. However, beyond the contribution that this foundation represents for understanding the origin of social inequality, it is not, however, sufficient to understand and explain the different forms that social inequality adopts throughout history in each society and in each epoch. This foundation of the origin of inequality allows us to understand inequality in ancient Greece as well as in feudal society or capitalism but not the different forms and dimensions that social inequality adopts and represents in each of these social formations.

In this regard, Marx answers this question with his thesis of the modes of production. By mode of production, he refers to the forms adopted by the social relations of production and which arise from the historical form of the labor process in each society, that is, to the social forms adopted by the ownership of the means of production, the social forms of labor and labor power, the social forms of control of the conditions of labor, and the social forms of appropriation of the surplus of the production process. Thus, for example, in feudal society the mode of production is characterized by the fact that the labor force—peasants—is subject to a set of extra-economic coercions that fix it and bind it to certain social institutions (servility, submission to a king or feudal lord, etc.). Likewise, the economic surplus generated by peasants is subject to private appropriation by the feudal lords, precisely on the basis of this system of extra-economic relations of coercion against peasants. Although the means of production remain in the hands of the direct producer—the worker or laborer themselves—they are not always the owners of that property, the same as the land and the other conditions of production. What is relevant in any case is that the labor process and the relations of production generated in it are subordinated to an external system of coercion and forms of power that regulate and control the labor process, as well as the production and surpluses that emanate from it.

In the capitalist mode of production, on the other hand, "the economic surplus is also subject to private appropriation, but as distinct from feudalism, ownership of the means of production is severed from ownership of labor-power; it is what permits the transformation of labor-power into a commodity, and with this birth of the wage-relation" (Laclau, 1986: 182). Here what is relevant for our discussion is the separation of the means of production from the direct producer, that is, the dissociation between means of production, labor, and conditions of the labor process. Capitalism is based on a particular and historically determined form of labor: the wage laborer. This is a worker who has been stripped of both the ownership and possession of the means of production, as well as of the control and appropriation of the conditions of the labor process and of the surplus generated there.

Labor in its wage form exists neither in nature nor in society but is a historical construct, arising from the dispossession of the worker of their means and conditions of labor (Marx 1977). Likewise, capital in its capitalist form does not exist either in nature or directly in society but is a historical construction that arises from the transformation of money into capital and from the same process of dispossession of the worker of their conditions and means of production; this, of course, derives from the appropriation of them by the capitalist class, owners of capital and money. In this sense, what is relevant is the historical process that allows the transformation of private property into capital and of labor into wage labor. It is this process that gives rise to the formation of the capitalist mode of production and the consolidation of a system of social relations of production that sustain it and its particular form of development of the productive forces. It is a mode of production that is based on a specific form of exploitation of labor and that allows not only the generation of surplus, but also its appropriation by capital and its reinvestment, that is, its capitalization. This process requires the salaried form of labor, as well as the capitalist form of ownership of the means of production.

Faced with the dispossession of all means of production as well as of other resources and the conditions of the labor process, the worker has only their labor power. But it is of no use to them by itself since for them it no longer has any use value, as they have no way of using it productively. It only remains to sell it to others, who are the possessors of the means of production. The formation of the labor market contributes to this and, as Polanyi points out, constitutes one of the pillars on which the market economy and society—i.e., capitalism—are based. In this labor market, the worker alienates their labor power for a wage, which allows them to cover basic survival needs and those of their family. This is the exchange value at stake, determined by the social cost of the goods required for social reproduction as a worker and the labor force.

Through the purchase of labor power in the form of wages—its exchange value—the capitalist appropriates the use value of that commodity, as they do with any other. The key point is that the use value of labor power is labor itself, that is, its capacity to perform work and, therefore, to transform the other means of production, inputs, and working conditions into products that can be commodified so that the capitalist can sell in different markets. The core of all this is that the exchange value of labor power—its wage—need not correspond in quantity and quality to its use value, that is, the labor time materialized in the commodities it produces. To the extent that the exchange value (wage) is greater than the use value (labor embodied in the commodities), the capitalist will incur a loss, since they will have paid a wage that exceeds what they can obtain from the sale of the products of that labor. Normally, in this case, the logical result would be that the capitalist will end up closing down their business, as they cannot render a profit from their enterprise. What usually happens, rather, is the reverse situation: the wage earned by the worker is placed at a rate that is less than the real use value of their labor, i.e., the value that labor embodies and materializes in the commodity produced. This difference is what is called surplus value and gives rise to the capitalist's profit. In reality, this difference corresponds to the surplus in its form of value that is generated by labor, which is appropriated by the owner of that labor, that is, the capitalist.

This surplus value is the basis and *leitmotif* of the whole process of production, as well as of the social forms it assumes. The transformation of the worker into a wage earner is for this purpose and this purpose alone, that is, to be able to generate surplus value that under the wage form of labor corresponds to property for the buyer of that commodity, i.e., the capitalist. In this sense, the capital-labor relation becomes a relation of surplus-value generation that sustains the process of value accumulation, that is, of capitalization of capital. In this sense, capitalism constitutes a mode of production, a system of social relations of production that gives rise to a system of social and productive classes: on the one hand, capital and capitalists; on the other, labor and workers. In the labor process, capital and labor are opposed. The logic of organization and functioning of the labor process is given by capital in terms of which the whole process is oriented to the generation of surplus value to feed the capitalization of capital.

However, this description only deals with their economic and productive forms. What is certain is that both fundamental categories of capital and labor concur under the form of concrete social subjects, in the form of capitalists on the one hand and workers on the other. In this sense, as economic categories they contribute to the understanding and functioning of production and its ultimate meaning: the accumulation of surplus in the form of capital. Likewise, as social subjects, they, therefore, concur as social classes, which contribute to the understanding and functioning of the economy and society. What opposes subjects in these processes of labor, surplus value, and accumulation in the greater social sphere or field confronts them as a struggle of differentiated class interests, taking shape as social inequality in its different manifestations: income, privileges, power, politics, culture, arts, sciences, etc. What is relevant, then, is that social inequality is expressed as a form of class inequality whose roots originate in the specific form adopted in capitalism by the social relations of production as we have defined them above.

In effect, this capital relation—understood here as a process of extraction of surplus value and its accumulation under the form of capital—requires the formation of two things: (1) the free worker, that is, the formation of individuals completely stripped of the possession and ownership of their working conditions and means of labor, such that they only possess in property their labor power, which obliges them to sell it for a wage in order to ensure their social reproduction as persons; and (2) capital itself, that is, the formation of the social form adopted by the ownership of the means of production and the conditions of labor, which, while concentrating these resources and commodities, does not possess neither the ownership nor the possession of labor power. In this way, it is a question of breaking and dissolving all forms of relationship with labor that are based on relations of servitude or slavery. All of them would be replaced and substituted by salaried forms of relation between the means of production (capital) and the labor force (labor), where one and the other (capitalists and workers) freely concur in the market for the purchase and sale of that particular commodity: the labor force. Indeed, as Marx (1973: 427) points out:

> The same process which placed the mass face to face with the objective conditions of labour as free workers also placed these conditions, as capital, face to face with the free workers. The historic process was the divorce of elements which up until then were bound together; its result is therefore not that one of the elements disappears, but that each of them appears in a negative relation to the other, the (potentially) free worker on the one side, capital (potentially) on the other. The separation of the objective conditions from the classes which have become transformed into free workers necessarily also appears at the same time as the achievement of independence by these same conditions at the opposite pole.

This, which for any inhabitant of the 21st century would seem to be something natural and normalized, is in fact only the product of a certain historical process. It was not always so nor should it always be so. Before capitalism—in particular before the formation of the labor market—labor was imbricated (embedded) with its conditions and means in at least two ways: (1) either the worker not only owned means of production but also had access to some extent to a form of control over the labor process itself; or (2) labor and the worker were some forms of property and possession of other social and economic subjects (Polanyi 2001). Whether it was the feudal lord (based on relations of serfdom) or whether it was the master (based on relations of slavery) in both cases the feudal lord and the master appropriated not only the labor of the peasants and slaves under their dominion but also the very means of production and the conditions of labor themselves. As Marx (1973: 413) critically states:

> In the relation of slavery and serfdom this separation does not take place; rather, one part of society is treated by the other as itself merely an inorganic and natural condition of its own reproduction. The slave stands in no relation whatsoever to the objective conditions of his labor; rather, labor itself, both in the form of the slave and in that of the serf, is classified as an inorganic condition of production along with other natural beings, such as cattle, as an accessory of the earth.

Thus, the field of production was mediated by a system of extra-economic and extra-productive social relations, which influenced and controlled the entire work process. In capitalism, on the other hand, all these relations are autonomized and transferred to mercantile forms, constituting for this purpose specific and unique markets where certain processes become mercantile forms, that is, merchandise exchanged for a price, even when their value is very complex. We are talking about the labor market, the land market, and the money market—three elements intrinsic to every labor process—that until before capitalism had not yet taken the form of commodities but depended directly on other social, cultural, and political forms that bound and signified them from other fields of social relations (Polanyi 2001).

In this sense, "the relation of labour to capital, or to the objective conditions of labour as capital, presupposes a process of history which dissolves the various forms in which the worker is a proprietor, or in which the proprietor works" (Marx, 1973: 421). It is a process of dissolution not only in relation to the ownership of land and instruments of labor but especially the dissolution of the social relations in which the workers themselves—as persons and individuals—are still included among the objective conditions of production and labor and, therefore, are susceptible of being appropriated not only as labor but also as persons by other subjects, whether in the form of slaves or serfs.

For capital, on the other hand, "the worker is not a condition of production, only work is" (Marx, 1973: 422). If the worker (as an individual) could be replaced by machines (as has been the constant in capitalism), so much the better for capital, since it does not appropriate the worker (the individual) but their labor, mediated by a process of exchange, that is, of wage-earning. Now, for this dispossession of labor from its working conditions to become a process of wage-earning, it requires an encounter with capital as a capital relation, not only as patrimony or hoarded money. In this sense, the same process that generates the dispossession of labor is that which allows patrimony-money to be transformed into capital. As Marx (1973: 430) points out:

> Capital does not create the objective conditions of labour. Rather, its *original formation* is that, through the historic process of dissolution of the old mode of production, value existing as *money-wealth* is enabled, on one side, to buy the objective conditions of labour; on the other side, to exchange money for the living labour of the workers who have been set free. All these moments are present; their divorce is itself a historic process, a process of dissolution, and it is the latter which enables money to transform itself into capital.

In synthesis, this process is not the result of capital, but on the contrary, it is the presupposition for the historical formation of the capital relation. The capitalist, thus, acquires the role of intermediary between property in general and labor and, as such, becomes a social class that, as the owner of the means of production, opposes and relates to the workers as the dominant social class that owns labor. Their different and opposed interest, are the basis of the historical conformation of capitalism, and their confrontations will determine the dynamics and destiny of this mode of production. This class opposition is the basis of the form taken by social inequality in capitalism.

CHAPTER 5

The Debate on Social Inequality in the 20th Century

> Our inequality—the extremes to which it has grown, the forms it has taken—is not inevitable; it is not the result of inexorable laws of economics or physics; it is a matter of choice, of our policies; and these in turn are the result of our politics.
> JOSEPH STIGLITZ, *The Great Divide* (2015: 295)

In this chapter, we focus on the review of three approaches to inequality that emerged in the first half of the 20th century: functionalist approaches, neoclassical theory, and Gunnar Myrdal's approach to the origin of social and regional inequalities. The first two are conservative, while Myrdal proposes a critical one. The term conservative is not gratuitous but is consistent with the principles that guide them, at least from two perspectives: On the one hand, for functionalism and neoclassicists, inequality is a necessary and inevitable social phenomenon and, to a certain degree, desirable for greater ends, such as social integration, social development, and economic progress. On the other hand, in both approaches, the debate on inequality is restricted to its forms and dimensions—in some cases even to its most immediate causes—but in neither case to its historical genesis. For the same reason, the debate in these two approaches is not about inequality per se but about its magnitude and consequences for society. It is a debate that falls on the quantitative/formal plane—discussing dimensions and forms—while leaving the qualitative/structural plane—analyses of social processes and history—absent.

Myrdal's approach, on the other hand, is critical of these two approaches as it places at the center of the debate the mechanisms that give rise to the structures of inequality, as well as their perpetuation and aggravation in capitalist society. He also establishes that the reproduction of inequality arises from the same processes that generate development and progress in the capitalist economy.

1 Functionalist Sociology

All social stratification refers to a classification of individuals that make up a society—people, institutions, subjects, classes, etc.—according to their position in that classifying social system, whether in higher strata, whether in lower strata. For this approach, social stratification, and the configuration of structures and forms of social inequality with it, are a phenomenon intrinsic to every society. Textually, Davis and Moore (1945:242) state that "no society is "classless", or unstratified," from which they infer that stratification would be a universal need of every society to sustain itself as a social system. Parsons (1974: 147), for his part, points out in the same sense that "social stratification ... is an aspect of the concept of the structure of a generalized social systems ... the system of stratification is intimately linked to the level and type of integration of the system as such."

From the functionalist point of view, social stratification is seen, then, as a social necessity that besides being a socially inevitable phenomenon is also functionally positive for any society, since it would fulfill a function in terms of sustaining modes of social integration and cohesion (Parsons, 1991). Social stratification is considered inevitable, as well as necessary and *functional*, and, therefore, desirable in terms of its effects on social life and society itself. Having said the above, it remains then to ask what these authors mean by stratification and inequality.

In this regard, Parsons (1974: 150) states that "stratification, in its evaluative aspect, is the hierarchization of units of a system according to the standards of the common system of values." In other words, for Parsons, all social stratification is configured on the basis of a process of social evaluation that assigns values to each individual according to the recognition made by others with respect to their contribution to the system as a whole, that is, with respect to their specific function within the system and their action within it. The substance of this definition refers to the concept of a "common system of values," on the basis of which the configuration of all social stratification rests.

For Parsons, all social stratification refers to a hierarchical classification of specific elements, the ordering of which would respond to the result of the operation of some common system of values in this sense. However ambiguous this definition may be, the central question is from where such strata are constructed and how their differentiation is determined in terms of their social valuations (Tumin, 1974). In this respect, neither Parsons nor other functionalists are dedicated to explaining the historical genesis of social stratification, that is, why one type of common values predominates in some societies and others in others. Given the confirmation and 'validity' of this common system of values in the form of social stratification, functionalism focuses its interests on analyzing the specific functionality of that hierarchies in a given society, therefore, on observing in each society the particular form adopted by the hierarchization into social strata. In this sense, Parsons affirms that all stratification is result of the form adopted by the division and distinction of social activities, which never are evaluated, judged, or valued as equally important and necessary for society, but as different and hierarchical. Thus, depending on the common system of values of each society, the hierarchy of activities, and, whit that, of the individuals who perform them, are determined.

Based on the division of labor, a structure of role differentiation is established in every social system (Parsons, 1991). This differentiation implies two levels of analysis: on the one hand, as a structure of roles, referring to the distinction of the functions and responsibilities that make up the social system; on the other, to the distribution of these social roles and functions among the population, referring to the ways and mechanisms in which these roles and functions are assigned—or assumed—by different persons, subjects, and social strata. The first refers to the analysis of the social structure, while the second refers to social stratification, that is, to the distribution of persons and subjects within such role structure, as well as to the distribution of rewards assigned and distributed to each role according to said structure. Both planes make up the social system, where stratification corresponds to a specific hierarchical ordering of roles and functions, which are based on the norms dictated by the common system of values indicated by Parsons (1974).

A corollary that follows this approach is that social stratification would be inherent to any industrial society and, therefore, is also part of the social systems of Eastern Europe. The generating structure of social differentiation would not be the character of capitalist exploitation—search for profit and private appropriation of surpluses—but something far much simpler and more abstract: the distinction of occupational roles and functions that arise from the industrial form of organization of the division of labor. And this occurs both in its capitalist and communist or statist modes (Parsons, 1949). In any society, there will always be social positions that are functionally more important than others and that require differentiated and higher-level skills and abilities. In view of this, social stratification to the extent that it is based on a common system of values and beliefs contributes to maintaining the integration of society by establishing a system of distribution of benefits, privileges, rights, and responsibilities according to this differentiated and unequal structure of positions. In this sense, social stratification should be analyzed based on the function it fulfills in the social system (Duek and Inda, 2014).

Davis (1963) adds that the debate on stratification systems cannot be restricted to the characteristics of individuals in different social positions, but must focus on the system of differentiation of these positions in a given society. It is not the same to discuss the characteristics of the different positions within a society—their differences in terms of status, prestige, rewards, and other aspects—as it is to discuss how and why certain individuals occupy certain positions within that social hierarchy. Indeed, with respect to the first type of stratification, societies can establish general frameworks and principles that legitimize the social differentiation that emanates from all stratification. On that basis, it is easier and more organic to discuss and apply criteria about the characteristics and attributes of the individuals who should occupy the different occupations in the social hierarchy established by the stratification of those positions.

Social stratification, understood as a structure of differentiated and hierarchically ordered positions, is established on the basis of two basic functional principles: (1) the function of each position for society, which determines its social importance; and (2) the talent or skill necessary for its realization, which determines the conditions and attributes of those who are suitable for each social function (Stavenhagen, 1974). In this sense, in any society the social stratification of positions is, thus, a product of the need to establish functional forms and mechanisms for the distribution of its members in the various social positions and to encourage them to carry out the activities, tasks, and responsibilities inherent to those positions.

Given the above, it is, therefore, inevitable and necessary for every society to establish in the first place a system of rewards that can be distributed in a differentiated manner according to the different positions that make up the social stratification of each society. Rewards and their distribution system, thus, become an intrinsic part of the social order, constituting a central factor in society's system of stratification and inequality. As Davis and Moore (1945: 243) point out:

> Social inequality is ... an unconsciously evolved device by which societies ensure that the most important positions are conscientiously filled by the most qualified persons. Hence every society, no matter how simple or complex, must differentiate persons in terms of both prestige and esteem, and must possess a certain amount of institutionalized inequality.

Thus, all social stratification is linked to and gives rise to a system of social inequality, insofar as rights, privileges, and rewards are distributed differently according to the function of each position and the talent required for its performance, and this is exactly what is meant by stratification. The regulating principle would be, then, the correspondence and proportionality that must be established between a person's merit and the reward they receive. In other words, the position of a person in a specific stratum is a function of their merits—skills and abilities—to develop the activity corresponding to that role defined for that stratum and, therefore, the retribution received will be a function of the value that this function has for society. Thus, "the position in the hierarchy is equivalent to a reward, and this depends on individual merit" (Duek and Inda, 2014: 156, our translation).

The corollary of this analysis is that, in any society, stratification and inequality are social phenomena and, while functionally positive for society, they are also equally necessary and inevitable. It is not possible to imagine a complex society without thinking of unequal forms of distribution and allocation of its resources, rewards, status, prestige, rights, and privileges among its members. Again, this conversation shows how the debate on inequality is reduced to its mere forms, magnitudes, and dimensions but not to its genesis, structure, or historical conformation as a social phenomenon.

Faced with this discourse of functionalist sociology regarding social inequality and stratification, different critiques and counter-arguments have emerged, all of them pointing to the character attributed to these social phenomena by functionalism (see Tumin, 1953; Mayntz, 1974). In this regard, we would like to return to two aspects of this critique: (1) the social function assigned to stratification; and (2) the necessary, inevitable, and even desirable character attributed to all social stratification under certain circumstances.

Regarding the first point, Duek and Inda (2014) point to the merit-reward duality from which they critique the scope of this perspective of inequality and stratification as a mechanism for sustaining political and ideological hegemony. For Parsons (1974 and 1991), the social function of stratification is that it contributes to generate mechanisms of social integration and stability, while at the same time reducing the degree of conflict inherent to all social differentiation. This is possible to the extent that stratification is built on the principle that rewards are proportional to the merit and function (role) performed. Thus, the position and reward corresponding to each stratum in the social hierarchy is assigned based on the function and social role of that position and on the individual merits required for performing that function and social role. On this point, Duek and Inda (2014: 174, our translation) question whether this social function is nothing more than a way of naturalizing and legitimizing social inequality. According to these authors, "the correspondence between social position and personal merit is a fundamental ideological representation for individuals to inhabit their own class situation without further questioning and, in this way, to reproduce the current production relations." In this sense, the function of social integration and stability does not refer so much to social stratification itself as it does to the ideological discourse built around it from functionalist perspectives. The stabilizing role of stratification would not lie in its role as a social phenomenon in itself but in its ideological and political representation, the latter being fundamental to maintain and reduce the degree of social conflict that arises from any process of social differentiation and inequality.

Indeed, the functionalist discourse affirms that social inequality expressed in any stratification process is necessary and functional for society, since it allows for the most important, responsible, and demanding positions and roles to be assigned to those people with the greatest merits, those who are the most qualified and prepared to perform them. In this way, the unequal distribution of rewards would be fair and necessary since the greatest benefits would be assigned to those who legitimately deserve them most given their abilities and merits, as well as the roles and functions performed by them. In other words, the principle of function-merit-reward proportionality is the basis for legitimizing social inequality.

However, the ideological basis of this discourse is not only that it justifies the allocation and concentration of rewards, power, and wealth in the hands of those who are positioned at the top of the social hierarchy but also that it naturalizes the inequality and precariousness to which the rest of the social classes are confined. In effect, the functionalist discourse on social stratification makes "the others convince themselves that the misery, contempt and impotence that correspond to them in the distribution are the just remuneration of the small part that their modest talents allow them to take in the progress of the human species" (Laurin-Frenete, 1989: 15, our translation). The ideological power of the functionalist discourse on stratification rests not so much in the arguments for the acceptance of the concentration of power and wealth in the hands of the few, as it does in the conformism it promotes among the unfortunate who do not enjoy the merits and capacities to access such roles and social strata.

As for the second point of critique of the functionalist theory of social stratification, questioning the thesis that assumes it as a necessary, inevitable, and even desirable phenomenon under certain circumstances. We have already pointed out that functionalism does not seek to explain the genesis of inequality and stratification but rather focuses on analyzing and theorizing its function within society. In this sense, it is paradoxical that from this approach a character of inevitability is granted to a social phenomenon, when its historical origin has not been explained as such that could give reason for such a description of necessity and inevitability in its characterization. Even if we assume, as Parsons and Davis did, that social stratification is a phenomenon intrinsic to every society, the question, however, should not be reduced to analyzing and explaining the function stratification assumes in each society but, rather, to discuss its origin, that is, the genesis of both the form adopted by the division of social labor and the common system of social values that gives legitimacy to the differentiation of the various social positions. Functionalism only points out the fact that inequality and stratification arise from society itself, without specifying the mechanisms, devices, structures, systems, and relations from which it is configured.

From our standpoint, we comprehend that social stratification, along with the value system that legitimizes and fosters social cohesion within contexts of inequality, emerges through an ongoing and persistent interaction among the individuals constituting society. These individuals engage in relationships and distinctions precisely due to their varied positions within a system of social stratification. Consequently, the hierarchy of values, which give support the hierarchy of positions in social stratification, is a product of these interactions (comprising confrontations, cooperation, conflicts, and agreements) between individuals unequally positioned in the social hierarchy. Thus, in essence, opinions and hierarchy of values regarding stratification arise from the very conditions of social stratification, resulting in a somewhat tautological argumentation. The critical lies not only in the inherent tautology of the functionalist perspective, but also in the absence of a viable way to overcome it. The example of social differentiation and stratification based on gender proves particularly insightful in illustrating this point.

According to the functionalist approach, social stratification between men and women—i.e., gender inequality—would correspond to the fact that there would be a social system of values that would give more preponderance to certain activities (positions) than to others. Thus, the division of labor between domestic-reproductive activities and extra-domestic and productive activities entails a differentiation in terms of the value and social function of each of them. In any society, productive activities usually have a higher social value than reproductive activities: they concentrate greater status, privileges, power, community esteem, as well as greater benefits. However, in all societies this social division of productive and reproductive labor takes the form of a sexual division, where men tend to occupy the positions of production and women those of reproduction. This raises the question of whether this means that women are more apt and skilled for reproductive work, while men are more apt and skilled for productive work.

We know that this is not so, that there is nothing in the nature of men or women that makes them more suitable for one or another activity, but that these differences are socially constructed and, by the same token, reproduced in all societies (Federicci, 2004; Butler, 1999). The sexual division of labor, in reality, is constructed on the basis of relations of power and domination that women suffer from men, and it is this form of interaction—domination, exploitation, power—that determines the different value that all societies have assigned to one and another type of human work and activity.

In short, the stratification of positions, in this case of sexual and social division of labor, is not the result of a common system of values but of the imposition of interests, values, prejudices, etc., of some (men) on others (women). Likewise, this indicates that sexual stratification and inequality—like all forms of social stratification—is a process that has a specific historical and social genesis and, therefore, does not necessarily have to be that way.

The corollary of this reflection is that no social stratification is necessary or inevitable and even less desirable under any social and historical circumstance. On the contrary, every form of social stratification is a historical process and, therefore, avoidable and not necessarily desirable. Social stratification can, therefore, be reversed and reconfigured, both in the sense of establishing other formats of social inequality and domination and also in the form of dissolving all kinds of social inequality and, therefore, creating a social relation based on a process of emancipation.[1]

From a broader perspective, we can say that stratification, as a social process, is not determined but is continuously constructed and reconstructed, and, therefore, it is possible to be constructed and reconstructed from different historical formats; equally, we can sustain that no form of social stratification is valid in itself, but is always the product of a continuous and recurrent social and political confrontation between the subjects and classes that make up that same social stratification, that class structure of society.

Rousseau pointed out that private property is the genesis of social inequality and stratification. From Rousseau, we can, then, affirm that private property is the vector on which all forms of social stratification are built and from which derive such common systems of values and principles, which as discourses form the bases of legitimization of both the genesis and the form of social stratification. In this sense, we can point out that it is in the face of this

---

1 For one thing, feminism as a theoretical and political proposal promotes, precisely, a process of emancipation of women—and men—from the various forms of social inequality constructed on the basis of sexual division of labor and other forms of gender inequality that have been built and developed throughout the history of humanity.

phenomenon—private property—that it is possible to think of various forms of social emancipation, that is, of the construction of forms of social relations that do not imply private property as the matrix of the constitution of society and, therefore, do not imply the formation of classes, differentiated and unequal social strata. Later on, we will return to this line of reflection based on a proposal for social emancipation based on a discourse against inequality.

2 Neoclassical Economics

At the end of the nineteenth century, a revision of political economy emerged with force, taking up again some of Adam Smith's initial foundations. In contrast to the Ricardian and Marxist approaches to the labor theory of value, it put forward the principle of subjective value and the utility of goods and commodities as determinants of their value and prices. Its development is based on five fundamental principles, namely: (1) methodological individualism; (2) rational choice and the principle of *homo economicus*; (3) the principle of general equilibrium as the fundamental tendency of economic processes; (4) the principle of private property as the organizing axis of the production and distribution of resources; and finally, (5) the principle of perfect competition and free and self-regulated markets.

Based on these principles, the analysis of social inequality is developed at two separate levels. On the one hand, at the microeconomic level, we analyze how individual decisions contribute to an adequate and fair distribution of income, wealth, and privileges. On the other, at the macroeconomic level, the analysis of inequality is framed within the theories of economic growth and development.

At the end of the nineteenth century, J. B. Clark proposed a theory of distribution based on the principle of the marginal productivity of productive factors, a fundamental category in the neoclassical theory of production and allocation of resources. In 1899 he published his book *The Distribution of Wealth: A Theory of Wages, Interest, and Profits*, where he developed this proposal based on the advances of the Austrian marginalist school and the development of neoclassical economic thought. In this book, Clark theorizes the conditions for establishing when the distribution of income in wages, interest, and profits is really fair and equitable. In this regard, he questions the socialist formula that states that production and distribution should be governed under the motto "work according to ability and pay according need" (Clark, 1908: 8), arguing that it breaks with the principles of economic equity and distributive justice since it goes against what is normally considered a property right. As he points out in his text (9):

> [I]t is evident that a society in which property is made to rest on the claim of a producer to what he creates must, as a general rule, vindicate that right at the point where titles originate – that is, in the payments that are made for labor. If it were to do otherwise, there would be at the foundation of the social structure an explosive element which sooner or later would destroy it.

In his proposal, Clark argues that distribution cannot go beyond the principles of the economic science of production at the risk of falling into distortions of the markets that lead to generate more economic and social problems than those to be solved. Clark starts from the principle that labor as well as capital are commodities, and as such, the determination of their prices—wages and profit, respectively—is equally subject to the law of the marginal value of their productivities. In the particular case of wages and labor, he points out (180):

> We are to get what we produce—such is the dominant rule of life; and what we are able to produce by means of labor, is determined by what a final unit of mere labor can add to the product that can be created without its aid. *Final productivity governs wages.*

This principle of wage, profit, and interest determination is relatively simple and is based on the basic principles of neoclassical economic theory. In situations of equilibrium and wage non-discrimination, it is established that the remuneration of labor must equal the value of its marginal product, which is determined as the market value of what is produced by the final or marginal worker (Becker, 1971). If this value of marginal productivity were higher than the wage, the capitalist would have the economic motivation to hire more workers, since what they would earn from the sale of labor would be higher than the cost of hiring new workers (wages). Since the marginal productivity of labor is always decreasing—like that of any factor of production—and, therefore, as the hiring of workers increases, the productivity of the latter will tend to decrease and, with it, the market value of what they have produced. Thus, the capitalist entrepreneur will be incentivized to hire more workers up to the point where the value of marginal productivity equals the value of the wage. All of this is under the assumptions of perfect competition, homogeneity of the labor factor, diminishing returns of the factor, and other necessary assumptions of neoclassical theory.[2]

Based on this principle, it is to be expected that the wage differences that can be observed between one social group and another would be a direct function of the differences in their respective productivities. If this principle of proportionality were to be applied, we would be in the presence of a situation of economic and wage equity in the sense that each worker would receive a wage income in accordance with their specific contribution to production, which is expressed through the value of their productivity. According to Clark (1908), this principle, according to which it is productivity that ultimately determines the remuneration of the factors of production (labor and capital), not only meets the criteria of economic efficiency but also constitutes a principle of economic justice in the distribution of wealth. Based on this principle, what predominates and regulates the form of income distribution is the principle of economic equity and not that of social equality. In this context, then, inequality in income distribution is justified and legitimized as a result of this principle, according to which each person would be entitled to an income in accordance with their contribution to production and the economy.

Based on this argument, the neoclassicals return to theoretical and political positions from which they seek to give a scientific basis to the prevailing social inequality in our societies. Therefore, for the neoclassical perspective, inequality is not only inevitable but also fair and legitimate. To this end, they counterpose the principles of economic equity over the principles of social equality, choosing the former of the later. Since human beings are not equal, we do not have the same productive or economic capacity; therefore, according to the neoclassical approach, it is unfair that those with fewer capabilities have similar retributions and rewards to those with more capabilities. What is fair and equitable is to let the market allocate wages and income distribution according to the economic-productive conditions and capabilities of each individual.

If in sociological functionalism, inequality is justified by the differentiation of positions and occupations that sustain the social structure; in neoclassical economic perspectives, this differentiation is transferred from social positions to individuals and their capabilities, attributes, merits, or properties. Based on these differences, it is fair and legitimate for them to differentiate their rewards and remunerations. To act in the opposite direction would be discriminatory against the most capable and, therefore, an inequitable form of distribution

---

2 For a more detailed analysis on the marginalist theory of wage and employment determination, see Reisman, 1990; Krugman and Wells, 2006; Canales, 2019.

of remunerations and rewards, in addition to establishing distortions in the functioning of markets that would affect their efficiency as mechanisms for the allocation of resources, capital, and labor.

From a macroeconomic perspective, the analysis of inequality takes an important turn in that its dynamics and analysis are directly linked to the issues of economic growth and development. In this regard, economic and productive inequalities at the international level—further deepened by the world wars and the Great Depression of the 1930s—made it necessary to establish economic development alternatives that would contribute to providing positive responses to the problems of poverty and inequality that afflicted the economies of the Third World. It was not only necessary to promote and legitimize a developmentalist discourse but also to imbue it with positive attributes in terms of social development, progress, and welfare.

It is in this context that the proposal of Simon Kuznets (1955) arises. Based on his longitudinal and long-term analysis of the U.S. economy from the nineteenth century to the mid-twentieth century, Kuznets puts forward the thesis that the relationship between economic growth and inequality in income distribution marks a trend that takes the form of an inverted U-shaped pattern. In other words, in the early stages of development, when the economy begins its phase of industrialization and transition from an agrarian to an urban-industrial society, inequality in income distribution is relatively lower and is determined fundamentally by the form it takes in the traditional sectors (agriculture and rural areas). As the economy grows and industrializes, inequality tends to increase. However, at a later stage when the modern (urban-industrial) sector acquires greater weight and importance in the share of GDP and economic growth, inequality in income distribution begins to be affected, reversing its trend such that when the economy is fully industrialized and with an equally transformed and modernized agricultural sector income inequality returns to its initial levels.

Kuznets (1955) bases this model on two groups of forces that determine this particular tendency toward inequality in the long-run income distribution of developed countries. "The first group relates to the concentration of savings in the upper income brackets. ... The second ... lies in the industrial [intersectoral] structure of the income distribution" (7). To analyze and describe how these two forces operate, Kuznets takes up the two-sector model of economic growth with unlimited labor supply proposed by A. Lewis in 1954, which posits a scenario in which development results from the conjunction of these two economic forces. The model proposed by Kuznets analyzes the conditions for economic growth in a context of high intersectoral structural heterogeneity, which refers particularly to rural-urban differences in terms of their economic and productive structures, as well as to a dual scenario of high income and savings but with high inequality in income distribution.

With respect to intersectoral heterogeneity, a two-sector model is proposed: (1) the agricultural sector, based on a traditional economic structure, but with a high labor supply, very low productivity, low technological innovation and capital investment, and a high degree of population concentration; and (2) the urban sector, based on industrial activity, with a higher level of technological innovation and capital investment, higher productivity levels, but with a low labor supply.

Likewise, there is no minor sectoral heterogeneity in terms of income levels and personal income distribution. While the agro-rural sector has low levels of per capita income, it also has a more egalitarian income distribution. On the other hand, although the urban sector has higher levels of income, it also has higher levels of inequality in its distribution.

The model proposed by Kuznets and Lewis operates in this context. On the one hand, in terms of the factors linked to savings, given these structural conditions and rural-urban differences, it is to be expected that in the cities, where there is a greater concentration of income, there will, therefore, be a greater capacity for savings in the upper income strata. This higher level of savings would translate into greater funds for investment, which would help drive a process of industrial growth in the cities. To the extent that this occurs—given the structural differences in rural-urban productivity levels (agriculture versus industry) and considering the unlimited supply of labor in the countryside—a rural-urban migratory flow is to be expected, which in addition to providing labor for growing industrialization contributes to the economic development of the cities.

Now, in a context where inequality in intersectoral income distribution (rural-urban) is greater than inequality in intrasectoral income distribution—i.e., that which prevails both within the countryside and within the city—then this rural-urban mobility initially contributes to increasing the degree of inequality in income distribution, since it grows more in those areas with greater inequality. This would explain why in the first stage of economic development social inequality tends to increase.

However, as cities develop and advance in the next stages of the economic growth process in both productive sectors, the relative size of the agricultural sector (with low productivity) tends to decrease as the labor force becomes scarcer, due to their migration to the cities, thus creating the opportune conditions for greater capital investment, productive modernization, and, therefore, an increase in the rural sector's relative wages. In turn, the same rural-urban migration contributes to an increasing number of workers accessing jobs in industry with higher productivity and wages, thus increasing the proportion of the total population that has access to higher levels of per capita income in the process of economic expansion. The combination of both trends, in the agricultural and industrial sector, in this second stage of economic development finally leads to a reversal of the former relationship between growth and inequality, such that we enter the second phase of the Kuznets curve, according to which the levels and degrees of inequality in income distribution begin to fall.

This model was quickly and widely accepted and assumed almost as an intrinsic law of development. For one thing, it represented a beacon of hope for much of the Third World, which was mired in traditional economic structures with low growth and high levels of poverty and social inequality. It also immediately became a powerful argument in favor of assuming the problems of poverty, inequality, and economic inequity as a necessary yet ugly cost in the path of development, one that was in favor of a future hope for economic development, well-being, and greater economic and social equity. After all, in theory, this cost and suffering would have had to be paid even by the currently developed countries themselves, following Kuznets' model.

In this context, it is worth taking up Piketty's (2014) critique of Kuznets' model and its use with marked political and ideological overtones. In this regard—while at the same time recognizing Kuznets' great contribution to the design of the first ever studies on US national accounts and historical series on inequality—Piketty (2014: 15) points out, however, that Kuznets' greatest contribution, his "magic curve" relating growth and inequality, would have been formulated largely "for the wrong reasons, and its empirical underpinnings were extremely fragile." In the first place, Piketty reminds us that behind all the sophistication of Kuznets' macroeconomic model was a political intentionality. In fact, it would have been Kuznets (1955: 24) himself who explicitly recognized that the oversimplification of the model was, however, sufficiently realistic in terms of the objective of maintaining "the future prospect of underdeveloped countries within the orbit of the free world."

Secondly, Piketty also questions the methodological basis of Kuznets' model in terms of the solidity of the empirical evidence on which it is based. Specifically, he takes up Kuznets himself who in the conclusions of his 1955 paper explicitly recognizes that his model had a markedly hypothetical character, resting "perhaps [on] 5 percent empirical information and 95 percent speculation, some of it possibly tainted by wishful thinking" (Kuznets, 1955: 26). In other words, it is a model based mostly on conjectures and speculations with a great logical development, but a very weak empirical and without methodological consistency.

In spite of this double confession of guilt on the part of the author himself, the theory of Kuznets acquired a level of diffusion that does not correspond to its methodological fragility, although it does seem to be consistent with its explicit political intentionality. In fact, the data themselves demonstrated its fragility and weakness. As Piketty points out, the great reduction in income inequality documented by Kuznets, which he erroneously attributes to the economic development of the United States, was "due above all to the world wars and the violent economic and political shocks they entailed (especially for people with large fortunes). It had little to do with the tranquil process of intersectoral mobility described by Kuznets" (Piketty, 2014: 15).

Along with this methodological critique, Stiglitz (2001) raises a more radical questioning that points to the theoretical foundations of Kuznets' model. Returning to Polanyi, Stiglitz states that the entire neoclassical approach—and Kuznets' is undoubtedly within this category—is based on the thesis of market self-regulation—i.e., the idea that the free functioning of markets without state or social intervention (unions, etc.) would always lead to a situation of general equilibrium and economic efficiency in the allocation of resources. In this sense, according to Kuznets, it would be precisely the free functioning of markets that would explain the particular trend of inequality at each stage of a country's or region's development. The fact that inequality tends to decrease and reduce is a direct consequence of the free movement and displacement of labor and capital, processes that are promoted precisely by an economy of free and self-regulated markets and which result in a boost to economic growth, productive transformation, and social development.

However, nothing seems to be further from reality: In the same years that Kuznets proposed his model of growth and inequality, Polanyi published his book on the great transformation, in which he demonstrates not only that the famous self-regulation of markets has never worked, but also that the opposite is true to what neoclassical theory claims in this respect. According to Polanyi, the liberal model of a society of free and self-regulated markets is in a practically unsolvable dilemma. His thesis is that "the idea of a self-adjusting market implied a stark Utopia. Such an institution could not exist for any length of time without annihilating the human and natural substance of society; it would have physically destroyed man and transformed his surroundings into wilderness" (Polanyi, 2001: 3). Faced with this possibility of destruction, society has adopted historically various measures and providences that have involved different modes of protectionism. The point is that any of these self-saving measures went against the self-regulation of markets, supposedly disorganizing industrial life and with it endangering the economy but in a different sense than the one derived from self-regulated markets. This dilemma, where leaving markets free and self-regulated led to the collapse of society, while any form of regulation impeded the functioning of capital and with it economic and social growth and development, poses a highly unstable scenario, which explains the stagnation and crisis of the market system that led to the great crisis of the 1930s as well as the world crises that followed in the 20th century and are reappearing in the 21st century. Everything seems to indicate that the market economy is based on an irresolvable structural dilemma, whose only constant are the recurrent crises of the markets that demand, paradoxically, continuous and novel forms of intervention and extra-economic regulation.

For his part, Stiglitz (2001: VII) is equally emphatic in stating that "self-regulating markets never work; their deficiencies not only in their internal workings but also in their consequences (e.g., for the poor), are so great that government intervention becomes necessary." Thus, it is common practice for governments and states to continuously intervene in markets; this is not precisely to favor a better distribution of income or to reduce poverty but to solve various problems that capital itself cannot assume, generally acting in favor of industrial interests that have always promoted government intervention when they have needed to achieve their own interests.[3] The great transformation of today's developed and industrialized countries cannot be understood and would not have been achieved without the active role of governments, both in protecting their industries and in promoting technological innovation, research, and development and, not infrequently, in applying various measures to rescue companies, capital, and entire industries.

As if this critique of the theoretical foundations of Kuznets' model were not enough, Stiglitz also targets his darts at its methodological deficiencies, pointing out that the inequality curve described by this author is also misinterpreted. Curiously and paradoxically, the shape of the curve is not so much explained by factors of economic growth and the free action of markets as it is by different forms of government and state intervention in the functioning of markets and the conduct of the economy. Indeed, the decline in the levels of income inequality recorded especially in the post-war period—the 30 glorious years of which Piketty speaks—is not so much explained by the economic momentum of those years as it is by the constitution and formation of a welfare and social security state through which efficient and effective mechanisms were established to control and regulate markets. This especially included regulating the labor market and, by that means, the genesis of income distribution. It is not

---

3 The recent 2008 financial/subprime crisis in the United States and the State's response to rescue the large financial and real estate consortiums show that this policy of State intervention in favor of capital is a recurrent practice that continues to this day.

only a matter of redistributive processes and policies but, above all else, of direct intervention in the regulation of capital-labor relations that favor more egalitarian forms of power in the determination of wages, working conditions, and contracts, while at the same time defining various rights of labor and workers vis-à-vis capital.

In other words, it was the welfare state—and not the market—that made possible a distribution of surpluses and income based on criteria and principles of social security and labor protection through the promotion of a new configuration of the correlation of forces between capital and labor. What is relevant in this counter-argument, however, is that state intervention did not imply in any case the abandonment of the principles of profit and capital accumulation, undoubtedly necessary to maintain economic growth. On the contrary, the greatest achievement of this form of market regulation is manifested in the great growth and transformation of the developed economies in the post-war era. Likewise, the upturn in social inequality in recent decades—especially in the core countries—is also the result of the partial but progressive dismantling of these regulatory mechanisms and the implementation of a neoliberal economic model that is based on the Washington Consensus and the political strategy of giving markets complete freedom for their own self-regulation (Stiglitz, 2012).

Thus, the theoretical foundations of the inequality curve are quite different from those pointed out by Kuznets and the neoclassical approach. Likewise, the current trends of contemporary economic growth with increasing social inequality that characterize the developed world would be a total contradiction in terms of Kruznets' proposed model. How is it possible to explain from this model the realities experienced by the world economy in recent decades, where we have seen that once a level of development has been reached—formed on the basis of new economic and productive transformations—it leads, contradictorily, to an increase in inequality to levels even higher than those prevailing at the end of the nineteenth century and the beginning of the twentieth century. From this discussion, it is clear that it is not development that explains the trend in social inequality as the Kuznets curve seemed to dictate. It is, therefore, necessary to look for other arguments, determinants, and theoretical models to explain and understand the dynamics and forms of social inequality in capitalism.

Finally, and taking up the approaches of both microeconomics and the neoclassical school of growth theory with respect to inequality, we find an interesting contradiction in terms of the underlying conception of the phenomenon of inequality in both cases. In microeconomic approaches and in the neoclassical welfare theory itself, inequality is understood as an inevitable phenomenon;

it is not something desired, but neither is it something undesired: it simply exists and has its origin in innate differences between individuals. Unlike functionalist sociology—which emphasizes the inequality of socially defined positions—neoclassical economics emphasize the differentiation of individuals, particularly their productive capacities. The higher income of some is the result of greater aptitudes for work, which results in higher productivity. Differences in income are the result of a process of economic equity, which is enshrined above any ethical, moral, or political consideration of the social inequality that this may generate. In a way, inequality emerges as an inevitable but totally necessary phenomenon, since it constitutes both the best incentive for the improvement of people and their achievement of greater well-being.

This underlying conception contrasts with neoclassical approaches to inequality that are based on theories of growth and macroeconomics. In the models of Kuznets and Lewis, for example, it is evident that inequality is seen as an undesirable phenomenon that—although it could be understood as inevitable in certain circumstances—represents a problem to be solved, for which it is postulated that the best policy against inequality is the promotion of economic growth and development. In this sense, although the inevitability of inequality is accepted as fact, no legitimacy is attributed to it, to such an extent that it is assumed that in the horizon of economic growth inequality should be reduced to its minimum expression.

On the other hand, it is equally revealing that in both, microeconomic and macroeconomic approaches and those of growth theories, social inequality is confined to a matter of the individual order, that is, reduced to mere differences between individuals that are measured either by the remuneration and economic rewards received or by the distribution of income between individuals or families and not to a collective matter (social groups or classes). Class inequality is totally absent in these perspectives, both as a category of analysis and as a problem in itself. In fact, this absence corresponds to a historical-political condition that is typical of the post-war period, where a vision predominates economic perspectives of the time that denies the validity of class as a category of analysis and of the problematization not only of the phenomenon of social inequality but of any socio-economic problem.[4]

---

4 In the following chapter, we review and critique these approaches.

3 Gunnar Myrdal and the Principle of Circular and Cumulative Causation

In contrast to the neoclassical and functionalist models, Gunnar Myrdal turned the debate on its head when he proposed an analysis based on the mechanisms through which economic and social inequality is generated and reproduced, both at the international level and within each country. Myrdal's reflection is aimed at answering why some regions of the world develop while others remain underdeveloped as well as why conditions of ethnic and social inequality are perpetuated within societies, the latter exemplified in the case of racial discrimination in the United States.

In relation to unequal economic development, Myrdal argues that neither Ricardian international trade theory nor neoclassical economic theory can "provide much of an explanation in causal terms of how the fact of international economic inequalities have come into existence, and why there is a tendency for the inequalities to grow" (Myrdal, 1963: 9). The concept of stable equilibrium—a basic tenet in orthodox economic theory—is not only insufficient but also completely divorced from the processes of unequal development observed in the world economy.

According to neoclassical theory, differences in regional or national growth rates would tend to balance out with free trade and free mobility of production factors over time. Differences in productivity levels and factor endowments would be temporary issues, since to the extent that free competition and free international trade are encouraged market forces concur to establish macroeconomic equilibria.

In the first half of the 20th century, development economics—particularly driven by the work of Harrod (1939) and Domar (1946)—sought to explain how and why economic differences between countries, regions, and sectors are generated, as well as how and why they tend to reduce and disappear as market forces act freely. In the mid-twentieth century, A. Lewis (1954) put forward his thesis on economic growth in a scenario of structural differences in resource endowments and productivity levels. Even under these apparently unfavorable conditions, Lewis' model shows that the free circulation of factors of production is a sufficient condition for achieving economic growth in all regions and economic sectors.

In the same vein, it is worth mentioning the work of Solow (1956), who is perhaps the most cited author and obligatory reference in the field of economic growth and development. His work expanded on theories related to the dynamic extension of equilibrium in economies based on free competition and factor mobility (see León, 2013). Based on the assumption of diminishing marginal returns to capital, Solow points out that in an environment where technology is an exogenous factor freely available to all economies then all of them will tend in the long run to a situation of stable equilibrium.

The main critique of these neoclassical models is that they ultimately base growth and development on exogenous factors such as technology and innovation, from which their critics tactfully conclude that the models themselves lack a solid and consistent explanation of the economic bases that would drive economic growth, nor offer an adequate manner to explain the economic bases that generate, drive, and reproduce regional and sectoral inequalities in economic growth and development (Bastidas, 1996).

In contrast to these ideas, Myrdal puts forward the opposite thesis, according to which the market economy (capitalism) does not generate processes of economic convergence in the long term; on the contrary, the same mechanisms that drive development in a region or country and allow it to obtain some growth advantage over the rest will tend to sustain it over time, jump starting its growth and development so to speak. This is explained by the presence of *circular and cumulative causation* mechanisms that economic growth itself induces. More specifically, "migration, capital movements and trade are rather the media through which the cumulative process evolves -upwards in the lucky regions and downwards in the unlucky ones. In general, it they have positive results for the former, their effects on the latter are negative" (Myrdal, 1963: 27).

Like other economists of the time,[5] Myrdal considers that society and the economy are dynamic and changing, never static and even less stable. There are no equilibria but continuous imbalances, movements, and transformations that reproduce these imbalances and inequalities. In this sense, he distances himself completely from the theories of international trade—very much in vogue in those years as now—pointing out that they fail to offer a plausible causal explanation as to how and why international or interregional economic inequalities arise, let alone why these tendencies tend to increase cycle after cycle (Tomas Carpi, 1978). His critique is focused against the notion of general equilibrium, a basic and fundamental concept of neoclassical theory and its models of economic growth as we have already pointed out. For Myrdal (1963:22), this concept of general equilibrium seems to be "imbued with a teleological intent, and is related to powerful predilections, all rooted firmly in the

---

[5] Specifically, we refer to authors such as Paul Baran, Paul Sweezy, Joan Robinson, among others.

traditions of economic theory from its origins and in the philosophies which were, and continuously are, this theory's logical basis."

For him, the inadequacy of this perspective is why it fails to grasp the essence and basis of the constitution of social inequalities and economic imbalances in capitalist society. Social and economic disturbances do not generate reaction mechanisms that lead to the reestablishment of social and economic equilibria; this is because neither society nor the economy are governed by laws of self-stabilization, nor do they move by themselves towards any point of equilibrium and stability, but, on the contrary, they tend permanently to move away from such abstract positions and situations. Specifically, Myrdal (1963: 13, emphasis ours) points out that:

> The system is by itself not moving towards any sort of balance between forces, but is constantly on the move away from such situation. In the normal case a change does not call forth countervailing changes but, instead, supporting changes, which move the system in the same direction as the first change but much further. Because of such *circular causation* a social process tends to become *cumulative* and often to gather speed at an accelerating rate.

In this framework, he proposes the principle of *circular and cumulative causation* in opposition to the economic equilibrium approaches postulated by neoclassical models. For Myrdal (1963: 14, emphasis ours), the "essence of a social problem is that it is concerns a complex of interlocking, *circular* and *cumulative* changes." In this sense, the task that Myrdal imposes on himself, and bequeaths to all of us, is to unravel these circular and cumulative mechanisms present in every process of social change. Particularly interesting is the way in which Myrdal makes sense of this process. It is not just any process of interaction but a phenomenon of cumulative causation, based on a principle of circular interdependence. Both terms, *cumulative* and *circular*, give meaning to this principle of *causation*. Economic and social inequality at the global level—as well as at regional levels and between social classes—is explained by this principle:

1. On the one hand, there is a reciprocal causation between development and underdevelopment (poverty and wealth, welfare and precariousness, etc.). This circular causation makes one factor (development) the cause of its opposite (underdevelopment), and vice versa.
2. On the other hand, it is cumulative in the sense that development generates and *accumulates* development, while underdevelopment reproduces and *accumulates* underdevelopment. This unequal accumulation

is in turn caused (explained) by this development-underdevelopment circularity.

According to Myrdal, underdevelopment not only reproduces itself but in that same process causes the reproduction (accumulation) of development; inversely, development not only reproduces itself but in that same process causes the reproduction (accumulation) of underdevelopment. This is what we could call the principle of *cumulative circularity* on which the reproduction of economic inequality is based at the international and regional levels—as well as at the social level—in the reproduction of inequality and the class structure of each society.

It is evident that Myrdal's concern is not only the underdevelopment of some regions or inequality at the international and regional levels, but also how these situations are reproduced and perpetuated over time: why is it the case that in spite of the economic growth experienced by underdeveloped regions they remain underdeveloped? In fact, with few exceptions, the regions today classified as underdeveloped are practically the same as those that have existed since the nineteenth century and even before. And vice versa, the regions today classified as developed are practically the same as those we have identified for more than two centuries. Why is it the case that throughout these two centuries some regions have grown and accumulated development, while others have remained stagnant and accumulated underdevelopment?

In this respect, the proposal of *circular and cumulative causation* is based on a perspective of analysis that seeks to articulate and integrate in the same model of understanding the conditions of some (developed) with the conditions of others (underdeveloped); more precisely, as a theory it seeks to explain how the reproduction of the situation of development of some is influenced and conditioned by this relationship of inequality that opposes it to the situation of underdevelopment of others. Thus, the context—the relation of inequality—becomes a structuring factor in the reproduction of what some have and others do not; by this means, it becomes a factor of self-reproduction of itself as a context of inequality between developed and underdeveloped regions.

Myrdal had previously developed this same principle of circular and cumulative causation in his analysis of the racialized, social situation of African-American population in the United States (Myrdal, 1944). More than a decade before the civil rights mobilizations that changed the face of the country, he analyzed the persistence of white racism and its impact on the condition of discrimination and social exclusion affecting black populations. From his analysis, Myrdal establishes a model of dynamic interrelationships that allow him to explain and understand the reproduction of both the situation of privilege of some—the whites—and that of exclusion and discrimination of others—black populations. In this regard, Myrdal constructs his model on the basis of the reciprocal action and interaction of two factors: factor A, which would be the *prejudice of whites*, which sustains racial discrimination against blacks in its different forms; and factor B, which would be the *low standard of living* of the black population—that is, the condition of poverty, supposed patterns of behavior, and ways of life associated with this situation of vulnerability and social precariousness that is a consequence of the same ethnic discrimination to which it is subjected.[6] According to Myrdal (1944: 1066):

> We take, as given, a mutual relationship between our two variables, and we assume this relationship to be such a type that, on the one hand, the Negroes' plane of living is kept down by discrimination from the side of the whites, while, on the other hand, the whites' reason of discrimination is partly dependent upon the Negroes' plane of living. The Negroes' poverty, ignorance, superstition, slum dwellings, health deficiencies, dirty appearance, disorderly conduct, bad odor, and criminality stimulate and feed the antipathy of the whites for them.

This example vividly illustrates the operation of the two aforementioned principles: circular causation and cumulative causation:

1. In the case of the former, we see, on the one hand, that factor A (white prejudice) is caused by factor B (black poverty, behavior patterns, and lifestyles). But, in turn, factor A (prejudice) is a social condition that generates and causes factor B (ways of life). In this way, both factors determine each other reciprocally in a system of circular causation ad infinitum. It is "*a cumulative process* of mutual interaction in which the change in one factor would continuously be supported by the reaction of the other factor and so on in a circular way" (Myrdal, 1963: 16, emphasis ours).
2. This process is also *cumulative*, since this situation of inequality generated by the condition of ethnic-racial discrimination is self-reinforcing in two ways. At the first level, the initial positions reproduce themselves: the poverty of blacks causes them to reproduce themselves as poor, while the prejudices of whites reproduce their discrimination against blacks.

---

6 This is quite a useful model when thinking of inequality, although some of the language of Myrdal's initial proposal may a bit outdated.

At the second level, the reproduction of these initial positions mutually reproduces each other: as blacks accumulate poverty, behaviors, and lifestyles that oppose them to whites, this in turn causes whites to accumulate prejudices and behaviors that reproduce the condition of ethnic discrimination. Inversely, the accumulation of prejudice and discrimination on the part of whites causes their counterpart, blacks, to reproduce and accumulate poverty, lifestyles, etc. This makes the circular, interactive causation of one (racism and discrimination) and the other (precariousness and poverty) also cumulative of one and the other.

At some point, there was a tendency to associate this notion of circular and cumulative causation with the vicious circles or cycles idea expressed by both Winslow (1955) and Nurkse (1955). The former refers to a circular process in which a negative factor is both cause and effect of other negative factors. Such is the case of illness and poverty. The poor become sicker because they are poor, and as they become sicker, they remain poor, thus closing the vicious circle or cycle of poverty-illness-poverty.

For his part, Nurkse refers to the "vicious circle of poverty" to explain the underdevelopment of countries in contrast to developed countries, exemplifying it with the case of capital formation (Fontela and Guzmán, 2003). According to this author, underdeveloped countries have capital formation problems due to the persistence of a low level of real income. Without capital formation and capitalization, however, it is not possible to increase production nor the level of real income, thus closing the vicious circle that restricts the capacity for capitalization and economic growth in underdeveloped countries.

In his book *Economic Theory and Underdeveloped Regions*, Myrdal confronts these criticisms and points out that in both cases we are dealing with notions of an eventual vicious circle, but this fact or characteristic of development is far from constituting a general theory of development and underdevelopment, and in any case, the two propositions are theoretically and methodologically very distant from his proposal on circular and cumulative causation. Although the notion of a vicious circle makes it possible to highlight the causal circularity of a situation such as poverty or underdevelopment, it does not establish a relational system, that is, a comprehensive vision that accounts for the situation of poverty and underdevelopment beyond its own characteristics: deprivation, precariousness, vulnerability, among others. In other words, it is not true that poverty reproduces itself and even less so that this process is a circular and cumulative continuum. For Myrdal, circular and cumulative causation establishes a relational system, not a self-centered process. He establishes this both in his book on the situation of discrimination affecting the

African-American population in the United States (Myrdal, 1944), and when he analyzes the conditions of development and underdevelopment of economic regions worldwide (Myrdal, 1963).

Indeed, the great difference of Myrdal's proposal with respect to this traditional notion of the vicious circle is that, in his theorization, the particular situations of poverty of a social group, the condition of discrimination affecting African Americans, or the level of underdevelopment of a country or region, does not produce or reproduce themselves; in contrast, they are formulated in relation to what they are not, that is, to their opposites, with whom structures of relations and social, economic, and political inequality are established. This vision is what we believe gives a qualitative leap in Myrdal's proposal, since it allows us to understand the process of circular and cumulative causation as a mechanism of social reproduction at three simultaneous levels, namely:

1. the social reproduction of subjects and agents (classes, countries, regions);
2. the social reproduction of their situations and positions within a social structure—that is, as rich or poor subjects, developed or underdeveloped regions;
3. the reproduction of the system of social, economic, and political relations between these same subjects and social structures.

In the case of poverty, its reproduction is in opposition to the reproduction of wealth and welfare conditions of other social subjects. In the case of the African-American population, the reproduction of their situation of discrimination is in opposition to and in relation to the reproduction of the situation of social welfare and social privileges enjoyed by the white population in the United States. Finally, the reproduction of the conditions of underdevelopment in some regions of the world is in relation to and in opposition to the reproduction of the levels and conditions of development in other regions of the world. One cannot exist without the other.

In all these cases, what is relevant is not only the situation of each pole of the relationship—nor is it the reproduction of that situation in itself—but what is fundamental is the relationship that opposes and links them: the relationship that constitutes them as opposite poles and configures their positions in a social structure of inequality. It is not poverty that reproduces poverty: it is the position of the poor in relation and in opposition to the rich that reproduces poverty and, therefore, that produces and reproduces wealth. It is, in short, the structure of social inequality, the structure of classes, and class relations (domination, exploitation, subordination) that reproduces some and others and in the same process reproduces itself as a social structure.

Thus, what derives from this model of analysis is not the reproduction of the poor, purely and simply, nor the reproduction of the rich, but the reproduction of the system as a whole and, in particular, the reproduction of the social structure of differentiation and inequality between rich and poor. Thus, what circular and cumulative causation entails is not only the reproduction of one or the other, nor of their particular positions and situations (of wealth-well-being, of poverty-vulnerability), but what binds them together as a social whole—i.e., the social structure.

In the case of regional development-underdevelopment, the mechanism of circular and cumulative causation, then, refers to the reproduction of economic relations and unequal exchanges and transfers of value between some regions and others, which is, in short, what generates and reproduces the situation of development of some regions as opposed to the situation of underdevelopment of others. In this sense, the circular mechanism defines a cumulative process of structures and relations of inequality between some regions and others, inequality that is based on relations of exploitation and unequal exchange, among other mechanisms of economic relations.[7]

In the context of the social inequality structure between African-Americans and the white population in the United States, the principle of circular and cumulative causation not only perpetuates the privileged status of some (whites) and the vulnerability and lack of protection of others (African-Americans) but also reinforces the racialization of social inequality. This extends to the class structure, encompassing both its economic-productive foundations and its cultural, social, and political manifestations that uphold the system of prejudice and patterns of racial discrimination exercised by whites against African-Americans.

In all these cases, we see how the mechanism of circular causation defines cumulative processes of social, economic, and political inequality, whether between classes, ethnic groups, or economic regions. The reproduction of some is, at the same time, the reproduction of their opposites—their others— and the reproduction of both is the reproduction of the system of relations that places some in positions of privilege, well-being, and development, and

---

[7] Similar approaches would be developed a couple of decades later by Latin American dependency theorists. See F. Cardoso and E. Faletto, (1978), *Dependency and Development in Latin America*. Berkeley, University of California Press; F. Hinkelammert, (1972), *Dialéctica del desarrollo Desigual* [*Dialectic of uneven development*], Chile, Universidad Católica de Chile; A. Gunder Frank (1967), *Capitalism and underdevelopment in Latin America*, New York, Monthly Review Press; and R. M. Marini, (1977), *Dialéctica de la dependencia* [*Dialectic of Dependency*], México, Era.

others in positions of precariousness, lack of protection, and underdevelopment. It is not only the reproduction of the subjects and agents involved but also the reproduction of the structures that constitute and mutually link them; it is the reproduction of the system of inequality that constitutes them as subjects, classes, and regions.

CHAPTER 6

The Death of Class and the Historical Resilience of a Social Category

> So many times, they killed you, so many times, you will be resurrected.
>
> MARÍA ELENA WALSH

∴

The concept of *class* is one of the most controversial in the Social Sciences and in social and political analysis. Due to its origin and history, class refers directly to a positioning in relation to society, which is based on a complex interweaving of theory and politics, of moments of understanding and moments of praxis, which dilutes the limits between one and the other. When we talk and debate about classes, we will always be left with the question of when we stop talking about their theorization and when we move on to a political and ideological debate proper.

On various occasions and from different contexts and paradigms, its eventual historical death has been decreed in some cases, or theoretical obsolescence in others. However, from each decree of death, the *class* is resurrected to continue portraying—like no other category in social analysis—the histories of inequality in our societies. Paradoxically, there is no better indicator of the strength and relevance of class as a category of sociological analysis and social category of political praxis, than the permanent need of its antagonists—theoretical and political—to decree its death and historical overcoming.

However—and perhaps just as ironically—the resilience of the category lies not so much in its theoretical and methodological construction as in the fact that it is the product of social and historical processes. It is not so much the strength of Marxist theory as the stubbornness of society to bring *class* to the forefront of political and academic debate time and time again. Nothing seems to make more sense than the oft-quoted phrase that classes are constructed in class struggle. But not only in the sense attributed to it by Marx, but also in the fact that it is the same social conflict that causes class to be reborn again and again as a fundamental category of analysis to understand any class society.

In this sense, the resilience of the concept of *class*—as well as of the Marxist approach to its analysis—should not lead us to draw happy accounts in this regard. For one thing, we cannot but recognize that Marx's strength in theorizing on the formation of classes on the basis of the relations of production and exploitation contrasts with his theoretical weakness in analyzing and theorizing on the formation of those classes on the basis of the modes of political and social domination. As Lukács (1969: 46) points out, "Marx's chief work breaks off just as he is about to embark on the definition of class." This implies that Marx's references to class formation maintained a certain ambiguity that makes it difficult to study and describe the concept of classes used by him.

In this respect, Giddens (1975) helps to unravel this difficulty by pointing out that in Marx there would be at least two perspectives of analysis: on the one hand, an abstract or pure model of class domination, which applies to all class social modes and which normally implies a dichotomous notion of classes; and, on the other hand, descriptions of various levels of concreteness used to analyze particular characteristics of classes and class structure at particular times and in particular societies, as is the case of his analysis in works such as *The 18th Brumaire of Louis Bonaparte* or *The Civil War in France*. In this sense, the question to be resolved "is the relationship between the dichotomous class system presupposed by the abstract model, and the plurality of classes which, as Marx admits, exists in all historical forms of (class) society" (Giddens, 1975: 30). This is not a minor issue and in the face of which important discrepancies arise within Marxism itself. Some (Althusser, 2009; Poulantzas, 1975) emphasize the abstract model as a framework of analysis of the class struggle in capitalism. Others (Lukács, 1969; Gramsci, 1992; Luxemburg, 2020) opt for more complex views on the constitution of classes based on historical processes, where the conditions of economic and political domination are equally relevant, considering that classes and class struggle refer not only to a confrontation between exploiters and exploited but also to a political antagonism between oppressors and the oppressed (Giddens, 1975).

Considering the above, in this chapter we present a review of the debate on the so called, *death of class*, a thesis initially promoted by Nisbet, Davis, Dahrendorf, and others in the early post-war period, referring to the consolidation of industrial, Fordist, and welfare state capitalism; the thesis was later taken up again by Lipset, Pakulski, Waters, and others in the late 1980s in the context of the fall of socialism and the advent of a post-industrial and global capitalism. In the face of this thesis, we present various arguments that contribute to its debate and will allow us in the following chapters to take up again the proposal of Marxist and non-Marxist authors on the constitution of social classes in contemporary societies.

1 The Death of Class

In the 1950s, various attempts were made to decree the obsolescence of Marxism as a social theory and of class analysis as a valid sociological category for the understanding of contemporary society. This occurs in a context of consolidation of functionalism in American sociology, as well as a historical context characterized by the consolidation of industrial capitalism and Fordism and Keynesianism as regulatory frameworks of production and the economy. Further, this rhetoric appears during the formation of a welfare state as a framework for regulating the capital-labor relationship, as well as during the context of the Cold War, which resulted in the polarization not only of politics and society but also of the theoretical and sociological frameworks for analyzing it. Interestingly, those same years correspond to the three golden decades of capitalism, as Piketty (2014) calls them, a time when, in addition, class conflict in advanced societies is institutionalized in the frameworks of a society and economy of regulation, which drastically reduce its radicality and level of conflict (Boyer, 1992).

In those same years and in that context, Lipset (1960: 403, 406) even went so far as to question whether we might not be in the presence of "the end of ideology,"[1] thereby reflecting "the fact that the fundamental political problems of the industrial revolution have been solved," including in the first place the question of class struggle as formulated by Marx in the nineteenth century. For the time being, Lipset (ibid.) continues, in this capitalist society, "the workers have achieved industrial and political citizenship; the conservatives have accepted the welfare state; and the democratic left has recognized that an increase in over-all state power carries with it more dangers to freedom than solutions for economic problems." According to this thesis, everything would indicate that in this golden context of advanced capitalism a substantive and transcendental change in Western political life would have been consolidated, resolving all the problems and contradictions that would have characterized capitalism and that were theorized and questioned by its various critics.

---

1 It is no coincidence that this thesis is very similar to the one that 30 years later resurfaced under the format of postmodernity and neoconservative thought and which was synthesized in the phrase of the so-called "end of history," promulgated by Francis Fukuyama in 1992.

2   Argument 1. From Class Structure to Social Stratification

In the aforementioned context, several intellectuals questioned whether in view of the end of class differences experienced in these golden decades of capitalism we might not also be reaching the end of the political and partisan conflict between left and right. In this respect, Bullit (1959: 177) expressed it quite explicitly, when he pointed out that "the economic class system is disappearing, [and the] redistribution of wealth and income is compressing to a pancake the cone of economic ranks ... and the truncation of the tip has ended economic inequality's political significance."[2]

For his part, Nisbet (1959: 11) was equally precise and direct. Beyond the question of whether class is a good or bad category of social analysis—and even beyond whether it is good or bad that society is divided into social classes—for him the pertinent question was whether "can American society today reasonably and objectively be called a class society." He thought not, suggesting that changes in advanced societies already in those years made "the term social class useful for the time being in historical sociology, in comparative, or popular sociology, but of almost no value in analyzing the data on wealth, power, and social status in the United States and much of Western society in general."

Although he warns that his position does not imply any prejudice about the value of a class society or a classless society, it is evident that Nisbet's argument is based on a certain political and intellectual position regarding the concepts of social class as categories of analysis of society. In particular, it is an argument that goes directly against Marxism and the theories of social change to which it gave support. Nisbet, as well as other sociologists before and after him, attempt to question the validity of Marxist theory and, in particular, the class approach as an analytical framework for understanding social inequality. From functionalist and Weberian paradigms, they elaborate various proposals that seek to explain and analyze social inequality without including the class dimension but from other categories of social differentiation that are supposed to predominate in the structuring and formation of social inequality in the industrial societies of the time (1950s).

Given the similarities it presents, it is somewhat surprising that thirty years later in the context of the end of the Cold War, the fall of the Berlin Wall, and

---

2   In those year, Lipset (1960: 407) was more cautious and wondered if these authors were not confusing "the decline of ideology in the domestic politics of Western society with the ending of the class conflict which has sustained democratic controversy." Thirty years later, however, Lipset abandons this caution to adhere completely to the thesis of the end of class conflict, albeit now in the context of the advent of post-industrial society.

the collapse of real socialisms, as well as the advent of post-modern and post-industrial societies,—that is, in a context unthinkable in the 1950s, when those first attempts to declare the obsolescence of social class as a category of analysis became popular—the same arguments are reborn. In some cases, the arguments made were raised by the same authors as before, who were now raising once again the thesis of the death of social class.

However, they no longer claimed it was due to the effects of Keynesian capitalism of the welfare state but of global and postmodern capitalism. It was no longer attributed to the effects of the Fordist mode of industrial production but rather to the consolidation of a post-industrial and post-Fordist economy. Furthermore, it was no longer attributed to the consolidation of national states but rather to what has been their overcoming, a global economy in the midst of the Information Age.[3]

In this respect, Clark and Lipset (1991) are explicit in pointing out that at the time of their writing new forms of social stratification and the configuration of inequality are emerging that are not only substantially different from those that prevailed in the nineteenth century, which corresponds to the period analyzed and theorized by Marx and Weber, but also from those that characterized the industrial societies of much of the twentieth century. Returning to the thesis that Nisbet put forward 30 years earlier in the framework of industrial societies and with the regulatory capacity of the Welfare States, Clark and Lipset (1991: 397) again point out that:

> Social class was the key theme of past stratification work. Yet class is an increasingly outmoded concept, although it is sometimes appropriate to earlier historical periods. ... Class analysis has grown increasingly inadequate in recent decades as traditional hierarchies have declined and new social differences have emerged.

The decline of class as a structuring factor of social inequality and political conflict would be reflected in the multiplication of other forms of hierarchization of society, that is, the emergence of other dimensions from which differences in social status between individuals are constructed and which, therefore, determine the differentiated and unequal position of persons and subjects in society. As these authors point out, contemporary societies would

---

3 As can be seen, the social and historical context of the argument of the end of class and class analysis does not really matter, since it is a thesis based more on ideological paradigms about society and politics than on sociological and theoretical paradigms of understanding society and political conflict.

be characterized by a growing fragmentation of the forms of social stratification in advanced societies, which not only hinder the social and political constitution of large class formations, but also imply the fragmentation of the origins of social inequality and political conflict.

In other words, the fragmentation of the forms of social stratification reflects the decline of class relations in the determination of traditional forms of authority and social hierarchization, diluting their capacity as a category of analysis and explanation of the social and political behavior of individuals and social subjects. However, both authors are clear in pointing out that this decline of class as a factor that constructs and determines social conflict does not mean that conflict as such disappears, but that it is organized and reconstructed on the basis of other emerging factors and fields of social differentiation and inequality, such as, for example, gender (Clark and Lipset, 1991).

It is revealing, paradoxically enough, that in this discourse of the end of class, gender, race, religion, status, and other similar fields are appealed to as emerging factors of differentiation, when these are fields of social inequality and political conflict even as much or even earlier in history than social class itself. Indeed, neither gender nor race are emergent fields of social inequality any more than they are emergent as catalysts of social conflict. This would imply ignoring not centuries, but millennia of ethnic-racial conflicts (slavery, among them) as well as gender conflicts (*machismo* and patriarchy, to name but a few), not to mention religious conflicts and wars. The question remains as to how such obvious aspects can be overlooked in a scientific discourse that seeks to explain the origin of inequalities and antagonism in contemporary society.

3   Argument 2. From the End of Class to the End of Marxism

Although in their analysis Clark and Lipset refer to class analysis in general, the foundation of their critique is fundamentally oriented against the Marxist theory of social classes and class struggle, both as an approach to explain social inequality and as a category for analyzing social conflict in capitalism. In the same vein, Pakulski (1993: 282) points out that the thesis regarding the death of class does not refer to "the utility of any particular concept of class (however defined), but [to] the relevance and utility of the Marxist conceptual and theoretical tradition in analyses of stratification patterns, identity and political action in advanced societies."

According to this author, Marxism seeks to explain social inequality in capitalism by linking it to property patterns and labor relations.[4] On this basis, Marxism would identify the key generators of economic conflict, which would take shape in the now classic class struggle. In this regard, Pakulski points out three points that, for him, would be basic to Marx's concept of classes:

1. The centrality of labor and property relations, which form the class structure, in shaping social inequality, distribution of resources, benefits and privileges, status and power. Here, what Pakulski criticizes is the widely cited economic determinism that seems to characterize Marxism, thus adding to the same criticism that others even before him—and even from within Marxism itself from the likes of Luxemburg, Lukács, Gramsci, among others—have made of simplified and orthodox views of Marxism.

2. The centrality of the class structure in the formation of other social structures, acting as a matrix for social structuring. This also implies what Wright (2004 and 2015) calls as class formation, that is, the correspondence between a particular situation in the class structure that is constituted by certain patterns of social, political, and cultural behaviors of subjects. Here, the critique refers to a structural one, which assumes a necessary correspondence between the conditions of the infrastructure and its forms of representation at the level of the social superstructure—that is, the direct passage from class situation to class consciousness.

3. "The centrality of class structure in structuring social antagonism and overt conflict" (Pakulski, 2005: 154). By this he refers to the central place occupied by the class position in the participation of social conflict and class struggle, from which the impulse of revolutionary social change is constituted. The critique refers to the oversimplification of Marxism in the face of the complexity assumed by social conflict and political antagonism in contemporary societies, which go beyond the simple bourgeoisie versus proletariat contraposition, however fundamental they may be for industrial capitalism.

---

4 Although Pakulski (1993) does not explicitly point it out or describe it, he is referring here to the ownership of the means of production and the salaried means of production and the salaried labor force as a system of labor relations between capital and labor. It should be noted, however, that the failure to mention these terms and ideas explicitly is not accidental but rather reflects a certain confusion and misunderstanding of the Marxist theoretical framework itself. We will see this in more detail later on.

In his critique of Marxism, Pakulski points out that this paradigm of social inequality and class conflict competes with other theoretical frameworks that from non-classist approaches and analyses offer alternative explanations of both social inequality and the forms of social and political conflict in advanced societies. These approaches are based on the proposals of Weber, Durkheim, Tocqueville, and other authors. On the one hand, it refers to theories that replace the class approach with approaches to occupational stratification and the division of labor based on the dynamics of labor markets. On the other hand, it also refers to theories that locate the sources of social inequality not in class but in other social categories such as gender, race, or ethnic-national identity. Finally, it refers to theories that explain the concentration of political power (and discrimination and domination) not on the basis of social class but in the organizational hierarchies of authority and the social tensions and struggles that accompany them.

Taking up these authors and these alternative theories, Pakulski questions the validity and relevance of Marxist class analysis, insofar as, according to this author, this approach assumes that class, being an essentially economic phenomenon, is also expressed in patterns of social grouping and collective action. Thus, "class location is reflected in social consciousness, identity, and antagonism, and ... it generates forms of action in the economic and the political fields that have a potential to transform capitalism" (Pakulski, 2005: 152).[5]

Based on this definition of Marxist class theory, Pakulski proposes two planes from which its eventual historical obsolescence and eventual theoretical death (theoretical overcoming, we would say, rather) can be sustained: its empirical validity—its contrast with concrete social processes—and its analytical capacity as a category that accounts for and explains social inequality,

---

5 In this definition, Pakulski falls into an important conceptual error. For him, class consciousness derives directly from the position of groups in the class structure, when according to the Marxist approach—and in this agree the structuralist Marxists such as Althusser, Poulantzas, and others such as the critical Marxists like Lukacs, Gramsci, and Luxemburg—class consciousness is constructed precisely from social processes and the conflict and antagonism of class. In a word, class consciousness is constructed in the class struggle, thus establishing that in the social relations of production, although it has an economic-productive base, its constitution as a social phenomenon takes place in the political and social field, and it occurs as a social and historical construction—that is, its constitution is also determined by the historical conditions that define the forms adopted by social conflict and class antagonism. This implies that the passage from one field to another (economic-productive to socio-political) is not direct but mediated by other historical, cultural, and political processes (Lukács, 1969). We will return to this examination of Pakulski's critique later on.

as well as social and political conflict and antagonism. In both cases, Marxist class theory would show an eventual disadvantage vis-à-vis other theoretical schemes, especially for analyzing inequality and conflict in contemporary societies.

Regarding the first point, Nisbet (1959), Clark and Lipset (1991), and Pakulski (1993, 2005) agree that Marxism and the theory of social classes were perhaps an adequate framework of analysis for the understanding of past societies, including industrial capitalism, but that they do not constitute a valid and pertinent theoretical and methodological tool for the analysis and understanding of contemporary societies. Social transformations and the advent of post-modern, post-industrial, and globalized societies have rendered Marxism's categories of analysis—constructed and developed for other historical and social contexts—obsolete.

We have already seen the critique of Nisbet, who described Marxism as useful only for historical sociological analysis but of no value for the analysis of modern societies. For his part, Pakulski is clearer and more precise in this thesis. He proposes to reduce class as a category circumscribed to a particular historical mode. According to him, "this involves locating class within a historical-developmental sequence as a particular social configuration of inequality typical of the industrial era. ... [T]herefore the relevance of class analysis, var[ies] historically. ... 'Classness' reached its peak in industrial society and has been declining while postindustrial and postmodern trends intensify. Contemporary advanced societies remain unequal, but in a classless way. These increasingly complex configurations of classless inequality and antagonism ... call for more comprehensive theoretical and analytic constructs"(Pakulski, 2005: 154).

4 Argument 3. The Historical Obsolescence of Class

This critique of the obsolescence of Marxism leads us to the second point made by Pakulski, which refers to the forms of inequality and political antagonism in contemporary advanced societies. In this respect, both Clark and Lipset and Pakulski agree that the main characteristic of postmodern and post-industrial societies refers to the decline of the traditional forms of social inequality (classes) and the emergence of new matrices from which social inequality and political conflict and antagonism are constituted and take shape in modern societies, where the keynote is the reduction of the level of confrontation, on the one hand, and the fragmentation and proliferation of various mechanisms of social differentiation and political action of the subjects, on the other.[6]

On this plane, it is Clark and Lipset (1991) who make a more solid and complex analysis, proposing their thesis on the fragmentation of the class structure. For these authors, social stratification and the construction of hierarchical differentiations in advanced societies cannot be reduced to such a simplistic scheme of capitalist-worker conflict, when both (entrepreneurs, capitalists, as well as workers and employees) face diverse processes of fragmentation and differentiation, which cannot be reduced or explained by the basic categories of class (workers and capitalists). Following Giddens (1975), the basic argument of these two authors is that both social inequality and political conflict have multidimensional bases in which class (considered as a mere economic basis) seems to have less and less explanatory capacity. In this respect, these authors highlight both the changes in occupational stratification within the workplace and the transformations in social relations outside the workplace, which are increasingly important for the configuration of stratification and social inequality.

This fragmentation of the class structure leads to an eventual decomposition of classes in post-industrial and post-modern Western societies, giving rise to new social strata and, fundamentally, new stratification patterns that increasingly diversify and complexify the social structure. In this regard, different factors that contribute to this greater complexity of social stratification are usually mentioned. In our case, we have organized them into two large groups: (1) those that refer to changes in the relationship between ownership of the means of production and domination and hegemony of the labor process and society; (2) those that refer to new components and factors of social distinction and differentiation that go beyond ownership of the means of production or wage-earning of the labor force.

In the first group, four situations are worth mentioning:

1. The growing weight and importance of a new class of managers, business executives and CEOs of large corporations, professionals and high-level technical personnel, commonly referred to as an emerging corporate class (Urrutia León, 2017) or as an emerging transnational elite (Sassen, 2007). Without directly owning the means of production and capital, this

---

6 As we mentioned earlier, it is curious that Nisbet in 1959—more than nearly 30 years before these other authors discussed above—proposed very similar arguments, however referring not to the post-industrial society that was still not emergent at the time but, rather, to industrial capitalism and the welfare state that predominated in those decades in advanced societies.

is a class that exercises the greatest economic power at the global level, which questions the thesis that it would be property the basis and origin of power.
2. The anonymization of property, especially of large corporations, where capital is no longer directly identified with an individual or their family but with conglomerates formed by large shareholders. In this case, large ownership not only persists but has increased its concentration. However, it no longer refers to specific individuals but to large shareholders and owners who act not directly but through their intermediaries on the boards of directors of these large conglomerates, allied to the new corporate class formed by top executives.
3. Also noteworthy is the proliferation of both small autonomous owners of different types who are oriented towards the provision of highly specialized services (information technology, knowledge industry, and the like) and small and medium-sized family businesses formed with small capital and oriented towards the provision of services and trade subordinated to larger companies.
4. Finally, equally important are the changes within the proletariat. What is relevant here is the growing internal heterogeneity of the working class, which is manifested in employment inequality reflecting differences in access to social protection systems, contractual regulation, and labor flexibility. In post-industrial and global societies—along with the decline (but not disappearance) of the traditional industrial working class—there is an increase of new labor subjects, or workers, immersed in conditions of high labor precariousness. They are what Standing (2011) calls *precariat,* a term that combines the precarious and the proletarian form of the worker, or what Sassen (2007) refers to as a new global class of the disadvantaged. This is a heterogeneous collective in formation, but like the collectives of the corporate class, they are part of the new global forms of production and accumulation. What is relevant is that the wage relationship, while defining a situation of exploitation, does not, however, generate a direct link between capital and labor, as was the case with the industrial proletariat. The highly flexible forms of labor—subcontracting, relocation of industrial plants, and exportation of jobs—end up weakening the link of the direct worker with their means of work and the work process itself. Thus, wage-earning does not ensure a social or occupational status and by the same token implies a greater weakness and fragmentation in their links within the particular society to which this group of workers belongs.

In these four cases, the traditional way of configuring class—defined on the basis of subject relationships with the means of production—no longer seems to be sufficient to describe and analyze it. It is this situation that leads these authors (Clark and Lipset, Pakulski, Nisbet and others) to propose the disuse of class as a category of analysis. However, as we have seen, this seems to be real nonsense, insofar as it is precisely the changes in the forms of property and in the reconfiguration of social relations within the labor process that are giving rise to these new social forms of class. In other words, the forms of exploitation of labor by capital have undoubtedly been transformed, but this in no way implies that all forms of exploitation of labor by capital have been eliminated, and, therefore, the eventual disuse and decline of class as a category of analysis of social inequality cannot be concluded from these changes. We will return to this argument later.

In relation to the second group, three other situations should be noted:

1. The growing importance of education and higher education for the accreditation and credentialing of skills and the professionalization of occupations, generating new modes of distribution and concentration of privileges, benefits, and income from work. This, in turn, means that access to these benefits and privileges is no longer necessarily dependent on the social class of origin but on the merits and capabilities of each individual, all of which is supported by a greater intensity of social mobility (Goldthorpe, 2012).

2. The growing importance of consumption as a factor of social differentiation and the configuration of forms of inequality and distinction among the population. If in industrial society, stratification was marked and determined by the position of individuals in the production process; in post-industrial society, stratification is determined by their position in the sphere of consumption and the market. Likewise, a fundamental feature of postmodern society is that consumption ceases to be a function of the satisfaction of material and concrete needs, and what becomes relevant is the object of consumption—to become above all a symbolic relationship—where through consumption forms of representation and social and cultural differentiation between subjects are constructed (Baudrillard, 1981). The consumer society ceases to have shear economic meaning attributed to it as it once did, moving to acquire a sociological and cultural sense that is typical of postmodernism, where consumption—like society itself—becomes a liquid process in constant flow and becoming but also in a constant dilution and fading of the same social existence of the subjects (Bauman, 2000). Consumption only satisfies consumption, no longer the consumer,

although in this process it continues to valorize capital and increase the capitalist's profits. What is relevant, in any case, is that this postmodern consumption—individualized and liquid—contributes to dilute the traditional forms of social stratification to reproduce them as forms of social differentiation and socio-cultural distinction (Bourdieu, 1984). Class is no longer given by position in production but by distinction in consumption.

3. Finally, in contemporary societies, other fields of inequality, conflicts, and antagonisms emerge that are not necessarily based on the division of society into social classes. Gender, race, citizenship, human rights, among many others, are new forms of social inequality. It is not that these forms of inequality were not present before, but that their manifestation as such would always have been mediated by the realities of class and subordinated to the preeminence of the class approach to inequality. Indeed, gender, race, citizenship, among others, are forms of social discrimination and political domination, which are not necessarily constituted on the basis of the relations of production—i.e., the forms of property and labor—but rather can influence them, configuring, in some cases, diverse forms of racialization of occupational structures, as well as in other contexts forms of sexual division of labor. In both cases, ethnic, gender, and/or citizenship conditions, for example, tend to present themselves increasingly as forms of inequality that affect and determine access to work opportunities and ownership of means of production, as well as forms of discrimination in terms of options and access to political and social power and the social mobility of individuals. Around these axes of differentiation and inequality, various social and political movements tend to be formed, which acquire great capacity to influence social and political conflict, reconfiguring the traditional class struggle between capital and labor. Social and political struggles no longer necessarily pass through the capital-labor antagonism but through other forms of social antagonisms, such as the recognition of difference (Fraser, 1995). To this must be added the emergence of virtual and global communities that are supported by new information and communication technologies and constituted around supranational issues, such as the environment, the health of populations, and other phenomena that arise with the same economic globalization. This leads to the formation of groups with interests and political positions and social behaviors that do not depend directly or indirectly on the class origin of individuals, nor on the capital-labor antagonism.

5   Class Is Dead, Long Live Class!

Undoubtedly, all these processes described above are real and refer to dynamics and transformations inherent to contemporary societies. In general, they refer to the transition towards postmodern and post-industrial societies within the framework of the globalization of contemporary capitalism (Beck, 1998; Harvey, 2010). However, none of these trends and transformations characteristic of contemporary societies necessarily implies the abandonment of the centrality of class in the configuration of both social inequality and social and political antagonisms. To propose the end of class—that is, the death of a social category to analyze and understand the forms of social inequality in today's world—entails the risk of falling into visions of society as "sheer heterogeneity, random difference, a coexistence of a host of distinct forces whose effectivity is undecidable" (Jameson, 1991: 6). This would lead us to an analysis and description of contemporary social phenomena (inequality and social antagonism, for example) without the possibility of unraveling their genesis, without referring to anything beyond their changing and random morphology.

Face with the transcendental question of what explains social inequality, the problem is that approaches to the decline of class only offer descriptions and proposals that allow locating and classifying people into different social strata based on status criteria, behavioral patterns, aspirations, and other similar indicators, when what is really important is to transcend these *ad hoc* descriptions and stratifications in order to "identify ... causal mechanisms that help determine salient features of that system [as inequality]" (Wright, 2005: 185). No one doubts or denies the existence of social inequality. However, the question at bottom of this discussion remains to what extent class retains its explanatory power and understanding of social inequality.

In contrast to these former approaches, there are many other authors who point, on the contrary, to the persistence of class as an explanatory factor of social inequality, as well as of class conflict and antagonism in advanced societies. In this regard, Giddens (1998: 364) supports this thesis, explicitly pointing out that "class divisions are crucial in the economic inequalities of modern societies," although he adds that social inequality is not only of class but also of gender, race, citizenship, geography, and other dimensions, to which he devotes several chapters and sections in his work *Sociology*.[7]

---

7   We review Giddens' analysis in more detail below, taking up his text on class structure in contemporary capitalism, as well as his critique of the Marxist approach.

Likewise, for Requena and Stanek (2015), social class does not cease to be one of the crucial variables for understanding inequalities in contemporary society. In particular, in their study on the case of Spain, they show "how location in the class structure conditions people's life opportunities in terms of their education, employment status, income and health" (490, our translation).

Likewise, Therborn (2013) points to social class as one of the main types of inequality, which is expressed in inequality in terms of the resources available to the different social strata, resulting in inequality of opportunities and social mobility. This author (2013: 57) points out four mechanisms through which social inequality is constructed in advanced societies. Among them he mentions "inequality by exploitation", that is, inequality based on the fact that "capitalist production is built on the asymmetrical appropriation of the fruits of human labor" and, therefore, on the configuration of differentiated social classes structured on the basis of these asymmetrical relations, which originate in the access or deprivation of private property—in this case, of the means of production. As an example, Therborn (ibid) specifically points out that no one could deny "that the workers of Chinese, Bangladeshi or other tricontinental sweatshops producing for Walmart and other American or European retailers and brands are exploited."

In addition to reinforcing the thesis of the persistence and relevance of social class, this quote is interesting because it allows us to illustrate a form of exploitation of labor that is very characteristic of post-industrial society. This facet of contemporary post-industrial society is, nevertheless, systematically made invisible in the thesis on the decline of class as a category of analysis, despite the fact that this same thesis is supported by the recent transformations brought about by post-industrial society itself. As we have pointed out in other works (Canales, 2019; Castillo, 2016), the exploitation of labor carried out by large transnational entities no longer refers solely and primarily to the local labor force of advanced societies, but to a type of globalized proletariat. In other words, the globalization of capital brings with it the globalization of forms of exploitation, hence the globalization of the labor force and of the proletariat. It is paradoxical that the same process (the development of the post-industrial economy) that was thought to imply the decline of class antagonism and the decline of the proletariat as a class is, in reality, what is actually doing its reconfiguration as a global category. In fact, the processes of industrial relocation from the central to the peripheral economies, while implying a significant reduction of the industrial working class in advanced societies, actually corresponds to a relocation of that subject to the peripheral economies. However, we must not overlook the fact that it is a reconfiguration under a very different format, especially in terms of their working conditions and constitution as a social class as a proletariat, whose main characteristic is precisely an increase in the levels of exploitation to which they are exposed as a working class for capital.

For his part, Urrutia León (2017) offers an interdisciplinary perspective that takes up different texts that seek to analyze social inequality vis-à-vis criminality, health and death, education, and social mobility, coming to the conclusion that all these separate analyses could never account for the forms of global inequality if they ignored an analysis of the class condition of the subjects involved. In other words, "social class continues to be a major determinant of life chances for many people throughout the global world" (75, our translation).

In this debate on the existence or not of social classes, we cannot fail to mention Bourdieu's proposal. As a way out of the impasse involved in discerning whether classes are part of social reality or whether, on the contrary, they are a theoretical construct, Bourdieu (1987: 4) appeals to the concept of multidimensional social space, whose structure "is given by the distribution of the various forms of capital, that is, by the distribution of the properties which are active within the universe under study—those properties capable of conferring strength, power and consequently profit on their holder." In this sense, the economy and its productive and distributive structures (classes), although undoubtedly necessary, are not in themselves sufficient to understand the reproduction of the class structure in modern society. Likewise, social, cultural and symbolic structures—the bases of the formation and distribution of the corresponding capitals—are as necessary as they are insufficient in themselves to account for the reproduction of social inequality in contemporary societies.

Faced with this, the need arises to incorporate into the same analytical and conceptual framework the set of dimensions and spheres of social life that shape and give meaning to social reproduction. This is a framework of analysis that is built from a vision of totality—that is, of the articulations of the different dimensions that make up the social space. A framework of analysis where class (economy) is not only production relations but also kinship relations, marriages, fertility, family structures, education, inheritance systems, symbolic and cultural structures, among many other things, and where all of them are equally bearers of structures of inequality (Bourdieu, 1990).

We could continue citing other authors who reinforce and vindicate the role of class as a category of analysis of social inequality in the era of global capitalism, but we believe that this would be redundant.[8] In this sense, we are rather

---

8 See, for example, the texts of Castells (2020), Sassen (2007), Piketty (2015), Carroll and Sapinski (2016), Stiglitz (2012), among others.

interested in presenting a series of arguments from which we refute both the scope and the theoretical underpinning of the thesis of the decline and decay of class as a sociological category. Rather than presenting arguments in favor of class, we would like to refute the arguments that Pakulski and other authors elaborate to support their attempt to decree the death of class as a sociological category and, with it, of Marxism as a social theory.

6   The Death of Class: Ideology or Theory?

As Bourdieu (1987: 2) points out, class analysis is one of the major principles of division within the political field. For the same reason when faced with the question of the existence or not of classes and, therefore, of their validity as a category of analysis, every possible answer rests on political options. In this case, the question does not pertain to whether or not the proposal on the death of the class is based on a political and ideological position vis-à-vis the class itself, but, rather, how much of that position is traversed and constructed by these ideological principles and how much by theoretical and methodological arguments as such.[9]

In our view, the argument of the death of class has been constructed on the basis of a political-ideological distortion that leads it to confuse a legitimate critique of Marxism as a theoretical framework and political proposal, with a critique of a category of analysis that arises before Marxism and that has a theoretical-methodological validity that transcends it. In this sense, our first point of critique is oriented to unveil this political-ideological distortion behind the critique of Marxism and the eventual "death sentence" of the class.

Although Clark and Lipset are somewhat ambiguous and include their critique of Marxism in a more general critique of the concept of class, including Weber to some extent in their discussion, it is clear that in their reconstruction of the analysis of inequality and social conflict they recover substantive elements of Weberian thought. On the contrary, Pakulski is more explicit in pointing out that his critique is fundamentally directed at Marxist class theory as a theory of social inequality, placing special emphasis on the eventual obsolescence of the thesis that links the structuring of social inequality and political antagonism in the configuration of the class structure that arises from

---

9 For one thing, it is suspicious that those who speak of the death of class are referring only to the subordinate classes, annulling any reference to the ruling classes. This curious oversight is indicative of the class character of the political-ideological position that underlies the named "theoretical" move towards the death of the class and class struggle.

property relations with the means of production. According to Pakulski (1993 and 2004) and Pakulski and Waters (1996), in contemporary societies (postmodern and post-industrial) social inequality and political antagonism would no longer be explained by the relationship of subjects with the means of production, but by other fields and dimensions of society such as social status, consumption, culture, or education.

We argue that this argumentation and critique suffers from a double flaw. On the one hand, it attributes to Marxism the origin of class as a category of analysis and, in particular, its constitution on the basis of property relations. On the other, it overestimates the weight of the transformations of contemporary society and their eventual impact on the structuring of classes in global and post-industrial capitalism. Here we will focus on the first of these failures, leaving the second for later.

Although class is usually associated as an essentially Marxist category, the truth is that Marx was not the first to sustain the thesis that both social inequality and the structuring of society into social classes arise from private property. As we have argued and described in previous chapters, much before the writings of Marx, Rousseau pointed out that same thesis and used it to analyze social inequality throughout history. Likewise, Aristotle argued the role of property in the constitution of classes, estates, and social strata in Ancient Greece. Let's start with the latter.

Aristotle (2012) held as natural the division of society into social classes. In the field of the *OIKOS*—of the household economy and the homestead—inequality is given by property relations. The father, as well as the master, embodies the ownership of the means of production and even of the forms of labor (slaves). Likewise, in the field of the *POLIS*, property relations reappear not only as a division between free citizens and non-citizens but even within the former also as a division between rich and poor—that is, between those who live off the labor of others and those who live off their own labor (laborers, day laborers, etc.). The conjunction of one field and the other—of the *OIKOS* and the *POLIS*—is established in Aristotle's idea that the government of the *POLIS* should preferably fall on citizens who enjoy full economic self-sufficiency; or, put in another way, those who, based on their property, have the possibility of dominating others so that with their work they can provide them with material sustenance and, thus, have all the time necessary and be free of all material concerns to devote to the proper cultivation of the virtues necessary for the good government of the *POLIS* (Campilo, 2012).

If Aristotle thought that social inequality and the formation of classes were something natural to any society, Rousseau proposes the opposite thesis, pointing out that class inequality is a social construct that arose historically with the emergence of private property—that is, when some men exercised the right to property, depriving others of access to land and other means. Rousseau's *Discourse*[10] (Rousseau, 1761) is essentially a rational argument against religious views that posed a divine origin of inequality. For him, inequality—as well as other social institutions—arise from historical processes and social conventions constituted on the basis of differences of power and domination of some over others. Among these differences and power relations, he points to private property as one of the fundamental ones, insofar as when it arises and is constituted it is what gives rise to the constitution of civil society as such—that is, as a social form that is substantially distanced and differentiated from the communitarian forms of primitive and natural societies.

When private property is constituted, civil society is founded. This is the thesis with which Rousseau begins the second part of his essay. But property does not arise as a spontaneous or random process. It is the product of the development and control of the productive forces—that is, of the capacity of human beings to generate productive surpluses beyond those necessary for their direct and indirect maintenance. As Rousseau (1761: 97–98) explicitly points out:

> [T]he idea of property depends on several prior ideas which could only spring up gradually one after another, it was not formed all at once in the human mind: Men must have a great progress; they must have acquired a great stock of industry and knowledge, and transmitted and increased it from age to age before they could arrive at this last term of the state of nature.

It is this conjunction of *progress, industry,* and *knowledge (enlightenment)* that gave rise to economic forms of surplus generation and opened the way for the formation of various forms of social division of labor. Progress and industry allowed the surpluses generated to give way to forms of division of labor that were no longer based on strictly natural factors (direct domination of the strongest) but on social forms—that is, forms of domination of the most powerful both in terms of the social forms of labor (slave, servitude, salaried) and also in the sexual division of labor between men and women (Rousseau, 1761: 107). In all these cases, it is not the strongest but the most powerful who

---

10 I refer to the text *Discourse on the Origin and Foundations of Inequality among Men* (1761) in which Rousseau sets out his approach to the social and historical origin of inequality.

dominates, and power ceases to be a matter of natural forces to become one of social and political relations.

With the generation of surpluses and the social division of labor that this makes possible, the foundations are laid for the emergence of private property. Property and surpluses allow some to appropriate the labor of others, generating various types of bonds and dependencies among them. Thus, the bonds of servitude, for example, arose only when the situation of some did not allow them to survive without depending on others, and this occurred when they had been deprived of the means necessary to sustain their own reproduction— that is, when private property of the means, land, and the product of labor had arisen and been implemented, and, therefore, there was nothing left for them but to work for others. The social form of this work for others varies historically, but in all epochs, the same relation of exploitation is maintained: one of appropriation by some of the labor surplus of others.

This asymmetrical situation vis-à-vis property is the basis of social inequality and the formation of social classes. These are forms of inequality that go far beyond the natural forms of differentiation and inequality among sheer individuals. The concentration of means, land, and labor expresses at the same time concentration of power of some over others—of owners over nonowners—generating not only relations of exploitation but also of domination and discrimination in terms of access to benefits and privileges, power and wealth. This distancing in the conditions and situations of bodies leads, therefore, to processes of dehumanization that contradict and threaten the essence of the human spirit. In this way, human civilizations, with all their development and gain in economic terms, of sciences and philosophy, with all their progress, their industry and their enlightenment, end up losing their humanity (Rousseau, 1761). The equality that prevailed in the natural world of the human being is transformed into inequality in the social world that "civilized" it.

This thesis of class inequality—and its foundation in the private ownership of the means of production and the appropriation of the labor of others— went from being an Aristotelian argument to a Rousseauian one and later a Marxian one. It is evident that what differentiates one from the other is not the thesis of classes and class structure as a factor of articulation of society, nor the thesis that the structuring of classes arises from private property and, in particular, from the appropriation of the labor of others. What differentiates them, rather, is their corollary—that is, the conclusion they reach from this thesis on the constitution of societies as intrinsically unequal and classist. While Aristotle saw class inequality as a natural form of every society, which even allowed the achievement of forms of good government and, by that means, the attainment of human happiness, Rousseau saw the opposite, characterized by forms of alienation and dehumanization, which distanced human beings from the equality and equity proper to their original communities, from their natural life. Marx, on the other hand, saw in the structuring of society into social classes the necessary force that allows the development and evolution of human history. This force takes shape in the widely known and a thousand times cited thesis of the class struggle as the motor of history.

This conclusion is relevant to our discussion since it allows us to situate the real scope of Pakulski's and others' critique of Marxist class theory. At bottom, their critique is not so much directed at class as the foundation of social inequality as it is at Marx's reading of that foundation to support his theory of social conflict and political antagonism. The problem is that in attempting to question this Marxist corollary of class theory they end up rejecting the entire premise of class. In a certain way, this critique of the class struggle ends up disguised as a critique of the theory of classes. Which, again, is nonsense, since it only serves to clothe an eminently political and ideological discourse in theory, thus discarding the categories of analysis that would allow an adequate understanding of society even from conservative positions, as Aristotle himself did in his time. Undoubtedly, it is totally legitimate to disagree with Marx and to confront Marxism both in terms of its theoretical and methodological positions and in terms of its political and ideological approaches. What is not valid, however, is to want to pass off one critique as another—that is, to want to pass off an ideological critique as a theoretical one. These are different planes of thought and action that require very different forms of argumentation and intellectual construction—as much as the distance that separates science from politics—and this is for two main reasons:

1. The theory of private property and the appropriation of the labor of others as the foundation and origin of classes comes from Aristotle to Rousseau. This does not give more validity or legitimacy to the argument of classes, but it does detract from the validity and legitimacy of its criticism and "death sentence" when this is done by distorting the origin of such theory. For one thing, the least that would have been expected from a frontal critique of the theory of class is to recognize its historical origin. The problem is that in doing so they would have had to recognize that it comes from conservative thought (Aristotle), liberal thought (Rousseau), and socialist thought (Marx), something too complex to articulate in such a "radical" critique of a concept.
2. The critique of class struggle can be maintained even if we continue to think that classes have their origin in relations of exploitation. This has been developed by Giddens and other non-Marxist authors with a much greater elegance and depth than that presented by Pakulski and others.

It is to argue that social conflict and political antagonism have origins that go beyond social classes. In other words, while class status vis-à-vis property and exploitation is fundamental, it is not the sole determinant of social inequality. Bourdieu, Tilly, and others have made the same point with great intellectual depth and stature without the need to fall into theoretical reductions of the debate on class, inequality, and politics.

In summary, the critique of Pakulski and other authors discussed above is essentially ideological and, paradoxically, very similar to its other side, that is, the critique that from the left and official communism was usually made to Western sociological schools non-Marxist, qualifying them as *bourgeois science*. In both cases, it is an attempt to disqualify the other. The difference is that, while from Marxism the qualification of "bourgeois sciences" was made precisely to endorse that it was an ideological confrontation, those who propose the *death of Marxism* do so disguising their political confrontation as a theoretical critique. What is criticized is not the theory itself, but the political-ideological position that sustains that theory. In both examples, the critique is not based on logical, historical, or empirical arguments, but on foundations closer to political philosophy. In both cases, it is not theoretical critique but a form of theoretical confrontation with a political and ideological opponent. In Pakulski's case, it is not by chance that the term used is that of the "death" of a theory and not that of theoretical refutation, overcoming, or obsolescence, which would be more in line with a scientific debate. It is a discourse that reflects more the conditions and interests of a political and philosophical confrontation than a debate of scientific ideas and theories.

7 Critique of the Alleged Obsolescence of Class Analysis

Another argument that is often reiterated as a critique of social class is its supposed historical obsolescence. Already in the 1940s and 1950s, Nisbet (1959), together with Davis and Moore (1945), pointed out that if the term social class retained any usefulness, it was only in the context of historical sociological analysis. This was supposedly because class no longer seemed to have heuristic value for understanding and analyzing social inequality, stratification, and social antagonisms in modern industrial societies. Thirty years later, Clark and Lipset (1991), referring to post-industrial society, point to the same argument, qualifying both, Marxism and class analysis, as an "outmoded" mode of analysis that would only be valid for previous historical periods, no longer for contemporary advanced societies. Likewise, Pakulski and Waters (1996) and Pakulski (1993 and 2005), while recognizing that this is a questionable argument, end up enthusiastically joining this approach to the supposed historical obsolescence of Marxism and class theory for the analysis of contemporary society.

In the same line of reflection but from a different field of analysis, Drucker (1993) addresses some key changes in contemporary society that leads him to propose the advent not only of a post-industrial and post-modern society, but even a post-capitalist one, both in terms of the organization of production and the organization of society and politics. According to this author, we would be arriving at a social structure based on new categories of social stratification, whose nucleus of organization would be knowledge as a productive resource that would replace capital, land, and labor in the control and organization of the production process. In this way, private ownership of the means of production would cease to be the axis around which social classes would be constituted, instead to be replaced by the role of knowledge as a factor of production in itself (1993: 11). The obsolescence of Marxism, as well as of Rousseaunian thought, is thus declared. Without property, classes cease to be the factor on which the social structure rests, and with it, the class struggle will have become a concept in total disuse.

However, beyond the attractiveness of his rhetoric, Drucker does not develop or conceptualize a fundamental aspect in his argumentation: what constitutes a society as capitalist and what would make the current era a post-capitalist era. In this respect, his thesis is ambiguous and superficial, to the point that he affirms that capitalism has existed practically forever. Textually, he states (1993: 20) that:

> capitalism, in one form or another, has occurred and reoccurred many times throughout the ages, in the East as well as in the West. And there have been numerous earlier periods of rapid technical invention and innovation—again in the East as well as the West—, many of them producing technical changes fully as radical as any in the late eighteenth or early nineteenth centuries. What is unprecedented and unique about the development of the last two hundred and fifty years is their speed and scope.

As we see, Drucker falls into a no lesser confusion with generic statements that lead him to confuse the technical and technological organization of the process of production and labor with the mode of production—that is, with the class relations that arise from the mode of exploitation of the living forces of the production process: nature and labor. This leads him to think that technological change—conceptualized as industrial or productive revolutions as he calls them—is the basis of the transition from one mode of social organization to another. Based on this ambiguity and conceptual confusion, his thesis is nothing but an apologetic discourse of contemporary society, especially with regard to the role of information and knowledge technologies in the organization of the production and distribution process.

It is interesting to note that these arguments about an eventual obsolescence of Marxism and the approach to social classes are perhaps the most reiterated among the critics of the use of class as a category of analysis. However, it is also one of the weakest and most superficial both in logical-analytical and historical-empirical terms. Indeed, to accept this argument is to affirm that in the second half of the twentieth century, society would have made a historical leap equivalent to the transition from feudalism to capitalism between the seventeenth and eighteenth centuries. Undoubtedly, there have been very profound transformations in capitalism that have allowed the advent of post-modern, post-national, and even post-industrial forms. However, none of these allow us to argue that we are in transition to a *post-capitalist* society.

Indeed, even in contemporary sociology, all these terms have been widely debated. For one thing, post-industrial society remains, in essence, an industrial and manufacturing economy where the major transformation refers to the growing role of information technologies and, in particular, of knowledge in the organization of the work process (Lash and Urry, 1998). Likewise, although postmodern societies are spoken of, in any case they are always referred to as profoundly modern, and the term *post* refers more to an ultra-modernity (Touraine, 1995; Harvey, 1997) and not so much to a society that is situated as post-modern (Dussel, 2017). Finally, as for the post-national constellation, in terms of Habermas (2014), it has not implied a dissolution of national forms. Despite the great progress of economic and social globalization, the interests of nation states, especially of the great powers, remain predominant in the organization of world society (Hardt and Negri, 2000).

In capitalism, more than in any other social-historical formation, class—that is, economics—is central to unraveling its genesis. And within the world of the economy, the starting point of capitalism that gave rise to the new industrial order was what Marx and Polanyi called the separation of workers from their sources of livelihood to transform them into what we know today as wage laborers. Indeed, as Bourdieu (1987: 8,9) points out, "the working class as we perceive it today ... is a *well-founded historical artefact*." This historical foundation from which the formation of the proletariat—of the wage worker—is sustained is what Polanyi (2001) called the *Great Transformation* and corresponds to the historical process from which production and exchange—the political economy of society—are constituted as spheres separate and disembedded from other aspects of social life and structures of society. For the first time in history, the relations of production and exchange—the economy—were presented directly as what they are without the need for social and cultural mediations that symbolize them and at the same time constitute them.

In Marx's terms, this separation corresponds to the process of formation of the working class—of the wage worker—who has been stripped of all ownership of means and instruments of labor, leaving only labor power for subsistence and material reproduction (Marx, 1975). It is about the formation of workers "free" of all ties to be able to move and be moved—better said, to be used by and for others—for purposes and plans that are constituted independently of the purposes of material reproduction and subsistence of the worker. In a word, it corresponds to the formation of workers as a social class. This required that labor—together with money and land—be transformed into commodities, even though in the case of labor it corresponds to a vital activity of human life and indivisible and inseparable from their very condition as human beings. Therefore, it was required to transform this activity—labor and the potentiality of the worker, constituted as labor power—into a fictitious commodity, which allowed to forge the divorce—*disembedded*—of labor from the rest of the objectives of human life (Polanyi, 2001). This *disembedded* allowed, then, labor and the product of labor, to be objectified and reified, taking the form of a phenomenon in themselves.

If this disconnection of labor from the rest of human activity had not occurred, "there would be little chance for the idea of labour to be mentally separated from the 'totality' to which it 'naturally' belonged and to be condensed into a self-contained object" (Bauman, 2000: 142). In other words, if this *disembedding* of labor from the social had not occurred, the constitution of the wage-earner and the owner—the worker and the bourgeois—as such social classes would not have been possible, instead being subsumed and trapped in other social forms and, therefore, unable to deploy all the transforming potential that both Polanyi and Marx attribute to them.

This basic and fundamental structure of capitalism has not been modified in its essence, only in its forms. Its historical overcoming would imply the historical overcoming of capitalism as a social formation. Thus, there is nothing to indicate that we are in transition to a post-capitalist and, eventually, post-classist society. Considering the above, it is illogical to suppose that a theoretical framework that is recognized as a model of analysis and understanding of the foundational matrix of capitalism has theoretical validity in one moment of the history of a society but not in another, when the differences between one phase and another are not substantial and do not attend to the foundational matrix of capitalism as a mode of production and social-historical formation.

If we are moderately consistent with the critique and accept the obsolescence of Marxism, then we would have to extend it not only to the current phase of development of capitalism but also to its origins and previous phases. That is to say, we would have to assume that Marxism never had any validity to explain or understand capitalism in all its historical manifestations. However, no one until now has been able to assume such a radical position, since it is evident that given its lack of foundations it could not withstand even the slightest criticism. In fact, even the very precursors of non-Marxist sociology (Weber, Durkheim, Parsons, among others) as well as the main contemporary theorists (Giddens, Bauman, Beck, among others) all recognize in Marxism a valid and legitimate theoretical framework for analyzing contemporary society, although they obviously do not share its postulates.

8   Against Determinism

A no less weighty basis for the critique of Marxist class theory is the critique based on its mechanistic view of social life and the eventual determinism found in its formulation. As Pakulski (2005: 152) points out, Marxism usually assumes that "class is a fundamentally economic phenomenon, that it is reflected in patterns of social "groupness", that class location is reflected in social consciousness, identity and antagonism, and that it generates forms of action in the economic and political fields that have a potential to transform capitalism." According to this approach, the objective position in the production process—either as an owner of means of production (capitalists) or as an owner of labor power (proletariat)—would define objective and antagonistic interests attributable to those positions and are the basis of the capital-labor confrontation. From this basis, many Marxists consider that these objective interests generate forms of collective action—that is, social and political behaviors that reflect and reproduce in the political field this contradiction and opposition of interests generated in the economic-productive field (Pakulski, 1993).

In this context, class consciousness is posed as the mediation between one camp and the other—between the conflict of interests in the face of the process of exploitation and its manifestation as social and political conflict at the level of society. The point is that many Marxists see this rise of workers' class consciousness as a process not only inevitable, but practically almost direct (Pakulski, 1993). History, thus, we would add, is practically determined by the contradictions of the economic-productive structure, and its becoming is directly linked to the destiny of those contradictions. We end up, then, with a history constructed without subjects, practically determined by the structural conditions of society. If the class struggle is the motor of history, and classes emerge and are forged according to their position in the social relations of production, it is, therefore, logical to suppose that it is the contradictions of the economic-productive field—of the structural conditions—which ultimately determine the formation of classes and of the class struggle. However, the question seems to be neither so logical nor so simple.

Undoubtedly, more than a few Marxists have contributed to this mechanistic formulation of Marx's thinking on social classes and class struggle. Thus, for example, Poulantzas (1973: 27) pointed that "the economic place of the social agents has a principal role in determining social classes. ... Marxism states that the economic does indeed have the *determinant role* in a mode of production or a social formation; but the political and the ideological (the superstructure) also have an *important role*." Here, the point is establishing the ontological difference between *determinant role* and *important role*. That is to say, while the social relations of production are *determinant*, political and ideological factors are considered in a *secondary role* in the analysis of the class position and the social and political behavior of classes. Frequently, these Marxist authors end up analyzing class and the structuring of classes in capitalism, focusing almost exclusively on the economic-productive conditions. In fact, in that same text by Poulantzas as well as in those of Althusser, the "political and ideological factors" simply appear as something given, never as a concept to be analyzed and investigated in its historical constitution and making. Likewise, the analysis always ends up placing these factors in a subordinate role to the weight of economic-productive determinants. For one thing, in spite of formally recognizing the importance of the political and ideological superstructure, none of these authors develops a theorization in this respect that would allow us to understand its forms of structuring and its links with other levels of class analysis, such as the economic-productive one.[11]

It is on these authors and these readings—and their particular theoretical constructions of Marxism—that the critics of Marxism usually base their critique and, in this case, their death sentence as a theoretical body. What these critics overlook, however, is that from within Marxism itself have emerged perhaps the most grounded critiques of these readings of class and class struggle.

---

11   Contrast this structuralist strand of Marxism, which focuses on the phenomena of economic-productive infrastructure, with some of its contemporaries such as Gramsci, Lukács or Heller, who from different angles precisely take up the challenge of theorizing on the political-ideological superstructures and propose analytical models that imply theoretical and methodological integration (*embeddedness*, we would call it) of both levels of analysis.

This absence of references to these self-critique does not seem to be a simple slip but, rather, is part of a resource that contributes to their purposes of confronting (disqualifying, in fact) theoretical and political paradigms with which they have great ideological differences. This superficiality in the critique of authors such as Pakulski is even greater if we consider that even Clark and Lipset (1991: 398) explicitly recognize that in the face of this mechanistic understanding of class in these Marxist readings, "Marx never actually said that there would necessarily have to be a relationship between class position and the attitudes of class members." That is to say that even equally radical critics of Marx, recognize that the determinism and mechanicism exposed in class theory is rather the product of readings of a particular sector of Marxism and later Marxists, and that it does not necessarily concern the entire Marxist intellectual world, at the same time that it seems to be at odds with Marx's own statements on these points.

Notwithstanding the warnings of these authors, their very critique ends up yielding to the radicality of their political-ideological position, assuming likewise that social and political behavior would not be determined—neither in the first nor in the last instance—by the class situation in the labor process—that is, that the objective class situation does not determine or ensure a conscious position of class. According to this critique, the economic-productive and the political-social correspond to independent spaces and fields that are not relatively but completely autonomous of each other. To this end, it is argued and documented that the formation of the subjectivity and consciousness of subjects obeys more to market factors, consumption, status, as well as to extra-economic forms of identity (gender, race, citizenship, etc.), than to the class.

The point is that this critique of Marx and of the Marxist thesis of class consciousness starts from a common confusion even in some Marxist thinkers. I am referring to confusing the ideological consciousness of the proletariat, which is linked to its particular and concrete behaviors, with the class consciousness of the proletariat. In this sense, it is convenient to take up again, the analysis made in this respect by Lukács (1969), which, interestingly, is systematically forgotten and relegated by both critics and defenders of Marxism.

Lukács' analysis is based on two fundamental categories that, moreover, reflect the depth and complexity of his methodology and theorizing: on the one hand, the notion of totality and, on the other, that of alienation. Put very briefly (and, undoubtedly, in a reductionist manner), we can affirm that for Lukács (and for us as well) class consciousness—not just any consciousness—opposes the forms of alienation, unveiling their very exploitation. This requires that the subjects become conscious of social phenomena (and of their situations within them) as concrete totalities—not only as partialities, nor of their forms and appearances, nor only of their particular social, economic, or political position or situation. Only on the basis of this form of consciousness of society as a concrete totality can one act accordingly and, thus, transform consciousness *of* itself into consciousness *for* itself.[12] Let us look at this in more detail.

For Marx, the concept of alienation refers to the situation of the worker in the process of exploitation. Alienation refers to the separation (alienation) of labor and the fruit of labor from the worker. In capitalism, labor and its product (commodities) cease to serve the satisfaction of the needs of the direct producer—the worker—to serve the needs of other actors, in particular to satisfy the need of capital accumulation. The product of labor becomes an object alien to the worker, who is thus alienated in various ways by the transformation of their labor and the product of that labor into commodities. In this regard, in the *Economic and Philosophical Manuscripts*, of 1844, Marx (1964) points out four forms of this alienation of the worker, namely:

1. Alienation with respect to the work process. The meaning, purpose, and forms of the work process are beyond the control and domain of the worker.
2. Alienation with respect to the product of labor. The sale of labor power to capital is the alienation of the worker's productive capacity and, therefore, of the fruit of that labor capacity that, in turn, is presented to the worker as commodities and no longer as objectified forms of labor.
3. Alienation with respect to their nature as a human being. With the sale of labor power, the worker alienates their essence, their spirit that differentiates them from other animal species.
4. Alienation from other workers, to the same extent that they are alienated from their labor. What is valid for the relation of the worker to their own labor and the product of it is also valid in relation to the labor and the product of labor of others.

---

12 Luxemburg, from a different perspective, puts forward something similar. For her, theory—that is, the understanding of history and society—is an essential, fundamental part of the proletarian subject and its revolutionary action. It is from where its revolutionary potential must be sustained. In her view, theory—as a mode of understanding and apprehension of society—also functions as a process of consciousness that considers the world as a concrete totality and, therefore, of consciousness of the position and situation of the class in society and of the revolutionary sense of its project of transformation— that is, as forms of consciousness of *class in itself* and *class for itself*. It is in this logic that it makes sense Luxemburg's famous phrase where she (2020 [1908]: 3) points out "The entire strength of the modern labour movement rests on theoretic knowledge".

The basis of this whole process of alienation in its various forms is the constitution of the worker as a wage earner and of their labor power as a commodity. It is a form of existence of labor and labor force that is proper and characteristic of capitalism. Polanyi illustrates it clearly when he points out the necessity of capitalism to transform labor power into a commodity—a tradable object in a market—and, therefore, alienable from its possessor, the worker. But this can only occur as a fiction, since labor is an intrinsic part of the human being. Work cannot be understood as anything other than an activity proper to the nature of human beings; it cannot be separated from the human condition (Polanyi, 2001).

Thus, the historical constitution of the worker as a wage laborer and of labor power as a commodity, is the historical basis of the alienation we experience as human beings. What Polanyi calls the *fictitious* form of the commodity is what for Marx would represent the form of *alienation* of the worker from their labor. In both cases, the emphasis is placed on this separation of labor—and its product—from the worker as a human being. In both cases, this separation (alienation) constitutes a *fictitious* act—not a real one—a form of *alienation*. The difference between the two lies in the fact that while Polanyi focuses on the formation of the labor market as the historical mechanism of this alienation, Marx focuses his analysis on the relations of production that demand this constitution of labor as a *fictitious* commodity in a market, constructed *ex profeso* to give form to the relation of exploitation.[13]

In the case of wage labor, alienation is twofold: on the one hand, because of the separation that the worker suffers from labor due to its wage-earning form; and, on the other, because of the non-consciousness of this phenomenon that takes on the appearance of its opposite. In the labor market, the wage—that is, the price of labor power—takes the form (appearance) of the price or value of labor itself. This makes both worker and capitalist (seller and buyer) assume the appearance that what is paid is what corresponds to the totality of the work performed—that is, the intentional and performed confusion between the *exchange value* of labor power (its wage) and its *use value* (the work performed) (Marx, 1975).[14]

---

13 This is not a minor difference, although it refers more to the corollaries than to the foundations of each author. For example, Polanyi's emphasis on the formation of the labor market leads him to sociological and economic considerations in the transformation of society, while Marx, focusing on the social relations of production, emphasizes economic and political considerations in the mode of production and the constitution of classes and class struggle.

14 This is a confusion, however, that does not appear in the same way in other modes of production. In slavery, there is no separation between work and the worker, since the entire

Faced with this situation, Lukács (1969) points out that the consciousness of the worker regarding this process of alienation is at the same time a consciousness concerning the process of exploitation that underlies the alienation of labor itself—that is, the appropriation by capital of the labor and the product of the labor of the worker. For the same reason, it is a consciousness in relation to one's class situation—as a worker, as a proletarian—lacking the means of production. Finally, it is at the same time a consciousness of their function and of the meaning of their work and of them as a worker in the process of capitalist production and, therefore, in opposition to the function and meaning of capital and of the capitalist as owners of the means of production.

In this sense, we can add that the function of class consciousness is precisely to unveil this world of exploitation and inequality, hidden behind this world of appearances that come to life in the market. It is to unveil the relations of production, class inequality, and the constitution of classes on the basis of social relations of production (private property, exploitation), which are hidden and made invisible in the relations of buying and selling of labor power and in the mercantile relations of the labor market, where buyers and sellers usually concur supposedly on equal terms to transact (buy and sell) a commodity. However, as we have seen, it is not a real commodity but a material that hides in its mercantile form relations of exploitation, social inequality, and class.

This way of approaching the formation of class consciousness opens two lines of reflection. The first is a critique of those versions that vulgarize the idea of class consciousness, reducing it and assimilating it to the forms of thought and self-perception of individuals—in this case wage workers. Class consciousness does not refer to "men's ideas about their position in life, empirical-factual ideas, describable and psychologically explicable" (Lukács, 1969: 55). In other words, class consciousness does not refer to, nor is it measured by, the individual behavior of each person by their aspirations, attitudes, and personal or collective values. This is part of their daily life, of their lifestyle. On the contrary—and this is the second line of reflection—class consciousness refers to an objective *possibility* in capitalism of reaching a conception of society and its economy (forms of production, exploitation, distribution, reproduction, etc.) as a totality and, therefore, not only of the position of each class, each subject, and each individual, but of the whole of these positions and, most relevantly, of the structures and relations that give rise to these class positions and situations.

---

person is the property of the master, while in the feudal mode the separation is evident in its form, insofar as the peasant divides the times of work on their piece of land (or the one assigned to them) and on the land of the master (Marx, 1975).

Lukács points out that it is in capitalism that this principle of perceptibility is possible—that is, of the construction of a consciousness of the economy and of society as totalities. This would be feasible because the triumph of the bourgeoisie and the advent of capitalist society would have been constituted, precisely, from the destruction of the Stadial structures of pre-capitalist societies (feudal and slave-owning), which would have made possible the conformation of capitalism as "a social order in which the stratification of society tends to be a stratification in classes purely and exclusively" (Lukács, 1969: 59).

This perspective is what allows us to uncover the theoretical and methodological weaknesses of both Marxist determinism and its critics. In both cases, they abandon Marx's basic principle of analyzing social reality from its reconstruction as concrete totalities (Zemelman, 1987). From this perspective of totalities, we can critique both the prevailing economic determinism in the construction of social classes and class consciousness in Poulantzas, Althusser, and other Marxists and the superficiality of the critique of authors such as Pakulski, Clark, Lipset, and others.

As Cardoso (1979) points out in his comments to Poulantzas (1973), the very formulation in concrete terms of some type of *ultimate economic determination*—as well as the *relative autonomy* of the political-ideological superstructure—entails a methodological form of reconstruction of reality that departs from the method developed by Marx. As Cardoso points out, the distinction between an economic-productive and a political-ideological field is *fictitious*, being more a heuristic resource of thought than a concrete social form. For the same reason, it makes no sense to establish hierarchies or levels of determination of one over the other, neither to claim relative autonomies of one over the other. Society is one whole in unison, and the only way to apprehend it is from its reconstruction as a concrete totality. In this logic, Cardoso (1979: 144, our translation) continues: "For Marx, it was not a question concerning the distinct fields of human practices and diverse areas but of levels of complexity of the real that were articulated in complex totalities of thought."

In the same perspective, we would add that it makes no sense to establish the eventual existence of an economy independent of the existence of a politics or a socio-cultural world. The distinction between OIKOS and POLIS only makes sense if they are used as categories that allow us to apprehend society as a concrete totality—that is, as mediations to access a global and totalizing understanding of society. This would be the sense of class consciousness in Lukács' logic, as a mediation to access an understanding of society as a concrete totality, as a way to access an understanding of class, and of its conditions of existence and reproduction as a structure and social relation and, by the same token, as opposition to another class.

Having said this, in Marx the relevance of the economic is not casual but refers to the fact that we have already commented: that it is the relation of private property that historically gives rise to the conformation of human society in social classes. It is not only a question of the position or place of each person in relation to the private property relations of the means of production but, rather, a position—one of class—as a fundamental structure in the founding and constituent of society itself. As Castells (1979: 165, our translation) points out when referring to the capitalist mode of production, "if the structural 'places' of generator of value and appropriator of surplus value are fundamental, it is because they are those capable of arousing in their own dynamics a general social organization. That is to say, not just any 'place' in the economic structure defines a class, but those pairs of contradictory 'places', each capable of organizing the whole of a social formation around its specific interests."

It is not that other social classes or classifications do not exist but that they would not have the capacity to structure a form of "general social organization," and, therefore, they cannot be defined either as ascending or descending classes, in Castells' terms—that is, as *classes that struggle for the organization of society as a whole*, either to consolidate an existing social form or to stimulate its revolutionary transformation that leads to other forms of general social organization.

This is what gives meaning to the concept of class consciousness as a way of understanding this fundamental contradiction of all social-historical formation. It is a way of understanding society and its history (becoming) as a concrete totality in which class and class struggle constitute the motor of that history. Having said this, it is evident, then, that the very notion of class and class struggle corresponds to levels of abstraction and analysis that go far beyond its empirical manifestation in each historical conjuncture. Class consciousness derives in an argument against economicist determinism present in some Marxist texts as well as in some of its most radical critics. Class consciousness configures a category of high complexity, not only because of what it refers to, but also because of its methodological demand to think of it as a theoretical-ideological mediation to access forms of understanding society and classes and class struggle as concrete totalities. This concept and this Marxist theorization of class consciousness undoubtedly contrast both with the mechanistic notions of Althusserian structuralism and with the superficiality of the critique that has been made of this notion of Marxism from other paradigms.

Class consciousness is based on a complex thought that starts from the premise of society as a totality and where its function as a concept is nothing more than the apprehension and comprehension of society in its sense of totality. Consciousness, thus, serves as a *moment, momentum*, of mediation between the social subject—determined by class—and society as a totality. It is the moment of comprehension: of apprehension of society in its totality, not only in its direct, formal form—of its appearances—nor of individual positions, but as collectives. It is an understanding of the meaning and historical movement of any society. For the same reason, it is about the consciousness of the classes in any society that have the possibility of transforming themselves into subjects with a project of organization (whether conservative or transformative) of that society. Consciousness, in short, is conceived on the basis of the class struggle understood at this level of abstraction of society—that is, of the struggle for the forms and modes of organization of society.

If we live and exist in a world of alienation, consciousness is a moment of discovery and unveiling of these various types of alienation. In this sense, it is absurd to argue against the triad *Totality-Alienation-Consciousness* with arguments based on very minor levels of abstraction, such as that of individual or subjective consciousness. It is not that it is not relevant or unimportant to the conversation. On the contrary, the triad is fundamental for understanding individual and subjective action. The question is the confusion between one and the other level of analysis. With this discussion, we want to take up Lukács' critique of the individual and subjective level, largely psychological, of the concept of consciousness used in the critique of Marxism, which attempts to refute the notion of class consciousness by placing individual and collective behaviors of the workers and middle class populations before consumption, electoral politics, socioeconomic careerism, and other mechanisms and practices of distinction that individuals normally develop both to distance themselves from some and to approach others.

It is not that these mechanisms and practices do not exist or are only appearances. On the contrary, they are phenomena so real and material that they determine people's ways of life. What we want to point out is that we are dealing with a notion of subjective and individual consciousness that does not refer to the notion of class consciousness, since one and the other are located at different levels of abstraction and correspond to different planes of apprehension of social reality—of its totality. If we may be allowed the license, we can say that we are dealing with different levels of consciousness; subjective and individual consciousness in one case, and class consciousness of society as a totality in the other.

In this context, we can take up again the discussion on the role of consumption as a mechanism of social distinction, which according to class critics would lead to questioning this notion of class—and class consciousness—and its role in the structuring of contemporary capitalist society. In this view, it is consumption and not class what sustains the process of institutionalization of social hierarchy. It is, therefore, a question of reconstructing a political economy of consumption. It is true that for this hierarchizing function of consumption to manifest itself as such, it needs the mediation of production, that is, the manufacture of these goods of differentiation in consumption that function no longer as material objects full of the use-value/exchange-value dialectic—but as *signs and symbols of distinction*. In this new political economy, consumption determines the production of objects of consumption. This is not as the neoclassical economists point out in terms of their use values (goods for the satisfaction of needs), nor as political economy says in terms of their exchange values (objectification of labor as value for its accumulation as capital), but in terms of the signs and meanings they represent as objects of consumption. It is not the object that matters, but the *sign* associated with that commodity. It does not matter the material need it will satisfy but the need for *symbolic differentiation*. The use value of merchandise is no longer the satisfaction it generates but the *distinction* it produces. Consumption ceases to be a process in itself to become a mediation in the construction of social hierarchies, inequalities, and distinctions. Material objects are not consumed, but symbolic distinctions are consumed. Hence, "an accurate theory of objects will not be established upon a theory of needs and their satisfaction, but upon theory of social prestations and signification" (Baudrillard, 1981: 30).

But what does the need for distinction really mean, if not the need to differentiate oneself from some in order to resemble others? The question here is threefold: (1) Who are some and who are others? (2) Who defines those categories of some and others? and (3) Why can consumption be a means to establish distinction over others, as is the case with class origins? Our idea here is that, in reality, the denial of class origins by focusing on the thesis of distinction in consumption is nothing more than a form of affirmation that classes do, in fact, exist, to such an extent that the distinction that one wants to establish through consumption is nothing more than to establish a distance or a differentiation with respect to their original class of origin based on various processes that give the idea of some upward mobility—that is, of ascent and access to other classes through consumption.

It is *careerism* and *aspirationalism*, the illusion of mobility and social ascent, of distinction through consumption. But here lies the paradox: This need for distinction through consumption is but a reaffirmation of the existence of classes and of the social inequality based on them, which is precisely what the critics of Marxism and class theory wanted to deny. Since differentiation according to class origin is not desired and is rejected, consumption is used as a means of establishing other modes of distinction, forging the possibility— or at least the illusion—of access to other class situations, of an aspired and expected social ascent. Today's *aspirationalist* is no less yesterday's *déclassé*. As such, social subjects reaffirm their position in this complex dialectic by denying their class origins in the illusion of ascending to a higher class through consumption. In this sense, the only way to be declassed is for there to exist a class of which one renounces and another to which one aspires. The mere existence of the declassed and the *aspirationalist* are, thus, the reaffirmation of class inequality and, therefore, of the very existence of social classes.

Distinction through consumption and taste does not deny the existence of social classes but, rather, reaffirms it to such an extent that some seek through consumption a way of distinguishing themselves or at least symbolically distancing themselves from their peers—that is, from their equals in terms of their class of origin. To this end, they uncritically adopt (and very probably without awareness of it) the hegemonic cultural patterns of consumption and taste—that is, those of the dominant classes. In this way, this desire for distinction reflects a very weak consciousness of class origin that seeks to deny and overcome itself through consumption, as well as a strong influence of the consciousness of the dominant class that it aspires to reach. We are faced with forms of alienation that do not allow us to recognize the relations of exploitation and alienation that sustain them, precisely because we adopt the ideology of the dominant and their class consciousness as such (Moulián, 1997).

This type of distinction is a reflection of the capacity of some (the dominant class) to organize society through consumption and other mechanisms of symbolic reproduction. This is so much so that the lifestyle and consumption patterns of the dominant classes set the guidelines for the consumption patterns of others, establishing the model to be followed in order to distance and distinguish themselves from others and become part of the class of the distinguished. It is evident that the power of the ruling class does not arise from its peculiar taste but from the economic power that allows it to pay for the pattern of consumption that expresses that peculiar taste. Its power and its constitution as *powerful* do not arise from the subjective that distinguishes it in consumption—that is, from its good or bad taste—but from the economic power that distinguishes it in production—that is, from its particular position in the relations of production and exploitation.[15]

---

15   For one thing, we cannot overlook the fact that consumption is impossible without income, i.e., that consumption (its level, form, pattern, style, etc.) is materially underpinned by the income received by the population and, therefore, its position in the distribution structure of the product of labor and its surplus. In other words, the possibility of making consumption a process of distinction is a direct function of the position of each subject in the process of the exploitation of labor, that is, of the extraction of value and

In this sense, the powerful are not powerful because they have good taste in their consumption but, rather, because they have the necessary economic and political power to impose their taste as good taste. The *aspirationalist* is just that, one that aspires to be like the powerful; however, this aspiration is nothing more than an illusion, as such mobility will never be achieved. Deep down, every aspirationalist knows that it is only an aspiration, never a process of true social ascent, a mere attempt to distinguish oneself from their origins, which only in a few select exceptions allows the arrival to a higher social destiny. In most cases, it ends up as a dream, the aspiration to be like someone one can never be, but it does, however, allow one to symbolically distance oneself from one's class equals.

The banal nature of consumption, thus, reflects the levity of its liquid existence in terms of the absence of any true greater transcendence—social or material—than in the mere distinction of one with respect to their equals in terms of class. Further, the banality of consumption suggests a total renunciation of change, an affront to the real possibility of any social transformation, as these ideas are no longer convincing to the masses. Faced with the evidence of the defeat already experienced (politically, socially, culturally)—that is, of the impossibility of a real ascent, whether by economic-productive means (social mobility) or by political means (reforms or revolutions)—there remains only the illusion of ascent: the aspiration to be what one is not through the negation of what one is. But, again, these ideas are just that: illusions and aspirations. Truthfully, deep down, the aspirationalist knows that they will never be like the powerful, based on their everyday experiences in a world in which they have been defeated time and again, restricting dreams of transformational projects. From this reality, it only remains for the aspirationalist to imagine, to dream of being like the other: There are no paths for change. It is the aspiration to be, one that will constantly be unfulfilled. This is because to be able to be like the powerful and to be a member of the powerful, good or bad taste is not enough. It is necessary to have the resources to sustain that particular good or bad taste, and this can only come from the social field itself, such as the economy through acts of direct exploitation—that is, the appropriation of surplus labor. One can only be powerful if one belongs to the social class of the powerful.

---

surplus in the labor process. In this way, we can affirm that class distinction in consumption is limited by social position, that is, socioeconomic status, and, therefore, by position in the labor process. The distinction in consumption is only a way of hiding this other form of social differentiation: class inequality vis-à-vis the labor process.

Consumption—and distinction through it—is but a form of affirmation of the existence of classes and of the power that emanates from them. This is not only in terms of the wealth of some and the poverty of others—gross inequalities of income—but of the power of classes themselves to become one of the structuring vectors of society through their power. Thus, the power of the capitalist is not only their possibility of appropriating the wealth of others—of surplus labor—but also the very ability to make this relation of exploitation a structuring vector that is constituent of capitalist society itself. In this way, cultural hegemony through taste and consumption is but an expression of the power and domination of one class over others and a clear expression of a permanent class struggle, where, except for exceptional moments, the winners, as Warren Buffett used to say, always seem to be the same: the powerful (Stein, 2006).

9   Class: Critical Function of a Concept

Returning to Jameson (1991), we can argue that today, as in previous epochs of capitalism, every position we take on class—as well as those issues related to culture, society, consumption, labor, and economy—is at the same time, and necessarily, a political position on the nature of contemporary capitalism. To deny the importance of class as an analytical category is not only to deny a theory: It is also—and especially in this case—to deny the legitimacy and validity of Marxism as a critical theory of society, to deny the validity of an opposing political position. What is relevant in any case is that this critique of Marxism is made from a no lesser theoretical weakness, which reflects the levity of its very critique as we have argued.

Rejecting the alleged demise of class and scrutinizing assertions proclaiming its obsolescence, however, does not suggest a lack of acknowledgment for the challenges posed by the ongoing transformations in contemporary class-analytic society. These evolving articulations necessitate a reevaluation of class as both a social category and an analytical tool to comprehensively grasp the implications of these changes.

Assuming the relevance and theoretical and political validity of Marxism does not imply that it is not open to critique or debate. In this sense, our analysis is based on two premises to be taken into account:

1. While class is present in every social process (inequality, conflict, consciousness, etc.), it does not mean that class explains everything about every social process.

2. The fact that class does not explain everything does not mean that it does not explain anything.

Following Lukács, it is a matter of thinking of social phenomena as totalities and, in this way, overcoming both deterministic analyses and those centered on their morphologies. Society and the social phenomena that make it up are totalities—that is, they are constituted by multiple dimensions and processes. Thus, more relevant than establishing unilinear causal determinations in our sociological analyses is to establish the fields and levels of mediations between the social processes that constitute the dynamics of society. Thus, for example, social inequality is a form of totality in the sense that its structuring is not reduced to economic-productive factors but neither to its forms in terms of positions and distributions of objects, devices, and/or other forms of power and domination. Inequality as a totality is constructed from the mediation between different social fields, such as class, gender, race, citizenship, age, geography, territory, religion, etc. In each specific case, these social forces are combined and articulated in processes that are not free of tensions and conflicts.

In the case of the analysis of social inequality, for example, wanting to deny the validity or relevance of class—that is, of the economic-productive moment (relation of exploitation)—is as absurd as claiming the opposite, that is, that class always and everywhere determines the forms of social inequality. We can assume—and this would have to be demonstrated theoretically—that in capitalism class has a central role, but even in that case, it does not mean that it has a deterministic, unilinear role in the conformation and structuring of social inequality and class antagonism.

Every social conflict, every class antagonism, has an economic-productive substratum, just as it also has a political-ideological substratum, a gender-based substratum, a geographical substratum, etc. It is equally absurd to believe in the linearity and mechanicism of social conflicts as it is to deny their substrates. Conflicts are the expression of a social matrix of class constitution, and in this case, we use the term matrix in a double metaphor. On the one hand, we refer to matrix as genesis, origin, maternity, which gives birth to a new being. The components, constituted by previous elements, merge and give rise to the genesis of something new: economic-productive class interests, political-ideological principles, patriarchal relations, racism, etc. These various substrata together form the matrix from which classes, class structure, and class conflict/antagonism/struggle are born and reproduced.

On the other hand, we use the term matrix according to its use in mathematics—that is, as a moment of transformation. As a transformation device, it is formed and constituted by a set of vectors that can be read—and act—simultaneously vertically and horizontally, whose mutual interaction is what produces the mathematical transformation themselves. A vector—economic and productive class interests, for example—does not manifest itself directly as social conflict but, rather, is mediated by the social matrix, that is, by the matrix of vectors that constitute each society, the matrix of social inequality, and the matrix of classes in each society (determined by interactions of gender, race, geography, generations, classes, castes, etc.). This matrix, therefore, acts as a mediation of the conflict—that is, as a social device of transformation of the conflict of economic-productive (class) interests into a social and political conflict.

Following this logic, *OIKOS* and *POLIS* form two moments of society. The reconstruction of the latter as a Totality is not the sum of both—the mere aggregation of the economic (exploitation) and the political (domination)—but their articulation and imbrication in the construction of each social process. This articulation can only be reconstructed through processes of *mediation*. In this sense, we understand a mediation not as an intermediate field—or processes that inter-mediate between one and another level—but as a *moment* of reconstruction and transformation of one level and another level of analysis; in particular, this is a moment of reconstruction of one level of analysis *embedded* within other levels of analysis. Social processes are total and totalities. Our problem is that we cannot access them, apprehend them directly as such, except through abstractions. Therefore, their reconstruction as totalities requires thinking based on mediations—that is, reconstructing the forms of totality of the phenomenon.

In the case of social inequality and political conflict as social phenomena, their reconstruction as social totalities require thinking about their mediations. In this sense, class, race, gender, consciousness, age, geography, among many others, are those processes of mediations that allow us to reconstruct the particular social phenomenon (inequality) as a totality that articulates one and another level—*OIKOS*, *DEMOS*, and *POLIS*. Herein lies the foundation of our premises and its main corollary: *to want to reduce all social struggle to a conflict/antagonism of economic-productive interests—of classes—is as absurd as pretending that economic-productive interests, of classes are not present in any social conflict/antagonism.*

In this sense, we maintain that the function of class as a category of analysis is its capacity to critique society. Likewise, the function of class as a social category—that is, as a social reality—is also in its capacity to critique theories about society. Normally we use class as an *argument to force* (Maturana, 1997), that is, to impose on others our particular reason for things, either because the death of class is proposed, or its opposite, the universal validity of class.

What we want, instead, is to use class as an *argument for critique*, and this on a double plane: On the one hand, as a critique and discovery of reasons and rationalities present both in social reality and in theories. On the other, as a critique of the social, of society and its horizons of reason and historical possibilities (Zemelman, 1992). The challenge is none other than to orient our reflections regarding class and inequality towards *arguments of understanding and social transformation*, rather than petty debates of theory. This is the basis of our approach to class as an argument *against* inequality, understood as an argument for *social emancipation*.

CHAPTER 7

The Return of Class

The theses on the end of class and the obsolescence of Marxism are, in general, guilty of the same double characteristic: their superficiality in critique and the caricaturing of Marxism as a social theory. We are not the first to point out these weaknesses of the critics of Marxism. In a much more elegant and profound way, Giddens makes similar points. Referring to Dahrendorf, for example, he points out that his critique "do not contain an acceptable formulation of [his] theory; nor do they offer a satisfactory appraisal ... of the weaknesses in the Marxian standpoint" (Giddens, 1975: 81).

In our case, the critique of Pakulski, Clark, Lipset, and Nisbet, among others, is based on the same essential observations made by Giddens in the work of Dahrendorf: The weak construction of Marxist theory from which the critique of these authors starts makes the critique itself become distorted and, therefore, loses validity as a theoretical exercise, although, undoubtedly, very useful as a political and ideological one. Abandoning the politically correct discourse, we can point out that it is always very easy to criticize an author on the basis of a partial and caricatured reconstruction of thought because, like any caricature, it undoubtedly takes up the most fundamental and characteristic aspects in its articulation.[1] But also like any caricature, it does so by distorting them and taking them to extremes that distort their meaning and essence. In a drawing, this is essential, since what is sought is a humorous representation, for which the main features of a person are highlighted and distorted. However, in the theoretical and political plane, this method never leads to good results, since it not only distorts the object of critique but also the very critique it is trying to elaborate in the process.

In this sense, it is relevant to compare these shallow and weak criticisms with other authors who have developed valid critiques of Marxist thought from greater analytical and theoretical depths, which has allowed them to present alternative analytical frameworks. While in the first cases discusses above, it is obvious that the critique of these authors is basically aimed at decreeing the obsolescence of an author; in the second, on the other hand, the process of critique is part of a proposal that seeks to renew sociological thought and, in this

---

1 Quite a few Marxists have contributed to this caricatured version of Marx's thought, although, in any case, this does not exculpate the superficiality of the critique already mentioned.

attempt, to critically recover relevant aspects of Marxist thought. Undoubtedly, this gives it greater transcendence and sustenance in the current era.

Taking into account the above, in this chapter we present four approaches that we consider relevant for their contributions to the understanding of social inequality in the contemporary world and that are based in different ways on social class as a category of analysis. We begin with the proposal of Anthony Giddens and his thesis of class structuring and social inequality. We continue with the approach of Eric O. Wright, who establishes a recovery of the category of social class in sociological analysis from a renewed vision of Marxism. We also present Charles Tilly's proposal on durable inequality and the role of categories in its configuration. Finally, we analyze Pierre Bourdieu's approach on the role of economic, social, and cultural capitals in the formation of classes, as well as that of the modes of accumulation of these capitals in the reproduction of social inequality. What is relevant and unifies all these authors and their proposals is that in all of them class occupies a preponderant role both as a social category and as a sociological category for the analysis of social inequality.

1 Giddens and Class Structuration in Contemporary Capitalism

Two aspects of Giddens' reflection are worth highlighting: (1) his proposal to analyze social processes based on their modes of *structuration* and (2) his analysis of the conformation of class structures in advanced societies, where his writing on the new middle class stands out, as well as his work concerning the changes in the structuring of the working class.

In relation to the first point—that is, his perspective of analysis and way of thinking society—Giddens begins by pointing out that although it is necessary to develop new starting points and foundations for contemporary social theory this cannot under any context or pretext imply the abandonment of what "is a long-standing problem in sociology—one might say, *the* problem in sociology: the question of classes and class conflict" (Giddens, 1975: 19, emphasis original). This is the fundamental presupposition on which he bases his theorems and proposals on class structure in contemporary capitalism.

For Giddens, beyond the alleged errors and questionings of Marxist thought in mainstream critique, it is clear that class and class analysis do not lose validity or relevance for the understanding of society. However, this does not necessarily imply a defense of Marxism. On the contrary, Giddens argues that class and class analysis have been faced with the dilemma of developing as a method of thought, as these ideas and categories exist as a set of already established and incontrovertible statements on society and capitalism, consolidating an orthodoxy that has curbed its very theoretical and comprehensive potential of capitalism and its evident transformations. In fact, this even seems a contradiction in terms, insofar as for Marx the object was precisely to develop a framework of analysis and understanding of social change and social and historical transformations, where human potentialities were key to understanding and acting on these transformations.

However, as Giddens (1975) points out, the greatest problem of Marxism—both as critical theoretical thought and as political-ideological principles for revolutionary action—was that in the twentieth century, an internal orthodoxy was consolidated that distorted its founding principles, a theory open to history and change, thus preventing any significant progress in the understanding of society and its continuous transformation.[2] In this sense, he states that "rather than speaking of the 'existence' or 'non-existence' of classes, we should speak of types and levels of what I call *class structuration*" (Giddens, 1975: 20, emphasis original). With this, he is explicit. Societies are class based—that seems a truism. What is essential for sociological analysis, therefore, are the factors that determine the *structuration* of classes and class structure in each historical context—that is to say, what is relevant is the process of formation and constitution of classes and class conflict, not their mere ascertainment or description.

In the case of capitalism, it mandates an intrinsically class-based society for its operations. Although advanced societies have undergone profound productive, technological, social, cultural, and political transformations, they continue to be essentially capitalist and, therefore, essentially classist or class-based. However, this does not imply that in capitalism the structuring of classes is a homogeneous and standardized process, following the same patterns at all times and in all places. The way classes are structured in contemporary advanced societies is very different from the way they were structured in the industrial capitalism of the nineteenth century, even if they still have, more or less, the same social classes and class structures. This is because their articulation not only operates on objective and structural factors—invariants of capitalism—but also on their historical contingency—that is, their objectification as historical and concrete processes that opens spaces for social and economic heterogeneity.

---

2 We can say that in the same situation would be found the dominant currents in academic sociology (functionalism) in its repeated effort to pronounce the end of ideologies, classes, and class analysis. There is no doubt that in these approaches the political-ideological principles underlying these sociological theories predominate over the principles of scientific and academic rationality.

For Giddens, the structuration of classes starts from at least two different planes or social fields, although intimately connected. He maintains that the conditions of the economic-productive infrastructure as defined by Marx continue to have a relevant weight. However, in opposition to Marxist orthodoxy, Giddens argues that the political conditions of society are equally relevant— that is, that the conditions of the political superstructure are also fundamental in the processes of structuration social classes and, therefore, in the historical configuration of inequality and class conflict and antagonism. As Giddens (1975: 21) notes:

> To point to the existence of chronic differences in infrastructures between societies is not to accord a necessary and universal causal primacy to infrastructural factors themselves. On the contrary, I shall argue that specifically political influences, which both condition and express such differences, must be allocated a primary role in interpreting the formation and development of class structures.

Now, although Marx also states that economic domination, which arises from the social relations of production, is intrinsically linked to political domination, Giddens distances himself from the Marxist approach in the sense that he does not establish a deterministic relationship between the two planes of domination. Nor is Gidden's perspective a question of recognizing a "relative autonomy" of the plane and forms of political domination with respect to those of economic domination: The issue is more complex and refers, rather, to the role of one and the other social field in the structuration of class systems in capitalist society. In this respect, Giddens puts forward a theory of classes that emphasizes their structuration process rather than the class structure itself. This allows him to identify fields, moments, and factors from which this structuration is generated as a social process, which allow Giddens to go beyond an economic-productive determinism.

A good example of his proposal is when he analyzes the structuration of the working class in advanced societies in contemporary capitalism (Giddens, 1975).[3] For him, as for Marx, a fundamental factor in the structuration of classes

---

3 Giddens' analysis is based on the 1970s, considering the dynamics of advanced societies in those years. However, the relevance of his proposal transcends that moment, in such a way that both the categories of analysis, as well as his way of understanding the structuring of classes, offer us a framework for analysis in contemporary societies. In many cases, to Giddens' analysis we add reflections that incorporate our own appreciations of these changes in the structuring of classes in contemporary capitalism.

refers to the formation of class consciousness. In this respect, Giddens proposes two levels of constitution of the class consciousness of the workers: a first one referred to what he calls "conflict consciousness", and a second one that he calls "revolutionary consciousness", and refers to the separation of what would be the "industrial" conflict as such from the "political" conflict, which accounts for the separation of the economy and politics (the field of the *OIKOS* and that of the *POLIS*, as we have called them in previous chapters). These are not only different fields of constitution but also different planes of analysis and action with different scopes and dimensions than traditional Marxist approaches. The first, conflict consciousness, "although influenced by the specific forms of structuring of the working class, is in a certain sense inherent to the worker's perspectives in capitalist society" (Giddens, 1975: 200). The second, revolutionary consciousness, on the other hand, would correspond to specific moments and historical conjunctures that would make its constitution possible, impelling the structuration of the working class towards other directions.

In a certain way, the revolutionary consciousness pointed out by Giddens corresponds to the same plane that Castells (1979) mentions regarding the role of the class as the bearer of a project of social organization that transcends it as a social class and as a historical moment of constitution. That is to say, we would add, class and class consciousness as an *historical possibility* and not only as a mere determination derived from the position and contradictions in the economic-productive infrastructure. We, therefore, understand the notion of historical possibility in a double plane, as both the possibility of a particular constitution of class and as a revolutionary transformation of class society.

What is relevant in this discussion is that based on this distinction according to planes of formation of class consciousness—conflict consciousness and revolutionary consciousness, economic plane and political plane, "industrial conflicts" and "political conflicts"—Giddens distances himself from Marx and Marxist orthodoxy as well as from his staunchest critics, such as Dahrendorf and other authors that we have already reviewed in previous chapters. With respect to the former, Giddens distances himself from the mechanicism implicit in the notion that a cumulative development of conflict and a sharpening of the contradictions inherent in the infrastructure of capitalism would necessarily arise with its maturation (Giddens, 1975: 237); and with respect to the latter, he particularly questions the thesis that in "post-capitalism" economic and political conflicts would separate and take autonomous forms, reducing their potential as forces of change and transformation. On the contrary, Giddens explicitly points out that "the institutional separation of (the manifestations of) class conflict in the industrial and political spheres, far from marking the transcendence of capitalism, *is the normal mode of the structuration of class conflict in capitalist society*" (Giddens, 1975: 202, emphasis original). With this, he demolishes the thesis of an eventual advent of a post-capitalist society, a thesis defended by Dahrendorf (1959) and other authors.

Considering this distinction, Giddens focuses on analyzing the structuring process of the working class, paying special attention to its conflict consciousness, without going into greater detail regarding the structuring of the class around its revolutionary consciousness. In this regard, he points out different fields from which to analyze the structuring of the working class. These fields can be differentiated into two large planes: those referring to the *paratechnical*[4] conditions and relations, and those referring to contextual, political, and social conditions.

Regarding the first, he takes up two aspects of the paratechnical relations proposed by Marx, which would be "the congregation of workers in large plants" and "their subjection to routinised forms of productive activity" (Giddens, 1975: 203). Both conditions contribute to the formation of class consciousness, insofar as they allow two fundamental issues: on the one hand, the congregation of bodies and, on the other, the communion of interests and class situations. For the same reason, they acquire a relevant weight in the ways of structuration the working class in contemporary capitalism. It is evident that by themselves they are not sufficient, but they do constitute a fertile field for the emergence of collective action and by that means the structuring of a particular class.

To these aspects, Giddens adds a third, which Marx had already raised but in the opposite sense. I refer to the persistence and deepening, in many cases, of the division between skilled labor and unskilled manual labor. For Marx, the development of capitalism would lead to the reduction and eventual elimination of the former, something which, as Giddens notes, has not occurred in industrial capitalism nor in post-industrial capitalism but, rather, has consolidated its position within the productive process and increased its capacity of control. This works against the structuration of classes itself and the formation of its class consciousness as such, since it contributes to generate an important differentiation within the working class. It translates into different ways of structuration as class, where these accented distinctions among the members of the working class conform a mode of social and political division rather than unity. This division is installed in the very basis of the structuration of the

---

4 Paratechnics is a term that emerged in the nineteenth century, and refers to conditions, processes, relations constituted through, or by means of, technical processes, in this case, the concrete—technical—organization of the work process, and also refers to science and its role in the organization of production and the development of productive forces.

working class itself and the conformation of its class consciousness as such (Giddens, 1975).

Regarding the second field, Giddens points to different spaces from which class relations are constituted but which go beyond the borders of the directly productive spheres. These are "mediate structuration factors" from which processes of construction of class identity can develop and, by this means, constitute forms of class consciousness and the structuring of class itself (234). Giddens' analysis focuses on three factors of mediate structing. First, based on the division between manual and non-manual workers, he points out the importance of the existence of a "buffer zone"[5] between them that reduces the scope of inter- and intra-generational mobility, which contributes to the mediated structuration of the working class. To the extent that this mobility does not go beyond this "buffer zone," while it tends to concentrate mainly in the category of skilled manual workers, its mediated effect is the consolidation of various elements that contribute to the constitution of manual workers—especially unskilled—as a collective with class identity and consciousness.

Secondly, it refers to settlement patterns and eventual residential concentration as a factor in class structuration, something that not only works in the case of the working class but, in general, of other social classes. Spatial concentration—which in extreme cases acts as a process of residential segregation—acts by configuring spaces and territories of relatively homogeneous collectives in terms of their class situation and their position within social structures. This contributes to the formation of collective identities as a type of self-identity, one that is at the same time differentiated from other collectives in other class positions who are located in other territories. The extreme cases are undoubtedly mining operations, which tend to concentrate their workers either in camps or in small towns and cities, isolated from the rest of the urban system and close to the operation. It is often thought that the formation of large cities and metropolitan cities could cause a de-structuring of class, insofar as they favor anonymity, high daily spatial mobility, and neighborhood disengagement, all of which contribute to dilute the structuring of class. However, this does not seem to be the case, especially in large cities in European societies and in North America. On the other hand, the very conformation of new urban ghettos, where immigrants and social minorities

---

5 The notion of a buffer zone refers to the fact that, given that virtually "all movement, whether upward or downward, inter-or intragenerational, across the non-manual/manual division, is 'short-range': that is to say, takes place in such a way as to minimize achieved differences in market capacity. Thus, there is some ... sort of 'buffer zone' between the two class groupings" (Giddens, 1975: 181).

preferentially settle, contributes to resignifying the spaces of the city. This, thereby, strengthens the mechanisms for the construction of collective identities and class consciousness in opposition to other urban collectives located in other spaces, where the very configuration of the urban landscape—its architecture, the urban design of its spaces, as well as the way of inhabiting them (with their smells, colors, and sounds)—form mechanisms of social and class differentiation and, by that means, of structuring class and class consciousness.

Thirdly, Giddens points out how union organization and the axes of its constitution also shape the structuring factors of the working class, especially in terms of its awareness of economic and political conflict. In this respect, he takes up the already known differentiation in terms of unionization in the United States and Europe, pointing out the predominance of industrial conflict in the constitution of the former, as opposed to the greater degree of politicization in the case of European labor unionism. Beyond the stereotypes that may prevail, what is relevant is to recognize the union and, in general, the role of the organization of the working class as a field of its very constitution and of the character of its class consciousness as such.

Giddens takes up this approach to class structuring in order to analyze the formation of what has been called a "new working class" (196). To this end, he considers three different modes of structuring, which refer to aspects of different types of social and economic structures. He begins his discussion by analyzing the conformation of an underclass, which would correspond to diverse socio-demographic groups that emerge in contemporary capitalism such as immigrants, young people, women, and other ethnic and social minorities. It corresponds to a downward differentiation mode, through the pauperization and precariousness of these groups in the face of the new conditions of employability and social reproduction that emerge in capitalism due to its transition to a global and post-industrial economy. In this sense, processes of social and demographic discrimination acquire great importance, built from the predominance of cultural and social forms such as racism and xenophobia. This generates two types of differentiation: (1) the differentiation of these groups from society as a whole—constituted as postmodern strangers (Canales, 2021) or as collateral damage of globalization (Bauman, 2011)—; and (2) the differentiation of these groups from the traditional working class, whose members commonly form part of the ethnic majority of advanced societies. In this way, it is not only an underclass in terms of its subordinate, discriminated, and vulnerable position, but also in the sense that it shapes a way of structuring themselves and of constituting class consciousness that is traversed by relations deriving from one's specific position in the economic-productive structure—their class situation—as well as from their position in social structures and cultural representations that are predominant in contemporary society.

As well, Giddens considers the reverse case of upward differentiation, in which the upper strata of the working class increase their real income, tending towards an eventual middle class. Giddens refers to white-collar workers, who would form a type of middle class very different from the one Marx spoke of, which referred rather to a petty bourgeoisie. Other authors speak of a type of working-class *gentrification*—an unfortunate category—which refers more to a way of stigmatizing a phenomenon than to describing and understanding it. In any case, it is a process that entails a certain erosion of the existing class structure and modifies the modes, character, and scope of the structuring of the working class and the formation of its class consciousness.

These processes refer to modes of de-structuring the working class that imply a process of fragmentation as a class and, therefore, of its identity and consciousness as such. To these Giddens adds a third process that complicates the structuration of the class and that would imply, rather, its transition towards liquid and less structuring forms. It corresponds to the "separation that has taken place between the position of a worker as producer and [their] position as consumer" (Giddens, 1975: 216). This contributes to generate new fields of structuration class distinctions, which would no longer pass through the productive and labor structures and relations but through the sphere of distribution relations. What at first operated through mass consumption now operates as its inverse, as a mode of social distinction and differentiation through consumption. In both cases, a double process of equalization/inequality operates through consumption. On the one hand, subjects and individuals are equalized as consumers, diluting the inequality structured in the economic-productive field. On the other hand, they are, again, made unequal through the distinction in consumption and the income it demands. In both cases, what is relevant is that the moment of consumption—and, therefore, of income and the market—configures a fundamental mediation in the structuring of classes and class consciousness, as well as its translation into the modes of conflict and tensions that arise from it.

A similar process of reflection is developed when Giddens analyzes the ways of structuring the *new* middle class in advanced societies A first aspect to consider is his explicit rejection of the thesis that advanced societies would move towards becoming middle class societies, regardless of the relative and absolute increase in the volume of white-collar workers, technicians, and professionals. This position that Giddens takes with respect to capitalist society in the 1970s is, in our opinion, equally valid today for analyzing contemporary, global, and postmodern societies. For one thing, the question of the middle classes is more complex than the mere variation in the quantitative composition of the labor mass and alludes precisely to the ways of structuring the middle classes in advanced capitalism.

The central question remains how to define what is called the "middle class." In this regard, there is often a double confusion in the discussion, which comes from defining the middle class as the supposed space that mediates between the worker—the direct producer—and the capitalists and landowners. Attempting to create a classification for what the middle classes is by what it is not—workers or capitalists—is not only imprecise but also lacks the slightest trace of theoretical and methodological soundness. By merely defining the middle classes as the middle-income population, what is between capitalist and the working class, the term falls into an even more serious imprecision and methodological bias by reducing the conceptual and theoretical definition to only one of its possible measures and calculations.

This "confusion" when we refer to the middle class—to call somehow this theoretical-methodological deficiency—arises from the absence of a definition of class in general and of what makes it a mediating force in society. In this sense, Giddens distances himself from the notion of class as an actor (in reference to Touraine's definition of this category of analysis) and even states that "[a] class is not even a 'group'; the concept ... refers to *a cluster of forms of structuration* based upon commonly shared levels of market capacity" (Giddens, 1975: 192). In the case of the middle class, this approach to class structuration is even more pertinent and necessary, since we are dealing with individuals who normally lack paratechnical conditions that precisely define a class situation, as well as mediated conditions that contribute to the generation of a clear and indubitable class identity. Giddens adds that even in the case of being unionized, middle-class people are usually characterized by not taking a clear form of conflict consciousness, which would otherwise allow them to assume defined and consistent positions in the face of conflict, negotiation, and politics that go beyond their immediate interests.

Hence, it is a methodological requirement to analyze the constitution of the middle class (and of the middle classes, in plural, we would add) based on their modes of structuration and not so much as the result of a process of hierarchical qualification derived from the form adopted by the function of distribution of resources, capital, status, etc., even though this distribution is directly related to and conditioned by the form adopted by the class structure and its structuring at each historical moment.

In relation to the new middle class, it is a category that encompasses important class differences in terms of the way it is structured. The most relevant refers to its origin and function in the process of production and economic distribution, as well as its situation in relation to the labor process itself. In this respect, Giddens, together with other authors, distinguishes two large sectors, which, moreover, acquire relevance at different moments in the development of capitalism itself: (1) the so-called white-collar workers, consisting mainly of clerks, office workers, salesmen, and administrative support staff, who become relevant in the early stages of capitalism's development, especially in the twentieth century; and (2) technicians and professionals, who show a more pronounced growth and development in contemporary capitalism, especially since globalization, the advent of a post-Fordist and post-industrial mode of organization of the work process (Fazio, 2011) and the consolidation of a knowledge and information industry as a new engine of capital accumulation (Mattelart, 2003; Blondeau, 2008).

These are, in fact, two middle classes that are very different from each other, both in terms of their class position in the labor process and in terms of their ways of structuring themselves as social classes, including the formation of their awareness of conflict and negotiation. Likewise, these are social and labor sectors exposed to different working conditions and exploitation that also imply significant differences in terms of their situation as classes in terms of the structure of risks, vulnerabilities, as well as the precariousness and social protection to which they may have access. Within this middle class in general in this case, we could advance that a process of polarization is configured, which not only refers to living and income conditions but also to work conditions and the structuring of themselves as social classes.

In the case of white-collar workers, there are two types of activities: (1) administrative support workers for the production process—secretaries, clerks, employees, cleaning and maintenance, among others—and (2) support personnel for the distribution and consumption process—salespersons, retail workers, personal services, among others. In both cases, these are, in general, support personnel who provide support but do not necessarily participate in the production process.

In the case of technicians and professionals, on the other hand, we are dealing with personnel who participate directly in the work process through the organization, management, and control of production. Likewise, it acquires more and more weight in the face of the predominance of a new mode of productive organization, where the motor of the process is transferred to the moment of information and knowledge processing, sustained by the development of new technologies that facilitate the flexibilization of work processes, as well as the separation and relocation of its parts in geographically distant points. They are the architects of the global knowledge industry, a sector of activity around which is organized not only the global work process but also the whole process of accumulation together with its counterpart, the financial sector (Harvey, 2005; Lash and Urry, 1998).

In this way, we can begin to see that in contemporary capitalism—global, informational, postmodern—the middle class is, in reality, an ambiguous category that hides a great differentiation and polarization within it, the same that accounts for completely different ways of structuring itself as a social class. In fact, these two major aspects of the shaping and structuring of middle classes indicate that the commonly assumed notion of a service economy is, in reality, an ideological construction that hides the new forms of construction of class inequality, which are added to and articulated with the forms already known from the industrial capitalism of the nineteenth and twentieth centuries. This new form of the global and informational economy—although based on the development of services as a sector of economic activity that concentrates the greatest growth in employment and, in general, the greatest volume of workers—contains a profound social and class division, which is reflected in the growing polarization of the occupational structure in developed countries. In other texts (Canales, 2021 and 2019), we have shown how in European countries and in the United States the growth of the service sector is structured on the basis of a deep occupational polarization. Along with the increase and consolidation of a class of high-level professionals and technicians—directly linked to the new demands imposed by the knowledge economy on the production process—there is also an increase and consolidation of a new class of unskilled service workers, who face a highly disadvantageous labor market insertion, characterized by high levels of labor precariousness and social vulnerability in terms of their living and working conditions.

In the first case, this is exactly what Sassen (2007) refers to when she describes a new transnational elite: These are workers who participate in the management and control of the global work process and in the provision of various productive services to transnational companies and corporations. This is both in terms of the work process itself—technical and technological support, provision of services and computer support, among others—and in administrative support and control activities—accounting, marketing, business organization, among others.

In the second case, these are workers in a situation of high social vulnerability and job insecurity, who are engaged in various services both for companies and for individuals. Those included in the group are individuals who offer cleaning and maintenance services for buildings, offices, and factories, as well as other unskilled services, which are equally essential for the functioning of these other activities carried out by technicians and professionals. In addition, it includes personal services—also of low qualification—such as domestic service, food preparation, transportation, and other services that are equally necessary for the social and daily reproduction of these same technicians and professionals in the global industry (Hondagneu-Sotelo, 2007).

It is equally relevant that this new division of labor takes the form of a racialization of the occupational structure (Canales, 2019), where top management, professional, technical, and similar positions are occupied by white workers or workers from the ethnic-national majority of each country. In contrast, positions in unskilled services are usually filled by immigrant workers, women, and other social and demographic minorities. In this sense, ethno-national origin, gender, and other fields of constitution of social inequalities also form spaces from which the difference in class structuring is established.

In both cases—professionals and technicians, as well as unskilled workers in various services—we are referring to "white-collar" workers, who could be included in the broad category of "middle classes." However, as we see, they are very different social subjects in terms of their modes and conditions of structuration themselves as a class. In both cases, both the paratechnical conditions and the social contexts refer us to modes of structuration that are very different from each other, although in both cases they are modes and conditions of structuring that also distance them from manual workers and laborers, in one case, and from businessmen and owners of capital, in the other. What is relevant is that the model of analysis proposed by Giddens almost 50 years ago is, nevertheless, very pertinent for the understanding of the modes of structuring of these new classes—middle and popular—in contemporary capitalism.

In synthesis, this vision of classes as structuration processes proposed by Giddens, opens the analysis to the heterogeneity of class structures in capitalist societies. It is a non-deterministic approach to class structuration and social conflict, while allowing us to understand and analyze the differences between different capitalist societies in terms of their class structures and the forms of class struggle at each moment in their history. For example, Giddens uses this line of thinking to illustrate the differences between American and French society with respect to the structuration of classes and, in particular, the meaning and significance of class struggle in both countries. These differences refer not only to factors linked to the economic-productive infrastructure but also, and equally fundamentally, to questions related to the political superstructure and the formation of the State. Thus, economy and politics, infrastructure and superstructure, are fields from which the process of structuring social classes in each society is forged.

This approach is interesting because in a certain way it distances itself completely from Tocqueville's (1963) approach, who uses the North American case as a parameter to measure and analyze the situation and state of European democracies (and of the structuring of classes and class conflict, we would add). For Giddens, such an exercise would make no sense, since the analysis must be made on the basis of the particular economic, social, and political conditions of each society and of its own time. Comparative models would only serve to analyze differences, never to establish patterns or models of behavior to be followed.

Likewise, it is equally interesting to note that this same idea is already implicit in the Marxist thesis that classes are constituted in the class struggle—that is, in the field of praxis where the conditions of the productive infrastructure are just that, conditioners of a social praxis and not its determinant, neither in the first nor in the last instance. Rather, contrary to the determinism of Marxist orthodoxy, we can affirm that the class struggle is the *field of possibility* of the constitution of classes, not necessarily of their determination as such; this is to recognize that the constitution of every subject—and classes—always operates on the dialectic between *existence* and *potency* (Zemelman, 1998)— that is, between the *determination of being* and its *possibility of being*, from which arises the construction of history. Thus, if the class struggle is evidently a historical process, whose form, structure, and dynamics are characteristic of each society and of each historical moment of that society, then it is logical to suppose that the class structure and the formation of classes must be equally dynamic and changing, a characteristic of each society and of each historical moment of that society that struggles between the determinants of its existence and its possibilities of being.

Every society is classist or based on class, yes, but each society has its own particular way of constitution and structuration the classes that make it up. For the same reason, general theories of the structuration and formation of classes—such as those established by Marxist orthodoxy—serve as a general illustration but never as a method and theory to understand class struggle in each historical moment of each society. What a theory of classes and class struggle should aim at is understanding the form of this dialectic between *existence* and *potentially*, determinations and possibilities. In the case of Giddens, it is a dialectic that can be approached from the *structuration approach*, while, in the case of Marx, it was approached from the concept of *praxis*. The main difference between the two approaches lies in the fact that Giddens' approach focuses on the mode of understanding the social phenomenon, while Marx's approach focuses on its continuous transformation, for which, as Luxemburg (2020 [1908]) pointed out, a mode of understanding and theoretical comprehension is indispensable.

2   Erik Olin Wright: Marxism and Social Classes Revisited

Wright made important contributions to the renewal of Marxism and its adaptation to current times, without losing sight of the critical and contesting sense of Marxist thought. He not only reflects and contributes theoretical elements on the constitution of classes in advanced societies but also offers specific models on how classes are structured, establishing the relevant axes and dimensions for their conformation as categories of analysis in empirical research and statistical measurement. In our case, we chose to analyze and reflect on his theoretical proposal for the construction of social classes rather than on his analytical and empirical proposal.

From his first studies, Wright positioned himself as an alternative to the dominant current in sociology, especially in the North American tradition where functional-structuralism and, to a lesser extent, Weberian thought usually predominate. On the one hand, he takes up class and Marxist analysis as the theoretical body from which he bases his thinking. On the other hand, and following this line of reflection, Wright focuses his analysis on the constitution of classes in the sphere of production and not so much in the field of distribution, distancing himself from the sociological mainstream. Finally, while recognizing the weight and importance of other fields of inequality such as male domination, racism, citizenship, or human rights, Wright maintains the Marxist principle that the social relations of production are the central sphere for understanding the capitalist system. In this respect, he pays more attention to relations of exploitation than to relations of domination as the starting point of his class analysis.[6]

Although he starts from the Marxist thesis that class struggle is the motor of history, Wright takes distance from both critics of Marxism and not a few Marxists themselves, pointing out that this use of Marxist theory does not imply that historical materialism and class analysis are a framework that can explain everything that happens in history. His proposal may seem somewhat more restricted, but it is nonetheless ambitious. Like Marx, he considers that "the overall trajectory of historical development can be explained by a properly constructed class analysis" (Wright, 2004: 1). The question, then, is how to construct such an *adequate* model of class analysis. In this regard, Wright proposes a model of class analysis based on four elements, namely:

---

6   More recently, however, Wright has put forward some revisions in this regard, proposing a model he calls "pragmatic realism" and with which he seeks to integrate (unify) the main theoretical bodies on society and social classes. In this regard, see Wright (2015).

1. the concept of *class structure*, which refers to the forms that class differentiation and inequality take and that give rise to class interests;
2. the concept of *class formation*, which refers to the way in which collective actors organize themselves;
3. the concept of *class struggle*, which refers to the practices of the actors around their class interests;
4. the concept of *class consciousness*, which is the self-understanding of actors of their class interests.

The objective of this model "is not simply to understand class structure and its effects, but to understand the interconnections among all these elements and their consequences for other aspects of social life" (Wright, 2004: 2). To this end, Wright emphasizes in his theorization the first of these concepts, that of *class structure*, which constitutes the central pivot in his version of class analysis. His reformulation of the idea of class structure is what allows clarifying the general logic of class analysis as a whole, establishing the interconnection with the other elements of his model of analysis. In order to differentiate class formation, class consciousness, or class struggle from any other formation, consciousness, or struggle of social groups, the key point is the definition of class as the articulating axis of the formation, struggle, and consciousness of social collectives. It is necessary, therefore, to define what constitutes them not as mere groups but as *social classes*. For Wright, the concept of class structure is what allows this constitution and gives meaning to the use of the term class as an adjective for its formation, consciousness, and struggle.

The key point Wright makes in this classification refers to the *class interests* that are shaped by the constitution of classes in a class structure. It is these class interests that give meaning to the formation of groups as social classes, to their social struggles as class struggles, and to the form of consciousness of their interests as class consciousness. In each of these three moments—formation, struggle, and class consciousness—it is fundamental to start from a prior definition of class structure that gives them meaning. For Wright, the elaboration of a clear and precise concept of class structure is "an important conceptual precondition for developing a satisfactory theory of the relationship between class structure, class formation and class struggle" (Wright, 2004: 3).

According to Wright, what structures society as classes is the relation of exploitation established between them in the production process. This argument, eminently Marxist, implies three elements to be taken into account: (1) classes are not given but are structured and, therefore, are historical processes; (2) this structuring of classes is based on relations of exploitation, which refers not to technical-productive processes but to social relations and structures of power and domination; and (3) these relations are not constituted in any social sphere but in the labor process, which takes the form of a social process of production in a double sense: on the one hand, it is determined by social-historic situations and structures, and on the other, it is in itself a process of social production—of the production of civil society, as Rousseau would say—which arises from these relations of exploitation and the constitution of classes.

On this Marxist foundation of class analysis, Wright establishes his model both in its theoretical and methodological forms for the empirical analysis of classes in contemporary capitalist society. The central pivot in this model is the concept of *exploitation*, from which he takes theoretical distance with respect to other models of class analysis elaborated from other conceptual matrixes (Weberian, functionalist, and even eclectic theorizations). Figure 3 illustrates this centrality of the concept of exploitation in Wright's model.

This figure identifies three dimensions from which social classes can be defined in sociological analysis. First, Wright posits that social classes can refer to a value of a distribution (income, for example) or to a position in a relationship. Considering the relational approach over the distributive one, a second aspect must, therefore, be resolved: whether classes are analyzed on the basis of market relations or on the basis of production relations. In the latter case, it would then be necessary to decide whether classes refer to positions in the technical division of labor, or to relations of authority with respect to the labor process, or to a system of exploitation of labor. Although it is recognized that there are other dimensions from which to construct the concept of social class, this model reflects more faithfully the dimensions that underpin the Marxist approach to social classes. This is because it recovers the central aspects to be taken into account: a relational approach that is centered on production and on the concept of exploitation as the foundation of the capitalist process of production.

Various controversies arise around the term exploitation, usually based on interpretations that come from positions of ethical and moral principles that tend to qualify it as something unjust. While this may be the case, it is a term that refers to something simpler in a Marxist perspective: the ability of some to extract or appropriate the labor and the fruits of the labor of others.[7] Based on this meaning of the term exploitation, Wright (2004: 9–10) establishes

---

7   In reality, Marx was not so much referring to the appropriation of the product of labor as to the extraction (appropriation) of the value of labor power by capital, as does an owner of any agricultural property, who, on the basis of the application of labor, extracts valuable products from the land, or the owner of a mine, who extracts minerals from which they appropriate value. In these two cases, it is not so much the products themselves that are of interest as their value, whether for direct use or for commodification. In this sense, it is interesting that Wright refers exploitation to the appropriation of the fruits of labor and not so much to the

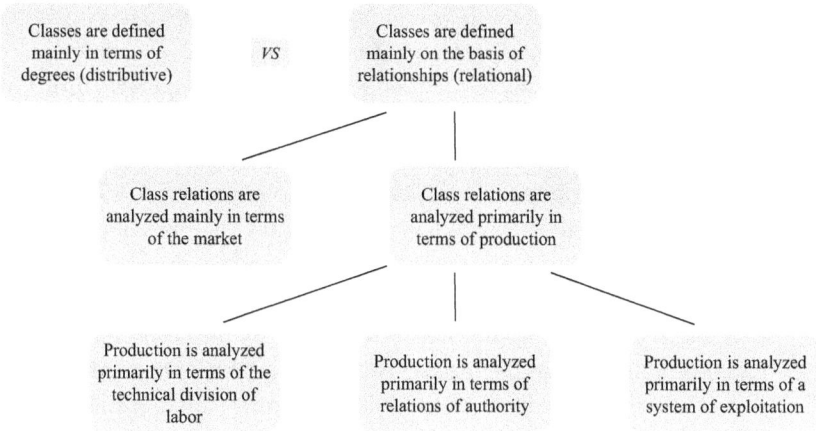

FIGURE 3   Erik O. Wright's typology of class definitions
SOURCE: ERIK O. WRIGHT (1979: 5)

three principles that allow him to define different spheres of the exploitation process:

1. The principle of *inverted interdependent welfare*, which refers to the fact that the welfare of the exploiter and the exploited are inversely related. The greater welfare of one is the counterpart of the lesser welfare of the other. Thus, the wealth of the rich is the counterpart of the poverty of the poor.
2. The *principle of exclusion*, which refers to asymmetrical relations with respect to access to and control of certain fundamental resources, such as the means of production. Exclusion responds to private property rights—that is, it deprives some of property rights in favor of others.
3. The *principle of appropriation*, which refers to the fact that those who own or control the means of production have the capacity to appropriate the fruit of the labor of others or the surplus product. This concept of appropriation by exploitation differs from other modes of appropriation by dispossession or expropriation, insofar as it is based directly on a relation of production and not on a relation of extra-economic power that gives rise to forms of oppression.

Based on these three principles, Wright establishes the basic form assumed by this fundamental antagonism between the material interests of classes

---

concept of extraction of value. We will return to the importance of this distinction later on in our critique of Wright's model.

in capitalism: the exploiters (capitalists) and the exploited (workers). Interdependence based on asymmetrical conditions of power allows some (capitalists, owners of the means of production) to appropriate the fruits of the labor of non-owners (workers). As Wright (2004: 14) himself points out,

> [b]ecause of the power relation between capitalists and workers, capitalists are able to force workers to produce more than is needed to provide them with this subsistence. As a result, workers produce a surplus which is owned by the capitalist and takes the form of profits. Profits, the amount of the social product that is left over after the costs of producing and reproducing all of the inputs (both labor power inputs and physical inputs) have been deducted, constitute an appropriation of the fruits of labor of workers.

In this way, the welfare of capitalists depends not only on the privations it can generate for workers but also on the effort it can demand from them in their work. In this way, we can point out that the first principle highlighted by Wrights of inverse interdependence in the welfare of capitalists and workers is reinforced by these other principles of asymmetries of power that allow the capitalist class to reinforce the exploitation of labor—that is, the appropriation of surplus product generated by the worker.[8]

An important contribution of Wright is his conceptualization and operationalization of the category of *middle classes*, a term undoubtedly full of ambiguities that calls into question not only the Marxist approach but almost all social class analysis. In fact, Marx never spoke of middle classes, at least not as a category of analysis in itself but only as a metaphorical reference. For him, classes are defined in terms of their relation to the means of production. In this sense, he defined three classes fundamentally: (1) the capitalists, who are owners and hire workers; (2) the proletariat, who have no means of production and are hired for a wage; and (3) the petty bourgeoisie, who, having means of production, do not hire workers, but use their own labor power. In

---

8 As we shall see below, this thesis is not free from discussion, insofar as it establishes a direct relation between profit as income of the capitalist, without considering the mediation imposed in this respect by the role of profit as surplus value in the process of the expanded reproduction of capital. This is not a minor element, since, by not considering this mediation of accumulation in the class structure, it makes abstraction of the meaning of class antagonism (capital-labor) from the perspective of political economy. In the end, Wright's thesis, by not including this other dimension of the capitalist production process, poses a distortion of the Marxist thesis on the structuring of social classes and of their fundamental antagonism in capitalism. We will return to this argument later.

this scheme, the so-called middle class—an ambiguous and multifaceted figure, but undoubtedly very characteristic of modern societies—simply has no place as a category of analysis in the traditional Marxist understand of class structures. However, as Wright points out, everything indicates that there is a social subject that can be assimilated to a notion of middle class, which also poses quite a few contradictions and paradoxes to class analysis. For one thing, although they could be conceptualized as part of the wage labor force (working for wages), they are normally associated in class conflicts with the interests of capitalists and in opposition to those of wage earners.[9]

In the face of this ambiguity, Wright proposes the theoretical construction of the middle classes as subjects situated in contradictory class relations and who, by the same token, generate equally contradictory class interests. On the one hand, they are employees and, therefore, wage earners who sell their labor power and do not own or possess the means of production. But, on the other hand, they usually occupy relatively strategic positions within the production process, which gives them varying degrees of power over the production and distribution of economic surplus. Likewise, these are positions that allow them to distance themselves and establish different ways of distinguishing themselves from traditional workers, both in symbolic terms and in relation to their living conditions, resource endowment, consumption levels, life patterns, and lifestyles.

Whether because they access positions of authority and control of the work process (managers, CEOs, executives) or because they have professional training and experience (engineers, supervisors, technicians, administrators, among others), the fact is that they manage to access positions of planning, organization, direction, or control of the production process. In this sense, the key concept in understanding contemporary class relations for Wright is that of authority and dominion over the production process exercised by the capitalist. This is because "[c]apitalists do not simply *own* the means of production and hire workers; they also *dominate* workers within production" (Wright, 2004: 16). This underlies the role of authority, which refers to the role of domination of the capitalist over labor—that is, the power that allows the capitalist to demand the greatest possible effort from the worker to generate surpluses. To this end, capitalist production always involves an apparatus of domination, in which various employees participate, even those considered part of the middle class. However, because of their function of controlling and

---

9 These would be workers with a weak consciousness of class conflict, who, in Giddens' terms, are the very definition of the middle class. See the previous section in this chapter.

directing the production process, they simultaneously occupy a double and contradictory role: on the one hand, they are wage employees and, as such, part of the proletarian class, but, on the other, they act in the interests of the capitalist, the owner of the means of production, exercising the authority conferred upon them as if they were part of the capitalist class.[10]

The basic question is that this contradictory class location also defines contradictory class interests. For the same reason, its position in the class structure cannot be directly and mechanically assimilated neither to the social class of the exploiters nor to that of the exploited, defining rather a complex intermediate field of variable and changing situations and interests in the face of specific historical circumstances.

2.1 Discussion Points on Erik Olin Wright's Approach

Wright's approach constituted an important contribution to Marxist thought and to the debate on social classes and inequality in contemporary capitalism. However, it is not exempt from controversy. In our case, we want to take up his approaches from a critical perspective in an attempt to deepen the Marxist theory of classes and social inequality. This critical reflection is organized around two axes that seem relevant to our own discussion.

The first refers to the concept of exploitation used by Wright, which seems to us to entail a certain distortion with respect to the approach developed by Marx. This discussion is undoubtedly relevant, since Wright himself takes it as the central pivot in his theory on class structure and the formation of class interests, from which his entire conceptual model on the formation and consciousness of class struggle in capitalism is built.

On more than one occasion, Wright refers to exploitation as the appropriation of surplus labor by capitalists. Likewise, he also points out on more than one occasion that this relation of exploitation is the basis on which class interests are defined, which would put capitalists and workers in opposition in two areas: (1) the distribution of that surplus or surplus labor; and (2) the dominion of the capitalist to impose greater efforts on the worker in the generation of that surplus. In these two aspects, we believe that Wright's argument is incomplete and generates a certain distortion as to the scope of Marx's proposal.

---

10 Figures such as the middle class thus defined, that is, in contradictory class positions, are not exclusive to capitalism. In Latin American *haciendas*, for example, based on forms of servile labor, there was also the figure of the foreman, who, although he was a worker, his function was to exercise the authority conferred on him by the *hacienda* owner in defense of his class interests.

Wright's principle of inverse interdependence, which puts in opposition the welfare of the capitalist to the welfare of the worker, does not refer exactly to the relation of capitalist exploitation defined by Marx, strictly speaking. For one thing, this way of posing the question suggests that the conflict of interests between one class and the other is situated in the sphere of the distribution of surplus, while presupposing that the central object of exploitation is the generation of wealth appropriable by the capitalist as a subject and not as a relation of capital—that is, its *accumulation*. Both arguments are fallacious, since they do not consider the crucial fact that the final object of the production process is the *accumulation of capital*, a concept which is absent from Wright's approach.

Based on this principle of the inverse interdependence of welfare, Wright establishes that class interests and class antagonism are structured in terms of the distribution of surplus and, therefore, of the distribution of wealth generated in the labor process. The point we want to highlight here is that class interests are not restricted to the modes—and metrics—of surplus distribution. The contradiction between capitalists and workers is not only defined by their power, as the former can become richer and richer, accumulating wealth and surplus, as rich as no other social class has ever been before in history. Nor is the question that the capitalist classes exercise a power of domination and control of the process of production and exploitation as a function of this concentration of wealth for themselves. Capital—not only the capitalist—is the dominant factor in the labor process to the extent that it organizes it as a process of *capital accumulation*, based on the extraction of value from labor—of surplus value—which, as such, is what *accumulates* as capital, as accumulated value.

It is not just the concentration of wealth in the hands of the capitalist—which, undoubtedly, it also is—but also the concentration of value as accumulation of capital—that is, the *capitalization of surplus value*, which is the essence of the capitalist production process and which defines and gives meaning to the process of exploitation. Likewise, it is not only a process of exploitation—that is, of appropriation of the product of the labor of others, purely and simply, but of *alienation* of labor and of the product of labor. The surplus-value generated by labor and the worker is not only taken from them and appropriated by capital, but also that same already capitalized surplus-value is placed before them as its counterpart, its antagonist in the labor process: as capital.

If we look at the question in terms of its sheer measures and volumes, there is no doubt that the small part of the surplus labor—of the surplus—that is appropriated by an individual of the capitalist class as a social subject (the capitalist's collected rent) really pales in magnitude and power compared to that part of the *surplus* that is equally appropriated (*accumulated*) by capital itself as a factor and subject of production, for the purpose of its own accumulation and capitalization. To put it in simpler terms, it is evident that the wealth of any business professional and their family—that is, the income and rents that sustain and finance their lifestyle and material tastes, however sumptuous and wasteful they may be—pales in comparison with the wealth of their capital—that is, the value of their companies and their productive, financial, commercial, and technological assets. This is precisely why wealth in surveys, like the famous Forbes list of the wealthiest, is not measured by disposable income used in direct consumption but, rather, by income plus the value of capital in their companies and financial and productive assets.

In a word: the meaning of capitalism lies within this *capital relation*—that is, the continuous and permanent *valorization of capital*, its capitalization, what Marx analyzed as the extended reproduction of capital. The wealth and welfare of capitalists become a mere corollary in the matter, a minor externality for capital, though certainly not minor for the structuring of social and class inequality in capitalism in particular social contexts.

The theoretical and methodological consequence of our critique is that class antagonism and class interests, therefore, are not only constituted around the distribution of surplus between social subjects but also, fundamentally, between economic-productive subjects. It is not only the distribution of income (rents and wages) between capitalists and workers but also the organic composition of value between capital and labor. These are the class interests around which the class struggle is structured. Class antagonism is not only structured on the basis of the struggle for the distribution of surplus, but also around the process of capital accumulation—that is, around capital as a social relation of production: its *capitalization* based on the *alienation* of labor.

The class interest of the capitalist is never to increase their direct welfare and wealth (in itself always high) but, rather, to ensure its perpetuity and maintain the accumulation of capital, expanding the reproduction of capital and the capitalization of surplus labor. For its part, the class interest of the proletariat is not only or exclusively to improve their living and working conditions and increase the value of their labor power (of their wage): its main class interest is against the *alienation* of their labor (Lukács, 1969). Therefore, Marx refers to the abolition of the ownership of the means of production as the central focus of the proletarian struggle, since that ownership is the genesis of the exploitation and alienation of labor and of the capitalization of its surplus.

Hence, the struggle of the proletariat is against capitalist alienation and for an emancipation and liberation from the property relations on which it is established, while the strategy of capital and the capitalist is to maintain and reproduce these forms of alienation of labor and continuous and permanent capitalization of surplus. The struggle for the distribution of surplus—that is, the struggle for the distribution of income, wealth, privileges, lifestyles, status, consumption, etc.—is undoubtedly valid. But this does not imply that it is the fundamental contradiction of capitalism. In fact, this struggle refers a much older debate within Marxism, which arose within socialist strands in the first half of the twentieth century, a debate centered on what Luxemburg aptly synthesized as *Reform or Revolution*. The struggle for distribution is part of projects of reform and antagonism *in* capitalism but not necessarily a path that works *against* it in a revolutionary sense. Undoubtedly, these struggles are part of the triumphs of the workers' movement in capitalism, especially in the twentieth century, but this does not imply that all the struggle of workers' movements should be restricted to these domains.

However, this distinction does not imply a confrontation of exclusions. From our perspective, it is rather a matter of levels of class conflict from which we can define different scopes in terms of class interests. That the general and transcendental interest of the working class is the abolition of capitalism as a form of exploitation and alienation of labor (in which it has an obvious direct interest) does not imply that it cannot assume class interests within capitalism, reflected in a struggle over the distribution of economic surplus, surplus labor, and its living and working conditions. The point is that neither one can deny the other, nor subsume one into the other. It is a matter of differentiated fields and levels, which have to be established as such, referring to each sphere in its proper measure.

The second axis of our critique of Wright is a corollary of the previous one. Wright points out that, given this confrontation over the distribution of the surplus, the domination that the capitalist has over the production process allows them to demand a greater effort from the worker for the generation of economic surplus. In reality, this thesis is questionable. It is true that there are relations of domination in the labor process that contribute to the employer and foremen being able to exercise this control and imposition on the worker, but this is not so relevant in terms of the generation of surplus value. On the one hand, it refers rather to industrial engineering—that is, to the form of organization, direction, and control of the production process—than to its form as a political economy of the exploitation of labor and accumulation of capital. And, on the other hand, the formula that capital utilizes to increase its rate of surplus value does not have so much to do with the greater physical exploitation of the worker but, rather, a greater type of *organic exploitation* that accompanies a continuous increase in the organic composition of capital—that is, the relation between constant capital and variable capital.

Certainly, the portion of profit—indicative of the surplus value generated by labor over the cost of labor—is influenced by the level of advancement in productive forces. Additionally, it is shaped by the social and historical factors that determine the value of labor power and the value of the goods and services essential for the worker's reproduction of that labor power in the production process. The development of the productive forces refers to the productivity of labor and is achieved as a result of technological innovation and the application of scientific knowledge to the work process, a phenomenon that gives rise to the industrial revolutions and sustains the development of capitalism and its productive forces. In fact, the research and application of knowledge and technologies to the labor process operates as a counter tendency to the fall of the rate of profit in a double sense.

On the one hand, it represents a continuous increase in the organic composition of capital—that is, the composition between constant capital and variable capital—which is what gives constant movement to capital as a relation of accumulation. Although, it is important to note that this same process of increasing the organic composition of capital is the structural basis of the decreasing tendency of the rate of profit. In this sense, it also contributes to increase the technical composition of capital—between fixed capital and labor power—thus contributing to an increase in the productivity of the worker through technological advancement, not only in terms of greater commodity production but also of greater generation of value per unit of labor.

The determination of wages is a historical and social process, which depends on the correlation of forces between capitalists and proletarians and other classes and social strata. It refers directly to the distribution of income and productive surpluses destined to the reproduction of the population—that is, of social classes—and indirectly to the distribution of surpluses between the spheres of expanded reproduction of capital and the social reproduction of classes.

In the first case, as a struggle for income distribution, it is part of the dynamics of any capitalist society, which, as we can see throughout history, goes through different moments according to the correlation of forces, alliances, hegemonies, and domination of some classes over others. On this point, Wright's contribution to clarify class interests and class formation is of great value, especially in terms of how to identify the interests of the middle classes and the possibilities, therefore, of building alliances and hegemonic historical blocs, as was the case with the social blocs of the 20th century that supported the welfare state model with a Fordist mode of production and the Keynesian model of organization of the economy, market, and society. Likewise, in the second area, regarding the confrontation between the interests of capital reproduction (not only of capitalists) and social reproduction (the struggle for income distribution), nothing exemplifies it better than the continuous affirmations from neoliberalism and neoclassical economic thought, which argue that any wage increase above labor productivity entails risks to investment and economic growth.

3   Charles Tilly and Categorical Inequality

Charles Tilly, an American sociologist, proposed an interesting twist in the understanding of social inequality. His proposal focuses on studying what he calls *durable inequality*—that is, those inequalities "that last from one social interaction to the next, with special attention to those that persist over whole careers, lifetimes, and organizational histories" (Tilly, 1999: 6). Throughout our lives, human beings spend time immersed into different social relationships, all of which always generate some form of social distinction and differentiation. Durable inequality refers to those distinctions and differentiations that transcend the times and spaces of each circumstantial relationship and form part of central aspects of individuals, of their social identities. To this end, he introduces the concept of *categorical inequality*, understood as those lasting and systematic inequalities that manage to generate persistent and structural distinctions between members of different social categories.

The categories to which Tilly refers, are those organizational mechanisms that make it possible to establish systems of closures—that is, to define the boundaries of social inclusion and exclusion that organize individuals into categorical forms. In this sense, it is worth making two clarifications that, from our perspective, are fundamental for understanding Tilly's analysis of categorical inequality. On the one hand, that a social category acts by establishing social boundaries between individuals, agglutinating and including those who are considered to be similar to one other, while at the same time dividing others who are considered dissimilar, excluded from the first priority category and agglutinated to a second (or third) category. On the other hand, despite these agglutinations, "[c]ategories are not specific sets of people or unmistakable attributes, but standardized, movable social relations" (Tilly, 1999: 66).

This emphasis on social relations as the origin and sustenance of categorical inequality is, in our view, fundamental in Tilly's approach and refers to an equally radical critique of approaches based on methodological and phenomenological individualism, as well as structuralist approaches. The theoretical construction focuses on the links that relate objects (social categories, structures, behaviors, etc.) and not on their ontological essences. The object of study is, thus, the system of social relations and links that generate inequalities, analyzed in terms of categorical pairs such as man/woman, black/white, citizen/foreigner, youth/adult, rural/urban, aristocrat/plebeian, among many other categorical pairs that generate social differentiation.

Based on this relational and categorical approach, the analysis of inequality no longer focuses on distributions of a continuum—such as rich ... poor, high ... low or similar—but on categories that represent qualitative differences—social closures of inclusion/exclusion—where the categorical limits not only act as boundaries of separation between them, but also as social relations that link and construct these social distinctions themselves, shaping categories of distinction on which inequality is sustained and generated. We are referring to identity limits and frontiers between categories, but, at the same time, identities that are founded on their relationship with a socially designed other, the other category. The identity of the included is constructed in relation to their opposition to that of the excluded. The same happens with inequality in welfare and power: the power of some is based on their power over others.

In this sense, for Tilly, categorical boundaries play an important organizational role into the society and, in particular, in social inequality, to such an extent that, in his view, it would be these categorical differences that would really explain a large part of what ordinary observers assume as individual differences in terms of talents, training, efforts, or personal histories of individuals. They are, therefore, categorical distinctions that contribute to social organization. Taking up Weber's thesis on what he called "social closures," Tilly points out that categorial limits, while enabling and facilitating the action of the powerful to exclude others from the benefits and full enjoyment of the exercise of their power, also and simultaneously promote the action of the underprivileged—of those excluded from power—to organize themselves and establish forms of action for access to those benefits and enjoyment of power that are denied them. Based on this, Tilly (1999: 7) expresses his central thesis in this way:

> Large, significant inequalities in advantages among human beings correspond mainly to categorical differences such as black/white, male/female, citizen/foreigner, or Muslim/Jew rather than to individual differences in attributes, propensities, or performances. In actual operation, more complex categorical systems involving multiple religions or various races typically resolve into bounded pairs relating just two categories at a time, as when the coexistence of Muslims, Jews, and Christians

resolves into the sets Muslim/Jew, Muslim/Christian, and Jew/Christian, with each pair having its own distinct set of boundary relations. Even where they employ ostensibly biological markers, such categories always depend on extensive social organization, belief, and enforcement.

And to reinforce the social and historical character of categorical inequality, Tilly (1999: 9) explicitly points out the following:

> Much of what observers ordinarily interpret as individual differences that create inequality is actually the consequence of categorical organization. For these reasons, inequalities by race, gender, ethnicity, class, age, citizenship, educational level, and other apparently contradictory principles of differentiation form through similar social processes and are to an important degree organizationally interchangeable.

But it is not just any social differentiation or inequality, but forms of distinction that involve power relations between categories. For Tilly, durable inequality between categories allows those who control power and access to value-generating resources (the dominant category in the relationship) to solve organizational problems, establishing precisely these categorical distinctions, generating with them forms and systems of social closure, of borders and limits that define the spaces of inclusion and exclusion and, therefore, that determine who belongs to one or another social category. At the base of all categorial inequality, there is always some form of power relation that allows one of the categories to define and use these closures to resolve the question of distribution, appropriation, and exploitation of values and resources; its very constitution as inequality contributes to its social reproduction.

The persistence of inequality is the result of the institutionalization of categorical inequality—that is, of the normalization of the system of categorical pairs of social distinction. In an organizational sense, the system of paired and unequal categories plays a fundamental role in the configuration of societies. Through this categorical system, long-lasting forms of differentiation and inequality are produced and recreated in relation to access to and appropriation of goods, values, welfare, power, and other socially valued resources. It is true that not all the categorical pairs of this system of social inequality operate always and in the same way in all social and historical contexts. However, it is also true that in every social and historical context inequality is configured on the basis of these systems of categorical differentiation. Likewise, these systems of categorical differentiation may not always be able to explain the origin and genesis of social inequality, but in any case, social inequality always operates on the basis of these systems of categorical distinction. Although they do not always explain the origin of social inequality itself, they do explain its *persistence* in each historical context as a structural phenomenon.

It is common for people to tend to normalize categories of inequality, naturalizing them and even attributing their categorical distinction to possible genetic or physical profiles or other directly perceptible attributes of differentiation. However, this is nothing more than a social construction. The limits and boundaries established on the basis of categories such as gender, race, or age, for example, although they appear to have some natural substratum, are in fact socially constructed. However, the limits established as well as the conditions that characterize each categorical pair on either side of those limits may vary significantly throughout history and may be constructed differently in each society. But, in all of them and in every epoch, the categories refer to forms of social inequality—in other words, methods of socially constructing boundaries and divisions that result in inequality within each categorical pair.

Categorical inequality is not an exclusive product of modern societies but has been around for thousands of years, when human beings formed the first communities and social organizations. The persistence of categorical inequality is due to two reasons: (1) it facilitates the exploitation and hoarding (concentration) of resources, opportunities, and power among the most favored in an organization; and (2) once categorical inequality has been institutionalized, its modification and transformation into new organizational models would imply too high transaction and adaptation costs. Once a form of categorical inequality is established, it is itself part of the forces that sustain its reproduction and of the social organization to which it gives rise. Patriarchy, for example, as a form of male-female categorical inequality not only establishes gender difference but its own reproduction and, by that means, the reproduction of society organized around gender inequality. Likewise, the enduring presence of gender inequality for over a millennium, organized on the basis of patriarchal forms, bestows upon it a powerful force for reproducing and structuring social life. Its eventual transformation requires, therefore, the deployment of an equally powerful force that can subvert this mode of reproduction and organization of social life, from its most everyday confines to its most fundamental structures.

Advancing in his proposal, Tilly (1999) identifies four causal processes through which categorical inequality is constructed, namely:

1. *Exploitation*, which refers to the appropriation and disposition of resources generated by others. It is a concept taken directly from Marxist literature, although Tilly generalizes the concept beyond the economic-productive spheres.

2. *Opportunity hoarding*, which refers to the concentration in the distribution of resources, values, power, and well-being. In this case, concentration contributes to the reproduction of categorical inequality.
3. *Emulation*, which refers to the copying and transplanting of unequal relations from one sphere to another.
4. *Adaptation*, which consists of the elaboration of daily routines that refer to the role of social networks and other mechanisms that contribute to maintaining the boundaries and closures of each category between those inside and outside them.

While exploitation and hoarding act directly in the installation, constitution, and genesis of categorical inequality, emulation and adaptation act by generalizing and reproducing it in other spheres and contexts. Exploitation and hoarding provide the means to achieve the unequal appropriation of benefits, values, and powers and, therefore, to constitute inequality between categories. However, these mechanisms do not ensure their permanence and the maintenance of the distinction between the included and the excluded—i.e., that social closures and boundaries between categories endure. In this sense, "[e]mulation and adaptation lock such distinctions into place, making them habitual and sometimes even essential to exploiters and exploited alike." (Tilly, 1999: 11).

When analyzing the causal mechanisms and processes that produce, sustain, and alter categorical inequality over time, explanatory models face at least four drawbacks, corresponding to *particularism, interaction, transmission*, and *mentalism*. Let us explore these critiques and qualms.

First of all, the idea of particularism refers to the essential question of why, if each form of categorical inequality seems to be explained by its own factors and not those of the others, it nevertheless shows very striking similarities in terms of the mechanisms of inclusion/exclusion in almost every society. This is so because in the configuration of each form of categorical inequality there are more causal factors than those pointed out by particularistic explanations. What lies behind this is that we are not dealing with inequalities produced by naturalized forms of individuals, but by social processes of distinction and differentiation between subjects and collectives, processes that are very similar in terms of the ways and strategies of constituting categorical closures and borders. And this is true both for patriarchy, in the case of gender inequality, and xenophobia, present in the state forms of distinction of citizenship/foreigners, or racism, inherited from slavery in inequality by ethno-racial origin, to cite three very current examples of categorical inequality.

The second drawback refers to the difficulty of the most common explanations to account for the interactions between various forms of categorical inequality. Here we are dealing with a double type of difficulty. On the one hand, there is the conjunction in the same process of various modes of categorical inequality. In the case of labor insertion, for example, it refers to how economic exploitation in global capitalism tends to combine different conditions of categorical inequality. Thus, as Parella (2003) points out, migrant women in advanced societies are three times discriminated against and exploited: first, because of their class condition; second, because of their gender condition; and, third, because of their migratory condition. In this case, the conjunction—interaction—of categorical inequalities results in enhanced forms of social inequality.

A further complication in the discourse arises when interaction transitions into the interchangeability of categorical inequality. Here, similar jobs are exposed to different forms of categorical inequality, depending on the social, historical, and geographical context, so that they end up being exclusively female in some cases, for immigrants in others, or for ethnic-racial minorities in a third sphere (Tilly, 1999). Such is the case of seasonal work in modern, globalized agriculture. In California, for example, this precarious work is developed by Mexican migrants, many of them undocumented (Hernández, 2015). In modern export agriculture in northern and western Mexico (Sinaloa, San Quintín, Sayula, among others), these same jobs are occupied by indigenous people from the southern states of Mexico (mainly Oaxaca) (Lara, Sánchez and Saldaña, 2014). In a different context in the Central Valley of Chile, but still in the area of export agriculture, women instead of migrants are employed to develop these same jobs and occupations (Canales, 2001). In these three cases, we are dealing with the same structure of social inequality in relation to work, but is adopts different forms of categorical inequality, which are literally interchangeable depending on the geographic and social context.

The third drawback facing explanatory frameworks on the causes of inequality is the transmission of categorical inequality to new members. If one accepts the perspective that inequalities refer to individual differences, the question then becomes how these attributes are inherited by the new members of each category. The case of gender is eloquent in this respect. If the situation of women implies a condition of social vulnerability, then why is this situation only inherited by their female daughters and not by their male children? The question is evidently more complex and alludes to the processes of reproduction of categorical inequality that are equally the product of social and historical relations. Categorical inequality is transmitted not as an inheritance pure and simple but as the reproduction of the social conditions that generated the same categorical inequality in the first place. Thus, women's inequality before men is not inherited from women to their daughters but is socially transmitted to the extent that the social relation—patriarchy—is socially reproduced from one generation to the next. Again, this process is not one of mere mother-daughter transfer but of sociohistorical transmission—that is, of reproduction of power relations between men and women that account for the relations of exploitation, monopolization, emulation, and adaptation already mentioned above and which are part of the causation—and, in this case, transmission—of categorical inequalities. Just as categorical inequalities are a reflection of social relations of inequality, their transmission is equally the result of the reproduction of these same social relations. Inequality is not inherited directly but transmitted through the social reproduction of its causal factors and relations.

The fourth drawback is mentalism, which refers to mental states as "fundamental sources of inequalities" (Tilly, 1999: 17). Tilly's analysis here is much more complex than the previous ones dealing with inequality, since it refers not only to mechanisms of the phenomenon but also to what Tilly calls ontological foundations, from which different ways of explaining social inequality are constructed. In this regard, he identifies four ontologies, namely: (1) methodological individualism, (2) phenomenological individualism, (3) system theory or structuralism, and (4) relational models, which is the one Tilly defends and argues for in his proposal. For Tilly, the fundamental difference between these ontologies is that, while the first three focus on the essences of individuals or of systems, the fourth is based on bonds, which make it possible to combine both aspects of the subjects involved (the individual level) and of the social contexts and structures (systems).[11]

Methodological individualism is based on the idea that social life is the product of people's individual actions, motivated by their own interests. Categorical inequality—gender, age, ethnicity, citizenship, etc.—is explained, then, by the differences in individual attributes between those who belong to one or another social category. The causal mechanism of inequality corresponds to mental events—i.e., the decisions made by individuals based on particular rationalities. The problem is that this ontology does not formulate a plausible theory of how these mental events result in social and categorical inequality.

For its part, phenomenological individualism postulates the conscious mind as the ultimate social reality (Tilly, 1999: 20). In this sense, it supports an

---

11 Hence, the title of the first chapter of his book *Durable Inequality* (1999) is, precisely, "Of Essences and Bonds", as a way of reflecting the transcendence of this distinction in his theoretical proposal.

explanation of inequality based on consciousness and the forms of communication between the mental constructions of individuals with respect to the social. For this ontology, people's behavior is based on the meanings attributed to categories, and based on this, they act categorially—that is, disseminating their own conception of themselves, their categorial identities, to others. The problem is that so far this ontology has not provided a coherent explanation of how the mental and conscious states of individuals provoke alterations in social structures, such as the categorial construction of inequality.

The system perspective, on the other hand, appeals to the role of social structures as generators of inequality, abstracting from the conditions of individuals, their attributes, consciences and mental constructs. Gender inequality, for example, is explained by the weight of social structures that construct gender difference, such as patriarchy and the sexual division of labor. These are explanations based on structures without subjects, where the mechanisms that allow us to understand how the social structure really articulates categorical inequalities are not established. The structure becomes a noun but never a verb, never the action of subjects. The structure, therefore, acts by itself, without further mediation. Although social structures are relevant and have a primordial weight in the gestation and reproduction of categorial inequalities, what is needed is to move from the analysis of the structure of categorial inequality to that of the social structuring of categorial inequalities, as Giddens rightly points out.

Relational analysis, on the other hand, considers the categories of inequality as social constructs and, in particular, as by-products of social interaction. Although this ontology supported the initial development of the social sciences—and of economics in particular—from the second half of the nineteenth century onwards, it tended to be displaced by individualistic approaches, which predominate in the theoretical and methodological construction of contemporary social sciences. For Tilly, however, this approach, although a minority one, represents an alternative with greater potential than the essentialist approaches, both individualist and structural. It is curious to note that in the case of Political Economy, for example, both Adam Smith and Karl Marx built explanatory frameworks based on categorical relationships. In the case of Smith, based on the relationship between land, capital, and labor, which in Marx are reduced to the relationship between capital and labor. Beyond the particular arguments and theories of each case, what is relevant is the ontological substratum from which they start: the relational system between economic and social categories. In both cases, the categories of analysis refer not only to economic processes and categories but also to social categories—that is, to subjects and social classes.

It was in the second half of the nineteenth century, however, that this ontological approach was replaced by individualistic models. It corresponds to the rise of the neoclassical school, which emphasizes the rational behavior of economic actors (capitalists, consumers, workers) and no longer the links and relations between social categories, such as capital-labor, bourgeoisie-proletariat, among others, which gave rise to processes such as exploitation, private property, alienation, and accumulation. With this change in the ontological paradigm, the explanation of inequality shifted from the particular configuration of links and categorical relations to the attributes and profiles of individuals and their rational decisions. As a consequence, the idea that social inequality is the result of variations at the individual level and not of structural coercions linking one and other categories of social inequality tends to prevail.

An example of this situation is the explanation of social mobility as a response to processes of categorical inequality. In human capital approaches, for example, as well as in modern sociology based on individualistic models, mobility is assumed to be self-promoted by individuals themselves and not as a result of categorical relations and inequalities. Indeed, in neoclassical and functionalist approaches, social mobility is explained by various individual mechanisms, such as education, merit, effort, or other attributes of individuals. This leads to the erroneous idea that social inequality, although real and persistent, can be overcome through individual mobility processes, when, in fact, categorical inequality is maintained precisely because of the persistence of the social relations that structure social inequality. In the face of this, both human capital and social and cultural capital, although they can enable social mobility processes at the individual or family level, do not necessarily resolve the conditions of categorical inequality that underlie the social situation of each individual.

According to Tilly, these individualistic approaches characteristic of neoclassical economic thought, as well as of functionalism and methodological individualism in Sociology, "fail, however, to the extent that essential causal business takes place not inside individual heads but within social relations among persons and sets of persons. ... If so, we have no choice but to undertake relational analyses of inequality—whether or not we finally couple them with individualistic elements of relevant decision processes" (Tilly, 1999: 33–34).

Along with this radical critique of individualistic approaches, Tilly considers that relational analysis must take into account at least two other warnings: relational analysis does not deny the analysis of individual characteristics, but it does demand their contextualization, and people have multiple categorical identities, as many as the number of social relationships they can maintain. This poses two demands for relational analysis, making it a challenging sociological framework. It cannot reduce the individual to one aspect or relation but must consider this multiplicity of identity and categorical dimensions of individuals; in this sense, such a perspective challenges "any ontology that reduces all social processes to the sentient actions of individual persons" (Tilly, 1999: 35).

4 Reproduction and Social Inequality in the Thought of Pierre Bourdieu

Bourdieu's proposal on the formation of social classes and social inequality starts from two ontological principles, as Tilly would call them, namely: (1) understanding all practice as a *total social fact*, in the sense given by Mauss (Bourdieu, 2005); and (2) the *reproduction* of the social world as the central object of Sociology (Bourdieu, 2011, and Bourdieu and Passeron, 1990 [1970]).

In relation to the first principle, Bourdieu takes up Mauss' (2002) thesis on exchange as a total social fact to extend its use to all social practices, beyond only economic relations.[12] As Bourdieu points out, sociology, in its most complete and general definition, refers to the set of practices involved in production and reproduction, not only economic but also social and cultural. Even contemporary neoliberal economics, with its enormous power to dictate political norms at a global level and to present itself as universally valid, owes its fundamental characteristics "to the fact that it is immersed or embedded in a particular society, that is to say, rooted in a system of beliefs and values, an ethos and a moral view of the world, in short, an *economic common sense*, linked, as such, to the social and cognitive structures of a particular social order" (Bourdieu, 2005: 10).

The economy, as we usually understand it, is actually constituted from a process of abstraction that dissociates "economic" practices from the social order of which it is a part. The requirement of the analysis is, then, to recover this totality of dimensions of the social that are immersed in all social practices, including economic ones. It is to take up Polanyi's concept of *embeddedness*, according to which the economy refers not only to economic relations but also to those *embedded* in social, cultural, and political relations, and vice versa—that is, that the same economic relations (production-distribution) are *embedded* in social, political, and cultural relations.

---

12   On this notion of Mauss's total social fact and our interpretation and use of it, see Chapter 3, where we reflect on the structuring of social inequality from the perspective of totality and mediations.

Nothing expresses this idea better than the concept of fictitious commodity that Polanyi (2017) uses to refer to the construction of labor and the labor market in capitalism. According to Polanyi, even when labor and labor power, can be traded in the market for a price and be part of economic exchange practices. In reality, this represents a fictitious act, since work is in itself a human activity that cannot be detached from all the cultural, social, demographic, family, political, and human dimensions that constitute it. In this sense, work as a human activity can never detach itself from its other senses and meanings, which define it beyond the economic-productive sphere. Only through an act of imposition and power was it possible to create this fiction of labor as a commodity in itself. Based on this, we would say then that, for Polanyi, work as a human activity is a total social fact—that is, constituted and constituent of a totality of social practices that determine it.

Thus, in work, as in all economic and social practice, the social world is present in its totality. Therefore, the epistemological and methodological exigence is to undo the economicist abstraction present in neoclassical theories in order to recover the social, cultural, and political world that gives meaning to each economic and social practice. To this end, it is necessary to equip ourselves with instruments of knowledge that highlight "the multidimensionality and multifunctionality of practices, enable us to construct *historical models* capable of accounting, with rigour and parsimony, for economic actions and institutions as they present themselves to empirical observation" (Bourdieu, 2005: 3). In this sense, Bourdieu's concepts and theories are placed at the disposal of the analysis of the social from this general statement on human practices as total social facts. The concepts of field, habitus, capitals, among others, are, from this perspective, conceptual mediations, instruments of knowledge used for the understanding of the social totality that surrounds each social fact.

In the case of inequality, it is a matter of thinking of it as a totality in itself and, therefore, not reducible or constrained to any of its dimensions, no matter how fundamental they may be. As a social fact, inequality is not economic, class, gender, ethnic-racial, generational, geographic, or other dimensions that we may add. It is all of them at once and none of them in particular. As a total fact, it is the articulation of all its dimensions, each one *embedded* in the others. The categories of analysis that we usually use (economic capital, social capital, classes, gender, ethnicity, citizenship, among so many others) are only partial and restricted modes of reconstruction of the social fact itself: inequality. Although these mediations contribute to its understanding, they can never achieve its total apprehension, only in a partial and disjointed way. The demand, then, is from these categories to initiate a process of critique and reflection that takes us beyond them, to discover step by step diverse aspects of the totality embedded in inequality as a social fact. It is a exigence of thought—that is, to think of concepts and theories as categories of mediation between the concept itself and the social fact to which it refers—questioning the concept, the theory, for what it does not make explicit directly of the social fact but which, in a certain way, has included it as an abstraction. It is a demand of thought to theoretically reconstruct the social fact as an articulated totality, in the understanding that we will never be able to recover it as a real totality (Zemelman, 1987).

Returning to the example of labor as fictitious merchandise, it is then a matter of understanding the economic activity of working—that is, economic occupation as a social occupation—and not only nor fundamentally economic (in the neoclassical sense of the term). The exchange of labor power not only turns labor into a commodity for someone else but also activates various social aspects inherent in work during the process of buying and selling, even if this transaction may be considered a symbolic or fictitious act.

Only in capitalism is this social form of labor and labor activity stripped of the social clothing that constitutes it. In pre-capitalist societies, this was not necessarily so. In feudalism, for example, the labor relation was in itself a social relation, not only an economic-productive one. It set in motion not only productive processes but also social and cultural relations. The peasant was not only a form of existence of labor and labor power but a total social subject in itself—a subject whose existence referred to society as a whole. It was not possible to imagine the peasant in the absence (abstraction) of the feudal lord, and vice versa. In capitalism, on the other hand, the conformation of the labor market has institutionalized this separation—dislocation—between labor as an economic act and the worker and their labor power as social facts. Economic occupation refers only to the act of working—that is, of generating value for capital. In this act, the worker is abstracted from their social world as a human being and becomes an abstract entity; they become undifferentiated from other individuals as mere workers and, therefore, interchangeable with any other from one position to another, from one job to another, from one economic activity to another, since what matters is not them as social subjects but, rather, their labor as value, as abstraction. The labor of the wage-worker, unlike the labor of the peasant, no longer refers to society, to the other social classes, but as mere economic abstractions of social facts. However, all this is nothing but a fiction, an abstraction, which, at the point of becoming routine and reiterated over centuries, is presented to us today as concrete social facts. But they never cease to be what they truly are: abstractions of total facts and, therefore, fictitious representations of a totality. This fiction is what neoclassical economic theory has instituted, which has become hegemonic in social thought.

It is the basis of an economistic construction of society and, therefore, of social practices, to such an extent that economic theory has now been extended to explain the most diverse social practices, such as having children, studying, staying healthy, getting married, forming families, and even reproducing. Although in every social practice, as a total social fact, we can recognize an economic dimension, this does not mean that the economic is the constituent and structuring factor of each and every social practice. Precisely, the notion of total social facts goes in the opposite direction, in terms of understanding practices as multidimensional and multifunctional social facts, including economic practices.

Even under capitalism, in addition to an economic-productive activity, labor is a human social activity. It establishes the position of subjects in society precisely on the basis of their position in a founding and structuring social relation of the social: the place occupied in the buying and selling of labor power, on the one hand, and the place occupied in its consequence, the exploitation of labor and the alienation of the fruit of that labor. But, in order to occupy those places and positions in the labor market and in the economic-productive process, both the buyer (capitalist) and the seller (proletarian) must assume a social form of existence and, therefore, of a social position. Capital, labor, exploitation, and alienation are historical and social constructs, as well as the relationships that links them. Neither one nor the other are objects in themselves but the fruit of social and historical processes; in that same sense, both capital and labor are equally total social facts.[13]

The second ontological principle, the reproduction of the social world, is, from our perspective, one of the fundamental concepts in Bourdieu's theory and allows us to organize and give meaning to his entire theoretical proposal on society. For Bourdieu, one of the basic and fundamental questions that sociology must resolve is that of "knowing why and how the social world lasts, perseveres in being, how the social order is perpetuated, that is to say, the set of relations of order that constitute it" (Bourdieu, 2011: 31; our translation).

In order to answer this basic question of social science, Bourdieu distances himself from structuralism, according to which it is structures that, as bearers

---

13   Although we exemplify with labor, this idea of the economy as a total social fact is present in all economic and exchange practices. Thus, for example, Baudrillard (1981) points out that all consumption is not only of material goods, but also of cultural and social signs and meanings embedded in the objects of consumption. Likewise, Bourdieu (1984) indicates to us that through consumption we not only consume products, but in that same process we produce social and cultural distinctions. Consumption is produced distinction and, therefore, is based on a political economy of signs and tastes.

of a principle of perpetuation, reproduce themselves with the collaboration of agents subjected to their structural conditions and constraints, as well as from symbolic interactionism and methodological individualism, according to which the social world is the product of the acts of construction carried out at each moment by agents in a sort of continuous creation.

Faced with these visions that reduce the analysis of the social functioning and reproduction of society to only one of its pillars, Bourdieu proposes a perspective that implies a paradigm shift. Regarding social reproduction, Bourdieu (2011: 31, our translation) puts forward the following thesis:

> The social world is endowed with a *conatus*, as the classical philosophers said, with a tendency to persevere in being, with an internal dynamism, inscribed, at the same time, in the objective structures and in the "subjective" structures, the dispositions of the agents, and is continuously maintained and sustained by actions of construction and reconstruction of the structures that in principle depend on the position occupied in the structures by those who carry them out. Every society rests on the relationship between these two dynamic principles, which vary in importance according to societies and are inscribed, one in the objective structures, and more precisely in the structure of distribution of capital and in the mechanisms that tend to guarantee its reproduction; the other, in the dispositions (to reproduction). It is in the relationship between these two principles that the different modes of reproduction are defined, in particular the strategies of reproduction that characterize them.

This theoretical perspective of reproduction becomes more complex if we understand, for example, that the economic system is not only productive and distributive regimes but also social relations and structures of class and inequality, power structures that underlie these regimes of production and distribution. In this sense, the economy and its productive and distributive structures (classes), although undoubtedly necessary, are not in themselves sufficient to understand the reproduction of the class structure and social inequality in modern society. Society, as *modes of reproduction* and not only *modes of production*, is not only economics, although it is also economics. Likewise, class is not only economic, determined and produced by economic processes (production and distribution), but is also a cultural, symbolic, political, social, demographic category. Class is not only relations of production, which it also is, but also relations of kinship, marriages, fertility, family structures, education, systems of succession, symbolic and cultural structures, among many other things, all of which are also bearers of structures of inequality.

In view of this, the need arises to incorporate into the same analytical and conceptual framework the set of dimensions and spheres of social life that shape and give meaning to social reproduction and that have different ways of distancing themselves from structural determinisms. We refer to the spheres of culture, politics, social, demographic, education, among many others (Bourdieu, 1998a). In these other dimensions, class structures, social structures of differentiation, and inequality are also reproduced. In this sense, Bourdieu argues that in these social fields forms of capital and capitalization are also constructed, not under economic formats but as social, cultural, symbolic, and other forms that also participate and form a fundamental part of the reproduction of the class structure and social inequality (Bourdieu, 2011).

In the social world, understood as a multidimensional social space, social inequality is structured on the basis of different factors of differentiation that can be categorized as those "powers or *forms of capital* which are or can become efficient, like aces in a game of cards, in this particular universe, that is, in the struggle (or competition) for the appropriation of scarce goods of which this universe is the site" (Bourdieu, 1987: 4). From this it follows that social inequality results from the form of concentration of the various forms of capital—that is, from those capital relations that give strength, power, and profit to their possessors, who are positioned as dominant and powerful actors against the others, who are positioned as dominated and in an underprivileged situation.

In this framework, Bourdieu incorporates the concept of *capital* to refer to these fundamental social powers that give rise to the formation of social classes. Specifically, Bourdieu identifies four forms of capital that refer to different dimensions of the social embedded in each economic and social act, and, in particular, in the structuring of class inequality and its social reproduction.

In the first place, *economic capital* is mentioned in all its forms and species, which is perhaps the most widely diffused and theorized. It refers to forms that can be directly or indirectly convertible into money, which is of particular importance in the institutionalization of property rights and control of economic and productive resources, making it an important source of political power and hegemonies in capitalist society.

Secondly, he mentions *cultural capital*, which, as its name indicates, refers to the accumulation of culture by each class, and which is transmitted through forms of inheritance, as well as through socialization and formal education. It refers, therefore, to forms of information, knowledge, education, and other acquirable skills that confer advantages (or disadvantages, as the case may be) and status vis-à-vis others. Under certain conditions, it can become economic capital or, rather, a generator of economic capital. Although it is associated with academic and educational qualifications, it differs substantially from the concept of human capital developed by Becker (1966). Beyond the individualistic and economistic reductionism that underlies Becker's model, the point is that this author places all the emphasis on the economic returns of investment in education, without considering "the fact that the scholastic yield from educational action depends on the cultural capital previously invested by the family. Moreover, the economic and social yield of the educational qualification depends on the social capital, again inherited, which can be used to back it up." (Bourdieu, 1986: 17).

In other words, the concept of cultural capital is broader, more complex, and multidimensional than mere academic-professional training—that is, than human capital as an investment in education and academic degrees. Cultural capital is fundamental not only because it contributes to the formation of social classes and social inequality, but also because in this same process, it establishes and institutionalizes the social and cultural mechanisms of its reproduction, including the role of the educational system itself as an institutionalization of social and class inequality, while ignoring the role of other institutions, such as the family and cultural inheritances, in their reproduction.

Thirdly, he mentions *social capital*, which consists of the material and symbolic resources that arise from the relationships and connections that establish modes of group belonging. These are relationships of mutual knowledge and recognition based on systems of trust, reciprocity, and solidarity among members of the same community. The social capital possessed by the members of a group is based precisely on belonging to that group and, therefore, serves them all, jointly. It is also a capital that accumulates as it is used and deployed in actions and practices of support, solidarity, trust, and reciprocity. Likewise, the network of relationships is not a natural or social phenomenon, established once and for all, but is the result of a continuous effort of institutionalization. This requires a continuous effort and investment of time, dedication, and commitment to keep social capital alive, to maintain the network of relationships that sooner or later will provide some material or symbolic benefit. In this context, the individual and collective reproduction strategies that are woven to maintain, reproduce, and accumulate social capital are fundamental.

To these three types of capitals, Bourdieu adds a fourth, which is *symbolic capital*, which he defines as "the form the different types of capital take once they are perceived and recognized as legitimate" (Bourdieu, 1987: 4).

Based on this perspective of analysis, the structuring of inequality in a social space—that is, the location of each agent within the social structure—is manifested as the distribution of the agents in that social space according to three fundamental variables: on the one hand, the overall volume of capital they possess; on the other, the composition of their capital, that is, the relative weight of each of these three types of capital; finally, the trajectory in the social space, that is, the evolution over time of these two variables, volume and composition of the capitals.

This approach to the forms of capital (economic, social, cultural) has been widely disseminated, reproduced, and used. However, little attention is paid to the concept or notion of capital that underlies Bourdieu's theory of the configuration of social spaces. In some cases, capital is even associated with resources, or stock of something, that can be possessed, whether in material or symbolic form. In many cases, this confusion is understandable, since Bourdieu himself speaks in terms of interchangeability of capitals, volumes, and others that may allude to these forms of capital as a resource. However, even when Bourdieu extends the use of the concept of capital far beyond the economic-productive spaces and beyond the social relations of production, the fact is that the notion of capital in Bourdieu is not very different from that of Marx. In both cases, the concept of capital is used not to represent a resource, a stock or a good but to refer to a social relation and, therefore, to make the structuring of classes and inequality between social subjects rest on that social relation. In this sense, the concept of reproduction, which is present in both Bourdieu and Marx and with which both refer to the structuring bases of capitalist society, is key to this understanding.

In Marx it is widely known and documented that the concept of capital refers both in its material form, to goods and means of production and, in its social form, to a relation of *accumulation* of value. The relation of exploitation is precisely that, extraction of surplus value from labor to be *accumulated* in the form of capital; that is the *relation of capital* that sustains the capitalist mode of production.

The same logic operates in Bourdieu, but it is used for all the forms of capital already outlined. The concept of social reproduction alludes precisely to this dynamic of capital accumulation. For Bourdieu, the social world does not operate in a historical vacuum, where each moment is independent of the previous one, but operates on the basis of processes of *accumulation*, which occur in and through time. In the social world, reproduction operates as a movement that generates its own social inertia, through which the accumulation of capital at one moment does not disappear at the next moment, but is transmitted and transferred from one generation to another. In fact, the practices of social reproduction (education, marriage strategies, systems of patrimonial inheritance, and the social networks themselves) are modes of transmission and accumulation of acquired capitals.

Contrary to the notion of individual decisions—identical in their essence to one another as proposed by the methodological individualism present in neoclassical economics and functionalist thought—the notion of social reproduction alludes precisely to these social processes of transmission and inheritance of class position and, therefore, of reproduction of social inequality and class structure. As Bourdieu (1986: 15) himself points out, in order to avoid the reductionism inherent in approaches based on methodological individualism and models of economic equilibria:

> [O]ne must reintroduce into it the notion of capital and with it, accumulation and all its effects. Capital is accumulated labor (in its materialized form or its "incorporated," embodied form) ... It is a *vis insita,* a force inscribed in objective or subjective structures, but it is also a *lex insita,* the principle underlying the immanent regularities of the social world.

This notion of capital as a social relation and of accumulation as a form of extended reproduction of capital is very similar to that proposed by Marx, but, unlike Marx, Bourdieu broadens it to incorporate not only the material and economic-productive relations—property, exploitation and alienation—but also the immaterial and subjective ones that being internalized in the capitals acquire their own social form as cultural, social, and symbolic capitals. In this sense, and although it may be paradoxical, this notion of capital in Bourdieu refers to a notion of it as a total social fact—that is, as a multidimensional and multifunctional social fact—and not reduced or reducible to only its economic manifestation, however relevant and determining it may be in certain historical contexts. I say paradoxical, since totality as a mode of thought is undoubtedly one of the main characteristics of Marxist thought.

In this sense, this double character of the notion of capital in Bourdieu, as a total social fact and as a process of accumulation and social reproduction, means that social practices and social spaces do not run as simple games of chance without memory or history but, on the contrary, as social processes where historical inertia is fundamental; the accumulation of capitals, as an extended reproduction of social and historic processes, is determinant for social becoming. The situation and position of each subject in a social structure in a given social world is not independent of the previous social structures, classes, and inequalities in the history of that same social subject, both as an individual and as a social class.

In this regard, we can point out two concrete examples where Bourdieu analyzes social reproduction based on this logic of capital accumulation as forms of reproduction of social inequality. The first is found in his study on marriage and succession practices in Kabilia and Béarn, where Bourdieu (2008) points out how the marriage strategies developed by individuals and their families not only allow the reproduction of lineage, positions of privilege and/or family economic capital, but through these same marriage strategies the structures of differentiation and social inequality on which these lineages, privileges, and economic capitals are built are reproduced. In this sense, marriage strategies are not only strategies of family reproduction, understood as family survival, but above all, they are mechanisms for the reproduction of the community and its social inequalities on which social differentiation and stratification are structured.

We also cannot fail to mention his study on the role of the French school system in the reproduction of social and class inequality. As a privileged field of production and accumulation of cultural capital, the school system acquires a unique function as a mode of reproduction of class relations and the structure of social inequality. In the words of Bourdieu and Passeron (1990 [1970]: 10–11), in the analysis of the education system " the classical theories tend to sever cultural reproduction from its function of social reproduction, that is, to ignore the specific effect of symbolic relations in the reproduction of power relations." In other words, traditional models, such as Gary Becker's human capital model, fail to link school and educational investment strategies with the set of social reproduction strategies deployed by agents. In doing so, human capital theorists fall into a double limitation. In the first respect, they lose sight of the fundamental role of the school as an institution for the production and accumulation of capital, which is none other than to act as a mechanism for the reproduction of class inequality. And, on the other hand, they neglect "the best hidden and socially most determinant educational investment, namely, the domestic transmission of cultural capital." (Bourdieu, 1986: 17).

The school, although it is a space for the production of cultural capital, is also a space for the reproduction and accumulation of previous cultural and social capitals. The agents do not form their cultural capital in school purely and simply, but rather, through education, reproduce and accumulate cultural capital that the agents carry from family and class spaces. In this way, the school not only produces individual academic titles and merits but, through them, reproduces in an expanded form the previous cultural capitals of the agents. The school is, in essence, a space for the transmission and accumulation of cultural capital.

But this theory of reproduction and of society in no case rests on a harmonious and conflict-free vision. On the contrary, as in Marx, in Bourdieu the notion of social reproduction must also be thought of on the basis of the recognition of a logic of inequality in the distribution of material and symbolic resources and, therefore, of a continuous struggle for access to them. In Marx it is evident that the reproduction of capital is the reproduction of the class structure that sustains the capitalist mode of production and, by this means, the reproduction of the class conflicts that arise from the same mode of capitalist production—that is, from the class struggle.

Bourdieu's perspective is more complex. Although, like Marx, he stresses the idea of the social world as an unequal space and as a space of struggle and conflict, he does so, on the other hand, by conceiving the existence of other forms of capital beyond economic capital and beyond the social relations of production. In this way, he expands the logic of Marxist analysis to other fields of social relations, where, as in production, class structures and social inequality are produced and reproduced (Rizzo, 2012). In this logic, Bourdieu defines the concept of social reproduction "as the reproduction of the structure of the relations of force between the classes" (Bourdieu and Passeron, 1990 [1970]: 11).

Returning to Giovanni Bechelloni (1996), we can also point out that the reproduction of class relations does not start from a *tabula rasa*: It develops from subjects positioned in a class structure and, therefore, from a structure of distribution of economic, cultural, symbolic, and political capital, which give rise to forms and relations of asymmetries of power and, at the same time, of subjects constituted as such—that is, with positions and discourses regarding these same phenomena of production and reproduction of social and class inequality. In this sense, in Bourdieu, unlike ethnomethodology, the construction of the social world of agents, classes, and social subjects is not done in a social vacuum but on the basis of the position occupied by them in the social space, established according to the structure and volume of capital possessed, making this the organizing axis of representations and positions (Bourdieu, 1991). In this way, Bourdieu opposes approaching social reproduction in static and linear terms; on the contrary, it must be linked to the dynamics of struggle and conflict (Rizzo, 2012). Specifically, the fields, as Bourdieu defines them, have a history that is the product of the permanent struggle within them—that is, of the specific existing relations of forces—which leads him to state that "[t]he permanent struggle within the field is the motor of the field" (Bourdieu, 1993: 135).

CHAPTER 8

Social Classes and Inequality in Global Capitalism

Stiglitz (2015 and 2012) documents how global capitalism has deepened the gap separating the very rich (1% of the population) from the rest of the world's population, as well as increasing the gap between rich and underdeveloped countries. Inequality has reached such levels that it is even counterproductive for maintaining economic growth and capital accumulation in developed countries. Even within the richest 1%, "increasing numbers of them realize that sustained economic growth, upon which their prosperity depends, can't happen when the vast majority of citizens have stagnant incomes" (Stiglitz, 2015: 7).

However, as he also points out, inequality is not inevitable, much less the product of laws or inexorable forces of the economy but is due to questions of policies and strategies: It is the result of the conjunction of political (domination and power) and economic (exploitation and appropriation of surpluses) processes that, together, determine this concentrated form of distribution of the fruits of economic growth. An expression of this, for example, is that in the 2008 crisis, the U.S. government, instead of supporting the indebted population and thus giving respite and sustenance to the banks and the financial system, opted for the easy option, giving support directly to the latter, leaving the bulk of the population defenseless. This strategy is not the result of the unrestricted application of the principles of economic theory but is due to the pressure and decision-making power of the big bankers and top corporate executives who exercise their dominion over the State and economic policies, even in the world's leading power. This would be leading to the fact that in the United States social and class inequality would already be undermining the bases of social cohesion that always characterized it and that, based on processes of social mobility and integration, allowed reducing the scope and manifestations of an eventual class struggle (Stiglitz, 2015).

Along the same lines, Piketty (2014: 26), in his analysis of the historical dynamics of the distribution of wealth and the structuring of class inequality, concludes that capitalism, both in its industrial-national and post-industrial and global formats, is a factory of inequality where social gaps tend to grow systematically to such an extent that "the concentration of capital will attain extremely high levels—levels potentially incompatible with the meritocratic values and principles of social justice fundamental to modern democratic societies."

But, as Piketty himself points out later in his book, these are not only forms of income inequality, as what lies behind them are forms of class inequality, which he illustrates empirically when he documents that the concentration of income, although growing, pales in comparison with the concentration of income from property. As he points out, "inequality with respect to capital is always greater than in equality with respect to labor. The distribution of capital ownership (and of income from capital) is always more concentrated than the distribution of income from labor" (Piketty, 2014: 244). If the rich are getting richer and richer, this situation is accentuated in the case of owners with respect to non-owners. This is not a particular circumstance of some time or place but a regularity that occurs in all the countries and periods he analyzes in his vast study. One factor that explains this regularity characteristic of capitalism is the specific weight of the inheritance of property and capital, which generates cumulative causation effects in the concentration of wealth and income. As a result, class inequality is not only evident but even obscene and gross.

In these texts by Stiglitz and Piketty, these authors, along with repositioning the issue of inequality as a social, economic, and political problem of our societies, confirm that inequality has not only increased, reaching unsuspected levels, but that this has occurred in the midst of the process of expansion and consolidation of global and postmodern capitalism. It would seem that the Information Age is also a new era of inequalities (Fitoussi and Rosanvallon, 2003), in which what has changed is not the existence of social classes per se, but the way in which they are structured and shaped as such, as well as their growing social and economic distancing. Contemporary capitalism may be defined as post-industrial, informational, reflexive, or cognitive in its attempts to distance and differentiate itself from industrial capitalism, but in any case, it remains a capitalist mode of production. As such, it is based on salaried forms of labor power in its relation to capital and, therefore, on modes of exploitation of labor and appropriation of surplus labor by capital. Likewise, capital, as a social relation, remains the fundamental relation that structures the mode of production. In this digital and reflexive, postmodern and globalized era, the capitalization of surplus remains the process upon which both the social process of production and the class relations that derive therefrom are founded.

What has changed are the conditions and modes in which this relation of capital is objectified—that is, of accumulation and capitalization of surplus value—but not the process itself. Unlike previous regimes of accumulation, we are witnessing one based on the flexibility and reflexivity of the labor process as founding processes. The first establishes the conditions that define the capital-labor relation and, therefore, of the constitution and structuring of classes and class struggle. The second establishes the conditions of the development of the productive forces and, therefore, the form of generation of surplus and surplus value. Considering these two founding processes, we present below an analysis of the constitution of social classes in global capitalism.

1   On Globalization and Class Inequality

The last few decades have witnessed profound transformations in the economy, politics, and society that have affected the entire planet. For the first time, we could truly say that world events are objectively planetary and global, both in their origins and causes and in their consequences and impacts. As never before, the "butterfly effect" has become a real possibility in the social world and not just a metaphor to explain the interdependencies of societies. It is so-called globalization—first as a metaphor and now as a concept and a powerful idea—that gives meaning to and describes the form assumed by social, political, and economic processes in the contemporary world.

In terms of its political economy, globalization refers to the new schemes of territorial organization of the world-economy, where the rules of oligopolistic competition and the international division of labor are substantially redefined (Petras and Veltmeyer, 2001; Preyer, 2016). This change has been driven by the development of new technologies and forms of organization of the work process, through which local, regional, and national productive specializations have been reformulated, as well as patterns of economic exchange at the international level. What is relevant in this sense is that globalization implies moving from a national scale of production with international exchanges to a fully globalized or worldwide scale of production and exchange. Until very recently, the production process, firms, plants, and industries were essentially national phenomena. In this framework, the prevailing international division of labor was an expression of the spatial form taken by international trade, which developed preferably as an exchange between national economies (Amin, 1996). In this sense, the international division of labor and international trade were exactly that, economic relations between nations. Likewise, their theorization and problematization, from Ricardo in the early decades of the nineteenth century until only few decades ago, was understood as just that, a productive specialization and commercial exchange between national economies. It is only in the last two decades of the 20th century that the form taken by world economic processes, as well as the way of understanding and analyzing them, requires reformulating them no longer as international relations but as global processes in the strict sense of the term. It is not only the internationalization of economies, something that has been going on even before capitalism, but the operation of companies, capital, finance, productive processes, labor, etc., which no longer operate within the limits imposed by the nation state and national economic frontiers. The operation is global, not because it involves the entire planet but because it is no longer necessarily based on a national basis but on trans local relations, in which the national has become just one more factor in the global economic equation (Canales, 2002).

Within this framework of globalization, one phenomenon is becoming increasingly important. It is the acceleration of the timing of social processes, economic exchanges, politics, information, and communications, all sustained by the so-called microelectronic revolution (Mires, 1996). This has caused the spatiality of social processes and networks of relationships to be disrupted and fragmented or simply to dissolve in the face of the revolution of temporalities derived from the new information technologies. All this allows the global economy to have the capacity to function as a unit in real time and on a planetary scale (Castells, 2010 [1996]). It is as if the acceleration of time annulled space.[1] Although, for the sake of precision, in reality it is not time that is accelerating but the movement of society, its exchanges, and its relationships. All this expresses a qualitative leap in terms of the fact that the rhythm of social movement represents a new organization of social space and time.

Various postmodernist and conservative texts have tried to conceptualize these processes of fragmentation and dissolution of space and time as the eventual end of geography (space), together with the virtual end of history (time). In reality, it is something different. It is the dissolution of the times and spaces inherited from the Enlightenment and liberalism, which materialized in practices and relations of groups and classes between nations and nationalities (Ianni, 1996). The speed of microelectronic processing has allowed the dissolution of the boundaries between there and here, between the external and the internal, the national and the international. However, just as there is no end of history, neither is there an end of geography in global society; rather, what is happening is a modification of the social forms of space and time inherited from the first modernity and whose main figure was the national society. As Giddens (1990: 64) points out:

---

1 "No human language can withstand the speed of light. No event can withstand being beamed across the whole planet. No meaning can withstand acceleration. No history can withstand the centrifugation of facts or their being short-circuited in real time ... It seems that, like cosmic space, historical space-time is also curved." (Baudrillard, 1994: 2; 10).

[g]lobalisation can thus be defined as the intensification of worldwide social relations which link distant localities in such a way that local happenings are shaped by events occurring many miles away and vice versa. ... what happens in a local neighbourhood is likely to be influenced by factors-such as world money and commodity markets-operating at an indefinite distance away from that neighbourhood itself. The outcome is not necessarily, or even usually, a generalised set of changes acting in a uniform direction, but consists in mutually opposed tendencies.

The instantaneity of events does not only refer to processes at high speeds—which, in the case of communications, are already almost close to those of light—but, through it, denote the loss of time as a factor of the event and, consequently, the devaluation of space as a dimension of the event. It is the passage from the age of hardware (industrial modernity) to that of software (post-industrial and post-modern society), where "'[i]nstantaneity' means immediate, 'on-the-spot' fulfilment, but also immediate exhaustion and fading of interest" (Bauman, 2000: 118). Both the speed of events and their spatial expansion derive in liquid forms of the social, in a seductive lightness of being.

The material basis of this acceleration of events in social processes is the microelectronic revolution that, through the productive use of microchip, has taken industry and the economy to levels never before imagined in terms of capacity and development of productive forces. The speed of information processing made possible by microelectronics has allowed, in practice, the simultaneity of events, thus erasing the frontiers that separated the *here* from the *there*, the internal from the external, the local from the global. For various authors, these changes are the most characteristic features of the transition from industrial society to a post-industrial or informational society (Kumar, 1995), opening a broad debate among the various theories on post-industrial society. Some authors, such as Daniel Bell (1973), emphasize the birth of a new social structure based on the transition from an industrialized to a service economy and, therefore, on the rise of executive and professional occupations, together with the disappearance not only of agricultural and primary-extractive jobs but also, and importantly, those in the industrial sector. Others, such as (Castells, 2010 [1996]), on the other hand, point out that the informational nature of contemporary societies is expressed not so much in the decline of industrial activities as in the new character of occupations. Emphasis is placed on the increasing content of information and knowledge required by the work process, which has repercussions on the structure of occupations and employment.

In this sense, however, the now classic approach that characterizes the current stage of the world economy as a post-industrial society is based on erroneous premises. For one thing, the relevant distinction is not so much between the industrial or non-industrial character of contemporary society but, rather, between two different ways of incorporating and organizing the process of knowledge and information in industrial, agricultural, and service production. In this sense, Castells chooses to speak of an *informational society* rather than a *post-industrial society* to refer to the character, meaning, and scope of the changes in today's world economy.

According to this author, what characterizes the information era is not the type of activities that are developed, but the "technological ability to use as a direct productive force what distinguishes our species as a biological oddity: its superior capacity to process symbols" (Castells, 2010 [1996]: 100). This shows the informational character of this new era that is no longer based on exchange and material relations but on the exchange and processing of information and symbols, which re-signifies the entire process of production and distribution of material goods and services.

Lash and Urry (1998), for their part, go further and point out not only the informational character of current accumulation processes but also emphasize their reflexivity. In the information age, accumulation acquires a reflexive character since it is increasingly based on the capacity to process information, not on its mere accumulation. This processing requires a hermeneutic—a process of interpretation and construction of senses and meanings—in the work process. For the same reason, the term flexibility is very limited to account for this hermeneutics so present nowadays in work processes. On the contrary, reflexivity emphasizes the increase in the cultural mediations of this material exchange. According to these authors, "the increase of reflexivity in the social work process indicates that an increasingly larger portion of individual labor processes are only indirectly linked to the basic function of the total work process, which is the fulfillment of the material exchange between men and nature" (Lash and Urry, 1998: 94).

In traditional agricultural societies, the work process was based on a direct exchange of energy for matter. Likewise, in industrial society, it corresponded to a machinist mediation, where matter was the means, object, and result of production. In the information age, on the other hand, it is a reflexive mediation in which the mediation of symbols and signs acquires an essential weight for the organization of the energy-matter exchange. For the same reason, in the information economy the process of accumulation is not only *flexible* but *reflexive*, insofar as it is based on processes of self-regulation that transform the labor process into an object of itself. The concepts of flexibility, deregulation, and post-Fordism are deemed insufficient as they harbor a productivist bias, preventing them from fully "capturing the depth to which production and consumption are rooted in discursive knowledge" (Lash and Urry, 1998: 91).

Other authors speak of the emergence of a mode of cognitive capitalism that, sustained by the global knowledge industry, makes knowledge and immaterial production the basis of capital accumulation. It is not a question of assuming the eventual disappearance of the production of material goods (merchandise) but rather the emergence of a new way of doing things and, in particular, of a new "continent of human practice," inscribed in a new form of capitalist economy, sustained in the production, distribution and use of services and immaterial goods (Blondeau, 2004: 31, our translation). The digital era allows what Negroponte (1996) called the passage from an economy of "atoms" to one of "bit". In the former, exchange value is a function of the material nature ("atoms") of the things being exchanged and, therefore, of the material labor required to produce them. In the second, in the knowledge and information economy, this is no longer the case. Value is not a function of the material but of the informational; it is not the hardware that is exchanged but contents and symbols. In some cases, production even materializes only in a virtual sense, never exists materially as such.

There is no doubt that all these phenomena have a direct impact on the ways in which classes and social inequality are structured in contemporary capitalism. In this sense, Mires (1996) points out that the microelectronic era not only defines a new economy or new productive and technological forms but also new social orders. Just as in its time the steam engine contributed to reconfigure the same social context from which it emerged—disciplining bodies and minds, times and movements, spaces and their symbolizations, from its hard and heavy forms, establishing solid forms of an emerging modernity—today, in the digital era, microelectronics does not only refer to a new economy or new productive and technological forms but also to new social orders; microelectronics refers not only to technologies embedded in machines and instruments but, through its ways of revolutionizing the times and spaces of economy and production, it also transforms the ways of observing, perceiving, feeling, and representing, of living the social reality that this new economy transforms into new modernities. In this way, the digital era defines a new social and historical mode of production, understood as "an order based on a specific technological set that imposes its logic and its rites on the social context from which it originated, that organizes and regulates the relations of production and work, consumption patterns, and even the predominant cultural style of life" (Mires, 1996: 17, our translation).

Thus, the social and historical significance of the microelectronic revolution is paramount; just as the Industrial Revolution in England was in its time, the current information and knowledge era defines not only another industrial revolution but also a radical and structural transformation in the social and political, sexual and cultural, ecological and spiritual, demographic and human spheres, among many others that make up contemporary social life. The digital age and microelectronics redefine and restructure all social forms, including class structure and social inequality.

In this regard, the changes affecting the structure of employment and occupations stand out for their importance since they would be the basis for the emergence of a new class structure and social stratification, as well as new ways of structuring these social classes and the forms of their conflict and opposition as such—in a word, the way of structuring class consciousness, as well as the class struggle itself. It is, in particular, the configuration of a new pattern of polarization and social differentiation based on two different and complementary processes: on the one hand, the restructuring of the labor regime based on the new structures of labor flexibility and deregulation, which result in what Beck (2000a) has called a regime of labor risk; on the other, the restructuring of the system of occupations and class status, in particular the growing segmentation of occupations and the social and labor differentiation and inequality that they imply. The first refers to the socio-political matrix of (dis)regulation of the capital-labor relation; the second, to the productive and labor matrix, which defines the new forms of economic-productive and occupational structures—that is, of classes.[2]

Based on these two processes (labor risk regime and employment segmentation), new forms of social differentiation and inequality and social stratification of the population are consolidated, which have economic and demographic bases that we are interested in taking up again. For one thing, if we consider that the social process of work is the basis of the social structure, it is to be expected that changes at this level will reflect and have direct repercussions on the structuring of society into classes, strata, and differentiated social groups. All this results in a twofold process, namely the recompositing of the class structure, on the one hand, and the genesis of new ways of constituting social classes and inequality in cognitive and reflexive capitalism, on the other. This will be discussed more in depth in the following sections of this chapter.

---

2 In Wright's terms, we can say that the latter refers to the form taken by the class structure, while the former refers to the conditions of class formation in global capitalism. In Giddens' terms, both shape new fields of class structuring and class struggle.

2 Neoliberalism and Globalization: Ideological Foundations in the Reconstitution of the Ruling Classes

Ruling classes exist, although we do not always perceive and conceptualize them as such (Therborn, 2008 [1978]). Nothing reflects the power of the powerful better than to go unnoticed, so that they are not identified with their dominance and power over others. The direct exercise of power can always remain in the hands of foremen, managers, law enforcement, politicians, bureaucrats or other figures of similar rank and power. However, the ruling classes are there and exercise political domination, economic exploitation, and social discrimination. As hegemonic classes, they are constituted around an ideology that gives them meaning and transcendence beyond themselves, making that ideology the dominant one, the one that orders and organizes society, economy, politics, culture. And, in the present times, this ideology has a name: neoliberalism, disguised as globalization and postmodernity.

More than three decades have passed between the coup d'état in Chile in 1973 and the war in Iraq that imposed a neoliberal model of invasion and dispossession. In this period, neoliberalism was first forged and experimented with by the Chicago Boys in Chile and then expanded and consolidated as the dominant ideology and project at the global level. Both developed and Third World countries and governments have reconstituted their societies and economies under the principles of economic and political neoliberalism. But this was not something natural; it is the result of historical processes, class struggles, and political and ideological confrontations.

In its expansion and consolidation, neoliberalism has developed a strategy of *creative destruction* (Harvey, 2005). It first needed to destroy pre-existing institutional and political frameworks, including alternative ideological and theoretical frameworks, in order to establish itself as dominant and proclaim itself as the *unique thinking* (Ramonet, 1995). Neoliberalism thus became the ideological support of "[t]his new kind of conservative revolution appeals to progress, reason and science (economics in this case) to justify the restoration and so tries to write off progressive thought and action as archaic" (Bourdieu, 1998b: 35).

Like any dominant ideology, neoliberalism is constituted on the basis of the domination of other frameworks of thought and, like any dominant ideology, it seeks to make them invisible, silenced, and delegitimized. From this constitution—invention—of neoliberalism as the dominant ideology, we are told again and again that there would be no possible or valid opposition to the neoliberal vision. In reality, all this discourse on the inevitability of neoliberalism is nothing but an attempt to try to "to impose as self-evident a neo-liberal view which, essentially, dresses up the most classic presuppositions of conservative thought of all times and all countries in economic rationalizations" (Bourdieu, 1998b: 30).

Until the seventies of the last century, an economic and ideological model prevailed based on a form of flanged liberalism (Harvey, 2005). It is a model in which the market and the State are constituted on the basis of a mutual and highly intertwined relationship. On the one hand, it is an essentially capitalist market, based on forms of exploitation of labor as a mechanism of capital accumulation; on the other, a State constituted, among other things, as a mechanism of regulation of that same market—that is, of constriction of the market to avoid its self-regulation, both at the level of production and finance and, especially, in the distribution of surpluses. But, all in all, it is still a capitalist state that protects and encourages the development of the market and capital.

The principles guiding state intervention and regulation were that self-regulated markets do not function as efficient mechanisms in the allocation of resources and generally end up leading to recurrent crisis scenarios and the concentration of economic power and wealth, generating economic forms that threaten the ultimate object of capitalism: the accumulation of capital (Polanyi, 2001 [1944]). Thus, the principle underpinning this flanged liberalism is that the market needs State regulation to avoid and overcome the crises of capital accumulation generated by its own functioning (Boyer, 1992).

In contrast to this ideological matrix, based on Keynesian and social democratic thinking in terms of distribution and equity, neoliberalism has arisen. As an ideological matrix and a matrix of economic and social thought, neoliberalism predates Keynesianism. However, for decades it was subsumed in the ideological and political dominance of Keynesian and regulatory thinking. In the 1970s, the Keynesian model and its state mode of regulating capitalist accumulation entered a phase of exhaustion. As an economic and political model, it was no longer efficient to solve and resolve the recurrent crises of capitalism, leading to a crisis of capital accumulation. It is the end of the three golden decades of postwar capitalism, as Piketty (2014) calls them.

Several economic and political factors converge in this scenario: on the one hand, the oil crisis and the weight of OPEC in price setting, which generated a crisis in the developed economies, highly dependent on this raw material; on the other, an economic crisis together with the exhaustion of the Breton Woods agreements as mechanisms for regulating the accumulation of capital on a global scale. This is accompanied by profound technological and productive changes, which radically transform the forms assumed by the labor and production process. We refer to the growing flexibility of work processes and the incorporation of knowledge and information as direct means of production, together with the globalization of production and the economy through the segmentation of the work process and its relocation in different contexts and territories at the global level (Lash and Urry, 1998; Fazio, 2011).

In this historical context, neoliberalism re-emerges and is constituted as a project that proposes to "disembed capital from these constraints." imposed on it by the State within the Keynesian ideological framework and social democracy (Harvey, 2005: 11). It is fundamentally a discourse that offers as its central message the idea that neoliberalism is synonymous with liberation. From Milton and Rose Friedman's famous "Free to Choose" to the notion of deregulation and liberation of markets, the message is the same: an attempt to convince us that flexibility, adaptability, competitiveness, self-regulation of markets, and individuality are the basis and sustenance of success and development.

In this sense, neoliberalism reformulates the concept of freedom on the basis of three axes or planes of action and liberation:

1. The *free market*, as a theoretical body that governs the functioning of the economy and as an ideological paradigm that guides economic policies in the broadest sense.
2. *Individual freedoms*, which point to the individual as the central subject of all freedom, understanding individuals as persons, companies, and institutions; and understanding freedom as the absence of restrictions and constrictions, whether they come from political and state institutions or from society itself (labor unions, community and civil society organizations, among others).
3. The *freedom of capital*, especially in terms of its mobility on a global scale. Markets are globalizing and require free capital to move from one place to another, a mobility that cannot be constrained by state interventions, however necessary they may be considered. Nationalist principles are nothing more than leftovers from other times that only limit the transforming forces of capital.

This idea of freedom is the founding force of neoliberalism as an ideological framework in current times (Hayek, 1960). The whole neoliberal discourse is articulated around this concept of freedom understood as economic freedom (of choice, mobility, action) and as political freedom—the principle of Western democracy—that stands against the still prevailing obscurantist forms, whether in fascist, communist, statist ideologies, or, more recently, in religious fundamentalism.[3]

---

[3] It is paradoxical and contradictory, however, that in this struggle to consolidate itself as the dominant ideology, it even appeals to highly religious rhetoric and arguments, as well as to

It is evident that neoliberalism, more than a theoretical paradigm, has become an ideological matrix from which economic policies for the Third World, as well as wars and invasions of countries, are sustained and founded. In the name of freedom, two wars have already been fought in Iraq, and a continuous exercise of US military dominance is maintained throughout the world. Likewise, various mechanisms and institutions are used to impose economic policies, structural adjustments, and economic models conducive to the entry of capital and transnational corporations.

Neoliberalism operates not only as an ideology but also as an economic program and a project of political and social transformations at the global level, which has contributed to the transformation and recompositing of the ruling class. It is a form of restoration of class power over the economy, society, and politics that functioned until the end of the nineteenth century but reconfigured and transformed by the new modes of domination and exploitation that are consolidated in post-industrial capitalism. In this sense, we are witnessing the refoundation of the State within the framework of neoliberal ideology. The State ceases to be a space in dispute—a field of struggle, confrontation, agreements, and negotiations between social classes on various aspects concerning the struggle between their interests (labor rights, economic franchises, taxes, benefits and social security, among many others)—to enter into a process of involution that reflects the triumph of the dominant classes, of their interests in the structuring of the State and its practical action (Bourdieu, 1998a). This suggests a division where, firstly, there is the presence of a State endowed with significant autonomy and direct intervention. Its role includes ensuring social guarantees and privileges for the ruling classes, as well as facilitating the expansion of capital and globalization. Conversely, on the other hand, there exists an equally interventionist State, but with a repressive and policing focus against the interests and mobilizations of the working and popular classes. This State is also highly active in international conflicts, consistently aligning itself with the interests of capital and advanced economies.

---

rhetoric typical of an idiosyncrasy based on manifest destinies. In this regard, suffice it to quote a few phrases from George W. Bush: "freedom is the Almighty's gift to every man and woman in this world. And as the greatest power on the face of the Earth, we [the United States] have an obligation to help the spread of freedom." (Bush, 2004). This legitimizes invasions, wars, dispossessions, impoverishments, expropriations and other forms of exercising power and domination on a global scale, in what would be a revised and updated version of the Monroe Doctrine.

3 The Reconstitution of the Ruling Classes in Global Capitalism

Capitalism and capitalists have always operated on scales beyond national boundaries. First, it was based on forms of colonial domination as a mechanism for extracting resources and wealth from the colonies. Then, it was based on forms of transnational corporations exercising their dominance through international markets and subordinating Third World economies in relations of domination and economic dependence. Presently, the control and utilization of resources and labor take shape through the globalization of production processes. This involves not only the relocation of various facets of the labor process, leading to diverse forms of labor exploitation, but also the resurgence of colonial extractivism and accumulation by dispossession. These elements frequently define the economic models prevalent in many Third World countries. (Harvey, 2003; Vivares, 2018).

In grasping the extent and significance of the restructuring of the class framework in global capitalism, we must begin with at least two premises that necessitate a reevaluation of traditional models in class analysis. First, acknowledging that capitalism operates within a global framework, we must also conceptualize the class structure and the formation of classes within this globalized context. Second, understanding class and its structuring involves recognizing them as intricate phenomena where various levels and social dimensions converge. This requires a holistic approach in terms of its totality, integrating the analysis of exploitation processes and relations with those of domination, recognizing their interplay, confrontation, and reproduction.

i) The formation of classes in global capitalism is an evolving process, making it challenging to capture using fixed categories and theoretical concepts. What proves most significant is the ongoing nature of their conformation and structuring, allowing for the identification of signs and emerging forms. It is undeniable that the globalization of capital is based on profound changes in the organization of the labor and productive process and, therefore, in the social and territorial forms adopted by the social relations of production. We refer, for example, to the growing diversification of occupations that entail new conditions for structuring social classes, which move away from traditional concepts and notions. In addition, the technological changes already described (microelectronic revolution, digital age, information age, cognitive capitalism, among others) are giving rise to new forms of class inequality. The globalization of production and the economy, sustained by new forms of organization of the process of exploitation of labor, has modified the formation of classes and the class structure, although the fundamental bases of the class structure and exploitation of labor characteristic of capitalism are maintained (Sassen 2007).

Thus, for example, the processes of productive delocalization expressed in the metaphor of the global factory (Ianni, 1996) imply not only the relocation of productive segments but with it the segmented and fragmented constitution of social classes; this is not only geographically but also socially, culturally, and politically, which significantly hinders their formation as social classes, whether at the local-national or global level. In Giddens' (1975) analysis, settlement patterns and the residential concentration of workers, differentiated by cultural and productive characteristics, were considered mediating factors in class structuring. However, envisioning the same factor in a globalized context reveals a transformation where industrial location and residence patterns of workers become disrupted, adopting a global-local format. In this global scenario, the characteristics of the local and the worker's community of origin play a pivotal role in the localization patterns of capital. This dynamic emerges as a primary factor in the very constitution of labor power as a commodity for global capital. Not only is it a local market for cheap labor, but it is also mediated by diverse social, cultural, demographic, and political factors that concur in the formation and structuring of that local labor force as a working class for global capital. In this sense, the diversity of the local constitutes a fundamental mediation to be considered in the social formation of the working class in this global capitalism.

Contrasting the global-local dynamic, it is noteworthy to emphasize the significance of translocal and global relations in shaping the class of professionals, technicians, and international civil servants. This class holds pivotal roles in organizing, directing, and controlling the processes of economic and productive globalization of capital. As Sassen (2007: 212) points out, "one of the characteristics of global classes is their settlement in a variety of economic, political and subjective structures, as is the case of the global networks that underlie each of these classes, networks that have different degrees of formalization and institutionalization."

Likewise, and as a result of the very globalization of productive processes and societies, the classic relationship between class and State acquires a new character, to the extent that both categories are constituted and act in spaces and territories that transcend national boundaries, although they never cease to be local and national. In other words, the relations of power and domination on which social classes and their links with national States are defined and constituted adopt an unprecedented dialectic that simultaneously combines and articulates the local and the global, the national and the supra- or transnational. What is relevant, in any case, is that the nation state is increasingly losing its capacity and power to shape the formation of global social classes, especially in terms of the constitution of their national identities and their sense of belonging.

These are, however, emerging modes in the process of consolidation, where the actions and power of one or the other—one or the other social classes, one or the other national States—are reconfigured but always reproducing the basic forms of power and domination. In this sense, to speak of global classes is no less a metaphor, inasmuch as we are dealing with classes that, although constituted on the basis of globalizing processes, maintain strong links and roots with densely local and national networks and relations. In this sense, Sassen (2007) chooses to call them partially denationalized classes.

ii) On the other hand, we know that the structuring of classes and class struggle refers not only to relations of exploitation but also of political and social domination, on which the very modes of exploitation of labor are based. While the class relation, namely between owners and producers, is inherently an exploitative relationship tied to the economic-productive infrastructure, the challenge has been that its emphasis has often overshadowed, or at the very least relegated to the background, another equally pivotal aspect in any exploitation process. This pertains to the relations of domination and power asymmetries that extend beyond the confines of the labor process.

In this sense, in a class society such as capitalism, the dominant classes cannot be defined solely in terms of the ownership of the means of production but must also include their position in terms of the relations of domination and control of both the labor process and society and the state. As highlighted by Therborn (2008 [1978]), the dominant nature of the ruling class is established through its ability to wield control over the primary modes and instruments of economic, political, cultural, and social dominance. This encompasses command over the means of production, thereby influencing the methods of exploitation, appropriation, and accumulation of surplus and surplus value. Additionally, it involves authority over the mechanisms of political reproduction, manifested through power over the State and the tools for the administration of political power and coercion. Lastly, it extends to governance over the mechanisms of production and reproduction of cultural and social hegemonies, encompassing not only the means of communication and consensus but also mastery and oversight of the arenas and domains where these consensuses and hegemonies are constructed, such as educational institutions, families, and communities.

Based on this notion of domination, we can argue that in global capitalism the ruling class would be formed not only by the owners of the means of production (capitalists and bourgeoisie) but also by the top executives and managers of large multinational corporations. Although they are not strictly speaking owners of capital, their position is equally one of control and domination of the labor process and capital accumulation. Although they are not part of the class of owners, they are not necessarily a class in opposition to them; on the contrary, they act and operate as agents extracting surplus labor. From our perspective, it would be a sector that, together with the owners of the means of production, make up the power elites in advanced capitalist societies. iii) Considering the two previous points, we can point out that in the recomposition and restoration of the ruling class in global capitalism we identify three main characteristics:

1) The globalization of capital is based on the formation of large corporations, which not only implies the merger of companies but also the integration of different forms of capital. A transnational corporation is not only the integration of various companies within the same sector but also the formation of economic groups with diverse and multiple interests. It is the integration of financial groups with monetary interests, with commercial groups and companies, productive and industrial companies, among others. The aim is to reduce the tensions and conflicts between the different forms of capital in order to favor its own globalization and its actions, therefore, constituting a global capitalist class. The post-industrial global society retains its industrial essence, with multinational corporations continuing to be founded upon industrial enterprises. However, the crucial distinction lies in their global manifestation, where they extend beyond mere manufacturing. Corporate interests now span diverse sectors, encompassing not only the production of various commodities but also the energy sector, finance, trade, technology, social services (particularly in health and education), and the provision of various services to the public sector, among other realms of capital operation.

2) Notwithstanding these fusions of interests between different forms of capital, this integration is based on the hegemony of finance capital.[4] What happens on Wall Street matters more and more and less what happens in factories and industries, even if they are highly globalized. The

---

4 Hegemony, in this case, does not mean domination or imposition of the financial sector over other sectors or forms of capital (commercial, industrial, etc.), but rather corresponds to the sector through which the process of capital accumulation is centralized. At the end of the day, it is the same conglomerate, the same corporation where all forms of capital come together, and with it, all its diverse interests converge.

global economy has a center of operations and these are the big stock exchanges, as well as the main financial and stock exchange centers of the global cities (Sassen, 1991). Nothing expresses this predominance of financial capital and the stock market world better than the 2008 crisis. Despite the fact that much of the economy and production was affected, the income, bonuses, prizes, as well as the profits of the financial sector, remained high and represented an important form of concentration of power and wealth (Stiglitz, 2015).

3) The new forms of production with high labor flexibility and reflexivity, sustained by the so-called global knowledge industry, have given rise to new forms of capital and new groups of professionals and entrepreneurs who join the upper echelons of the ruling class. We are referring to biotechnology and genetic engineering companies, as well as information technologies, digital applications and software for the automation of various segments of the work process and the production of goods, in addition to their distribution and consumption (David and Foray, 2002). Along with this, the weight of capital and entrepreneurs linked to the media in its various platforms and formats is increasing. In all these cases, these are highly dynamic industries with great and growing power over other economic sectors.

These changes imposed by globalization give rise to the restoration of privileges associated not only with the ownership of capital but also with its management and governance of the economy at the global level. Various authors refer to this as the emergence of new social classes or, at the very least, new social strata within the dominant classes in global capitalism, which are added to the capitalists and entrepreneurs—that is, to the direct owners of the means of production and capital. Along with this, anonymized forms of capital ownership are consolidating, expressed in the form of the constitution of large business corporations, where the ownership of capital itself is anonymized in shares and property titles that are continuously traded and exchanged on the global stock markets.

Along with the repositioning of large capitalist entrepreneurs, this new class of top executives, managers, and CEOs emerges and is embedded in the top management positions of multinational corporations and forming part of the boards of directors of large companies. Many times, these executives are recruited within the same families of the business classes and are usually trained in university and graduate centers of the social and political elite (Zimmerman, 2019). They are what Urrutia León (2017) calls the *corporate class*, which refers to senior executives of global companies who, without being direct owners of the capital of the companies and business corporations for which they work, directly exercise the power of capital, directing, planning, organizing, and controlling the process of exploitation of labor and accumulation of capital on a global scale.

Sassen refers to this emerging class as a new *transnational elite*. As she points out, with the development and consolidation of transnational corporations and their globalized territorial form, a transnational (global, in a certain sense) social space is configured in which this class of professionals and senior executives in charge of the management and control of global companies settles and mobilizes. For the globalization of the economy to exist and function, it requires a significant number of professionals, managers, executives, and technical personnel who can articulate and operate this economy of multi- and transnational companies and corporations. This "frontline workforce is quite mobile and can easily be considered as a new transnational class of professionals ... defined more by control than by ownership of the means of production" (Sassen, 2007: 217).

This emerging social class is characterized by its advanced professional expertise and remarkable hypermobility, enabling individuals to navigate the extensive economic and business landscape of over 40 global cities. These cities serve as the primary hubs for the management, control, and coordination of the corporate global economy, housing key financial centers that play pivotal roles in the contemporary world. This hypermobility reproduces their own globalized spatial form, while building and consolidating a dense network of relationships that articulates and constitutes them as social subjects with a labor, social, and cultural identity. Both because of their position in the management process of the global corporate economy and because of their cultural capital and social networks, they constitute a true transnational elite of professionals and senior executives on which the very operation of the global economy rests.

A defining trait of this emerging social class lies in the transformation of their income structure. It extends beyond conventional salary forms, which represent compensation for their work, to include what are known as stock options. These options grant them the rights to acquire shares in the very companies and corporations where they hold managerial roles or, in some instances, serve as members of their boards of directors. This means that their value as labor subjects is determined more by the value of those shares and corporate assets than by their eventual administrative effectiveness and efficiency in the management of the production of those companies and corporations. In this way, the social reproduction of this new emerging class (of its privileges, its social and political position, and status, among other aspects) is tied and directly linked to the reproduction of capital—that is, to the capacity to accumulate capital and not so much to its professional performance.[5]

On the other hand, unlike industrial capitalism, in global capitalism these ruling classes—both entrepreneurs and their corporate class—are no longer concentrated in the manufacturing and industrial sector of the economy but tend to exercise dominance and control over the accumulation of capital through the financial and speculative sector, as well as in technological development and the so-called global knowledge industry. They are a transnational class although not necessarily completely or fully cosmopolitan, since they maintain a local and national root that implies a dense network of local and national relations and interests. What constitutes them as a social class is, on the one hand, their narrowly utilitarian logic (Sassen, 2007), and, on the other, their position of power vis-à-vis the process of exploitation and accumulation of capital and control and domination of the labor process. What is relevant in all this is that under the protection of neoliberalism and globalization the power of the ruling classes is recomposed and restored, exercising their dominance over the accumulation of capital over the constraints and alliances that they had to accept during the period of the predominance and hegemony of the Keynesian and statist matrix of capitalist development.

The restoration of the upper classes as dominant classes is one of the pillars on which the new forms taken by the class struggle in advanced societies are built. And here is one of the most flagrant contradictions of the discourse on the death of classes: "Neoliberals, at the same time that they defend that social classes do not exist and accuse the left of practicing class struggle, decisively exercise the struggle against the working class" (Urrutia León, 2017: 77, our translation). In this regard, a relevant fact is that the existence of class struggle in contemporary society is not only a rhetorical resource of the left, but it is, above all else, a fact recognized even by some of the largest capitalists in the world such as Warren Buffett, who in 2017 was listed by Forbes magazine as the second richest man in the world. Despite his status as one of the wealthiest individuals, Buffett observed that he paid a notably lower tax rate compared to his own employees working in his office. This led him to ponder the fairness and ethical considerations surrounding this discrepancy, but the reason he gave himself was very simple and equally devastating: "There's class warfare, all right," Mr. Buffett said, "but it's my class, the rich class, that's making war, and we're winning" (Stein, 2006).

---

5 During economic crises of 2008, for example, this class of top executives received millions in compensation, even though they were largely responsible for the crisis (Stiglitz, 2012).

This is not the first time Buffett has argued against the injustice generated by class inequality. He had already questioned the asymmetry of power, showing that the state always ended up forgiving and pardoning the debts of the rich but very rarely those of workers and middle-class people. This is what happened, for example, in the 2008 crisis when the U.S. government was more interested in implementing policies to save the big banks and financial services than in financially supporting the large number of middle-class people who were trapped in a usurious and unfair mortgage system, which from the beginning was shown to be unfeasible to sustain. This strategy clearly expresses the political power and the capacity to influence the State of this new ruling class stratum and reflects the background of neoliberal ideology in which the freedom of big capital must always be placed above all other freedoms, even the freedom of markets for the middle classes. This is what Buffett questions when he asks "How can this be right?" (Stein, 2006), how is it possible to maintain a system with such injustices? Stiglitz takes a more precise and direct stance, characterizing these actions not as isolated circumstances but as routine practices of neoliberalism that signify the demise of fair play. This, according to him, results in a state of heightened immorality by "exploiting the poorest and least educated citizens of our country" (Stiglitz, 2012: 33), all to protect the wealthiest and most privileged members of the economy—an egregious manifestation of class struggle at its worst.

4   The Constitution of the Working Class in Global Capitalism

This manifestation of class struggle is evidenced in the social conditions defining the overall status of worker class. This extends to their vulnerability and weakness in constitution themselves as a relevant player in this scenario of class conflicts and social-political antagonisms.[6]

Starting from the late seventies, initiated by events such as the coup d'état in Chile—which served as an experimental ground for the initial implementation

---

6   By working class, we mean those whose only source of income is the sale of their labor power and whose income is essentially made up of wages, salaries, and benefits associated with their work. It corresponds to those workers who, through this market relationship, transfer to the capitalists and ruling classes the surplus labor they generate. As a class, it is extremely diverse, broad, and segmented into different strata according to occupations, qualifications, sex, race, ethnicity, religion, and other modes of social and political differentiation. As a working class, far from diminishing, it continues to increase over time, although the manufacturing-industrial component has been reduced as a result of the new forms of organization of the labor process.

of neoliberal concepts—, and continuing into the eighties with the rise of Thatcher in England and Reagan in the United States, a concerted strategy has been formulated, expanded, and solidified against the working classes and the middle sectors. It is not only a change in the force's correlation and a collection of the bill for all the privileges and benefits ceded or at least negotiated and conciliated in the previous Welfare State model. It corresponds to the consolidation of the neoliberal model in a framework of economic globalization and the advent of the post-industrial society. It is the transition to a new mode of capital accumulation in which the very conditions of class structuring, as well as the forms of conflict and antagonism between them, are rethought and reconfigured (Harvey, 2005).

What holds significance for our discussion is that it wasn't solely a political strategy aimed at undermining the working class, intending to diminish the influence of trade unions and their effectiveness in negotiations and collective endeavors, along with other entities and institutions advocating for workers' rights—although this was undoubtedly a component. Rather, a substantial portion of the strategy was rooted in the alteration of the structural foundations that define how workers constitute themselves as a social class. In essence, *Reaganomics* fundamentally entailed a shift in the methods of labor exploitation and, consequently, a transformation in the configurations of the production process within advanced societies. This transformation was a consequence of globalization and the establishment of new principles governing the organization and regulation of labor and productive relations within the labor process. Various authors call this the transition from industrial society to information society, the advent of cognitive capitalism. Beyond the terms used, what is relevant is that what characterizes this new era of capitalism is not the type of activities that are developed—industrial vs. services—but the way in which they are organized.[7]

A central aspect to this is the socio-labor and territorial impact of these new technologies and modes of work organization. In terms of their territorial forms, we refer to the globalization of capitalism. As noted in previous sections, globalization has implied new schemes and patterns in the territorial configuration of the world-economy. This territorial reorganization is based on two complementary processes:

1) Improvements in communications and transportation technologies allow the geographic reach of any industrial process to be amplified on a global scale (Mattelart, 2003).

---

7 For more details on this subject, see the first section of this chapter.

2) The new forms of organization of the production process (automation, division of operations, just-in-time production, etc.) have allowed the separability of the segments that make up the production system, thus making the spatial location of the different work centers more flexible according to their best options (De la Garza, 2012).

In short, we are dealing with a new logic of localization in which the principles of agglomeration that gave life to the large industrial cities of the 20th century are radically overturned by the development of telecommunications and information technology (Sassen, 1998). The new information technologies and the reflexivity of productive processes allow a growing fragmentation and separability of the different parts and segments that make up the work processes, making possible a greater flexibility in relation to the location of each productive segment and the forms assumed by the contractual relation of labor and the regulations of capital-labor relations, both in their technical-productive and socio-economic and labor dimensions (Lipietz, 1997).

This new mode of localization overturns one of the supposedly non-derogable premises of the work system of industrial societies. "Telecommunications have made this possible by removing what used to seem an inescapable part of the labour system of industrial society: that is, the need for people to work together at a certain place to produce goods or services. Jobs can now be exported" (Beck, 2000b: 17). What used to be manufactured in the same space today is deterritorialized, spatially fragmented, and its segments are located in different local spaces, directly articulating in a world system (supranational) local and regional economy territorially separated and distant. This is the emergence of the global factory, through which the process of geographical dispersion of production, productive forces, capital, technology, labor, planning, and the market itself is intensified and generalized (Ianni, 1996).

The relocation of productive segments follows the logic of the comparative advantages required for each segment. However, not all productive segments are relocalized equally. On the one hand, processes requiring high qualification based on processes of high reflexivity and information processing tend to be located in different productive areas of the First World. These include both technological generation and innovation processes (Silicon Valley, for example) and planning, management, and administrative and financial control (large financial and corporate centers in global cities). In all of them are concentrated officials, executives, and high-level professionals who make up the transnational elites of the global corporate class, which we have already mentioned in previous sections.

Conversely, production processes that do not demand reflexivity and hermeneutics in their progression—those characterized by repetitiveness and automation—tend to shift to peripheral and Third World economies. This relocation exploits social contexts marked by precariousness and vulnerability in labor, offering high flexibility in terms of contractual relations and regulations. In essence, these processes essentially involve the exportation of jobs, transferring the instability inherent in industrial employment to cities and communities in the Third World. Here, it intersects with the social and political vulnerability of workers in light of the influence wielded by local and national oligarchies, coupled with the absence of political protection mechanisms and institutions.

In a certain way, flexibility and reflexivity are the principles that, along with sustaining the new forms of production, also shape the new patterns of job location. Flexible jobs (deregulated, precarious, and vulnerable) are located in the periphery, while reflexive jobs (typical of the knowledge and information economy) are concentrated in the central economies. This would correspond to a new scheme of international division of labor. It is no longer a question of center-periphery relations pure and simple, which, as in the past, opposed developed and underdeveloped national economies, but of a social and class division through the configuration of production as a globalized fact. The global factory not only segmented and deterritorialized the productive process but with it also *deterritorialized the class structure* and thus the form of class structuring. If in industrial capitalism the factory was a space where all types of workers converged—from laborers and employees to administrators, engineers, and technical-scientists—in this era of globalization the metaphor of the global factory refers precisely to the disintegration of this space of confluence, deterritorializing and de-linking the different modes and categories of labor: unskilled, precarious, and flexible workers, on the one hand, and administrators, managers, technicians, professionals, and engineers in research and development, on the other. The global factory expresses on a global scale what is detached and disconnected at the local level. In any case, what is relevant is that this global articulation is made from positions of power and control over the labor process, thus configuring *a global form in the relations of exploitation of labor*—that is, of extraction and appropriation of surplus value. We are dealing, therefore, with *global forms of exploitation*, not because they are exercised by transnational institutions (companies and corporations) but *because the labor process itself is configured spatially as a global process*.[8] Both the technical

---

8 The existence of transnational consortiums and corporations and their role in the world economy are nothing new. Since the nineteenth century, transnational corporations have been operating in the Third World in the production of raw materials, energy resources, food, financial services, among many other commodities. Such is the case of banana plantations

division of labor, involving workers, employees, and engineers, and the social division of labor, encompassing classes and social categories of labor and workers, are now globalized. This means they are deterritorialized locally and re-linked on a global scale, consequently shaping the class structure within global capitalism.

In this sense, the labor flexibility promoted by neoliberalism configures not only the economic-productive context but also the social and political context in which the working class is constituted in global capitalism. As far as the world of labor is concerned, neoliberal policies, also known as structural adjustment policies, that have been promoted since the years of *Reaganomics* were based on a process of deregulation—that is, on the de-structuring of the previous regulatory scaffolding of labor and contractual relations, prevailing either in the labor market or in the labor process itself—which gave life to the so-called Fordist system of production and accumulation. This restructuring of the labor regime based on the new structures of labor flexibility and deregulation resulted in what Beck (2000a) has called a regime of labor risk, which replaces the labor regime and social institutions that emerged through the welfare state. As this author points out, in the informational society the Fordist regime of labor organization tends to be replaced by a regime of risk that through labor flexibility tends to blur "the boundaries between work and non-work are starting to blur, in respect of time, space and contractual content; paid work and unemployment are spread over larger spaces and therefore become less and less socially visible from positions on the margins" (Beck, 2000a: 77–78).

In this context, job instability stands as a constant in the realm of employment. Flexibility emerges as the term that most accurately encapsulates and simultaneously conceals this instability. On one hand, it signifies the imperative for capital competitiveness, forming the cornerstone of the triumphant narrative of the new economy. On the other hand, it underscores the worker's predicament—the realization of being a replaceable commodity, a pawn in the economic struggle between capitalists. This dynamic serves to bolster production, enhance competitiveness, and ultimately increase the profit and accumulation of capital. However, it also serves as the mechanism for preserving

---

in Central America, mining companies in South America, oil and energy companies in the Persian Gulf, to mention only the most relevant. However, none of them was sustained by the globalization of the labor process itself, which was their material of exploitation and accumulation. In many cases, they were enclave economies, which controlled and directed a large part of international trade in the peripheral economies and constituted an economic sector in itself, economically and productively disconnected from the rest of the local economy.

capital and corporate competitiveness, with workers bearing the full brunt of losses. In the competitive landscape, there are always both winners and losers, and flexibility functions as a lever that tilts toward workers in times of losses and toward capital in times of profits. As Bauman (2000: 147) points out,

> 'Flexibility' is the slogan of the day, and when applied to the labour market it augurs an end to the 'job as we know it', announcing instead the advent of work on short-term contracts, rolling contracts or no contracts, positions with no in-built security but with the 'until further notice' clause. Working life is saturated with uncertainty.

Thus, working life is nothing but pure uncertainty, permanent risk. The point is that losing one's job is not just any risk; it is one that is transferred to and envelops with uncertainty all the other areas of life of the worker and their family. Thus, occupational risk is a vital risk.

In this regard, there is often talk of the end of work or the end of the work society (Rifkin, 1995). In reality, what is in decline is not work, not even its salaried form in the strict sense, but the particular form that work assumed in industrial society throughout the 20th century, which was constituted around a social and welfare state that imposed various modes of protection and security on the world of work, as part of a social agreement or class pact between capitalists, workers, and the modern state. The "end of labor" refers, on the one hand, to the contractual forms of labor—that is, to labor agreements and contracts that established duties and rights for both worker and capital. On the other hand, it signifies the termination of work's social function as a privileged means of social and cultural integration, a process instrumental in shaping forms of social cohesion. This shift is attributed not so much to the nature of the work itself but rather to the regulations governing its contractual forms, duly sanctioned by the State. In the labor world of contractual flexibility and deregulation, work loses its function as the main letter of identity and access to forms of civility and social and democratic inclusion. The worker loses not only benefits and privileges but, more importantly, a means and a way of constructing meaning to their own lives, to their own humanity (Mires, 1996).

Let us phrase it this way: In the Social State in advanced societies of the twentieth century, work had regained a portion of its status as a fundamental element of human existence. It had, to some extent, moved away from the depiction crafted in the eighteenth and nineteenth centuries, where it was considered just another commodity—interchangeable and readily traded in the market (Polanyi, 2001 [1944]). During the twentieth century, despite retaining its structure as a salaried commodity, the contractual and commercial relationship of labor took on additional significance. It became embedded in a social and political context that attributed meanings beyond its economic-productive function as a creator of value and surplus value.

In the realm of flexibility, the social and cultural functions of labor, encompassing identity and politics, undergo disruption. Notably, it is not the commodity itself, nor the labor or its technical modes of production (such as the microelectronic revolution), that dictates this shift. Instead, it is the emerging social and political context. This context, buoyed by the ascendancy of neoliberalism as a political program and state ideology—and the subsequent decline of social democratic and socialist initiatives[9]—redefines the social and political terms (the power dynamics) that delineate the contours of the capital-labor relationship. It also shapes the opposition and structures the forms of wage-profit-accumulation. This transformation aligns with what Warren Buffett identifies as the triumph of capital in this contemporary iteration of the class struggle or war.

The strategies of flexibility and deregulation thus constitute new forms of exploitation of labor in global capitalism. The precarization of working conditions and contractual deregulation, as well as the labor instability resulting from the same flexibility, are the mechanisms normally used to reconfigure the correlation of forces and weaken workers' positions. In particular, labor flexibility operates on the basis of two mechanisms in its configuration as a mode of exploitation and domination. First, there is the so-called internal flexibility, which is basically based on new technical modes of organizing the work process (automation, reflexivity, and other modes characteristic of cognitive capitalism and the role of information and knowledge as the foundations of the production process, both in manufacturing industry and in other economic sectors). The direct effect of this flexibility mechanism is to increase the productivity of labor and, consequently, the rate of surplus value and capital accumulation.

Second, there is the so-called external flexibility, which refers to the forms of contractual relations that regulate the capital-labor relationship. Here arise the processes of precariousness of working conditions, which directly affect the labor rights acquired by the working class, as well as the increase in partial, piecework, forms of labor subcontracting, and other mechanisms that result

---

9 These setbacks are manifested in events such as the collapse of the Berlin Wall, the demise of authentic socialist systems, and the failure of the Third Way associated with European social democracy and English laborism. By the 1990s, neoliberalism had asserted its dominance over the political landscape and ideological discussions, positioning itself as the exclusive and prevailing ideology.

in greater instability and precariousness of employment. In turn, this process operates in two complementary ways.

On the one hand, the very segmentation and delocalization of work processes, along with favoring the mobility of capital, transfers important parts of production to geographical areas and countries with lower wages, lower social cost of worker reproduction, and other conditions that characterize a greater precariousness and social and political weakness of workers, which does not allow them to face the conditions imposed by modern capitalism. This is a strategy of capital that implies a globalized extension of competition among workers themselves (Bourdieu, 1998b).

On the other hand, there is the deregulation and *casualization* of working conditions within advanced societies themselves. In order to impose these new working conditions, advanced societies resort to the importation of workers in the form of labor immigrants, sustaining the precariousness of their intrinsic vulnerability, especially in anti-immigration political contexts that result in greater social and political weakness of migrants (Canales, 2019). Thus, we are increasingly witnessing a *racialization* of social and occupational inequality in which the occupational strata of lower social value (personal services, construction day laborers, among others) are occupied by immigrants from the Third World, while high-level jobs (professionals, technicians, managers, administrators, and other employees) are occupied by the 'native' population. Thus, on the occupational stratification that arises from the economic and productive model, an ethno-stratification is constituted where workers are discriminated and segregated according to their ethnic-racial and migratory origin.

In this sense, flexibility constitutes a *new mode of exploitation and domination*. Labor flexibility, and the precarization of labor that accompanies it, not only serve to increase labor productivity but, above all, act as a means of dispossessing workers' labor rights, reconfiguring the exploitation and appropriation of surplus labor based on new orders and forms of organization of the social and political domination of capital over labor. As Bourdieu (1998b: 84–86) points out:

> [Job] insecurity is the product not of an *economic inevitability*, identified with the much-heralded 'globalization', but of a *political will*. A 'flexible' company in a sense deliberately exploits a situation of insecurity which it helps to reinforce: it seeks to reduce its costs, but also to make this lowering possible by putting the workers in permanent danger of losing their jobs.

> ... Casualization of employment is part of a *mode of domination* of a new kind, based on the creation of a generalized and permanent state of insecurity aimed at forcing workers into submission, into the acceptance of exploitation ... [it] breaks resistance and obtains obedience and submission, through apparently natural mechanisms which thus serve as their own justification.
>
> ... So it seems to me that what is presented as an economic system governed by the iron laws of a kind of social nature is in reality a political system which can only be set up with the active or passive complicity of the officially political powers.

In a similar sense, Standing (2011) coins the term *precariat* to refer to this new way of constituting the working class, or at least some strata of it, in global capitalism. It is a neologism derived from the conjunction of the terms *preca*rious and prole*tariat*, thus emphasizing the context of precariousness that defines the new forms of structuring the working class. It does not an equivalent to the Marxist category of lumpenproletariat, since, unlike the latter, the precariat refers to a structuring situation of the mode of production and exploitation in global capitalism and not only to a deviation from it. Nor does it refer to the category of the working poor, since it is not only the level of wages or income that defines them as a social and labor category.

For Standing, the precariat corresponds to workers inserted in highly flexible and deregulated labor relations, which have implied the loss of different forms of labor security that were institutionalized in the context of welfare states and post-war European social democracy. The precariat refers not only to a labor condition but also to a social category—that is, to a social subject that is constituted as such in globalized capitalism from the imposition of neoliberal forms of (de)regulation of capital-labor relations. Thus, the *precariat* "is subject to pressures and experiences that lead to a precarious existence, to living in the present, without a secure identity or a sense of development that could be achieved through work" (Standing, 2011: 16).

The precariat referred to by Standing, although socially vulnerable workers, are nonetheless inserted in highly modernized and globalized economic sectors. Precariousness and labor flexibility are a strategy of capital to face the challenges of global competition, improving its conditions of competitiveness and productivity in all economic sectors; therefore, it is a reconfiguration of employment conditions that affects practically all industrial branches, as well as construction, commerce, and services.

What is relevant, in any case, is that, although precariousness and flexibility are strictly economic-productive processes, their constitution as a social phenomenon is mediated by a series of extra-economic factors that make this a highly complex phenomenon. For one thing, the distinction and construction of the social and labor identities of those who make up this kind of precariat do not follow a strictly economic-productive logic but are a function of processes of cultural, ethnic, demographic, gender, and migratory differentiation, among others. Hence, in contrast to the 20th-century industrial capitalism, where relations of exploitation were directly influenced by power dynamics negotiated politically through the State and various institutions of civil, economic, and labor society (such as unions, parties, and industrial chambers), contemporary global, flexible, and reflexive capitalism seems to have its relations of exploitation mediated by a myriad of alternative modes and structures of domination and power. These are neither political-state nor purely economic; instead, they are rooted in various spheres of social construction of inequalities and power structures. These include but are not limited to gender, race, culture, ethnic and migratory status, geographic and national origin, among numerous others.

It could be argued that this has always been the case—that in capitalism the exploitation of labor has always been sustained also in these other spheres of structuring the worker as a class and social subject. What is relevant, in any case, is the strength currently acquired by these spaces, as well as the weakness of the worker to assert their rights and interests from the same labor and productive spaces. The weakness of the unions, of the left-wing parties and, in general, of political and social institutions attest to this. The exploitation of labor in the sphere of production and the economy is constituted and structured on the basis of diverse modes of domination and discrimination structured in other spheres of social life. For the same reason, the formation of class consciousness, as well as the very structuring of the worker as a class, is mediated by these other forms of social construction of identities, consciousness, and construction as classes and social subjects. In a labor world characterized by flexibility, instability, and precarity, the shaping and structuring of class, ethno-national origin, gender identity, and various modes of social and cultural differentiation and self-identification hold greater significance and influence than the class situation determining one's placement in the labor market and production processes.[10]

---

10   Thus, for example, for a labor migrant, the fact that they are a member of their community, whether local or transnational, is more relevant and fundamental to their constitution as a social subject than their situation of exploitation vis-à-vis capital (Cordero, 2007). Something similar can be said of women seasonal workers in the agroindustry in

In this way, the precarization and flexibilization of labor (loss of forms and means of security of different kinds) arising from the post-Fordist mode of exploitation and production are socially articulated with the conditions of social and political vulnerability of individuals that configure them as different modes of social and demographic minorities. In this context, these same conditions that constitute them as social minorities (gender, ethnicity, race, national and geographic origin) cease to be risk factors that expose them to eventual economic and labor exclusion, and become the necessary condition for their inclusion in the flexible and precarious world of work (Canales, 2003 and 2021b).

In the current era of capitalism, unlike ever before, the methods of exploiting labor and workers are intricately linked with and supplemented by modes of domination, including discrimination and segregation, imposed among various social strata within the population. Unprecedentedly, the social makeup of the worker as an economic-productive class integrates social, cultural, and demographic elements, forming essential components of their identity as social and political entities. Contemporary capitalism, like never before, relies on non-economic and non-productive mechanisms to organize the economic exploitation of labor. Consequently, the working class today is configured based on internal processes of differentiation, hindering the development of a unified class consciousness and identity. The factors of ethnic, migratory, social, demographic, geographic, and political distinctions among workers create divisions that outweigh the common conditions of exploitation, such as flexibility and labor precariousness, rendering them indistinguishable and constituting them primarily as equally exploited labor.

Nothing exemplifies this situation better than the social and political attitude of 'native' workers towards labor immigration in advanced societies. Rather than seeing them as allies in the same struggle of interests as a social class, they see immigrants as aliens, their adversaries, an unfair competition, and do not hesitate to be the first to join anti-immigration policies, xenophobia, and racism, on which the current discourse and attitude of social unrest towards labor migrations is built (Canales, 2021). The case of Donald Trump and his 2016 electoral triumph clearly reflects this situation. White workers, although equally impoverished and precarious as migrant workers, did not hesitate to politically turn against them and support a representative of capital and corporations that, paradoxically, were responsible for their loss of

---

the export agro-industry in the Central Valley of Chile (Canales, 2001), to cite only two examples.

job security conditions, employment, wage reductions, and other forms of precariousness. In their discourse and awareness, these alternative forms of social differentiation, these varied structures of power and domination, took precedence. From these, their precarious situation was redefined, no longer perceived solely as an economic-productive phenomenon inherent to the capital-labor relationship, but rather as an issue stemming from migration and thus considered extra-economic.

Another example in which relations of exploitation are hidden from other forms of domination and power is the case of seasonal agricultural work, especially the packing of fruits and vegetables for export and sale in the central economies. Thus, for example, the same tomato and fruit that are offered in the supermarket chains of North American cities come from three different forms of exploitation and domination. On the one hand, export agriculture in Chile's Central Valley, where the exploitation of labor has been feminized (Canales, 2001). On the other, export agriculture in the valleys of northern Mexico, where the same exploitation of labor has been ethno-stratified, with workers from Mixtec communities in southern Mexico being in charge of the cultivation and harvesting of agricultural products exported to North American cities (Lara et al., 2014). Finally, in California agriculture, the same product (vegetables, fruits, etc.) is grown based on immigrant and undocumented labor most of the time, and, therefore, exploitation takes the form of migratory discrimination (Hernández, 2015). In these three instances, we observe how an identical productive activity, the same product or commodity (such as a particular fruit or vegetable available in the same supermarket), and the same mode of labor exploitation (involving the generation and extraction of surplus) assume distinct social forms. Nevertheless, across all cases, various forms of domination, discrimination, or social and political segregation come into play. In one scenario, gender conditions come into play, shaping the work with a feminized identity. In another, exploitation operates through forms of ethnic-racial discrimination, while in the third, social and political differentiation and inequality are based on the citizenship status of the workers.

What holds significance is that, for instance, in the case of women seasonal workers in Chile's Central Valley, their productive activity shapes a form of social and labor identity, and consequently, a social, cultural, and political integration into Chilean society. Similarly, exploitation is perceived not merely as exploitation but as gender discrimination. This pattern is replicated in the other two scenarios, where the worker's identity is not forged based on their economic-productive involvement and participation alone, but rather on non-economic factors and processes of social identity formation. These instances reflect alternative modes of domination not strictly confined to forms of economic exploitation. Instead, they complement and intertwine to such an extent that, at least superficially, they blur and obscure the economic-productive exploitation relationship, presenting it as a manifestation of social, cultural, and political domination.

Certainly, within this context marked by variations in the construction of class identity, it becomes exceedingly intricate and challenging to formulate strategies for class consciousness that transcend formal identities. It requires perceiving these identities as facets of class identity rather than as factors contributing to its fragmentation. In essence, it entails fostering an understanding and recognition among individuals as part of a unified global class. This unity stems from a shared mode of exploitation but is shaped by diverse forms of social and cultural domination.

However, despite the great diversity that constitutes them and the scarce interaction between these social minorities, their conformation as such stems from similar objective and material conditions that link them and allow us to conceptualize them as a single social class. Likewise, the conditions of precariousness and labor flexibility, which define their patterns of occupational and social insertion, are generated by the new conditions of organization of the labor process, in particular the forms of exploitation and domination of capital over labor that define the current pattern of capitalist accumulation.

Finally, a central aspect that cannot be overlooked in the constitution of the working classes in global capitalism refers to the impact of the strategy of fragmentation of production and relocation of each fragment in various local spheres, articulated in the form of a global factory. This process has generated, among other things, the relocation of industrial plants and with it the export of jobs from central economies to export processing zones in various Third World countries, taking advantage of the availability of cheap labor, the weakness of economic regulatory institutions, and the vulnerability and precariousness of the local workforce (Castillo, 2016).

From central economies, this phenomenon is seen as a reduction in the volume of manufacturing and industrial workers. However, if we look at the globalized form of production, we see that it is nothing more than a relocation of labor, which, at the same time, constitutes a recompositing of the social and political conditions of the constitution of the working class as such at the global level. It goes beyond mere relocation; it involves an intensification of labor flexibility, contractual deregulation, employment precariousness, and heightened social vulnerability for workers. In essence, it signifies the impoverishment and instability of the working class. Additionally, due to the territorial fragmentation resulting from this process, the working class lacks the essential tools to advocate for its collective interests.

The dispersed and divided nature of the global labor process is mirrored in the division and segmentation of the working class, encompassing both its social and economic status and geographical localization patterns. However, these two aspects—production delocalization and working-class fragmentation—currently exhibit distinct and even opposing implications. While the fragmentation and separability of production on a territorial and technical level represent just a phase within the global work process, with all components ultimately interconnected as a global entity, the fragmentation and delocalization of workers operate in the opposite direction. This hinders, and at times renders impossible, their reassembly as a cohesive social entity, as a unified working class. To overcome this, a shift from class fragmentation towards its recompositing as a global entity is imperative.

One example helps us to understand this situation that hinders the construction of a global class consciousness. Faced with the export of jobs and the deindustrialization affecting the core economies, the easy option for workers is to fall back on the old nationalist discourses advocating the interest of the nation, of the national economy, and the role of class in all of this. This is, in part, what has been used by the new right in the United States and took shape in Trump's discourse in his first election campaign. However, it is only a political strategy of the conservative right, which, with that nationalist discourse, hides the fact that the economy of the central countries, their industries and factories, already decades ago stopped operating with national criteria and nationalist logics, but they do it based on the reason of the globalization of the processes of capital accumulation. What this nationalist discourse of the new conservative right hides is that North American capitals and corporations, in reality, are only in name and are made up of global interests and capitals—that is, coming from different nationalities articulated around the same global interest: the accumulation of capital. As a basis for an electoral campaign, this discourse is highly effective; however, it is totally anachronistic in the face of the reality of the global economy. For the same reason, this nationalism is only a way to distort and cover up the objective forms of global production and economy and for the same reason to cover up and prevent the formation of a global working class. As a discourse, this nationalism aligns with the broader class struggle. However, contrary to the belief held by industrial workers in central economies, it does not work in their favor; instead, it serves to uphold the continued fragmentation of workers as a social class within the framework of global capitalism.

5 Class Structure and Social Antagonism in Global Capitalism

The rise of neoliberalism transcends mere academic discourse; it is fundamentally a political matter, serving as the primary ideological framework through which the ruling classes redefine and consolidate their positions in relation to the economy, capital, labor, and accumulation. In response to this, the working classes grapple with a landscape marked by significant fragmentation, both internally and in terms of geography. Simultaneously, class identity undergoes a transformation increasingly shaped by other forms of domination—such as gender, generation, race, ethnicity, citizenship, nationalities, and geographical distinctions—which are juxtaposed with new modes of economic and productive exploitation. These dynamics introduce greater complexity to the task of reconstituting and restoring their class identity.

The consequences in terms of social inequality and the shaping of class antagonisms are evident. One aspect to take into account is the difference in terms of the global-local constitution of capital and labor. While capital and capitalists are protagonists of globalization, labor and workers remain mere supporting actors, disarticulated as such and with a fragmentary existence as a class. This is because the labor process has lost its social, territorial, and cultural integration, so that, for example, the same merchandise is currently produced by workers located in different parts of the world, constituted in turn from different fields of identity construction that are juxtaposed and superimposed on their condition of being exploited by capital. The Fordist production chain has not only been dismantled, with each segment relocated to different countries with unequal labor contexts, but in each of these new production plants, labor is sourced locally. Although integral to the same global production process, these workers are configured merely as local workers, facing not only geographical distance but also social, cultural, and demographic differences. This configuration hinders their potential structuring as a unified global working class.[11]

In this way, the unity of class that was propitiated by the Fordist productive form is today fragmented and dissolved in the face of the delocalization and territorial separation of the different productive segments that form part of the global factory. Although both the commodity produced and the labor that produces it are global, the working class, the workers, therefore, have only a local

---

11   According to Fraser (2016), this implies that, within the context of class conflict, the emphasis is on demands and needs related to *recognition* (such as gender status, nationality, ethnicity, geography, among others) rather than on demands pertaining to the conditions of *redistribution* and labor exploitation (class situation).

existence. While capital and capitalization (accumulation of surplus labor) are organized and practiced globally, their counterpart, labor and labor power, is organized and takes shape only locally. Thus, we have an interesting paradox that expresses the hitherto unbridgeable contradiction in the making of the working class at the global level.

As *labor actors*,—i.e., due their role in the labor process, workers are global subjects. Both, their labor and the product of their labor, are an essential part of the economic and productive globalization of capital. They are an expression of a globalized form of surplus value extraction. However, as *social actors*, their constitution as a working class requires overcoming this territorial and social fragmentation imposed by the very globalization of capital and production. Although their labor is part of the great globalization of capital, in reality, it is so only as a consequence of their alienation as labor power, which has been sold to capital. As a singular worker, however, they do not manage to leave the local borders of their reproduction and social existence. While their labor, materialized in the most diverse products, artifacts, goods, services and merchandise, circulates throughout the world, crossing borders, forming part of the great entertainment of globalization, they, the workers, those who from below are the true architects of this process, are relegated to translocal displacements, to locally located and restricted spaces of reproduction, even exposed to various forms of territorial segregation and social and ethnic-racial discrimination.

In this way—and unlike the ruling class, which does constitute itself as a global class and, as such, is the driving force behind these forms of globalization—workers face structural obstacles that have so far prevented their constitution as a global class. For one thing, the very industrial localization of capital is based on relations of domination and power not only over the working class to be exploited, but also over the nation states with which they negotiate and agree these forms of exploitation associated with their location in those countries. In this sense, the ideology of neoliberalism is a weapon without counterweight, which, while legitimizing these conditions of localization of capital, prevents the constitution of the subaltern classes in confrontation with these forms of domination and exploitation.

The relation of exploitation—that is, of extraction of surplus value—is organized on the basis of global patterns of production and capitalization. Likewise, the ruling classes, which direct and organize the labor process of the global factory, are equally global. However, the worker and their labor force, which are the sustenance of all this, are constrained to local forms of existence, which facilitates their fragmentation, as well as their differentiation in terms of their forms of work and social identity, where the economic-productive basis of their condition of precariousness is hidden in the social and cultural forms of social vulnerability and differentiation. The asymmetries of power between capital and labor are now abysmal. Not only do they refer to differences of power of one over the other—that is, of domination and exploitation of labor by capital—but also to forms of social, territorial, and cultural discrimination that affect labor, violating and undermining its forms of existence and recognition as such. The dominance of capital extends beyond merely controlling labor; it also encompasses the *control of the ways in which labor reproduces and makes itself as a class in opposition to it*. Its domination over the class struggle is increasingly absolute, and there seem to be no social and political institutions that could counteract it. Faced with this, as Bourdieu (1998b) said, *the only option left is political struggle.*

In this framework, it is interesting to consider the proposal of Bauman (1998), who uses the term *"glocalization"* to refer to a new form of social stratification at the global level. For this author, globalization and localization are the driving forces behind a new stratification of the world population that takes shape in the opposition between the global rich and the local poor. What for some is free choice, for others is implacable destiny. Some are the dwellers of the global village; the others are the outcasts of globalization. *Glocalization* is thus a structuring of inequality that generates the distribution and accumulation of privileges for some and the absence of rights for others, of wealth and poverty, power and powerlessness. *Glocalization* is, in short, the spatial form assumed by social stratification at world level, where "the new frontiers of inequality generate ever greater separation between those who connect to supranational networks and those who take refuge in their local bastions." (García Canclini, 2014 [1999]: 15). What is relevant is that, in territorial terms, this differentiation between the globalized rich and the localized poor is built, however, in the same geography, in the same community. Both coexist in the same territories. Wealth and poverty, center and periphery, integrated and excluded, no longer break down into separate or discontinuous territories as in the recent past but intermingle both here and there, both between nations and within the same community. The global and the local are, thus, only two dimensions of the same process, the two faces in which the historical contradiction of capitalism currently materializes.

The novelty of this new form of social stratification is the form and role that space and time have for each social stratum. Social differentiation is thus a space-time differentiation. In the case of the dwellers of the global world, the constantly shrinking space suppresses the course of time. The globalization of their lives makes them live permanently busy, literally, they never have time for anything else (Bauman, 1998). Time is their greatest treasure, their main wealth. For them, space means nothing, since all distance, at the end of the day, is neutralized by the speed of exchanges, of information, of transfers (on our planetary scale, time has annulled space). They live in time, in an eternal present. On the contrary, the inhabitants of the local world live in space, and time is empty for them. They are subsumed in a superabundant and superficial time that they cannot fill. In their time, nothing ever happens, for, deep down, they do not control its course or its becoming. They are excluded from time, from the speed of events. The only thing left for them to do is to "kill time," just as they are inexorably consumed by it (Beck, 1998b).

Bauman (1998: 47–49) goes even further, pointing out that in the global era the nexus between poverty and wealth has also been lost. According to this author, the master-servant dialectic has been dissolved, as well as the bond of solidarity and mutual need that related one to the other and that integrated them in the same destiny. The new global rich no longer need the new poor; they are no longer a reserve army, nor are they potential consumers. This is undoubtedly a somewhat extreme view that we do not entirely share. We, on the other hand, maintain that the link of dependency between rich-poor, capital-labor, has not been broken; rather, it has been deterritorialized. In advanced societies, the wealthy elite, often referred to as the 1% highlighted by Stiglitz, remains just as reliant on the poor (workers) as in the past. However, unlike in industrial capitalism, in global capitalism the working class is scattered and fragmented, following the same dispersal and deterritorialization patterns of capitalist production. The distinction lies in the fact that while the deterritorialization of production and capital can be considered metaphorical, given its organization as a global factory, the working class struggles to transcend its identity as local and national subjects. In the case of the working class, other factors related to constitution and recognition take precedence over its role as an economic-productive class. The ties of capital-labor interdependence persist, but their formation and realization are obscured by various social processes, including the fragmentation of production and the working class. Workers are shaped not solely by economic-productive relations, but also by diverse forms of social differentiation and inequality, encompassing aspects such as gender, race, ethnicity, migration, generations, geographies, histories, and more.

This differentiation between globalized rich and localized poor constructs and reconstructs itself in the same geography, reconfiguring the spaces and territories of communities. Illustrative of this phenomenon is the evolving class structure in advanced societies, evident in the *racialization* of social inequality. This entails a structural scenario where ethnic background and national origin play a pivotal role in shaping disparities in living conditions, income distribution, economic resources, labor precariousness, labor market segmentation, occupational segregation, and various forms of economic and wage discrimination (Canales, 2019). Within this framework of social differentiation, migrants assume a distinct role as integral components of this emerging class of *glocal* workers. While their work connects them to the globalized context, their circumstances of discrimination, precariousness, and vulnerability relegate them to local spaces for their reproduction. Here, their migratory status carries more weight in shaping their identities and sense of belonging, overshadowing their class position and role in the economic-productive process.

CHAPTER 9

Final Reflections: for a Project of Social Emancipation

> The liberation of the individual and of all individuals from oppression and tutelage has been, and continues to be, the theme and political demand par excellence of modernity so far in existence.
> R. HITZLER (1999: 165)

∴

The purpose of this book is to support a discourse against inequality. Our critique does not dwell on the theoretical realm of inequality, exploring its causes, determinants, and historical conditions. Similarly, we do not position ourselves at a methodological level concerning the forms and instruments used for analyzing, describing, and measuring inequality. Instead, our analysis and reflection are grounded in a distinct approach, supported by a dual process of critique—namely, an epistemological critique and a political critique, the latter complementing the former.

Regarding the first plane, we take up both Santos' (2016) proposal regarding an *epistemology of the South*, and Zemelman's (1989) proposal regarding the *critical use of theories*. In both cases, it is a matter of sustaining a proposal considering the social and geographical coordinates from which we situate ourselves to make our analysis and critique of inequality. We know that every social science and, especially, every proposal for social transformation does not arise from the abstraction of the observer, nor from the theory on which it is based, but are socially and historically situated and, therefore, daughters of their time and of the society to which they refer in their analysis and to which they propose their transformation projects. This is especially valid when it comes to the question of inequality. In societies constituted on the basis of structures of inequality, there will always be more than one social position and more than one social situation from which to observe society and, therefore, to understand and act accordingly in the face of the forms of inequality that constitute it.

In the particular case of contemporary Social Sciences, we are prey to an epistemic hegemony, which Santos (2006), Quijano (2014), and other authors call the predominance of colonialist epistemologies, from which the major academic and disciplinary programs are designed. In certain instances, the primary research issues shaping disciplinary agendas are deliberated and formulated not exclusively within academic and scientific realms but also within intergovernmental forums. Examples include the United Nations and its diverse agencies, as well as multilateral global forums where political and social entities, predominantly from Northern countries, play a significant role. A case in point is the World Population Conferences, which often set the global demographic agenda. More recently, world forums addressing a range of issues such as international migration, climate change, or the development of Third World countries follow a similar pattern.

Undoubtedly, these agendas, theories, methodologies, and research problems are formulated from specific social and geographic perspectives. They not only dictate the subjects deemed relevant but also prescribe the methodologies and theoretical frameworks for understanding them. In the context of addressing inequality, our epistemic stance is doubly critical. On one hand, we position ourselves as individuals experiencing inequality within a social structure that assigns and positions us in such a manner. From this standpoint, we can scrutinize hegemonic, all-encompassing visions and models, recognizing them as modes of comprehension originating from dominant positions within these relations and structures of inequality. By standing outside these positions, we gain a clearer perspective, acknowledging them as theoretical and methodological constructs grounded in a Northern epistemology—a way of perceiving and comprehending the social from a vantage point of height and privilege conferred by their position within the framework of inequality. In contrast, we adopt a Southern epistemology, constructing an alternative approach to observing and understanding the social. It is from this perspective that proposals for social change and alternative visions for the future emerge.

Conversely, this epistemological perspective is accompanied by an alternative approach to the role and significance of theory and empirical analysis. It involves a reconstruction—and a critique—of theories, acknowledging that they have been shaped within a Northern epistemology. As analytical categories, these theories always imply a reconstruction from the specific epistemologies of the North, referencing social categories and historical processes rooted in those particular epistemologies. Consequently, the objective is not merely to dismiss these theories and methodologies outright but to engage in a critical utilization of them. The emphasis lies on using them while subjecting them to scrutiny, pushing them to their border zones—those zones where their meaning was initially constructed—thus paving the way for the development of new interpretations and meanings. In the context of concepts, the focus is on deconstructing their breadth and abstractions, unveiling through critique the aspects of the social that have been overshadowed within the hegemonic vision.

Regarding the second dimension, the political critique extends beyond a geographical critique of the South to encompass its social topography. Emerging from the vantage point below, within the realm of inequality, it takes shape as a political critique—a critique not solely of inequality itself but of society as a whole. Simultaneously, the critique of theories and perspectives on inequality is inherently political. It seeks to unravel the assumptions and frameworks that underpin these theories, shedding light on the hegemonic modes of comprehending and organizing the social. These frameworks constitute the foundation upon which such theories and methodologies are constructed. In this regard, our critique of inequality is structured along four key axes:

1) First of all, we are raising a discourse against inequality as a critique of Modernity. Modernity was presented to us as a hope for progress, based on reason as its main historical driving force. In its beginnings, philosophers such as Condorcet, Godwin, and others went so far as to affirm that there would be no possible obstacle that the power of human reason and progress could not finally resolve. However, already in the second half of the nineteenth century, and more appropriately throughout the twentieth century, Modernity has been presented to us as an incomplete project (Habermas, 2014). From our perspective, this unfinished character lies in one of the vectors that make up its own foundational matrix: persistent social inequality, which not only has not been brought down by progress and human reason but constitutes one of the pillars of Modernity itself. It is the foundational matrix of modern society that includes and reproduces different forms, which are structured on the basis of relations of exploitation, domination, and discrimination that sustain capitalist progress. Inequality is not a pending issue of Modernity; on the contrary, it is one of its underlying contradictions that cannot be resolved without a radical questioning of capitalist Modernity itself.

In this sense, it is the ethical, existential, and political consequences of all forms of inequality that persist in Modernity that configure it as an unfinished project with a great pending issue, that of social emancipation with respect to all forms of inequality. It is this historical debt of Modernity that forms the basis of a new political and social project in this era of reflexive and global modernity. The project and discourse *Against Inequality,* thus, constitutes the theoretical, epistemic, and ideological matrix from which we can support a project of emancipation and social liberation.

Our discourse against inequality is, above all, a discourse and a position of critique of Modernity. However, it should be noted that it is neither an anti-modern nor a post-modern position vis-à-vis progress and development. First and foremost, our position is not anti-modern because our critique doesn't stem from a desire to restore some pre-modern or anti-modern social and political order. In other words, it is not against progress or human reason as the foundation of modernity. On the contrary, our critique is inherently modern as it originates from critical aspects within the discourse of liberal Modernity itself. It emerges from a critical examination of the unresolved issues that capitalist Modernity has not only failed to address but has also used as vectors to construct its project of progress, development, and accumulation. Specifically, we are referring to class inequality and, by extension, its interconnectedness with various forms of social inequality such as gender, geographical, ethnic-racial inequality, among others.

Our critique is directed towards the capitalist and liberal Modernity that perpetuates various forms of social inequality. It unveils the contradictions inherent in this liberal Modernity, which, while espousing a discourse of equality, freedom, and fraternity, is paradoxically grounded in structures and relationships of domination, exploitation, and social discrimination. These structures directly undermine the very foundational philosophical principles that this modernity purports to uphold.

Secondly, this critique of Modernity does not align with a postmodern discourse on progress and development. It is not a conservative proposition aimed at preserving the existing social order by rejecting future possibilities and historical potentials. Quite the opposite, as a critique of Modernity, it not only exposes the inherent contradictions of liberal Modernity but also endeavors, in the same process, to construct a proposition for social emancipation and the political transformation of the current social order. It is a discourse that challenges the structures and relationships of inequality, yet it is rooted in the universal philosophical values and principles of equality, liberty, and fraternity.

In this sense, it is a critique and a posture of *transmodernity*, in the sense that Dussel (2017) gives to this term. This critique, stemming from within Modernity, transitions towards projects and proposals that go beyond its confines. In this transformative process, the critique assumes both intellectual and political dimensions. While constructing frameworks to understand Modernity, its boundaries, and contradictions, it simultaneously drives forward projects aimed at transforming Modernity itself. This progression leads to stages of social emancipation concerning the very contradictions that define it. Consequently, it constitutes an inherently political proposition, contributing to a transformative agenda for the present and the envisioning of potential future horizons.

In essence, if antimodern critique is primarily concerned with restoration and postmodern criticism tends to be conservative, transmodern criticism stands out as fundamentally emancipatory.

2) Secondly, the discourse against inequality has prompted us to draw a crucial distinction between projects focused on social equity and those centered on social emancipation. The discourse on equity, which has gained prominence in recent years, primarily revolves around establishing situations and conditions of equality. It is rooted in principles of social justice and follows a rights-based approach. On the other hand, the discourse of social emancipation is more comprehensive. It can be characterized as an equity project, but within the context of freedom. The objective is to attain equity through a process of liberation from the structures of social inequality—meaning the elimination of the conditions and structures that give rise to inequality in the first place, rather than merely addressing its consequences. Consequently, it involves both an act of equalization (*equity*) and an act of liberation (*liberty*).

While the equity project is grounded in recognizing each individual as a subject of rights, aiming to identify inequality as an act that infringes upon individual rights and liberties, the emancipation project takes a structural approach. In this context, inequality is conceptualized as a framework contributing to the formation of disparate and differentiated social subjects. This introduces a dual level of distinction compared to the former perspective: first, inequality addresses social subjects such as classes, genders, ethnicities, generations, nationalities, among others; second, the critical focus is not solely on the social distance between these subjects, but rather on the connections—the relational structures—that define them as unequal to each other. Inequality is not merely a structure violating the rights of each individual—although it undoubtedly does so—but it also emanates from and is shaped by structural processes determining the distribution of resources, privileges, power, and hegemonies among these subjects, thereby establishing them as distinct and unequal social categories.

In this context, the discourse of emancipation is more extensive and profound, encompassing the discourse of equity within a framework that advocates for liberation from the shackles of inequality. This liberation involves freeing individuals from the relations of domination, exploitation, and discrimination that underlie all forms of social inequality. As we've emphasized throughout this book, a useful way to grasp the difference between equity and emancipation is to consider the unequal situation of enslaved persons in societies built on slavery. In such a setting, no matter how liberal or progressive, any proposal for master-slave equity would inevitably be rejected for not addressing the fundamental nature of slavery. Only an emancipation project allows the enslaved person to break free from the social, political, and economic chains that bind them to a subservient relationship with the master. In this process, emancipation signifies not only the abolition of the condition of the dominated subject—the enslaved person—but also of the subject in the dominant role—the master. Consequently, it entails dismantling the structural bonds that designate some as the dominated (slaves) and others as the dominant (masters).

Social emancipation involves establishing conditions of equality within contexts of liberty. Its foundation is not solely ethical, moral, or philosophical—although these aspects are also relevant—but fundamentally political. While equity is rooted in principles of social justice and ethics, emancipation is guided by a political principle of freedom among equals. It recognizes that true freedom cannot exist within structures of inequality. Mere equalization in rights, resources, or status falls short unless accompanied by acts of liberation from the structures that create disparate social categories and subjects. This is not a philosophical or ethical discourse on equality but rather a political discourse against inequality as a structural condition that imposes limits and restrictions on people's freedoms.

Figure 4 depicts this thesis and highlights the distinctions between egalitarianism, equity, and emancipation. Like any visual representation, it simplifies and abstracts the underlying idea to its most fundamental form.

Figure 4 illustrates the concept of equity. The context, represented by the fence, constructs inequality, turning differences among subjects into modes of inequality. Equality, or equalization, involves distributing the same resources to all, addressing the inequality generated by the context. The equity strategy goes beyond equal distribution to each subject; instead, it allocates resources based on the distance necessary to be equal to others. Equity corrects the distance resulting from the context but does not eliminate or dissolve it.

In contrast, emancipation tackles the root of the problem—the origin of inequality (hence its radical nature): the context. Instead of relying on a redistribution strategy (boxes) to equalize conditions of inequality, emancipation establishes a liberation strategy from the structural condition that generates inequality—it removes the fence. By doing so, it essentially "destroys" the structures on which inequality was previously built.

Equity, therefore, is not an act of liberation but rather an equalization based on an ethic of social justice: it distributes resources according to differentiated needs, differences generated by the condition of inequality. The structural condition fostering inequality is maintained, and equity acts to correct its effects.

FINAL REFLECTIONS: FOR A PROJECT OF SOCIAL EMANCIPATION

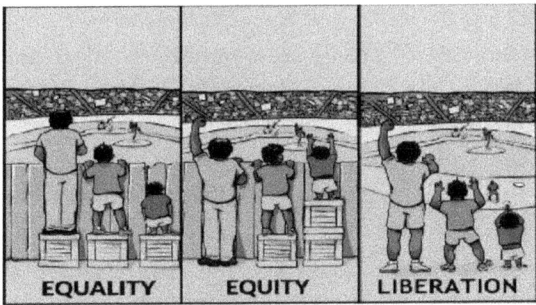

FIGURE 4   Graphic difference between equality, equity and emancipation
SOURCE: INTERNATIONAL WOMEN DAY, 2023. *EQUALITY AND EQUITY AS POLITICAL PRINCIPLES*, CONSULTED ON DECEMBER 15, 2023.

With the emancipation process, this structuring condition of inequality is eliminated, freeing subjects from the structures that render them unequal. The subsequent distribution of resources is no longer aimed at establishing conditions of equality or correcting structural situations but simply at generating greater well-being for the subjects—a means to better enjoy the view of the sporting spectacle.

3) In the context of advocating a project *Against Inequality*, we specifically *address all* existing forms of social inequality, placing emphasis on the comprehensive understanding of all these forms rather than singling out a select few, regardless of how fundamental or influential they may be perceived. What is essential is the development of a theory of inequality that not only enables the comprehension of its manifestations and consequences but also facilitates an understanding of its origins and social structuring.

In the 1970s and 1980s, amidst the ongoing reconstruction of the left and critical thought, the notion that *everything is politics* emerged. Some interpreted this as a devaluation of politics, suggesting that if *everything was politics*, then *nothing is political*—i.e., nothing held political significance. This perspective paved the way for an individualistic ethos that rejected political action—questioning and challenging power. In this view, everything seemed confined to the private and individual sphere. Consequently, if any emancipation project made sense, it was perceived to be solely for and from the individual, rather than for the collective or the public.

On the contrary, for another perspective, the idea that *everything is politics* entailed the necessity to discern a relationship of power and domination in every social interaction, every form of social action, and in the conditions and existence of individuals or collectives. This recognition emphasized the importance of subverting and transforming these power dynamics for the purpose of achieving social liberation and emancipation.

From this critical and radical standpoint, politics, pertaining to power and domination, is forged from the grassroots, emanating from the lower and internal realms of society itself. According to this perspective, power relations are not confined to specific spaces, situations, or forms of social interaction. Instead, they persist and renew in every situation and in every relationship among social subjects, as each interaction inherently carries political dimensions, involving projects of domination and counter-power. Politics, therefore, extends beyond the traditional realm of the *POLIS* and is interwoven into the spheres of *OIKOS* and *DEMOS*. Any act of exploitation implies an exercise of power, and similarly, all manifestations of discrimination are rooted in power relationships. In our context, aligned with this perspective, the notion that "everything is politics" should be interpreted as asserting that the political defines a

> [B]reath that *crosses all* human relationships. There is politics between man and woman, masters and servants, teacher and student, physician and patient, artist and buyer, and in any private relationships, just as in the public sphere there is a politics of law, of the economy, of culture and religion, and a social policy together with the politics of the State and parties in the proper sense.
> PLESSNER, 2018 [1931]: 86. Our translation

Put differently, in seemingly benign and everyday relationships such as doctor-patient, teacher-student, man-woman, or any other dynamic that involves a form of power and domination of one over the other, all other forms of power, domination, and discrimination are replicated. In settings like a doctor's office, the interaction between the doctor and patient goes beyond their roles and introduces additional layers of inequality. This relationship brings forth gender dynamics, influenced by the gender of both the doctor and the patient. Simultaneously, it incorporates class dynamics and intergenerational dynamics, along with relationships between individuals of different and unequal nationalities, and so forth. The rationale behind this is that, as we have argued throughout this book, every form of social inequality represents a comprehensive social phenomenon, inherently encompassing all other dimensions and fields that contribute to its constitution. What unfolds daily in various realms of social life is mirrored in the "grand" arenas of power. For instance, every instance of union-company collective bargaining, facilitated by specific individuals, inevitably carries with it the presence of other forms and modes of categorical inequality. These inequalities resurface within the domain of economic negotiation.

In alignment with our perspective on inequality, the notion that *everything is politics* is also interpreted as *inequality is everywhere*, extending beyond the realms of economy, politics, or the public sphere. However, the fact that social inequality is present in every corner of society does not mean, even remotely, that it is a project of contingencies—that is, limited to the partial, local, or individual concerns. On the contrary, it acknowledges that in every corner of society the various forms and modes of inequality are reproduced and, therefore, that the discourse against inequality requires the articulation of all of them in a proposal of mutual interdependence—that is, of totality. The struggle for the emancipation of women lacks meaning and significance if not intertwined with the fight for the liberation of indigenous peoples, which, in turn, needs to be connected with the struggle for the emancipation of workers, and so forth—encompassing every conceivable field of inequality. Likewise, the struggle for the liberation of labor from capitalist chains, to express it in orthodox Marxist terms, cannot be comprehended nor holds any significance unless it is linked with the struggle for the liberation of women, and both are connected with the struggles for the emancipation of peoples and ethnic groups facing racism and xenophobia. If inequality is considered a total social phenomenon, then emancipation struggle must be embraced as a total social process.

4) Finally, our proposition for a discourse against inequality, forming the basis of a project for social emancipation, is grounded in the thesis that inequality serves as the foundational relationship of society. Rousseau, among the first, argued that private property and the associated inequality are the roots of civil society, positioning economic inequality as the origin and bedrock of society. Building on this notion, Marx and subsequent thinkers supported the idea that throughout human history, societies have been shaped by diverse configurations of relations involving domination, exploitation, and social discrimination. Marx linked these to varying modes of production across historical periods.

From this perspective, we recognize that the current mode of constituting social inequality—modern, liberal, and capitalist—is also historical and, therefore, susceptible to transformation and transcendence. There are at least two possible perspectives for this: a conservative one, based on the emergence of alternative historical configurations of relations of exploitation, domination, and social discrimination; and a radical one, grounded in processes of social emancipation and liberation from the chains of social, political, and economic inequality binding subjects, classes, ethnicities, genders, and generations to relations of domination, exploitation, and discrimination. The first, we see as conservative, as it proposes overcoming liberal modes of inequality without necessarily transcending social inequality itself. The second entails a radical thesis, constituting a societal project founded on a continuous and ongoing struggle against all forms of inequality.

Historically, the predominant approach has been the first one, with human history marked by diverse modes of historical constitution of social inequality, blending different forms of class, gender, ethnic, racial, national, geographic, and generational inequality, among others.

However, this reflection and critique of history and its various modes of inequality provide an opportunity, as never before, to question these modes and envision alternative worlds rooted in processes of social emancipation. If inequality has been part of foundational matrix of society, critique inequality at this level can serve as a mediating force for a radical and more comprehensive critique against society itself. Therefore, at this plane, a discourse against inequality, operating on this dual epistemological and political level, also evolves into a project of social emancipation.

References

Althusser, Louis (2009 [1969]) "The Object of Capital", in Louis Althusser and Étienne Balibar, *Reading Capital*, London, Verso, pp. 77–225.
Amin, Samir (1996) "The Challenge of Globalization". *Review of International Political Economy* Vol. 3, No. 2 (Summer), pp. 216–259.
Aristotle (2012) *Politics*, Indianapolis, Joe Sachs.
Bárcena, Alicia, and Prado, Antonio (2016) *El imperativo de la desigualdad. Por un desarrollo sostenible en América Latina*, Buenos Aires, Siglo xxi and Economic Commission for Latin America and the Caribbean.
Bastidas, Alexander (1996) "Convergencia económica?", *Ensayos de economía*, Vol.7, Issue 11, pp. 79–99.
Baudrillard, Jean (1994) *The Illusion of the End*, Oxford, Polity Press.
Baudrillard, Jean (1981) *For a Critique of the Political Economy of the Sign*, Telos Press.
Bauman, Zigmunt (2011) *Collateral Damage: Social Inequalities in a Global Age*, Cambridge, UK, Polity Press.
Bauman, Zigmunt (2000) *Liquid Modernity*, Cambridge, UK, Polity Press.
Bauman, Zigmunt (1998) "On Glocalization: or Globalization for Some, Localization for Some Others", *Thesis Eleven*, Number 54, SAGE Publications.
Bautista, Juan José (2014) *¿Qué significa pensar desde América Latina?*, Madrid, Akal.
Bechelloni, Giovani (1996), "From the analysis of the processes of reproduction of classes and cultural order to the analysis of the processes of change. Introduction to the Italian edition", in Pierre Bourdieu and Jean-Claude Passeron, *La reproduction. Elementos para una teoría del sistema de enseñanza*, Mexico, Fontamara, pp. 15–24.
Beck, Ulrich (2000a), *The Brave New World of Work*, Oxford, UK, Polity Press in association with Blackwell Publishers Ltd.
Beck, Ulrich (2000b), *What is Globalization?* Cambridge, UK, Polity Press.
Beck, Ulrich (1998), *Risk Society: Towards a New Modernity*, London, Sage Publications.
Becker, Gary (1971), *The Economics of Discrimination*, Chicago, University of Chicago Press.
Becker, Gary (1966), *Human Capital. A Theoretical and Empirical Analysis, with Special Reference to Education*, New York, Columbia University Press.
Bell, Daniel (1973) *The Coming of Post-Industrial Society. A Venture in Social Forecasting*, New York, Basic Books.
Beriáin, Josetxo (1996), "El doble sentido de las consecuencias perversas de la modernidad", in *Las consecuencias perversas de la modernidad*, Barcelona, Anthropos. El acento apellido.
Bielschowsky, R. and Torres, M. (comps.) (2018), *Desarrollo e igualdad: el pensamiento de la Cepal en su séptimo decenio. Selected texts from the period*, Colección 70 años

(*series*), *2008–2018*, LC/PUB.2018/7-P, Santiago, Economic Commission for Latin America and the Caribbean.

Blaut, James Morris (1993), *The Colonizer's Model of the World: Geographical Diffusionism and Eurocentric History*, New York, Guilford Press.

Block, Fred (2001), "Introduction", in *The Great Transformation. The Political and Economic Origins of Our Time*, Boston, Beacon Press.

Blondeau, Olivier (2004), "Génesis y subversión del capitalismo informacional", in VV. AA., *Capitalismo cognitivo, propiedad intelectual y creación colectiva*, Madrid, Ediciones Traficantes de Sueños, pp. 31–47.

Bourdieu, Pierre (2011), *Las estrategias de la reproducción social*. Edited by Alice Beatriz Gutierrez. Buenos Aires, Siglo XXI.

Bourdieu, Pierre (2008), *The Bachelors' Ball: The Crisis of Peasant Society in Bearn*, Chicago, The University of Chicago Press.

Bourdieu, Pierre (2005), *The Social Structures of the Economy*, Cambridge, UK, Polity Press.

Bourdieu, Pierre (2000), *La dominación masculina*, Barcelona, Anagrama.

Bourdieu, Pierre (1998a), *Practical Reason: On the Theory of Action*, Stanford, Stanford University Press.

Bourdieu, Pierre (1998b), *Acts of Resistance Against the Tyranny of the Market*, Oxford, Polity Press and The New Press.

Bourdieu, Pierre (1993), *Sociology in Question*, trans. Richard Nice, London, Sage Publications.

Bourdieu, Pierre (1991), *First Lecture. Social Space and Symbolic Space: Introduction to a Japanese Reading of Distinction*, Poetics Today Vol. 12, No. 4, National Literatures/Social Spaces (Winter, 1991), pp. 627–638.

Bourdieu, Pierre (1987), "What Makes a Social Class? On the Theoretical and Practical Existence of Groups", *Berkeley Journal of Sociology*, Vol.32, pp.1–17.

Bourdieu, Pierre (1986), "The Forms of Capital." In Richardson, J., *Handbook of Theory and Research for the Sociology of Education*, Westport, CT, Greenwood.

Bourdieu, Pierre (1984), *Distinction. A Social Critique of the Judgment of Taste*, Cambridge, Massachusetts, Harvard University Press.

Bourdieu, Pierre and Passeron, Jean-Claude (1990 [1970]), *Reproduction in Education, Society and Culture*, London, SAGE.

Boyer, Robert (1992) *La teoría de la regulación. Un análisis crítico*, Valencia, Edicions Alfons el Magnanim.

Bronfman, Mario and Tuirán, Rodolfo (1984), "La desigualdad social ante la muerte: clases sociales y mortalidad infantil en la niñez", *Memorias del Congreso Latinoamericano de Población y Desarrollo*, vol. 1, Mexico, pp. 187–220.

Bullit, Simson (1959), *To Be a Politician*, New York, Doubleday & Co. Inc.

Bush, George W. 2004 (2004, April 13), *President Addresses the Nation in Prime-Time Press Conference*, US White House, Office of the Press Secretary. Press Conference of

the President: https://georgewbush-whitehouse.archives.gov/news/releases/2004/04/20040413-20.html.
Butler, Judith (2001), "The Question of Social Transformation", in Judith Butler, Elisabeth Beck-Gernsheim and Lídia Puigvert, *Women and Social Transformation*, vol. 242, pp. 1–28.
Butler, Judith (2000), "Restaging the Universal: Hegemony and the Limits of Formalism", in J. Butler, E. Laclau and S. Žižek, *Contingency, Hegemony, Universality: Contemporary Dialogues on the Left*, London, Verso, pp. 11–43.
Butler, Judith (1999), *Gender Trouble: Feminism and the Subversion of Identity*, New York, Routledge.
Callinicos, Alex (2003), *Igualdad*, Madrid, Siglo XXI.
Campillo, Antonio (2012), "Oikos and Polis: Aristotle, Polanyi and liberal political economy", *AREAS. Revista Internacional de Ciencias Sociales*, vol. 31, pp. 27–38.
Canales, Alejandro I. (2021), *El malestar con las migraciones. Perspectivas desde el Sur*, Barcelona, Anthropos.
Canales, Alejandro I. (2021b). "Demografía de la desigualdad", Nueva Sociedad No. 293, May-Jun., 154–166. https://nuso.org/articulo/demografia-de-la-desigualdad/.
Canales, Alejandro I. (2019), *Migration, Reproduction and Society. Economic and Demographic Dilemmas in Global Capitalism*, Leiden and Boston, Brill.
Canales, Alejandro I. (2003), "Demografía de la desigualdad. El discurso de la población en la era de la globalización", in A. I. Canales and S. Lerner (eds.), *Desafíos teórico-metodológicos en los estudios de población en el inicio del milenio*, Mexico, Sociedad Mexicana de Demografía, Universidad de Guadalajara and El Colegio de México, pp. 43–86.
Canales, Alejandro I. (2002), "El concepto de globalización en las ciencias sociales. Alcances y significados", in A. Canales, J. Arroyo and P. Vargas (eds.), *El norte de todos. Migración y trabajo en tiempos de globalización*, Universidad de Guadalajara, ucla, profmex and Juan Pablos Editores (Publisher), pp. 23–64.
Canales, Alejandro I. (2001), "Flexibilidad laboral y feminización del Empleo en el Agro Chileno. Un caso más de desarrollo sin equidad", *Revista de Economía y Trabajo*, 11, pp. 87–112.
Cardoso, Fernando (1979), "Althusserismo o marxismo? A propósito del concepto de clases en Poulantzas", in *Las clases sociales en América Latina*, Mexico, UNAM, pp. 137–153.
Carroll, William K. and Sapinski, J. P. (2016), "Neoliberalism and the transnational capitalist class", in Simon Springer, Kean Birch and Julie MacLeavy (eds.), *The Handbook of Neoliberalism*, London and New York, Routledge, pp. 39–49.
Castells, Manuel (2010 [1996]) *The Information Age: Economy, Society, and Culture. Volume 1: The Rise of the Network Society*, Oxford, Wiley-Blackwell.
Castells, Manuel (1979), "La teoría marxista de las clases sociales y la lucha de clases en América Latina", in *Las clases sociales en América Latina*, Mexico, UNAM, pp. 159–190.

Castillo, Dídimo (2016), "La deslocalización del trabajo y la migración hacia Estados Unidos. La paradoja de la 'migración de los puestos'", in Dídimo Castillo, Norma Baca and Rosalba Todaro (coords.), *Trabajo y desigualdades en el mercado laboral*, Mexico, clacso, cem, uaem, pp. 57–81.

Castoriadis, Cornelius (1979), "Reflexiones sobre el "desarrollo" y la "racionalidad"". En El mito del desarrollo. Varios Autores. Barcelona, Editorial Kairos, pp. 183–222. [Castoriadis, Cornelius (1985), "Reflections on 'rationality' and 'development'", *Thesis Eleven*, vol. 10–11 (1), pp. 18–36].

Clark, John Bates (1908) [1899], *The Distribution of Wealth: A Theory of Wages, Interest and Profits*, New York, Macmillan.

Clark, T. and Lipset, S. M. (1991), "Are Social Classes Dying?", *International Sociology*, 4, pp. 397–410.

Condorcet, Marie-Jean-Antoine-Nicolas Caritat (1795). Outlines of an historical view of the progress of the human mind. Philadelphia: M. Carey. https://oll-resources.s3.us-east-2.amazonaws.com/oll3/store/titles/1669/0878_Bk.pdf.

Cordero D., Blanca L. (2007), *Ser trabajador transnacional: clase, hegemonía y cultura en un circuito migratorio internacional*, Mexico, Benemérita Universidad Autónoma de Puebla.

Dahrendorf, R. (1959). *Class and Class Conflict in Industrial Society*, Stanford, CA, Stanford University Press.

David, Paul A. and Foray, Dominique (2002), "An introduction to the economics and society of knowledge", *International Social Science Journal*, 171.

Davis, Kingsley (1963), "The theory of change and response in modern demographic history," *Population Index*, 29 (October), pp. 345–366.

Davis, Kingsley and Wilbert E. Moore (1945), "Some Principles of Stratification", *1944 Annual Meeting Papers, American Sociological Review*, Vol.10 (2), pp. 242–249.

De la Garza Toledo, E. (2012). "La subcontratación y la acumulación de capital en el nivel global". In E. de la Garza et al, *La subcontratación laboral en América Latina: Miradas multidimensionales*, Buenos Aires, CLACSO. pp. 15–23.

Domar, Evsey D. (1946), "Capital Expansion, Rate of Growth, and Employment," *The Econometric Society*, Vol.14, Issue 2, pp. 137–147.

Drucker, Peter (1993), *Post-capitalist Society*, New York, HarperCollins.

Duek, Celia and Inda, Graciela (2014), "La Teoría de la Estratificación Social de Parsons: una arquitectura del consenso y de la estabilización del conflicto", *THEOMAI Journal. Critical Studies about Society and Development*, Vol.29, pp. 155–175.

Dussel, Enrique (2017), *Filosofías del Sur. Descolonización y transmodernidad*, Mexico, Akal.

Dussel, Enrique (2013), *Ethics of liberation: in the Age of Globalization and Exclusion*, Durham, Duke University Press.

Dussel, Enrique (1995), *Teología de la liberación: un panorama de su desarrollo*, Mexico, Potrerillos Editores.

ECLAC (2016), *The Social Inequality Matrix in Latin America*, Santiago, Chile, United Nations, Economic Commission for Latin America and the Caribbean, LC/G.2690 (mds.1/2).

Eco, Umberto (1986), *The Name of the Rose*, New York, Warner Books.

Faci Lacasta, Francisco Javier (1984). "El Policraticus de Juan de Salisbury y el mundo antiguo", *En la España Medieval*, vol.4, pp. 343–362.

Fazio, Hugo (2011), *¿Qué es la globalización? Contenido, explicación, y representación*, Bogotá, Ediciones Uniandes (Publisher).

Federici, Silvia (2004), *Caliban and the Witch. Women, The Body and Primitive Accumulation*, NY, USA, Autonomedia.

Fernández-Galiano, Manuel (1988), "Introducción", in *Platón, La República*, Madrid, Alianza.

Fitoussi, Jean-Paul and Rosanvallon, Pierre (2003), *La nueva era de las desigualdades*, Buenos Aires, Manantial.

Flores, María Victoria (2016), "Globalization as a political, economic and social phenomenon", *orbis. Scientific Electronic Journal of Human Sciences*, 34, pp. 26–41.

Flores Magón, Ricardo (1912), *Discurso del 1.º de julio de 1912, Discursos de Ricardo Flores Magón*, Mexico, fifth cybernetic edition, September 2006 [http://www.antorcha.net/biblioteca_virtual/politica/discursos/8.html].

Fontela, E. and Guzmán, J. (2003), "Círculos viciosos y virtuosos del desarrollo económico", *Estudios de economía Aplicada*, 21–22, pp. 221–242.

Fraser, Nancy (1995), "From Redistribution to Recognition? Dilemmas of Justice in a 'Post-Socialist' Era", *New Left Review*, Vol.1 (212).

Fukuyama, Francis (1992), *The End of History and the Last Man*, New York, The Free Press [El fin de la Historia y el último hombre, Barcelona, Planeta, 1992].

García Canclini, Néstor (2014 [1999]), *Imagined Globalization*, Durham: Duke University Press.

Giddens, Anthony (2006), *Sociology*, Cambridge, UK, Polity Press.

Giddens, Anthony (1998), *Sociología*. Madrid, Alianza Editorial.

Giddens, Anthony (1990), *The Consequences of Modernity*, Standford, Cal., Standford University Press.

Giddens, Anthony (1975), *The Class Structure of the Advanced Societies*, New York, Harper Torchbook.

Goic, Ramón Llopis (2007), "El 'nacionalismo metodológico' como obstáculo en la investigación sociológica sobre migraciones internacionales", *Empiria. Revista de Metodología de Ciencias Sociales*, n°13, pp101–120.

Goldthorpe, John (2012), "Back to Class and Status: Or Why a Sociological View of Social Inequality Should Be Reasserted", *REIS*, Vol.1 (137), pp.201–216.

González Casanova, Pablo (2015), *De la sociología del poder a la sociología de la explotación. Pensar América Latina en el siglo XXI*, México, Buenos Aires, CLACSO, Siglo XXI Editores.

González Casanova, Pablo (2006), *Sociología de la explotación* (Nueva edición corregida), Buenos Aires, Argentina, Consejo Latinoamericano de Ciencias Sociales.

Gramsci, Antonio (1992), *Prison Notebooks, Volume 1*, in A. Buttigieg (editor), New York, Columbia University Press.

Greenhalgh, Susan (2001), "Por uma abordagem reflexiva para estudos de população para o século XXI", in Ma. Coleta Oliveira (org.), *Demografia da exclusão social*, São Paulo, Editora da Universidade Estadual de Campinas, pp. 25–46.

Habermas, Jürgen (2014), *The Postnational Constellation*, Hoboken: Wiley Press.

Habermas, Jürgen (1985), "Modernity – An Incomplete Project", in Hal Foster (editor), *The Anti-Aesthetic Essays on Postmodern Culture*, Port Townsend, Washington, Bay Press.

Haraway, Donna (1988), "Situated Knowledges: The Science Question in Feminism and the Privilege of Partial Perspective," *Feminist Studies*, 14, 3 (Fall), pp. 575–599.

Hardt, Michael and Antonio Negri (2000), *Empire*, Harvard University Press.

Harman, Chris (2008), *A People's History of the World. From the Stone Age to the New Millennium*, London, New York, Verso.

Harrod, R. (1939), "An Essay in Dynamic Theory", *The Economic Journal* vol.49, Issue 193.

Harvey, David (2010), *The Enigma of Capital and the Crisis of Capitalism*, New York, Oxford University Press.

Harvey, David (2005) *A Brief History of Neoliberalism*. Oxford, Oxford University Press.

Harvey, David (2003) *The New Imperialism*. Oxford, Oxford University Press.

Harvey, David (1997), *The Condition of Postmodernity: an Enquiry into the Origins of Cultural Change*, Cambridge, Massachusetts, Blackwell.

Hayek, Friedrich (1960) *The Constitution of Liberty*. Chicago: The University of Chicago Press.

Hernández, Manuel Adrián (2015), "Los trabajadores agrícolas mexicanos en los campos de California: migración, empleo y formación de clase en una agricultura intensiva," *Revista Antropologías del Sur*, 4 (2015), pp. 13–33.

Himmelfarb, Gertrude (1984), *The Idea of Poverty: England in the Early Industrial Age*, New York, Knopf.

Hitzler, Ronald (1999), "El ciudadano impredecible. Acerca de algunas consecuencias de la emancipación de los súbditos", in Ulrich Beck, *Hijos de la libertad*, Mexico, Fondo de Cultura Económica, pp. 165–186.

Hondagneu-Sotelo, Pierrete (2007), *Doméstica: Immigrant Workers Cleaning and Caring in the Shadows of Affluence*, Los Angeles, CA, University of California Press.

Hopenhayn, Martín (1988), "El debate post-moderno y la dimensión cultural del desarrollo", in F. Calderón (comp.), *Imágenes desconocidas. La modernidad en la encrucijada postmoderna*, Buenos Aires, clacso.

Horkheimer, M. (2002), *Critical Theory, Selected Essays*, New York, Continuum.

Ianni, Octavio (1996), *Teorías de la globalización*, Mexico, Siglo xxi.

Iglesia García, Jesús de la (2006), "El debate sobre el tratamiento a los pobres durante el siglo XVI", in Francisco Javier Campos y Fernández de Sevilla (coords.), *La Iglesia española y las instituciones de caridad*, San Lorenzo de El Escorial, Instituto Escurialense de Investigaciones Históricas y Artísticas, pp. 5–30.

Jakubecki, Natalia (2013), "Juan de Salisbury: el Policraticus como bisagra entre la tradición y la innovación", in Luis De Boni and José Antonio C. R. de Souza (chairs), *XIV Congreso Latinoamericano de Filosofía Medieval: Filosofía Medieval: Continuidad y Rupturas*, Universidad del Norte Santo Tomás de Aquino and Fundación para el Estudio del Pensamiento Argentino e Iberoamericano (Congress), San Miguel de Tucumán, September 11–14.

Jameson, Fredric (1991), *Postmodernism or the Cultural Logic of Late Capitalism*, New York, Verso Books.

Krugman, Paul and Wells, Robin (2006), *Introducción a la economía. Microeconomics*, Barcelona, Reverté.

Kumar, Kishan (1995), *From Post-Industrial to Post-Modern Society. New Theories of the Contemporary World*, Malden, Mass., Blackwell.

Kuznets, Simon (1955), "Economic Growth and Income Inequality", *The American Economic Review* XLV, 1 (March), pp. 1–28.

Laclau, Ernesto (1986), "Feudalism and Capitalism in Latin America", in Peter F. Klarén and Thomas J. Bossert (eds.), *Promise of Development: Theories of Change in Latin America*, Colorado, Westview Press, pp. 166–190.

Lara, Sara, Sánchez, Kim, and Saldaña, Adriana (2014), "Asentamientos de trabajadores migrantes en torno a enclaves de agricultura intensiva en México: nuevas formas de apropiación de espacios en disputa", in Andrés Pedreño (coord.), *De cadena, migrantes y jornaleros. Los territorios rurales en las cadenas globales agroalimentarias*, Madrid, Talasa, pp. 150–169.

Lash, Scott and Urry, John (1998). *Economías de signos y espacios. Sobre el capitalismo de la postorganización*. Buenos Aires, Amorrortu. [*Economies of Signs and Spaces*. London: Sage, 1994].

Laurin-Frenette, Nicole (1989), *Las teorías funcionalistas de las clases sociales*, Madrid, Siglo XXI.

Lenski, Gerhard E. (1984), *Power and Privilege. A Theory of Social Stratification*. Chapel Hill and London, The University of North Carolina Press.

León, G. (2013), "Growth and economic convergence: a review for Colombia", *Revista Dimensión Empresarial* 11, 1, pp. 61–76.

Lewis, W. Arthur (1954), "Economic Development with Unlimited Supplies of Labour", *The Manchester School*, Vol.28, Issue 2, pp. 139–191.

Lipietz, Alain (1997) *The Post-Fordist World: Labour Relations, International Hierarchy and Global Ecology. Review of International Political Economy*. Vol. 4, No. 1 (Spring, 1997), pp. 1-41.

Lipietz, Alain (1986), "New Tendencies in the International Division of Labour: Regimes of Accumulation and Modes of Regulation", in Allen J. Scott and Michael Storper (eds.), *Production, Work, Territory*, Boston, Mass., Allen and Unwin, pp. 16–40.

Lipset, Seymour Martin (1960), *Political Man: the Social Basis of Politics*, New York, Doubleday & Co. Inc.

Lukács, Georg (1969) [1923], *Historia y conciencia de clase. Estudios de dialéctica marxista*. México, Editorial Grijalbo. [Lukács, Georg (1971), *History and Class Consciousness. Studies in Marxist Dialectics*, Cambridge, Massachusetts, The Mit Press.].

Luxemburg, Rosa (2020) [1908], *Reform or Revolution*, Paris, Foreign Languages Press.

Malthus, Robert (1966) [1798], *First Essay on Population*, London, Palgrave Macmillan.

Marini, R.M. (1977), *Dialéctica de la dependencia* [*Dialectic of Dependency*], México, Era.

Marx, Karl (1996) [1867], *Capital. A Critique of Political Economy*, New York, Penguin Books.

Marx, Karl (1975) [1865], *Wage, Labour and Capital & Value, Price, and Profit*, New York City, International Publishers.

Marx, Karl (1973) [1857], *Grundrisse. Foundations of the Critique of Political Economy (Rough Draft)*, London, Penguin Books in association with New Left Reviews.

Marx, Karl (1964) [1844], *Economic and Philosophical Manuscripts*, New York, International Publishers.

Mattelart, Armand (2003) *The Information Society: An Introduction*. London: SAGE.

Mattelart, Armand (1998), *La mundialización de la comunicación*, Barcelona, Paidós.

Maturana, Humberto (1997), *La Objetividad. Un argumento para obligar*, Santiago de Chile, Dolmen Ediciones.

Mauss, Marcel (2002) [1925], *The Gift: Forms and Functions of Exchange in Archaic Societies*, London, Cohen & West.

Mayntz, Renate (1974) "Observaciones críticas sobre la teoría funcionalista de la estratificación", in Claudio Stern (comp.), *La desigualdad social I. Teorías de la estratificación y movilidad sociales. Teorías de la estratificación y movilidad sociales*, Mexico, Secretaría de Educación Pública, Diana, pp. 189–218.

Miliband, Ralph (1987) "Class Analysis", in Anthony Giddens and Jonathan H. Turner (eds.), *Social Theory Today*, Cambridge, UK, Polity Press, pp. 325–346.

Mills, C. Wright. 2000. *The Sociological Imagination*. Oxford and New York, Oxford University Press.

Mires, Fernando (1996) *La revolución que nadie soñó, o la otra postmodernidad*, Venezuela, Editorial Nueva sociedad (Publisher).

Mossé, Claude (1984) [1976], "Los orígenes del socialismo en la Antigüedad", in Jacques Droz (editor), *Historia general del socialismo: De los orígenes a 1875*, Barcelona, Destino, pp. 89–91.

Moulian, Tomas (1997) *El consumo me consume*, Santiago de Chile, LOM Ediciones.

Myrdal, Gunnar (1963) *Economic Theory and Underdeveloped Regions*, London, University Paperbacks.

Myrdal, Gunnar (1944) *An American Dilemma. The Negro Problem and Modern Democracy*, New York and London, Harper and Brothers Publishers.

Negroponte, Nicholas (1996) *Being Digital*. New York, Vintage.

Nisbet, Robert (1980) *History of the Idea of Progress*, New York, Basic Books.

Nisbet, Robert (1959) "The Decline and Fall of Social Class," *The Pacific Sociological Review* Vol.2 (1), pp. 11–17.

Notestein, Frank (1953), *Economic problems of population change*, London, Oxford University Press.

Nurkse, Ragnar (1964), *Problems of Capital Formation in Underdeveloped Countries*, Oxford, Blackwell.

Ohmae, Kenichi (1995), *End of the Nation State: the Rise of Regional Economies*, London, Harper Collins Publishers.

Pakulski, Jan (2005), "Foundations of a Post-Class Analysis", in Erick O. Wright (ed.), *Approaches to Class Analysis*, Cambridge, UK, Cambridge University Press, pp.152–180.

Pakulski, Jan (1993), "The Dying of Class or of Marxist Class Theory?", *International Sociology* Vol.8 (3), pp. 279–292.

Pakulski J., and Walters M. (1996), *The Death of Class*, London, Sage.

Parella Rubio, Sonia (2003), *Mujer, inmigrante y trabajadora: la triple discriminación*, Barcelona, Anthropos.

Parsons, Talcott (1991), *The Social System*, London, Routledge Sociology Classics.

Parsons, Talcott (1974), "Un enfoque analítico de la teoría de la estratificación". En Claudio Stern (Comp.) *La Desigualdad Social I. Teorías de la estratificación y movilidad sociales*. México, Secretaría de Educación Pública, Diana; pp. 147–188. [Parsons, Talcott, (1940), "An Analytical Approach to the Theory of Social Stratification", *American Journal of Sociology*, Vol.45 (6), pp. 841–862].

Parsons, Talcott (1949), "Social Classes and Class Conflict in the Light of Recent Sociological Theory", *The American Economic Review*, Vol.39 (3), pp.16–26.

Petras, James and Henry Veltmeyer (2001), *Globalization Unmasked: Imperialism in the 21st century*, London, Zed Books Ltd.

Piketty, Thomas (2014), *Capital in the Twenty-First Century*, Cambridge, MA, The Belknap Press of Harvard University Press.

Plato (1992), *The Republic*, New York, Quality Paperback Book Club.

Plessner, Helmuth (2018) [1931], *Poder y naturaleza humana. Ensayo para una antropología de la comprensión histórica del mundo*. Madrid, Guillermo Escolar Editor. [*Macht und menschliche Natur: ein Versuch zur Anthropologie der geschichtlichen Weltansicht*. Junker und Dünnhaupt Verlag, 1931].

Polanyi, Karl (2001) [1944], *The Great Transformation. The Political and Economic Origins of Our Time*. Boston, Beacon Press.

Poulantzas, Nicos (1979), "Las clases sociales". In *Las clases sociales en América Latina*. México, UNAM, pp. 96–126. [Poulantzas, Nicos (1973), "On Social Classes", *The New Left Review*, March-April 1973, Vol.78 (1) 27–54].

Poulantzas, Nicos (1975), *Classes in Contemporary Capitalism*, London, NLB.

Preyer, Gerhard (2016), "Una interpretación de la globalización: un giro en la teoría sociológica," *Revista Mexicana de Ciencias Políticas y Sociales*, vol. LXI, núm. 226, enero-abril, 2016, pp. 61–87.

Pulido, Manuel L. (2007), "Fuentes filosóficas de la 'filosofía de la pobreza' en el pensamiento Bonaventurano," *Revista Española de Filosofía Medieval*, vol.14, pp. 161–172.

Quijano, Aníbal (2014), *Cuestiones y horizontes: de la dependencia histórico-estructural a la colonialidad/descolonialidad del poder*, Buenos Aires, CLACSO.

Ramonet, Ignacio (1995), "El pensamiento único," *Mientras Tanto* 61, Barcelona, Icaria, pp. 17–19.

Reisman, George (1990), *Capitalism. A Treatise on Economics*, Ottawa, IL, Jameson Books.

Requena, M. and Stanek, M. (2015), "Las clases sociales en España: cambio, composición y consecuencias," *Informe España 2015: Una interpretación de su realidad social*, Issue 22, pp. 487–517.

Rifkin, Jeremy (1995) *The End of Work: The Decline of the Global Labor Force and the Dawn of the Post-Market Era*. New York, Putnam Publishing Group.

Rizzo, Nadia (2012), "Un análisis sobre la reproducción social como proceso significativo y como proceso desigual," *Sociológica* 77, pp. 281–297.

Rodríguez Caballero, Juan Carlos (2003), *La economía laboral en el período clásico de la historia del pensamiento económico*, doctoral thesis, Universidad de Valladolid, Spain.

Rousseau, Jean-Jacques (1761) [1755], *A Discourse Upon the Origin and the Foundation of the Inequality Among Mankind*, London, Printed for R. and J. Dodsley.

Santolaria Sierra, Félix (2003), *El gran debate sobre los pobres en el siglo XVI*, Barcelona, Ariel.

Santos, Boaventura de Sousa (2016), *Epistemologies of the South: Justice against Epistemicide*, New York, Routledge.

Santos, Boaventura de Sousa (2006), *Conocer desde el Sur. Para una cultura política emancipatoria*, Perú, Fondo Editorial de la Facultad de Ciencias Sociales, Universidad Nacional Mayor de San Marcos.

Sassen, Saskia (2007), *A Sociology of Globalization*, New York, W. W. Norton.

Sassen, Saskia (1998), *Globalization and its Discontents*, New York, The New Press.

Sassen, Saskia (1991), *The Global City. New York, London and Tokyo*, Princeton, NJ, Princeton University Press.

Segato, Rita (2016), *La guerra contra las mujeres*, Madrid, Traficantes de Sueños.

Sen, Amartya (2009), *The Idea of Justice*, Cambridge, Massachusetts, The Belknap Press of Harvard University Press.
Sen, Amartya (1992), *Inequality reexamined*, New York, Oxford University Press.
Solow, Robert M. (1956), "A Contribution to the Theory of Economic Growth", *The Quarterly Journal of Economics*, Vol.70, Issue 1 (February), pp. 65–94.
Standing, Guy (2011), *The precariat. The new dangerous class*, New York, Bloomsbury Academic.
Stavenhagen, Rodolfo (1974), "Estratificación y clases sociales," in Claudio Stern (comp.), *La desigualdad Social I. Teorías de estratificación y movilidad sociales*, Mexico, Secretaría de Educación Pública (Publisher), pp. 46–70.
Stein, Ben (2006), "In Class Warfare, Guess Which Class Is Winning," *The New York Times*, November 26.
Stiglitz, Joseph E. (2015), *The Great Divide: Unequal Societies and What We Can Do About Them*, New York, London, W.W Norton Company. http://pinguet.free.fr/stigli15.pdf.
Stiglitz, Joseph E. (2012), *The Price of Inequality. How Today's Divided Society Endangers Our Future*, New York, W.W. Norton & Company.
Stiglitz, Joseph E. (2001), "Foreword", K. Polanyi, *The Great Transformation. The Political and Economic Origins of Our Time*, Boston, Beacon Press, VII–XVII.
Storper, Michael and Walker, Richard (1983), "The Spatial Division of Labor," *Cuadernos Políticos* 38 (October-December), pp. 4–22.
The New York Times (2017, January 10), "President Obama's Farewell Address," Full Video and Text. Retrieved from https://www.nytimes.com/2017/01/10/us/politics/obama-farewell-address-speech.html?_r=0.
Therborn, Göran (2013), *The Killing Fields of Inequality*, Cambridge, UK, Polity Press. https://download.e-bookshelf.de/download/0000/8397/52/L-G-0000839752-0002889368.pdf.
Therborn, Göran (2008) [1978], *What Does the Ruling Class Do When It Rules? State Apparatuses and State Power under Feudalism, Capitalism, and Socialism*. Brooklyn, NY: Verso.
Thompson, Warren S. (1929), "Population," *American Sociological Review* 34, 6, pp. 959–975.
Tilly, Charles (1999), *Durable Inequality*, Berkeley and Los Angeles, CA, University of California Press.
Tocqueville, Alexis de (2010) [1835], *Democracy in America*, Indianapolis, Liberty Fund.
Tomas Carpi, José Antonio (1978), "Notas sobre la noción de causación circular acumulativa y su utilidad en la teoría del desarrollo", *Cuadernos de economía*, Vol.6, Issue 16, pp. 347–369, Barcelona, CSIC, Centre of Economic and Social Studies, and University of Barcelona, Department of Economic Theory.
Touraine, Alain (1995), *Critique of Modernity*, Oxford, UK, Blackwell.
Tumin, Melvin M. (1953), "Some Principles of Stratification: a Critical Analysis", *American Sociological Review*, Vol.18 (4), pp.387–394.

Urrutia León, Manuel (2017), "¿Disaparición o transformación de las clases sociales en el siglo XXI?", *Inguruak*, Vol.63, pp. 70–94.

Villarespe, Verónica (2002), *Pobreza. Teoría e historia*, UNAM and Casa Juan Pablos Editores.

Vivares, Ernesto (2018) *Regionalism, Development and the Post-Commodities Boom in South America*, New York, Palgrave Macmillan.

Wallerstein, Immanuel (1999), *The Heritage of Sociology, the Promise of Social Science*, Presidential Address, XIVth World Congress of Sociology, Montreal, 26 July 1998. *Current Sociology*, vol.47 (1), pp1–37.

Wallerstein, Immanuel (1999b). *El futuro de la civilización capitalista*. Barcelona, Icaria.

Wallerstein, Immanuel (1995), *After Liberalism*, New York, The New Press.

Wimmer, Andreas and Glick-Schiller, Nina (2002), "Methodological nationalism and beyond: nation-state building, migration and the social sciences", *Global Networks. A Journal of Transnational Affairs*, vol. 2 (4), pp. 301–334.

Winslow, C. E. A. (1955), *What Disease Costs and What Health Is Worth*, Geneva, Switzerland, World Health Organization, Monograph Series No. 7.

Wright, Erik Olin (2015), *Understanding Class*, London, Verso.

Wright, Erik Olin (2005), "Conclusion: If 'classes' are the answer, what is the question?", in Erik Olin Wright (ed.), *Approaches to Class Analysis*, Cambridge, UK, Cambridge University Press, pp. 180–193.

Wright, Erik Olin (2004), *Class Counts (Student Edition)*, Cambridge, Maison des Sciences de l'Homme & Cambridge University Press.

Wright, Erik Olin (1979), *Class Structure and Income Distribution*, New York, Academic Press.

Zemelman, Hugo (1998), *Sujeto: existencia y potencia*, Barcelona, Anthropos.

Zemelman, Hugo (1992), *Horizontes de la razón. II. Historia y necesidad de utopía*, España, Anthropos.

Zemelman, Hugo (1989), *Crítica epistemológica a los indicadores*, Mexico, El Colegio de México, Jornadas Collection, No. 114.

Zemelman, Hugo (1987), *Uso crítico de la teoría. En torno a las funciones analíticas de la totalidad*, Mexico, United Nations University and El Colegio de México.

Zemelman, Hugo (1982), "Problemas en la explicación del comportamiento reproductivo (sobre las mediaciones)", en *Reflexiones teórico-metodológicas sobre Investigaciones en Población*, México, CLACSO/El Colegio de México.

Zimmerman, Seth D. (2019), "Elite Colleges and Upward Mobility to Top Jobs and Top Incomes". *American Economic Review*, 109 (1): 1–47. DOI: 10.1257/aer.20171019.

Index

abolition   XXIV, 8, 18, 21, 26, 204–5, 270
accumulation   XVIII, 6, 31, 37, 78, 82, 99, 110, 135, 137, 151, 175, 183, 193, 200, 203–6, 215, 221, 223–25, 228, 232, 236, 239, 244–45, 250, 259–62, 268
African-American population   135, 138
alienation   102, 161, 168–70, 174, 176, 204–5, 215, 219, 224, 261
  process of   170–71
alienation of labor   171, 203–5
Althusser, Louis   142, 148, 167, 172
analysis, relational   214–15
androcentrism   29, 34
antagonism   8, 81, 146, 148–49, 153–54, 166, 185, 205, 247
  capital-labor   153
approaches
  neoclassical   124, 128, 130–31
  relational   11, 198
appropriation, private   45, 107–8, 116
Argentina   63
Aristotle   45, 58, 76, 85–88, 158, 160–61
Austrian Marginalist School   122

Bárcena, Alicia   67
base growth   133
Baudrillard   152, 175, 219, 230
Bauman, Jean   23–25, 46, 152, 165–66, 189, 231, 251, 262–63
Bautista, Juan José   41
Béarn   225
Bechelloni, Giovanni   226
Beck, Ulrich   27–29, 36, 154, 166, 234, 248, 250, 263
Becker, Gary   225
Bell, Daniel   231
Beriain, Josetxo   36
Bielschowsky, R.   67
Black populations   3, 135–36
Blaut, James Morris   37, 39
Blondeau, Olivier   192, 233
Bolivia   3
Bourdieu, Pierre   23, 50–52, 68, 84, 103, 153, 156–57, 162, 164, 216–17, 219–26, 235–36, 238, 253, 262

Breton Woods   236
Buffett, Warren   178, 245, 252
Bush, George W.   238
Butler, Judith   31, 34, 121

Campillo, Antonio   86, 158
Canales, Alejandro   1, 9, 29–30, 50, 57, 74–75, 85, 114, 124, 141, 155, 182, 189, 193–94, 212, 227, 230, 253, 256–57, 264–265
capacities, reproductive   32
capital   XIX, XXI, 5–6, 13, 27, 50, 52, 76, 78–79, 81–82, 98–99, 103, 108–12, 123–25, 128–30, 133, 150–52, 155–56, 163, 169, 171, 175, 183, 191, 198, 200, 203–6, 214, 217–28, 230, 236–40, 242–46, 248, 250–53, 255–56, 258–63
  constant   206
  economic   52, 217, 221, 225–26
  global   240
  human   215, 222
  notion of   223–24
  owners of   108, 194
  reproduction of   204, 207, 226, 245
  social   52, 217, 222, 225
  symbolic   222, 224
  variable   206
capital accumulation   XX–XXI, 98, 130, 169, 192, 203–4, 223–24, 227, 233, 236, 242, 247, 252, 259
capital and labor   80, 110, 130, 147, 151, 153, 204, 214, 219, 260, 262
capital formation   137
capital investment   126
capitalism   XVII–XVIII, XXI–XXII, 2, 4, 23, 31, 45, 74, 78, 80–81, 94–95, 98–100, 102–3, 107–13, 130, 133, 139, 142, 146–47, 163–67, 169–72, 178, 183–84, 186, 189, 200, 202, 204–5, 217–19, 227–28, 230, 236, 239–41, 247, 255–56, 262
  cognitive   233, 239, 247, 252
  development of   187, 192, 206
  foundational matrix of   165
  golden decades of   143–44
  post-industrial   158, 187, 238
  postmodern   145, 228
  reflexive   234, 255

capitalist class   79, 108, 200, 202–3
capitalist entrepreneurs   13, 123
capitalist form   7, 108–9
capitalist Modernity   7, 28, 267–68
capitalist production process   200, 203
capitalists   7, 70, 76, 78–82, 109–10, 112, 116, 123, 150, 163, 166, 170–71, 178, 184, 191, 200–207, 215, 219, 236, 239, 241, 243, 246, 250–51, 260, 268, 273
capitalist society   6, 8, 45–46, 73, 75, 103, 114, 134, 143, 172, 178, 185–87, 190, 194, 206, 221, 223
capitalization   109, 137, 203–4, 221, 228, 261
capital-labor   200, 215, 263
capital-labor interdependence   263
capital-labor relations   XXII, 110, 228, 234
  regulation of   130, 248, 254
capital ownership   228, 243
capital relation   110, 112, 204, 221
capitals and corporations   256, 259
Cardoso, Fernando   139, 172
Carpi, Tomas   133
Castells, Manuel   156, 173, 186, 230–32
Castoriadis, Cornelius   39–40
categorical differentiation   64, 209
categorical inequality   12–14, 17–18, 21, 58, 61, 65, 83, 207, 209–15
  modes of   64, 212, 273
Catholic Church   89–90, 92, 94
causation, circular   134, 136, 139
Chalcedon   87
Chile   139, 212, 235, 246, 256
civil society   4, 68, 105, 159, 198, 273
Clark, T.   2, 61, 122–24, 145–46, 149–50, 152, 157, 162, 168, 172, 182
class analysis   143, 145–46, 149, 157, 162, 167, 183–84, 196–98, 201, 239
  model of   196, 198
class antagonism   148, 155, 179, 200, 203–4, 260
class conflict   XVII, 143–44, 148, 154, 183–86, 195, 201, 205, 226, 246, 260
class consciousness   147–48, 166, 168–69, 171–74, 176, 186–90, 197, 255, 258
class differentiation   89, 189, 197
class division   83, 154, 193, 249
classes   XVI–XVIII, XXI–XXIII, XXV, 2, 8, 10–11, 14–17, 20–21, 23–25, 41, 44, 47–48, 52–53, 58–59, 64–66, 69, 71, 73–76, 78–80, 82–84, 86–88, 98, 102–3, 107, 111, 115, 121–22, 131, 138–203, 205–7, 209, 211, 213–26, 229–30, 233–34, 239–42, 244–46, 250, 255, 259–60, 262, 269, 274
  structuring of   158, 160, 167, 184–85, 190, 195, 197, 223, 241
  working   77, 79, 97–100, 151, 156, 164–65, 183, 185–91, 205, 240, 245–47, 250, 252, 254, 256, 258–61, 263
class exploitation   73
class formation   142, 147, 197, 206, 234
class identity   188, 258, 260
  construction of   188, 258
class inequality   13, 15, 66, 73, 75–77, 80, 82, 87, 89–90, 102–3, 158, 160, 176–77, 221–22, 225–29
class interests   197, 202–6
  contradictory   201–2
  economic-productive   179
class opposition   73, 113
class origins   153, 175–76
class position   XV, 147, 167–68, 171, 188, 192, 224, 264
  contradictory   202
class relations   71–73, 83, 86, 138, 146, 163, 188, 199, 225–26, 228, 241
class society   1–2, 74, 141, 144, 186, 241
class status   162, 234
class structuration   183–84, 186, 188, 191, 194
class structure   2, 66, 78–79, 87–88, 94, 98, 102–3, 121, 135, 139, 142, 144, 147–48, 150, 154, 156–57, 160, 179, 183–85, 190–91, 194–95, 197, 200–202, 220–21, 224, 226, 234, 239, 249–50, 263
class structuring   183, 188–89, 194, 234, 240, 247, 249
class theory   161, 163, 168, 175
coercion   74, 108, 241
commodities   81, 99–102, 108–10, 112, 122–23, 165, 169–71, 217–18, 240, 242, 249–52, 257, 260
commodity labor power   101
composition, organic   204, 206
concentration   50, 119, 125, 148, 151–52, 160, 203, 210–11, 221, 227, 236
concentration of power and wealth   119, 243

INDEX

conditions
  historical-political   131
  necessary   61, 91, 256
  paratechnical   191, 194
  reproductive   74
  structural   126, 167, 220, 270
Condorcet, Marie-Jean-Antoine-Nicolas Caritat   2, 27, 35, 267
conformation   32, 62, 71, 75, 81, 100, 172–73, 179, 183, 188–89, 196
  historical   113, 118
confrontation, capital-labor   166
consciousness   XVIII, 23, 44, 168–69, 171–74, 176, 178, 180, 188, 190, 197, 202, 214, 255
  revolutionary   186–87
consumption   50, 52, 152–53, 158, 168, 174–78, 190, 205, 219, 233, 243
contemporary capitalism   154, 178, 183, 185, 187, 189, 192–94, 202, 228, 233, 256
contradictions   4, 22, 25, 27, 49, 130, 143, 166–67, 184, 186, 201, 203, 268
  fundamental   173, 205
  ontological   60
  structural   XVIII
  total   130
Cordero, D.   255
corporate class   151, 243, 245
corporations, transnational   238–39, 242, 244, 249
crisis   3, 5, 24, 96, 129, 227, 236, 243, 245–46
critique
  epistemological   6–7, 41, 48, 51, 265
  political   XV, 41–42, 265, 267
critique of development and progress   39–40
critique of inequality   6–7, 26, 42, 70, 267
critique of Marxist class theory   161, 166
cultural capital   68, 183, 215, 221–22, 225, 244
cumulative causation   134–39

Dahrendorf, Ralf   142, 182, 186–87
damages, collateral   23–24, 189
David, Paul   243
Davis, Kingsley,   15, 115, 117, 120, 142, 162
De la Garza Toledo, E.   248
Debates on Inequality   85–105, 107, 109, 111, 113
demography   42, 51, 71, 74–75

dependency   139, 160, 263
deregulation   232, 234, 237, 250–53
development, crisis of   40
development of productive forces   187, 231
differences, individual   15, 58–60, 65, 208–9, 212
dilemmas   4, 15, 26, 53–54, 128, 183
dimensions, economic   52, 219
discourse
  functionalist   119
  hegemonic   40, 46
  nationalist   259
discrimination   1–3, 8, 10–11, 13, 18–19, 42, 44, 62, 69, 71, 74–75, 79–80, 136–37, 255–57, 272
disembedding   102, 165
dispossession   108–9, 199, 235, 238–39
dissolution   18, 112, 164, 230
distortions, political-ideological   157
distribution, unequal   8, 12, 15, 61, 66, 73, 92, 119
distribution function   11–13, 15–18, 22, 50, 55, 57–58, 72, 191
division of society   73, 76–79, 83, 87–88, 90, 153, 158
dogmas   34–35, 39, 41
Domar, Evsey D.   132
dominance, male   23, 32–33
dominant classes   32, 45, 80, 87, 176, 238, 241, 243, 245
domination   XXIII, 22–23, 32–33, 39, 44–45, 71, 73–82, 102–4, 107, 121, 159–60, 178–80, 201, 205–6, 238–42, 252–53, 255, 257–58, 260–62, 272–74
  modes of   XX, 23, 41, 73, 77–78, 254, 256
  political   75, 79, 142, 153, 185, 235, 253, 258
  power of   22, 78
  relations of   11, 47, 78, 80, 86, 196, 205, 239, 269, 274
Drucker, Peter   163
dualism, radical   92
Duek, Celia   116, 118
Durkheim, Emile   148, 166
Dussel, Enrique   38, 43, 48, 94, 164, 268

economic crises   236, 245
economic development   XX, 126–28
economic equity, principles of   122, 124

economic growth   46, 98, 122, 125, 128–33, 135, 137, 207, 227
economic inequalities   133, 135, 144, 154, 273
economic policies   12, 227, 237–38
economic power   66, 78, 90, 92, 176, 236
economics, classical   99–100
economic sectors   132, 243, 250, 252, 254
economists, classical   97–99
economy   27, 46, 100, 102–3, 124–25, 128–29, 132–34, 143, 156, 164–65, 171–72, 177–78, 216, 219–20, 229–31, 233, 235, 237–39, 243–46, 259–60
efficiency   106, 125, 244
egalitarianism   5–7, 18, 270
emancipation   XXIV–XXV, 7–8, 18, 21, 40, 42, 45, 121, 204, 269–73
  project of   XXV, 26, 28, 267, 269–70
emancipation process   121, 271
Engels, F.   2, 97
equality   XXIV–XXV, 4, 6–7, 26–27, 35–36, 53–54, 56, 58, 60–61, 65, 67, 106, 160–61, 268, 270–71
equalization   XXV, 8, 21–22, 190, 269–70
equity   XXIV, 2, 5–7, 12, 18, 21, 48, 58, 61, 161, 269–71
equity project   269
exchange   50, 96, 112, 164–65, 216, 218, 229–30, 232, 263
  economic   229–30
exchange value   109, 175, 233
exploitation   XX, XXIII–XXV, 1, 8, 11, 13, 28, 42, 44–45, 47, 53, 55, 62, 69, 71, 73, 75–80, 82–83, 94, 107, 121, 138–39, 142, 155–56, 160–63, 166, 168–71, 176, 178–80, 192, 196–99, 202–5, 209–11, 213, 215, 219, 223–24, 227, 238, 241, 245, 249–50, 253–58, 261–62, 267–69, 272–74
  economic   212, 235, 256, 258
  inequality by   155
exploitation of labor   1, 73, 76, 109, 152, 155, 176, 198, 200, 205, 219, 236, 239–40, 244, 247, 252, 255, 257, 260
  modes of   228, 241
exploitation processes   199, 239, 241

Faci Lacasta, Francisco Javier   91
Faletto, E.   139
Fazio, Hugo   30, 192, 237

Federicci, Silvia   121
Fernández-Galiano, Manuel   87
feudal lords   100, 108, 111, 218
Feuerbach, Ludwig   XIX
fields, economic-productive   75, 77, 166–67, 190
Finland   3
Fitoussi, Jean-Paul   228
flexibility   228, 232, 237, 248–56
  precariousness and labor   254, 258
Foray, Dominique   243
Fordism   143
Fordist mode of industrial production   145
Fordist mode of production   206
Fordist production chain   260
formation, social-historical   79, 164–65, 173
fragmentation, working-class   259
framework, explanatory   212, 214
Franciscan order   92–93
freedom   XXV, 26–27, 36, 56–57, 61, 69–70, 82, 106, 143, 237–38, 246, 268–70
freedom and equality   26, 106
French school system   225
Fukuyama, Francis   143
functionalism   114, 116, 118–20, 143, 184, 215

García Canclini, Néstor   262
gender differences   58, 210, 214
gender equity   XXIV, 18, 21
gender inequality   XXIV, 3, 15, 18, 21, 23, 52, 55, 58, 68, 73, 82–83, 120–21, 210–11, 214
gender oppression   XXIV
gender relations   34, 59, 66, 73, 83
genesis of inequality   13
Giddens, Anthony   6, 142, 154, 161, 166, 182–92, 194–95, 214, 230, 240
Glick-Shiller, Nina   31
global classes   240–41, 261
global economy   145, 230, 243–44, 259
globalization   29, 31, 154–55, 189, 192, 229–30, 235, 238–40, 242–45, 247, 249–50, 253, 259–62
globalization of capital   155, 239, 242, 261
Glocalization   262
Godwin   2, 27, 267
Goic, Ramón Llopis   29
Goldthorpe, John   152
goods, primary   56–57

governments 86, 94, 129, 158, 227, 235, 246
Gramsci, Antonio 142, 147–48, 167
Gunder Frank, Andre 139
Guzmán, J. 137

Habermas, Jürgen 27, 37, 164, 267
Hardt, Michael 164
Harman, Chris 11
Harrod, R. 132
Harvey, David 154, 164, 193, 235–37, 239, 247
Hayek, Friedrich 237
Himmelfarb, Gertrude 95
Hinkelammert, Franz 139
historical conditions XV–XVII, XXI, XXV, 55–56, 104–5, 148, 265
historical determination XIX
historical materialism 196
Hitzler, Ronald 265
Hondagneu-Sotelo, Pierrete 194
Horkheimer, M. 40
human reason 27–28, 35–36, 38, 106, 267–68

ideological 92, 98, 119, 162, 167, 182, 236, 252
ideological matrix 20, 28, 236, 238, 267
income, concentration of 126, 228
income distribution 98, 122, 124–26, 129, 131, 204–7, 228
income inequality 52, 72, 128–29, 228
Inda, Graciela 116, 118
indicators 6, 17, 46, 141, 154
  quantitative 16
indigenous people 62, 79, 212
individualistic approaches 11, 53, 214–15
individualities 14, 55, 59–60, 64, 69, 237
industrial capitalism XVII, 97, 147, 149–50, 184, 187, 193, 228, 245, 249, 263
industrial societies 116, 144–45, 149, 152, 231–32, 247–48, 251
inequality
  categorical 209, 214
  classless 149
  class structure and social 88, 220–21, 226, 234
  conceptualize 58
  distributive 6, 17, 27
  durable 183, 207, 209
  ethnic-racial 3, 13, 15, 53, 68, 73, 82, 268
  existential 67–68
  interpersonal 65

master-slave XXIV
mechanism of 69–70
overcoming 7, 18, 70
persistent 75
political 86, 104, 138–39
productive 125
reducing 12, 70
structuring of 222, 262
systematic 207
women's 213
inequality curve 129–30
Inequality in Global Capitalism 227, 229, 231, 235–63
inequality matrix, social 66
information economy 232–33, 249
infrastructure, economic-productive 167, 185–86, 194, 241
institutions 27, 30, 89, 92, 99–100, 103, 217, 222, 225, 237–38, 249, 255
integration, social 114–15, 118–19
interests, global 259

Jakubecki, Natalia 91
Jameson, Fredric 154, 178
Jordan, Michael 63

Keynesian capitalism 145
knowledge XV, XIX, 32–33, 35, 38, 159, 163–64, 217, 221, 231–33, 237, 249, 252
  scientific 47, 206
Krugman, Paul 124
Kruznets 130
Kumar 231
Kuznets, Simon 125–28, 130–31
  Simon 125
Kuznets' model 127–29

labor
  cheap 240, 258
  conditions of 108, 110–11
  construction of 101, 217
  dispossession of 112
  division of 86, 106, 116, 120, 148, 159, 250
  fruits of 77, 169, 198, 200
  international division of 229, 249
  productivity of 206–7, 252
  product of 45, 101, 106–7, 160, 165, 169, 176, 198, 203
  reproductive 120

labor (*cont.*)
  sexual division of 10, 73, 82–83, 106, 121, 153, 159, 214
  technical division of 198–99
  unlimited supply of 97, 126
  wage 69, 77–78, 81–82, 98, 108, 170
  wage form of 77, 109
labor and money 81, 101
labor condition 254
laborers 76, 108, 158, 194, 249, 253
labor flexibility 151, 250, 252–54, 258
  new structures of 234, 250
labor force 97, 99, 102, 108–11, 126, 150, 155, 170, 261
labor identities 255, 257
labor market 66, 77, 81–82, 97, 99–100, 102, 109, 111–12, 129, 148, 170–71, 217–19, 250, 255
labor organization 100–101, 250
labor power 70, 76, 79, 97, 99, 101–2, 107, 108, 109–10, 165–66, 170–71, 200–201, 204, 206, 217–19, 228, 240, 246, 261
  exchange value of 109, 170
  exploitation of 76, 81–82
  sale of 169
  value of 198, 206
  wage forms of 76, 81
labor power inputs 200
labor precariousness 193, 256, 264
labor process XXII, 72, 77–79, 107–12, 150, 152, 168, 177, 192, 198, 203, 205–6, 228, 232, 239, 241–42, 245–47, 249–50, 258, 260–61
labor regime 234, 250
labor relations 147, 218
labour, objective conditions of 111–12
Laclau, Ernesto 108
Lara, Sara 212, 257
Lash, Scott 164, 193, 232–33, 237
Latin America 2, 48, 66–67, 139
Laurin-Frenete, Nicole 119
leaders, leftist XIV–XV
legitimacy 24, 47, 103, 120, 131, 161, 178
Lenski, Gerhard 11, 87, 89, 91
León 132
levels
  higher 16, 126–27
  subjective 174
Lewis, Arthur 125–26, 131–32

liberation XXIV–XXV, 7, 18, 37, 40, 42, 94, 99, 204, 237, 265, 269, 273–74
Liberation Theology 94
Lipietz, Alain 248
Lipset, Seymour Martin 142–46, 149–50, 152, 157, 162, 168, 172, 182
Luhmann 36
Lukács, Georg 142, 147–48, 167–68, 171–72, 179, 204
Luxemburg, Rosa XVIII, XXI–XXII, 142, 147–48, 169, 195, 205

male domination 23, 32–34, 83, 196
  modes of 33, 80
Malthus, Robert 97–98
marginalist theory 124
marginal productivity, value of 123
Marini, Ruy M. 139
market economy 99–102, 109, 129, 133
markets 25, 27, 98–103, 109–10, 123–25, 128–30, 170–71, 236–37, 246, 248, 251
  self-regulated 122, 128, 236
  self-regulation of 128, 237
Marx, Karl XVIII–XIX, XXII, 1–2, 8, 36, 44–45, 59, 76–77, 82, 97, 103, 108, 111–12, 141–43, 145, 158, 161, 164–65, 168–73, 184–85, 187, 190, 195–96, 198, 200, 202–4, 214, 223–26, 273
Marxism XVII–XIX, 142, 144, 146–47, 149, 157–58, 161–64, 166–68, 173, 178, 183–84, 196, 205
  critique of 148, 157, 174, 178
  obsolescence of 143, 149, 163, 166, 182
Marxist class analysis 148
Marxist class theory 148–49, 157, 161, 166
Marxist orthodoxy 185–86, 195
Marxist perspective 198
Marxists 142, 146–47, 166–68, 172, 182, 196–97
Marxist theorization of class consciousness 173
Marx's concept of classes 147
material interests XVI, 199
material reproduction XXII, 71, 86, 99, 165
Mattelart, Armand 192, 247
Mauss, Marcel 50–51, 216
Mayntz, Renate 118
mediations 10, 51, 53, 63, 65, 70, 166, 172–73, 175, 179–80, 200, 214, 216–17
  processes of 180

metadiscourses   29, 38, 41, 43
methodological individualism   122, 213, 215, 220, 224
middle classes   XVI, 190–94, 200–202, 206, 246
   new   183, 190–91
middle-class people   191, 246
migration   126, 133, 257, 263
migratory status   3, 74, 255, 264
Miliband, Ralph   74
Mires, Fernando   34, 36, 230, 233, 251
mobility   16, 57, 96–97, 175, 177, 188, 215, 237, 253
mobility processes, individual   215
modernity   2, 6–7, 20, 27–31, 34, 36–45, 265, 267–68
   critique of   43, 267–68
   project of   36–37
modernization   7, 24, 30, 36–39, 42–43
modes of domination and exploitation   XX, 79, 107, 238
modes of production and exploitation   75, 254
modes of social exclusion and discrimination   74, 79
modes of structuring   189, 194
money   81, 100–101, 108, 112, 165, 221
Moore, Wilbert   115, 117, 162
Mossé, Claude   88
Moulián, Tomas   176
Myrdal, Gunnar   114, 132–38

Nassau, William Senior   96
national economies   229, 259
nationalism   259
nationalities   XXV, 10–11, 14, 16–17, 20, 23–25, 31, 53, 58–59, 61, 64–65, 71–73, 259–60
national society   29–31, 230
nation-state   29–31, 41
natural differences   9–10, 12, 14, 85, 104–5
natural state   XXV, 104, 107
Negri, Antonio   164
Negroponte, Nicholas   233
neoclassical   61, 105, 122–24, 132, 207, 215, 218
neoclassical economics   59, 122, 131, 224
neoliberalism   XVI, XX, 98, 207, 235–38, 245–46, 252, 260–61
Nisbet, Robert   35–36, 142, 144–45, 149–50, 152, 162, 182

Oaxaca   212
Obama, Barack   26
obsolescence, supposed historical   162–63
Ohmae, Kenichi   30
oikos and polis   172
ontologies, individualistic   14–15, 54, 58, 105
origin and genesis of social inequality   66, 209

pairs, categorical   208–10
Pakulski, Jan   142, 146–49, 152, 157–58, 161–62, 166, 168, 172, 182
paradigms, individualistic   16
Parella, Sonia   79–80, 212
Parsons, Talcott   15, 115–16, 118, 120, 166
patriarchy   XXIV, 3, 8, 10, 18, 21, 58–59, 73, 83, 210–11, 213–14
peasants   86, 91, 108, 111, 171, 218
perspective
   critical   5, 19, 202
   neoclassical   124
Petras, James   229
Piketty, Thomas   127–29, 143, 156, 227–28, 236
Plessner, Helmuth   272
Polanyi, Karl   77, 81–82, 99–102, 109, 111–12, 128, 164–65, 170, 217, 236, 251
Policraticus   91
polis   71, 73, 75, 77, 79–80, 84–86, 88, 94, 102, 158, 172, 180, 186, 272
political conflict   145–46, 148–50, 153, 166, 180, 186, 189
political contexts   29, 250, 252–53
political economy   44, 95–98, 122, 164, 175, 200, 205, 214, 219, 229
political power   XVII, XXI, 78, 90, 93–94, 103, 148, 177, 241, 246, 254
Poor Laws   95–100
positions of inequality   XXV, 19, 22
positions of power   XVI, 24, 76, 245, 249
post-capitalist   163, 165
post-industrial society   76, 144–45, 149–50, 152, 154–55, 162, 164, 231–32, 247
Poulantzas, Nicos   142, 148, 167, 172
poverty   1–2, 49, 89–90, 94–95, 98, 125, 127, 129, 134, 136–38, 178, 199, 262–63
power   XV–XVIII, 8–10, 21–24, 73, 76–78, 80–82, 85, 91–94, 100–103, 119–21, 160, 178, 200–201, 203–4, 208–11, 235, 241, 243–46, 261–62, 271–73

power and domination   77, 159, 178–79, 238, 241, 272
  relations of   121, 240
power relations   62, 65, 77, 159, 200, 209, 213, 225, 272
power structures   34, 220, 255
Prado   67
praxis   XIV, XVII–XX, XXIII, 40, 44, 141, 195
  social   XVI, XVIII, XX, 44, 195
pre-capitalist societies   100, 103, 172, 218
precariat   254–55
precariousness   102, 134, 137, 140, 189, 192, 249, 252–54, 257–58, 262, 264
prejudices   38, 105, 121, 136–37, 139, 144
prestige   12, 64, 68, 117–18
Preyer, Gerhard   229
private property   10, 77, 85, 87, 105, 107–8, 121–22, 155, 158–61, 171, 173, 215, 273
privileges   5, 8–13, 15–17, 26, 50, 52–53, 116–18, 120, 122, 136, 139, 152, 225, 243–44, 247
processes
  constituent   46, 70, 75
  cumulative   133, 136, 139
  economic   30, 122, 214, 220, 229
  economic-productive   219, 254, 264
  founding   71, 75, 228–29
  historic   111–12, 224
  political   89, 148
  transformative   268
production
  capitalist mode of   99–100, 108, 173, 223, 226, 228
  factors of   123–24, 132, 163
production process   78, 108–9, 152, 163, 166, 191–93, 197, 201–3, 205–6, 229, 236, 239, 247–48, 252, 255
  social   1, 83, 198, 228
productive forces   77, 98–99, 106, 108, 159, 187, 206, 229, 231, 248
profits   109, 116, 122–23, 130, 156, 200, 206, 221, 243, 250–51
progress   XV, XIX, 2, 4, 7, 27–28, 34–35, 37–46, 114, 119, 125, 159–60, 267–68
  critique of   41–45
  discourse of   40, 43–44
  idea of   35–37
project
  colonizing   40–41
  socialist   XV–XVI
proletariat   151, 155–56, 164, 166, 168, 200, 204, 254
property relations   82, 88, 147, 158, 204
Pulido, Manuel   92

Quijano, Aníbal   39, 48, 266

Ramonet, Ignacio   235
Reagan, Ronald   247
Reaganomics   247, 250
reflexivity   228, 232, 243, 248–49, 252
regions, underdeveloped   135, 137–38
regulations   95, 129, 143, 234, 236, 247–49, 251
Reisman, George   124
relations
  economic   27, 50–51, 139, 216, 229
  system of   71, 139
relationships   XXIII, XXV, 10–11, 14, 21, 23, 30, 59, 61, 66, 69, 73–75, 79–80, 102, 110, 120, 125, 127, 135–36, 138, 142, 150, 158, 168, 197–99, 208–9, 214, 219–20, 222, 230, 244, 252, 268, 272
  capital-labor   143, 252, 257
  master-slave   XXIV, 21
relations of domination and power   241, 261
remunerations   61, 96, 119, 123–25, 131
reproduction   9–10, 32–33, 61, 65–66, 86–87, 97, 135, 137–40, 171–72, 210, 212–14, 216, 219–23, 225–26, 261
  modes of   210, 220, 225
reproduction of inequality   114, 135
Requena, M.   155
rewards   68, 117–19, 124–25
Rifkin, Jeremy   251
Rizzo, Nadia   226
Rodríguez Caballero, Juan Carlos   95–96
Rosanvallon, Pierre   228
Rousseau, Jean-Jacques   2 10, 45, 73, 89, 103–7, 121, 158–61, 198, 273
ruling classes   74, 76, 86, 157, 176, 235, 238, 241–43, 245–46, 261

Salisbury   91
Sánchez, Kim   212
Santolaria Sierra, Félix   95

Santos, Boaventura de Sousa 7, 44–45, 47, 265–66
Sapinski, J.P. 156
Sassen, Saskia 150–51, 156, 193, 240–41, 243–45, 248
Sayula 212
Scientific Discourses 31–49, 146
secularization 36–37, 89
Segato, Rita 23, 25
Sen, Amartya 4, 12, 17, 27, 50, 53–57, 59–61, 65
serfs 79, 91, 111–12
sex 54–55, 58, 75, 246
situation of inequality 46, 90, 136
slavery XXIV, 18, 21, 40, 78, 85, 90, 106–7, 110, 146, 269–70
  relations of 111
slaves XXIV, 18, 26, 69, 77, 79, 85–88, 90–91, 103, 111–12, 158–59
Smith, Adam 97, 122, 214
social antagonisms 147, 153–54, 162, 260
social classes 2–3, 69–70, 72–73, 75–79, 87, 89–92, 102–3, 144–46, 148–49, 152–53, 155–56, 158, 160–65, 172–73, 176–77, 183–86, 192–94, 196–98, 202–3, 238–41
social construction 14, 19, 21, 41, 58, 61, 63, 83, 210, 255
social differentiation 74, 79, 83, 116–20, 146, 150, 152–53, 208–9, 234, 257, 262–64
social division of labor 73, 75, 83, 99, 107, 121, 159–60, 250
social emancipation XIV–XV, XXII–XXIII, 7–8, 19, 21, 28, 34, 40–44, 48, 122, 267–70, 273
  processes of 18, 48, 274
  project of XV, XXI, 47, 265–74
social exclusion XXIII, 2, 19, 22–23, 48, 74, 79–80, 85, 135
social hierarchy 117–20, 175
social inequality
  categories of 21, 74, 83, 215
  persistent 28, 267
  reproduction of 156, 183, 224
  structures of 2, 4, 13, 21, 44–45, 47, 53, 74, 138–39, 212, 225
  structuring of 14, 157, 179, 216
  system of 117, 209
  theory of XXII, 157

socialism XVII, XIX, XXI, 31, 87, 142
social relations of production 72, 77, 99, 107–8, 110, 148, 167, 170–71, 185, 196, 204, 223, 226, 239
social reproduction XXII, 14, 109–10, 138, 156, 189, 206–7, 209, 213, 220–21, 223–26, 244
social stratification 15–16, 115–21, 144, 146, 150, 153, 163, 234, 262
social transformation XX–XXI, 34, 84, 149, 177, 181, 238, 265
society
  classless 144
  feudal 88, 107–8
  informational 231–32, 250
  market 99–100
  meritocratic 64
  post-capitalist 164, 187
  postmodern 23, 30, 152, 164, 190
  reproduction of 210, 220
  traditional 36–38, 50
Solow, Robert M. 132–33
Spain 79, 155
species XXII, 9–10, 61, 87, 106–7, 221, 232
Speenhamland Act 97, 100
Stanek, M. 155
Stavenhagen, Rodolfo 117
Stein, Ben 178, 245–46
Stiglitz, Joseph E. 4, 24, 114, 128–30, 156, 227–28, 243, 245–46, 263
strategies
  collective reproduction 222
  emancipatory 18–19
structural conditioning factors 64
structuration 185–87, 190–91, 194–95
structuration of classes 184–85, 187, 194
structuration processes 185, 194
structures of inequality XXIII, 6–7, 16, 22, 45–47, 55, 74, 114, 265, 270
subsidies 82, 96–98
surplus, distribution of 203–5
surplus labor 73, 178, 202–5, 246, 253, 261
  appropriation of 177, 202, 228
surplus value 76, 109–10, 173, 200, 203, 206, 228–29, 241, 249, 252
  extraction of 77–78, 99, 110, 223, 261
Sweezy, Paul 133

systems, relational   137, 214

technologies   37, 133, 206, 233, 242, 248
Thatcher, Margaret   247
Therborn, Göran   1–3, 19, 22, 56, 60, 67–70, 155, 235, 241
Third World   39, 46, 79–80, 125, 127, 235, 238–39, 249, 253, 258, 266
Tilly, Charles   11, 15, 17, 20, 53, 75, 105, 162, 207–16
Tocqueville, Alexis de   34, 148, 194
Torres, M.   67
totality   30–31, 51–53, 71, 83–84, 156, 165, 168, 170–74, 179–80, 216–18, 224
Touraine, Alain   36, 164
transformation, great   28, 100, 128–29, 164
transnational class   245
Trump, Donald   256
Tuirán, Rodolfo   2
Tumin, Melvin M.   115, 118

underlying economic exploitation   69
Urrutia León, Manuel   150, 156, 243, 245
utopias   XIV–XVI, 2

values, extraction of   73, 176, 199, 203
vision   4, 15, 30, 33, 38, 52, 54, 131, 138, 154, 156

wages   77, 81, 97, 99, 102, 109–10, 122–24, 127, 170, 200–201, 204
Wallerstein, Immanuel   29–30, 36–38, 45
Walsh, María Elena   141
wars   3, 24, 105, 146, 235, 238, 252
wealth   1, 8–9, 22, 50, 63–64, 67–68, 72–73, 86, 88–89, 92–94, 101, 119, 138, 144, 178, 203–5, 262–63
   concentration of   92, 203, 228
welfare state   95, 130, 143, 145, 250, 254
welfare state capitalism   142
Wells, Robin   124
winners   178, 251
Winslow, C. E. A.   137
workers   13, 77–82, 86, 96, 98–99, 101–2, 108–13, 123–24, 150–51, 164–66, 169–71, 186–88, 190–91, 193–94, 200–206, 218, 240, 246–47, 249–61, 263
work process   164, 169, 187, 192–93, 201, 206, 229, 231–32, 236–37, 243, 248, 252–53
   global   192–93, 259
world economy   130, 132, 232, 249
Wright, Erik Olin   147, 154, 196–203, 205

Zemelman, Hugo   XX, 6, 44, 48, 52, 84, 172, 181, 195, 218, 265
Zimmerman, Seth   243

www.ingramcontent.com/pod-product-compliance
Lightning Source LLC
Chambersburg PA
CBHW070611030426
42337CB00020B/3750